FOURTH EDITION

The Humanistic Tradition

Volume I

Prehistory to the Early Modern World

FOURTH EDITION

The Humanistic Tradition

Volume I

Prehistory to the Early Modern World

Gloria K. Fiero

Boston   Burr Ridge, IL   Dubuque, IA   Madison, WI   New York
San Francisco   St. Louis   Bangkok   Bogotá   Caracas   Kuala Lumpur
Lisbon   London   Madrid   Mexico City   Milan   Montreal   New Delhi
Santiago   Seoul   Singapore   Sydney   Taipei   Toronto

McGraw-Hill Higher Education

*A Division of The **McGraw-Hill** Companies*

THE HUMANISTIC TRADITION, VOLUME I
PREHISTORY TO THE EARLY MODERN WORLD
Published by McGraw-Hill, an imprint of the McGraw-Hill Companies, Inc.
1221 Avenue of the Americas, New York, NY, 10020.

This book is printed on acid-free paper.

2 3 4 5 6 7 8 9 0 WCK/WCK 0 9 8 7 6 5 4 3 2

ISBN 0-07-249382-8

Permissions Acknowledgments appear on page E1,
and on this page by reference.

Editorial director: *Phillip A. Butcher*
Executive sponsoring editor: *Christopher Freitag*
Marketing manager: *David S. Patterson*
Senior project manager: *Pat Frederickson*
Production supervisor: *Susanne Riedell*
Senior designer: *Jennifer McQueen*
Manager, publication services: *Ira Roberts*
Supplement producer: *Rose Range*
Media technology producer: *Sean Crowley*
Cover designer: *Kiera Cunningham*
Typeface: *10/12 Goudy*
Printer: *Quebecor World Versailles, Inc.*

http://www.mhhe.com

This book was designed and produced by
CALMANN & KING LTD
71 Great Russell Street, London WC1B 3BP
www.calmann-king.com

Senior editor: *Jon Haynes*
Picture researcher: *Peter Kent*
Designer: *Ian Hunt*
Cartographer: *Andrea Fairbrass*
Typesetter: *Fakenham Photosetting, Norfolk*

Front cover
Main image: Detail of *Thirteenth-Century Masons*, French miniature from an Old
Testament building scene, ca. 1240. 15 ⅓ × 11 ⅞ in. © The J. Pierpont Morgan
Library, New York, 1991, MS 638f.3.

Insets: (top left) Detail of pair statue of Mycerinus and Queen Kha-merer-nebty II,
Gizeh, Mycerinus, Fourth Dynasty, 2599–1571 B.C.E. Slate schist, height 4 ft. 6½ in.
(complete statue). Courtesy, Museum of Fine Arts, Boston. Harvard MFA
Expedition.
(middle left) "Herr Konrad von Altretten," detail of *Medieval Lovers*, from the
Manesse Codex, Zurich, ca. 1315–1330. Universitatsbibliothek, Heidelberg,
Germany, MS Pal. germ. 848, f. 84. Rheinisches Koln Bildarchiv, Cologne, Germany
(middle right) Lorenzo Costa, detail of *The Concert*, c. 1485–95. Oil on poplar, 95.3
× 75.6 cm. National Gallery, London.
(top right) Detail of terra-cotta soldier, tomb of the First Emperor of the Qin Dynasty,
221–207 B.C.E. Photo: Dagli Orti, Paris.

Frontispiece: Detail of Krater with "Geometric" decoration, ca. 750 B.C.E. Terra-cotta,
height 3 ft. 4½ in. The Metropolitan Museum of Art, New York.

Series Contents

Volume I Contents

MUSIC LISTENING SELECTION

CD One Selection 1

BOOK TWO

PART ONE

The shaping of the Middle Ages 175

PART THREE

The world beyond the West   319

Timeline   320

MAPS

MUSIC LISTENING SELECTIONS

CD One Selections 2 to 14

BOOK THREE

PART ONE

The age of the Renaissance   349

PART TWO

A brave new world 435

Timeline 436

MAPS

MUSIC LISTENING SELECTIONS

CD One Selections 15 to 23

"It's the most curious thing I ever saw in all my life!" exclaimed Lewis Carroll's Alice in Wonderland, as she watched the Cheshire Cat slowly disappear, leaving only the outline of a broad smile. "I've often seen a cat without a grin, but a grin without a cat!" A student who encounters an ancient Greek epic, a Yoruba mask, or a Mozart opera—lacking any context for these works—might be equally baffled. It may be helpful, therefore, to begin by explaining how the artifacts (the "grin") of the humanistic tradition relate to the larger and more elusive phenomenon (the "cat") of human culture.

The Humanistic Tradition and the Humanities

In its broadest sense, the term *humanistic tradition* refers to humankind's cultural legacy—the sum total of the significant ideas and achievements handed down from generation to generation. This tradition is the product of responses to conditions that have confronted all people throughout history. Since the beginnings of life on earth, human beings have tried to ensure their own survival by achieving harmony with nature. They have attempted to come to terms with the inevitable realities of disease and death. They have endeavored to establish ways of living collectively and communally. And they have persisted in the desire to understand themselves and their place in the universe. In response to these ever-present and universal challenges—*survival*, *communality*, and *self-knowledge*—human beings have created and transmitted the tools of science and technology, social and cultural institutions, religious and philosophic systems, and various forms of personal expression, the sum total of which we call culture.

Even the most ambitious survey cannot assess all manifestations of the humanistic tradition. This book therefore focuses on the creative legacy referred to collectively as *the humanities*: literature, philosophy, history (in its literary dimension), architecture, the visual arts (including photography and film), music, and dance. Selected examples from each of these disciplines constitute our *primary sources*. Primary sources (that is, works original to the age that produced them) provide first-hand evidence of human inventiveness and ingenuity. The primary sources in this text have been chosen on the basis of their authority, their beauty, and their enduring value. They are, simply stated, the great works of their time and, in some cases, of all time. Universal in their appeal, they have been transmitted from generation to generation. Such works are, as well, the landmark examples of a specific time and place: They offer insight into the ideas and values of the society in which they were produced. The drawings of

Leonardo da Vinci, for example, reveal a passionate determination to understand the operations and functions of nature. And while Leonardo's talents far exceeded those of the average individual of his time, his achievements may be viewed as a mirror of the robust curiosity that characterized his time and place—the age of the Renaissance in Italy. *The Humanistic Tradition* surveys such landmark works, but joins "the grin" to "the cat" by examining them within their political, economic, and social contexts.

The Humanistic Tradition explores a living legacy. History confirms that the humanities are integral forms of a given culture's values, ambitions, and beliefs. Poetry, painting, philosophy, and music are not, generally speaking, products of unstructured leisure or indulgent individuality; rather, they are tangible expressions of the human quest for the good (one might even say the "complete") life. Throughout history, these forms of expression have served the domains of the sacred, the ceremonial, and the communal. And even in the early days of the twenty-first century, as many time-honored traditions come under assault, the arts retain their power to awaken our imagination in the quest for survival, communality, and self-knowledge.

The Scope of the Humanistic Tradition

The humanistic tradition is not the exclusive achievement of any one geographic region, race, or class of human beings. For that reason, this text assumes a global and multicultural rather than exclusively Western perspective. At the same time, Western contributions are emphasized, first, because the audience for these books is predominantly Western, but also because in recent centuries the West has exercised a dominant influence on the course and substance of global history. Clearly, the humanistic tradition belongs to all of humankind, and the best way to understand the Western contribution to that tradition is to examine it in the arena of world culture.

As a survey, *The Humanistic Tradition* cannot provide an exhaustive analysis of our creative legacy. The critical reader will discover many gaps. Some aspects of culture that receive extended examination in traditional Western humanities surveys have been pared down to make room for the too often neglected contributions of Islam, Africa, and Asia. This book is necessarily selective—it omits many major figures and treats others only briefly. Primary sources are arranged, for the most part, chronologically, but they are presented as manifestations of the informing ideas of the age in which they were produced. The intent is to examine the evidence of the humanistic tradition

Our examination of the twentieth century has been expanded to include film, and each chapter in Book 6 now brings attention to landmark developments in that medium. The contemporary chapters have been updated to include a segment on the quest for ethnic identity, focusing on the Latino voice that has made a significant mark in the arts of the past two decades. In the newly organized chapter 38, electronic and digital art receive expanded consideration.

This new edition includes more color illustrations than previous editions, as well as new diagrams that assist the reader in understanding the content, function, or construction techniques of various artworks. The Rosetta Stone, the so-called Mask of Agamemnon, the Hellenistic Altar of Zeus, and artwork by Angelica Kauffmann, Henry Ossawa Tanner, Lucca della Robbia, Piero della Francesco, Fernand Léger, and Anselm Kiefer are among the many new illustrations. The treatment of ancient China has been updated to include the information yielded by recent excavations of early dynastic graves in the People's Republic of China. Two new audio compact discs replace the older cassettes. These listening selections illustrate the musical works discussed in the text. Music by Hildegard of Bingen and Aaron Copland, African call-and-response chant, and the Muslim Call to Prayer have been added to the earlier materials, along with an excerpt from Mozart's *Marriage of Figaro*. The revised *Science and Technology Boxes*, along with *Locator Maps* and new *Timelines*, provide useful and popular study aids. The revised timelines are not exhaustive, but show selected key works. Each chapter in the fourth edition opens with a key quotation drawn from the readings and focusing on the theme of the chapter. Updated bibliographies are appended to each individual chapter.

A Note to Instructors

The key to successful classroom use of *The Humanistic Tradition* is *selectivity*. Although students may be assigned to read whole chapters that focus on a topic or theme, as well as complete works that supplement the abridged readings, the classroom should be the stage for a selective treatment of a single example or a set of examples. The organization of this textbook is designed to emphasize themes that cut across geographic boundaries—themes whose universal significance prompts students to evaluate and compare rather than simply memorize and repeat lists of names and places. To assist readers in achieving global cultural literacy, every effort has been made to resist isolating (or "ghettoizing") individual cultures and to avoid the inevitable biases we bring to our evaluation of relatively unfamiliar cultures.

Acknowledgments

Writing *The Humanistic Tradition* has been an exercise in humility. Without the assistance of learned friends and colleagues, assembling a book of this breadth would have been an impossible task. James H. Dormon read all parts of the manuscript and made extensive and substantive editorial suggestions; as his colleague, best friend, and wife, I am most deeply indebted to him.

The following readers and reviewers generously shared their insights in matters of content and style: Professors Jill Carrington (Stephen F. Austin State University), Darrell Bourque (University of Louisiana, Lafayette), Enid Housty (Hampton University), Kim Jones (Seminole Community College), Juergen Pelzer (Occidental College), Denise Rogers (University of Louisiana, Lafayette), Ralph V. Turner (Florida State University), and my colleagues, Donald Liss and Robert Butler.

In the preparation of the fourth edition, I have also benefited from the suggestions and comments generously offered by Roy Barineau (Tallahassee Community College), Carol A. Berger (St. Louis Community College), Rodney Boyd (Collin County Community College), Judith Ann Cohn (West Virginia State College), Janet L. DeCosmo (Florida A&M University), Larry Dorr (University of North Carolina), Edward M. Frame (Valencia Community College), Grant Hardy (University of North Carolina), Cynthia Ho (University of North Carolina), Connie LaMarca-Frankel (Pasco-Hernando Community College), Robert J. G. Lange (University of North Carolina), Sandra Loman (Madison Area Technical College), Susan McMichaels (University of North Carolina), Lois L. McNamara (Valencia Community College), Ann Malloy (Tulsa Community College), Sharon Rooks (Edison Community College), Charlie Schuler (Pensacola Junior College), Gerald Stacy (Central Washington University), Elisabeth Stein (Tallahassee Community College), Patricia Gailah Taylor (Southwest Texas State University), Barbara Tomlinson (Kean University), Camille Weiss (West Virginia University), and Alice Weldon (University of North Carolina).

The burden of preparing the fourth edition has been lightened by the assistance of Christopher Freitag, Executive Editor, and by the editorial vigilance of Jon Haynes, Richard Mason, and Cleia Smith at Calmann & King.

SUPPLEMENTS FOR THE INSTRUCTOR AND THE STUDENT

A number of useful supplements are available to instructors and students using *The Humanistic Tradition*. Please contact your sales representative or call 1-800-338-5371 to obtain these resources, or to ask for further details.

Online Learning Center

A complete set of web-based resources for *The Humanistic Tradition* can be found at www.mhhe.com/fiero. Material for students includes study outlines, self-tests, interactive maps and timelines, and links to other web resources. Instructors will benefit from teaching tips, web activities and assignments, and access to material from the Instructor's Resource Manual. Instructors can also utilize PageOut, McGraw-Hill's own online course management tool. PageOut works seamlessly with the Online Learning Center resources and allows instructors to have complete control over the organization of online course content on their own course website. Instructors can register for this free service at www.pageout.net.

Compact Discs

Two audio compact discs have been designed exclusively for use with *The Humanistic Tradition*. CD One corresponds to the music listening selections discussed in books 1–3 and CD Two contains the music in books 4–6. Instructors may obtain copies of the recordings for classroom use through the local sales representative or by calling 1-800-338-5371. The recordings are also available for individual purchase by students; they can be packaged with any or all of the six texts. Consult your local sales representative for details.

Slide Sets

A set of book-specific slides is available to qualified adopters of *The Humanistic Tradition*. These slides have been especially selected to include many of the less well-known images in the books and will be a useful complement to your present slide resources. Additional slides are available for purchase directly from Universal Color Slides. For further information consult our web site at www.mhhe.com/fiero.

Instructor's Resource Manual

The Instructor's Resource Manual is designed to assist instructors as they plan and prepare for classes. Course outlines and sample syllabi for both semester and quarter systems are included. The chapter summaries emphasize key themes and topics that give focus to the primary source readings. The study questions for each chapter may be removed and copied as handouts for student discussion or written assignments. A Test Item File follows each chapter along with a correlation list that directs instructors to the appropriate supplemental resources. A list of suggested videotapes, recordings, videodiscs, and their suppliers is included.

MicroTest III

The questions in the Test Item File are available on MicroTest III, a powerful but easy-to-use test generating program. MicroTest is available for Windows, and Macintosh personal computers. With MicroTest, an instructor can easily select the questions from the Test Item File and print a test and answer key. You can customize questions, headings, and instructions and add or import questions of your own.

Student Study Guides, Volumes 1 and 2

Written by Gloria K. Fiero, two new Student Study Guides are now available to help students gain a better understanding of subjects found in *The Humanistic Tradition*. Volume 1 accompanies books 1–3 and Volume 2 accompanies books 4–6. Each chapter contains: a Chapter Objective; a Chapter Outline; Key Terms, Names (with pronunciation guides), and Dates; Vocabulary Building; Multiple Choice Questions; and Essay Questions. Many chapters also contain a Visual/Spatial Exercise and Bonus Material. At the end of each Part, Synthesis material helps students draw together ideas from a set of chapters.

mammoth and the woolly rhinoceros. Equally important, they document the culture of a hunting people. Painted with **polychrome** mineral pigments and shaded with bitumen and burnt coal, realistically depicted bison, horses, reindeer, and a host of other creatures are shown standing, running, often wounded by spears and lances (Figure 0.1). What were the purpose and function of these vivid images? Located in the most inaccessible regions of the caves, and frequently drawn one over another, with no apparent regard for clarity of composition, it is unlikely that they were intended as decorations or even as records of the hunt. It seems possible that, much like tools and weapons, cave art functioned as part of a hunting ritual. The following episode from Pygmy life in the African Congo, recorded by the twentieth-century German ethnographer Leo Frobenius, supports this hypothesis.

READING 1.1 The Story of Rock Picture Research

In 1905 we obtained further evidence from a Congo race, hunting tribes, later famous as the "pygmies," which had been driven from the plateau to the refuge of the Congo [an area in South-central Africa bordering the Congo River]. We met in the jungle district between Kassai and Luebonn. Several of their members, three men and a woman, guided the expedition for almost a week and were soon on friendly terms with us. One afternoon, finding our larder rather depleted, I asked one of them to shoot me an antelope, surely an easy job for such an expert hunter. He and his fellows looked at me in   10

astonishment and then burst out with the answer that, yes, they'd do it gladly, but that it was naturally out of the question for that day since no preparations had been made. After a long palaver they declared themselves ready to make these at sunrise. Then they went off as though searching for a good site and finally settled on a high place on a nearby hill.

As I was eager to learn what their preparations consisted of, I left camp before dawn and crept through the bush to the open place which they had sought out the night before. The pygmies appeared in the twilight, the woman with them. The   20
men crouched on the ground, plucked a small square free of weeds and smoothed it over with their hands. One of them then drew something in the cleared space with his forefinger, while his companions murmured some kind of formula or incantation. Then a waiting silence. The sun rose on the horizon. One of the men, an arrow on his bowstring, took his place beside the square. A few minutes later the rays of the sun fell on the drawing at his feet. In that same second the woman stretched out her arms to the sun, shouting words I did not understand, the man shot the arrow and the woman cried   30
out again. Then the three men bounded off through the bush while the woman stood for a few minutes and then went slowly towards our camp. As she disappeared I came forward and, looking down at the smoothed square of sand, saw the drawing of an antelope four hands long. From the antelope's neck protruded the pygmy's arrow.

I went back for my camera intending to photograph the drawing before the men returned. But the woman, when she saw what I was up to, made such a fuss that I desisted. We broke camp and continued our march. The drawing remained   40
unphotographed. That afternoon the hunters appeared with a

Figure 0.1 Hall of Bulls, left wall, Lascaux caves, Dordogne, France, ca. 15,000–10,000 B.C.E. Paint on limestone rock, length of individual bulls 13–16 ft.

Figure 0.2 Spotted horses and negative hand imprints, Pech-Merle caves, Lot, France, ca. 15,000–10,000 B.C.E. Length 11 ft. 2 in. Photo: Jean Vertut.

fine "buschbock," an arrow in its throat. They delivered their booty and then went off to the hill we had left behind us, carrying a fistful of the antelope's hair and a gourd full of its blood. Two days passed before they caught up with us again. Then, in the evening, as we were drinking a foamy palm wine, the oldest of the three men—I had turned to him because he seemed to have more confidence in me than the others—told me that he and his companions had returned to the scene of their preparations for the hunt in order to daub the picture with the slain antelope's hair and blood, to withdraw the arrow and then to wipe the whole business away. The meaning of the formula was not clear, but I did gather that, had they not done as they did, the blood of the dead antelope would have destroyed them. The "wiping out," too, had to take place at sunrise.

50

This reading illuminates two concepts that are vital to an understanding of prehistoric art, and perhaps the art of the ancient world as well. First, the arts of the ancient world were not primarily decorative or intended as entertainment, as is the case with most modern art. Rather, drawing, painting, music, and dance held a sacred function, usually related to ritual or celebration. Among our ancient ancestors, "art" was a form of prayer, a vehicle by which humans petitioned superhuman forces. The Pygmy enactment of the hunt was a ritualized kind of *sympathetic magic*: a method by which one gains power over an object by manipulating its name or physical characteristics. Second, in the performance of such rituals, the arts were integrated: The success of the ritual depended upon the proper combination of words (chanted, sung, or spoken), visual images, and gestures (perhaps dance). If the Pygmy

episode is taken as a model, it is likely that prehistoric cave paintings belonged to rituals designed for a successful hunt.

Faith in the power to alter destiny by way of prayer and the manipulation of proper symbols has characterized religious ceremony throughout the history of humankind, but it was especially important to a culture in which control over nature was crucial to physical survival. A motif commonly found on cave walls is the image of the human hand, created in negative relief by blowing or splattering color around the actual hand of the hunter, shaman, or priest who interceded between the human realm and the spirit world (Figure 0.2). Since the hand was the hunter's most powerful ally in making and wielding a weapon, it is fitting that it appears enshrined in the sacred precinct amid the quarry of the hunt. The precise meaning of many of the markings on prehistoric cave walls remains a matter of speculation. In that some cave paintings depict beasts and sea-creatures that humans did not hunt, it may be that these images were cult-related. Some scholars hold that certain prehistoric markings were lunar calendars—notational devices used to predict the seasonal migration of animals. The cave, symbol of the cosmic underworld and the procreative womb, served as a ceremonial chamber, a shrine, and perhaps a council room. No matter how one interprets so-called "cave-art," it is surely an expression of our early ancestors' efforts to control their environment and thus ensure their survival.

Women played important roles in Paleolithic culture. The Pygmy ritual described by Frobenius suggests a clear division of labor in the performance of ritual: As the male shoots the arrow into the image of the antelope, his female companion issues special words and pious gestures. It is

Year	Event
—12,000	domesticated dogs (descended from Asian wolves) appear
—10,000	goats are domesticated; herding begins in Asia and Africa
—8000	clay tokens are used in Mesopotamia to tally goods
—7000	cloth is woven in Anatolia (now Turkey)
—5000	crop irrigation is first employed in Mesopotamia

likely that similar kinds of shared responsibility characterized humankind's earliest societies. Women probably secured food by gathering fruits and berries; they acted also as healers and nurturers. Moreover, since the female (in her role as childbearer) assured the continuity of the tribe, she assumed a special importance: Perceived as life-giver and identified with the mysterious powers of procreation, she was exalted as Mother Earth. Her importance in the prehistoric community is confirmed by the great numbers of female statuettes uncovered by archeologists throughout the world. A good many of these objects show the female nude with pendulous breasts, large buttocks, and swollen abdomen, indicating pregnancy (Figure 0.3).

Figure 0.3 Venus of Willendorf, from Lower Austria, ca. 25,000–20,000 B.C.E. Limestone, height 4⅜ in. Museum of Natural History, Vienna.

Neolithic ("New Stone") Culture (ca. 8000–4000 B.C.E.)

Paleolithic people lived at the mercy of nature. However, during the transitional (or Mesolithic) phase that occurred shortly after 10,000 B.C.E., our ancient ancestors discovered that the seeds of wild grains and fruits might be planted to grow food, and wild animals might be domesticated. The rock art paintings discovered at Tassili in Africa's Sahara Desert—once fertile grasslands—tell the story of a transition from hunting to herding and the domestication of cattle and camels (Figure 0.4). Gradually, over a period of centuries, as hunters, gatherers, and herdsmen became farmers and food producers, a dynamic new culture emerged: the Neolithic. Food production freed people from a nomadic way of life. They gradually settled permanent farm communities, raising high-protein crops such as wheat and barley in Asia, rice in China, and maize in the Americas. They raised goats, pigs, cattle, and sheep that provided regular sources of food and valuable by-products such as wool and leather. The transition from the hunting-gathering phase of human subsistence to the agricultural-herding phase was a revolutionary development in human social organization, because it marked the shift from a nomadic to a sedentary way of life.

Neolithic sites excavated in Southwest Asia* (especially Israel, Jordan, Turkey, Iran, and Iraq), East Asia (China and Japan), and (as late as 1000 B.C.E.) in Meso-America, center on villages consisting of a number of mud- and limestone-faced huts, humankind's earliest architecture (Figure 0.5). At Jericho, in present-day Israel, massive defense walls surrounded the town, while tombs held the ornamented remains of local villagers. In Jarmo, in northern Iraq, a community of more than 150 people harvested wheat with stone sickles. Polished stone tools, some designed especially for farming, replaced the cruder tools of Paleolithic people. Ancient Japanese communities seem to have produced the world's oldest known pottery—handcoiled and fired clay vessels. But it was in Southwest Asia that some of the finest examples of painted pottery have come to light. Clay vessels, decorated with abstract motifs such as the long-necked birds that march around the rim of a beaker from Susa (Figure 0.6), held surplus foods for the lean months of winter, and woven rugs and textiles provided comfort against the wind, rain, and cold. Homemakers, artisans, and shepherds played significant roles in Neolithic society.

Agricultural life stimulated a new awareness of seasonal change and a profound respect for those life-giving powers, such as sun and rain, that were essential to the success of the harvest. The earth's fertility and the seasonal cycle were the principal concerns of the farming culture. A hand-modeled clay figurine from a Neolithic grave in Tlatilco in central Mexico (the region in which the Olmec—Meso-America's earliest culture—flourished)

---

*Also known as "the Near East" or "the Middle East." The geographic regions cited in this textbook are identified on the Key Map in the Preface.

Figure 0.4 Saharan rock painting, Tassili, Algeria, ca. 8000–4000 B.C.E. Photo: Sonia Halliday, Weston Turville, UK.

Figure 0.5 Isometric reconstruction of a neolithic house at Hassuna (level 4). Originally mud and limestone. The Oriental Institute, The University of Chicago.

Figure 0.6 Beaker painted with goats, dogs, and long-necked birds, from Susa, southwest Iran, ca. 5000–4000 B.C.E. Baked clay, height 11¼ in. Louvre, Paris. Photo: © R.M.N.

Figure 0.7 Eternal duality of birth and death, figurine, Tlatilco, central Mexico, 1700–1300 B.C.E. Clay, height approx. 12 in. Museo Regional de Antropologia e Historia, Villahermosa, Tabasco. Richard Stirling/Photo © Ancient Art and Architecture Collection, Harrow.

illustrates the eternal duality of birth and death (Figure 0.7): One half of the man-child appears plump and vigorous, but on the other the flesh is stripped away to reveal the skeletal remains of the body. The figure, like those of infants and dwarfs common in Olmec art, may be associated with rituals celebrating regeneration and the life cycle. Its startling conjunction of infancy and degeneration reflects a profound sensitivity to the course of birth and death that governs both the crops and the people who plant them.

The overwhelming evidence of female statuettes found regularly in Neolithic graves suggests that the cult of the Earth Mother may have become even more important in the transition from food-gathering to food-production, when fertility and agricultural abundance were vital to the life of the community. Nevertheless, as with cave art, the exact meaning and function of the so-called "mother goddesses" remain a matter of speculation: They may have played a role in the performance of rites celebrating seasonal regeneration or they may have been associated with fertility cults that ensured successful childbirth. The symbolic association between the womb and "mother earth" played an important part in almost all ancient religions. In myth as well, female deities governed the earth, while male deities ruled the sky (see Reading 1.5). From culture to culture, the fertility goddess herself took many different forms. In contrast with the "Venus" of Willendorf (Figure 0.3), for instance, whose sexual characteristics are boldly exaggerated, the marble statuettes produced in great number on the Cyclades, the Greek islands of the Aegean Sea, are as streamlined and highly stylized as some modern sculptures (Figure 0.8). Though lacking the pronounced sexual characteristics of the Paleolithic Venus, the Cycladic figure probably played a similar role in rituals that sought the blessings of mother earth.

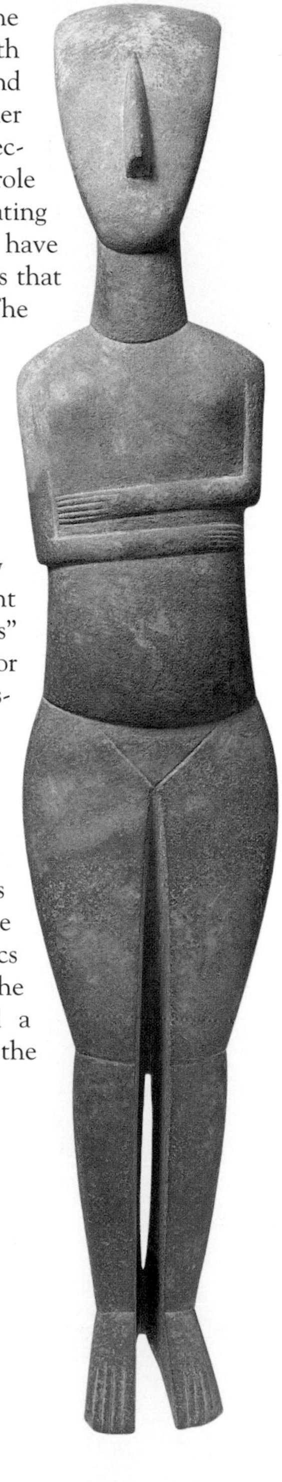

Figure 0.8 Female figure, early Cycladic II, Late Spedos type, ca. 2600–2400 B.C.E. Marble, height 24¾ in. The Metropolitan Museum of Art, New York. Gift of Cristos B. Bastis, 1968. 68.148.

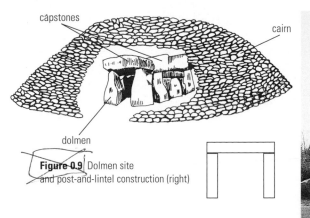

Figure 0.9 Dolmen site and post-and-lintel construction (right)

Figure 0.10 Burial site, Dolmen (upright stones supporting a horizontal slab), Crucuno, north of Carnac, France, Neolithic period. Ancient Art and Architecture Collection, Harrow.

To farming peoples, the seasonal cycle—a primary fact of subsistence—was associated with death and regeneration. The dead, whose return to the earth put them in closer touch with the forces of nature, received careful burial. Almost all early cultures regarded the dead as messengers between the world of the living and the spirit world. Neolithic folk marked graves with **megaliths** (literally, "great stones"), upright stone slabs roofed by a capstone to form a stone tomb or **dolmen** (Figure 0.9). At some sites, the tomb was covered over with dirt and rubble to form a mound (Figure 0.10), symbolic of the sacred mountain (the abode of the gods) and the procreative womb (the source of regenerative life). The shape prevails in sacred architecture that ranges from the Mesoamerican temple (see Figure 2.7) to the Buddhist shrine (see chapter 9). The dolmen tomb made use of the simplest type of architectural construction: the **post-and-lintel** principle. At ceremonial centers and burial sites, megaliths might be placed upright in circles or multiple rows and capped by horizontal slabs. One such example is the sanctuary at Stonehenge in southern England, where an elaborate group of stone circles, constructed in stages over a period of 2,000 years, forms one of the most mysterious and impressive ritual spaces of the prehistoric world (Figure 0.11). To this wind-swept site, 20-foot megaliths, some weighing 25 tons each, were dragged from a quarry some twenty miles away, then shaped and assembled without metal tools to form a huge outer circle and an inner horseshoe of post-and-lintel stones (Figure 0.12, 0.13). A special **stele** that stands apart from the complex of stone circles marks the point—visible from the exact center of the inner circle—at which the sun rises at the midsummer solstice (the longest day of the year). It is probable that Stonehenge served as a sacred calendar predicting the movements of the sun and moon, clocking the seasonal cycle, and thus providing information that would have been essential to an agricultural society.

Other Neolithic projects offer astounding testimony to ancient ingenuity. In the coastal deserts of Peru, enormous earthwork lines form geometric figures, spirals, and bird, animal, and insect designs, the meaning and function of which are yet to be deciphered. The giant hummingbird, whose wings span some 200 feet, is one of eighteen bird images pictured on the Peruvian plains (Figure 0.14). So complex are the designs of these earthworks that some modern writers have attributed their existence to the activity of beings from outer space—much as medieval people thought Stonehenge the work of Merlin, a legendary magician. Scientific analysis of the total evidence, however, severely challenges the credibility of such theories. Indeed, recent scholarship suggests that the Peruvian earthworks may have served as starmaps or astronomical calendars designed, like Stonehenge, to help ancient farmers determine dates for planting crops, for ritual celebrations, and thus for bringing human needs into harmony with the rhythms of nature.

—4500	sailboats are used in Mesopotamia
—4200	the first known calendar (365 days) is devised in Egypt
—4000	copper ores are mined and smelted by Egyptians; bricks are fired in Mesopotamian kilns
—3600	bronze comes into use in Mesopotamia
—3500	the plow, wheeled cart, potter's wheel, tokens with pictographic impressions, fermentation processes for wine and beer are all introduced in Sumer

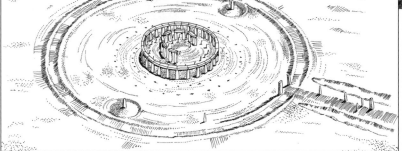

Figure 0.11 Stonehenge, Salisbury Plain, Wiltshire, England, ca. 3000–1800 B.C.E. Stone, diameter of circle 97 ft., height approx. 13 ft. 6 in. Photo: Aerofilms, Hertfordshire.

Figure 0.12 (left) Stonehenge's construction. Of the roughly eighty twenty-foot bluestones arranged in this horsehoe and circle formation, few survive. (below) Raising a sarsen stone into an upright setting. (bottom) Raising a lintel to the top of two sarsens.

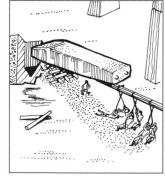
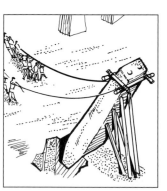
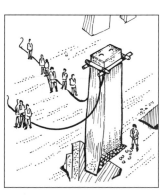

Figure 0.13 Stonehenge trilithons (lintel-topped pairs of stones at center). Height approx. 24 ft. (including lintel). © English Heritage Photographic Library.

Figure 0.14 Giant hummingbird, Nasca culture, Southwest Peru, ca. 200 B.C.E.–200 C.E. Wingspan, 900 ft. The geoglyph was created by scraping away the weathered surface of the desert and removing stones. Photo: Parabola, New York.

The Birth of Civilization

Around 4000 B.C.E., a new chapter in the history of humankind began. Neolithic villages grew in population and size. They produced surplus amounts of food and goods that might be traded with neighboring villages. The demands of increased production and trade went hand in hand with changes in division and specialization of labor. Advances in technology, such as the invention of the wheel, the plow, and the solar calendar in the earliest known civilizations of Sumer and Egypt, enhanced economic efficiency. Wheeled carts transported people, food, and goods overland, and sailboats used the natural resource of wind for travel by water. Large-scale farming required artificial systems of irrigation, which, in turn, required cooperative effort and a high degree of communal organization. Neolithic villages grew in complexity to become the bustling cities of a new era. The birth of civilization marks the shift from rural/pastoral to urban/commercial life; or more specifically, the transition from simple village life to the more complex forms of social, economic, and political organization associated with urban existence.

The first civilization of the ancient world emerged in Mesopotamia, a fertile area that lay between the Tigris and Euphrates Rivers of the Southwest Asian land mass (Map **0.1**). Mesopotamia formed the eastern arc of the Fertile Crescent, which stretched westward to the Nile delta. At the southeastern perimeter of the Fertile Crescent, about a dozen cities collectively constituted Sumer, the very earliest civilization known to history. Shortly after the rise of Sumer, around 3500 B.C.E., Egyptian civilization emerged along the Nile River in Northeast Africa. In India, the earliest urban centers appeared in the valley of the Indus River that runs through the northwest portion of the Indian subcontinent. Chinese civilization was born in the northern part of China's vast central plain, watered by the Yellow River. The appearance of these four river valley civilizations was not simultaneous. Fully a thousand years separates the birth of civilization in Sumer from the rise of cities in China.

By comparison with the self-sustaining Neolithic village, the early city reached outward. Specialization and the division of labor raised productivity and encouraged trade, which, in turn, enhanced the growth of the urban economy. Activities related to the production and distribution of goods could not be committed entirely to memory, but, rather, required a system of accounting and record keeping. Writing made it possible to externalize information and transmit images by means of symbols. The newest theories of the origins of writing suggest that this form of record-keeping evolved from counting. In centuries long before the birth of civilization, tokens, that is, pieces of clay formed in the shapes of objects, were used to represent specific commodities—cattle, jars of oil, tools, and so on. Such tokens became useful in keeping track of all aspects of production, distribution, and commerce. Eventually, these tokens were placed in hollow clay balls that accompanied shipments of goods; upon arrival at their destination, the balls might be broken open and the tokens—the "record" of the shipment—counted. By the fourth millennium B.C.E., traders simplified matters by pressing an item-token into wet clay and adding symbols to indicate the number of actual goods. Around 3100 B.C.E., on clay tablets from Sumer, the **pictograph** (pictorial symbol) began to take the place of the token (Figure **0.15**). In the following millennium, as scribes (using a stylus cut from a reed) found it difficult to execute the curves of pictographs on wet clay, these marks assumed a more angular and wedged

Map 0.1 Ancient River Valley Civilizations.

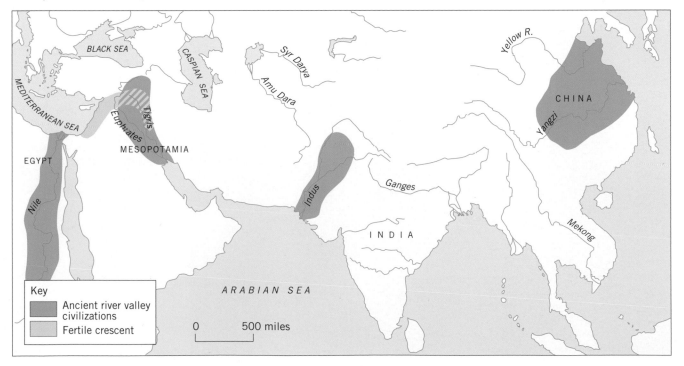

Figure 0.15 Reverse side of a pictographic tablet from Jamdat Nasr, near Kish, Iraq, ca. 3000 B.C.E., listing accounts involving animals and various commodities including bread and beer. Clay. Ashmolean Museum, Oxford.

inscription, written in two different types of Egyptian script and one Greek script, arranged in tiers, was understood only after a number of scholars, and ultimately Jean-François Champollion (1790–1832), matched the hieroglyphs for certain Egyptian rulers (such as Cleopatra) with their names in Greek.

The development of a written language is often isolated as the defining feature of a "civilized" society, but, in fact, complex urban cultures (such as those of the Pueblo and Andean peoples in the ancient Americas) have existed without writing systems. Writing in fact, was only one of many inventions mothered by necessity on the threshold of the urban revolution. For example, about the same time that systems of writing emerged in Mesopotamia, metal began to replace stone and bone tools. Metallurgy, which was first practiced around Asia Minor during the period 4000 B.C.E , afforded

Figure 0.16 The development of Sumerian writing from a pictographic script to cuneiform script to a phonetic system. Adapted from Samuel Noah Kramer, "The Sumerians," © 1957 by Scientific American, Inc. All rights reserved.

Earliest pictographs (3000 B.C.E.)	Denotation of pictographs	Pictographs in rotated position	Cuneiform signs ca. 1900 B.C.E.	Basic logographic values	
				Reading	Meaning
	Head and body of a man			lú	Man
	Head with mouth indicated			ka	Mouth
	Bowl of food			ninda	Food, bread
	Mouth + food			kú	To eat
	Stream of water			a	Water
	Mouth + water			nag	To drink
	Fish			kua	Fish
	Bird			mušen	Bird
	head of an ass			anše	Ass
	Ear of barley			še	Barley

shape. **Cuneiform** (from *cuneus*, the Latin word for "wedge"), a form of writing used throughout the Near East for well over 3,000 years, ushered in the world's first information age (Figure **0.16**). Of the thousands of clay tablets found in ancient Mesopotamia, the largest number are inscribed with notations concerning production and trade. In addition to inventories and business accounts, there are cuneiform texts recording historical events, religious prayers, and the names of local rulers. Essentially a practical means of record-keeping, writing was also a form of magic. As in rituals involving sympathetic magic, those who could make the marks that symbolized a thing might draw on its powers (see Reading 1.1)

In Egypt, slightly later than in Mesopotamia, a set of "sacred signs" known as **hieroglyphs**, answered similar needs. Ancient Egyptian writing remained a mystery to the world until 1822, when the Rosetta Stone (a black basalt slab discovered in 1799 in the Egyptian town of Rashid, or "Rosetta") was deciphered (Figure **0.17**). The stone's

–3100	cuneiform, the earliest known form of script, appears in Sumer; an early form of hieroglyphics appears in Egypt
–3000	candles are manufactured in Egypt; cotton fabric is woven in India; Sumerian math evolves based on units of 60 (60 becomes basic unit for measuring time)
–2600	Imhotep (Egyptian) produces the first known medical treatise
–2600	a lost-wax method of bronze casting is used in East Mesopotamia
–2500	the beginning of systematic standards in weights and measurement emerges in Sumer

Figure 0.17 Rosetta Stone, 196 B.C.E. Basalt, height 3 ft. 9 in. The same information is inscribed in Greek (1); demotic script, a simplified form of hieroglyphic (2); and hieroglyphic, a pictographic script (3); British Museum, London.

only to a small and well-to-do minority of the population. This minority formed a military elite who wielded power by virtue of superior arms. As the victory monument pictured in Figure 0.20 indicates, Sumerian warriors were outfitted with bronze shields, helmets, and lances.

The technology of bronze casting spread throughout the ancient world. Mesopotamians of the third millennium B.C.E. were among the first to use the **lost-wax** method of casting (Figure 0.18). Spreading eastward into the Indus valley, the lost-wax technique became popular for the manufacture of jewelry, musical instruments, horse gear, and toys (Figure 0.19). The ancient Chinese cast the separate parts of bronze vessels in sectional clay molds, and then soldered the parts together. Master metallurgists, the Chinese transformed the techniques of bronze-casting into one of the great artforms of the ancient world (see chapter 3).

People and Nature

Like their prehistoric ancestors, the inhabitants of the earliest civilizations lived in intimate association with nature. They looked upon the forces of nature—sun, wind, and rain—as vital and alive, indeed, as inhabited by living spirits—a belief known as **animism**. Just as they devised tools to manipulate the natural environment, so they devised strategies by which to understand and control that environment. *Myths*—that is, stories that explained the workings of nature—were part of the ritual fabric of everyday life. In legends and myths, the living spirits of nature assumed human (and heroic) status: They might be vengeful or beneficent, ugly or beautiful, fickle or reliable. Ultimately, they became a family of superhumans—gods and goddesses who very much resembled humans in their physical features and personalities, but whose superior strength and intelligence far exceeded that of human beings. The gods were also immortal, which made them the envy of ordinary human beings. Ritual sacrifice, prayer, and the enactment of myths honoring one or more of the gods accompanied seasonal celebrations, rites of passage, and almost every other significant communal event. In the early history of civilization, goddesses seem to have outnumbered gods, and local deities reigned supreme within their own districts. By means of specially appointed priest and priestesses, who mediated between human and divine realms, ancient people forged contractual relationships with their gods: In return for divine benefits, they lived as they believed the gods would wish.

humans a significant extension of control over nature by providing them with harder and more durable tools and weapons. At first, copper ore was extracted from surface deposits, but eventually metalsmiths devised sophisticated methods of mining and smelting ores. The result was bronze, an alloy of copper and tin that proved far superior to stone or bone in strength and durability. Since copper and tin were often located far apart, travel and trade were essential to Bronze Age cultures. (The 1995 discovery of Caucasian mummies in graves found in East Asia's Gobi desert argues for the existence of long distance trade and cross-cultural contact.) Metallurgy was a time-consuming process that required specialized training and the division of labor. Hence, bronze weapons were costly and available

Figure 0.18 The lost-wax process of bronze casting developed in Mesopotamia, third millennium B.C.E. A positive model (**1**) is used to make a negative mold (**2**) which is then coated with wax. Cool fireclay is poured into the wax shell; the mold is then removed (**3**). Metal rods are added to hold the layers in place, as are wax vents for even flow of bronze (**4**). The whole structure is immersed in sand; wax is burned out. Investment ready for molten bronze (**5**). Bronze head, ready for removal of gates and metal rods (**6**).

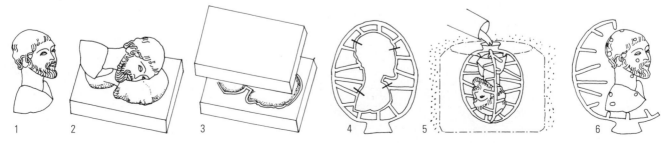

Figure 0.19 Chariot from Daimabad, Maharashtra, ca. 1500 B.C.E. Bronze, 8⅜ × 20½ × 6⅞ in. The Prince of Wales Museum of Western India, Bombay. Photo: Dirk Bakker.

Myth and the Quest for Beginnings

Today, no less than thousands of years ago, humans feel the need to explain the origins of the universe and define their place in it. While modern speculation on the origins of life takes the form of scientific theory (advanced by physicists, geologists, paleontologists, and anthropolo-

gists), the ancient quest for beginnings assumed the guise of myth. Ritually celebrated and repeated generation after generation, myths became fixed in the popular memory. As in the Pygmy ritual (Reading 1.1), words, gestures, and images formed the powerful amalgam of sacred ceremony.

In modern parlance, the word "myth" has come to suggest misconception; but, more accurately, myth describes a particular kind of speculation that, although prescientific, has enormous historical meaning. For while myth rationalizes the unknown in terms that may sound fantastic or quaint to modern ears, it constitutes the pattern of belief—the bedrock reality—of a given culture. Three further observations are note-worthy: First, the myths of ancient people are grounded in the evidence of the senses; thus, the imagery of myth is usually intensely visual. Second, the myths of a people are closely linked to that people's moral system, its rituals, and its religious beliefs, for what was taken as true was also held as sacred. Finally, the myths of humankind's earliest cultures show remarkable similarities, one of the most notable of which is the genesis of the first life forms from water.

In order to better understand these concepts, consider the following four creation myths. The first, a hymn from the *Rig Veda*—the oldest

Figure 0.20 The King of Lagash Leads His Phalanx into Battle. Detail of Eannatum's Stele of Victory, Tello, formerly Girsu, ca. 2450 B.C.E. Limestone, 70⅞ × 51⅝ in. Louvre, Paris. Photo: RMN.

religious literature of India—locates our beginnings in a watery darkness and in desire born of mind. The second is but one example drawn from the huge fund of creation stories told by African tribal people and transmitted orally for centuries. It situates the origins of life in the slender grasses that grow in wet, marshy soil. The third, an account of creation from the *Popol Vuh* ("Sacred Book") of Central America's Maya Indians, links creation to the word, that is, to language itself. Finally, from the Native American Iroquois Federation, a Mohawk tale recounts how the Good Spirit fashioned humankind in its diversity.

READING 1.2   Creation Tales

"The Song of Creation" from the *Rig Veda*

Then even nothingness was not, nor existence. **1**
   There was no air then, nor the heavens beyond it
   What covered it? Where was it? In whose keeping?
   Was there then cosmic water, in depths unfathomed?
Then there were neither death nor immortality, **5**
   nor was there then the torch of night and day.
   The One breathed windlessly and self-sustaining.
   There was that One then, and there was no other.
At first there was only darkness wrapped in darkness.
   All this was only unillumined water. **10**
   That One which came to be, enclosed in nothing,
   arose at last, born of the power of heat.
In the beginning desire descended on it—
   that was the primal seed, born of the mind.
   The sages who have searched their hearts with wisdom **15**
   know that which is, is kin to that which is not.
And they have stretched their cord across the void,
   and know what was above, and what below.
   Seminal powers made fertile mighty forces.
   Below was strength, and over it was impulse. **20**
But, after all, who knows, and who can say
   whence it all came, and how creation happened?
   The gods themselves are later than creation,
   so who knows truly whence it has arisen?
Whence all creation had its origin, **25**
   he, whether he fashioned it or whether he did not,
   he, who surveys it all from highest heaven,
   he knows—or maybe even he does not know.

(India)

An African Creation Tale

. . . It is said all men sprang from Unkulunkulu, who sprang **1** up first. The earth was in existence before Unkulunkulu. He had his origin from the earth in a bed of reeds.

All things as well as Unkulunkulu sprang from a bed of reeds—everything, both animals and corn, everything came into being with Unkulunkulu.

He looked at the sun when it was finished (worked into form as a potter works clay) and said: "There is a torch which will give you light, that you may see." He looked down on the cattle and said: **10** "These are cattle. Be ye broken off, and see the cattle and let them be your food; eat their flesh and their milk." He looked

on wild animals and said: "That is such an animal. That is an elephant. That is a buffalo." He looked on the fire and said: "Kindle it, and cook, and warm yourself; and eat meat when it has been dressed by the fire." He looked on all things and said: "So and so is the name of everything."

Unkulunkulu said: "Let there be marriage among men, that there may be those who can intermarry, that children may be born and men increase on earth." He said, "Let there be black **20** chiefs; and the chief be known by his people, and it be said, 'That is the chief: assemble all of you and go to your chief.'"

(Amazulu)

From the *Popol Vuh*

This is the account of how all was in suspense, all calm, in **1** silence; all motionless, still, and the expanse of the sky was empty.

This is the first account, the first narrative. There was neither man, nor animal, birds, fishes, crabs, trees, stones, caves, ravines, grasses, nor forests; there was only the sky.

The surface of the earth had not appeared. There was only the calm sea and the great expanse of the sky.

There was nothing brought together, nothing which could make a noise, nor anything which might move, or tremble, or **10** could make noise in the sky.

There was nothing standing; only the calm water, the placid sea, alone and tranquil. Nothing existed.

There was only immobility and silence in the darkness in the night. Only the Creator, the Maker, Tepeu, Gucumatz, the Forefathers, were in the water surrounded with light. They were hidden under green and blue feathers, and were therefore called Gucumatz. By nature they were great sages and great thinkers. In this manner the sky existed and also the Heart of Heaven, which is the name of God and thus He is **20** called.

Then came the word. Tepeu and Gucumatz came together in the darkness, in the night, and Tepeu and Gucumatz talked together. They talked then, discussing and deliberating; they agreed, they united their words and their thoughts.

Then while they mediated, it became clear to them that when dawn would break, man must appear. Then they planned the creation, and the growth of the trees and the thickets and the birth of life and the creation of man. Thus it was arranged in the darkness and in the night by the Heart of Heaven who **30** is called Huracán.

Then Tepeu and Gucumatz came together; then they conferred about life and light, what they would do so that there would be light and dawn, who it would be who would provide food and sustenance.

Thus let it be done! Let the emptiness be filled! Let the water recede and make a void, let the earth appear and become solid; let it be done. Thus they spoke. Let there be light, let there be dawn in the sky and on the earth! There shall be neither glory nor grandeur in our creation and formation **40** until the human being is made, man is formed. So they spoke.

Then the earth was created by them. So it was, in truth, that they created the earth. Earth! . . . they said, and instantly it was made. . . .

(Maya)

A Native American Creation Tale, "How Man Was Created"

After Sat-kon-se-ri-io, the Good Spirit, had made the animals, birds, and other creatures and had placed them to live and multiply upon the earth, he rested. As he gazed around at his various creations, it seemed to him that there was something lacking. For a long time the Good Spirit pondered over this thought. Finally he decided to make a creature that would resemble himself. **1**

Going to the bank of a river he took a piece of clay, and out of it he fashioned a little clay man. After he had modeled it, he built a fire and, setting the little clay man in the fire, waited for it to bake. The day was beautiful. The songs of the birds filled the air. The river sang a song and, as the Good Spirit listened to this song, he became very sleepy. He soon fell asleep beside the fire. When he finally awoke, he rushed to the fire and removed the clay man. He had slept too long. His little man was burnt black. According to the Mohawks, this little man was the first Negro. His skin was black. He had been overbaked. **10**

The Good Spirit was not satisfied. Taking a fresh piece of clay, he fashioned another man and, placing him in the fire, waited for him to bake, determined this time to stay awake and watch his little man to see that he would not be overbaked. But the river sang its usual sleepy song. The Good Spirit, in spite of all he could do, fell asleep. But this time he slept only a little while. Awakening at last, he ran to the fire and removed his little man. Behold, it was half baked. This, say the Mohawks, was the first white man. He was half baked! **20**

The Good Spirit was still unsatisfied. Searching along the riverbank he hunted until he found a bed of perfect red clay. This time he took great care and modeled a very fine clay man. Taking the clay man to the fire, he allowed it to bake. Determined to stay awake, the Good Spirit stood beside the fire, after a while Sat-kon-se-ri-io removed the clay man. Behold, it was just right—a man the red color of the sunset sky. It was the first Mohawk Indian. **30**

(Mohawk)

Civilization emerged not as a fleeting moment of change, but as a slow process of urban growth. By the operation of an increasingly refined abstract intelligence, and by means of ingenuity, imagination, and cooperation, the earliest human beings took the first steps in perpetuating their own survival and the security of their communities. Technology provided the tools for manipulating nature, while mythology and the arts lent meaning and purpose to nature's hidden mysteries. By such cultural achievements, the earliest human beings laid the foundations for the humanistic tradition.

SUGGESTIONS FOR READING

Chauvet, Jean-Marie and others. *The Dawn of Art: The Chauvet Cave*. New York: Abrams, 1996.

Clottes, Jean and D. Lewis-Williams. *The Shamans of Prehistory: Trance and Magic in the Painted Caves*. New York: Abrams, 1998.

Ehrenberg, Margaret. *Women in Prehistory*. London: British Museum Press, 1992.

Hadingham, E. *Lines to the Mountain Gods: Nazca and the Mysteries of Peru*. New York: Random House, 1987.

Hawkins, G. S. *Stonehenge Decoded*. New York: Dell, 1965.

James, E. O. *The Cult of the Mother Goddess*. New York: Barnes & Noble, 1994.

Johanson, Donald, and Blake Edgar. *From Lucy to Language*. New York: Simon & Schuster, 1996.

Jolly, Alison. *Lucy's Legend: Sex and Intelligence in Human Evolution*. Cambridge, Mass.: Harvard University Press, 1999.

Leakey, Richard. *Origins Reconsidered: In Search of What Makes Us Human*. New York: Doubleday, 1992.

Ruspoli, Mario. *The Cave of Lascaux*. London: Thames and Hudson, 1987.

Sandars, N. K. *Prehistoric Art in Europe*, 2nd ed. Baltimore: Penguin, 1985.

Schmandt-Besserat, Denise. *Before Writing: From Counting to Cuneiform*. Austin, Tex.: University of Texas Press, 1992.

Schwartz, Jeffrey. *What the Bones Tell Us*. New York: Henry Holt, 1993.

GLOSSARY

animism the belief that the forces of nature are inhabited by spirits

culture the sum total of those things (including traditions, techniques, material goods, and symbol systems) that people have invented, developed, and transmitted

cuneiform ("wedge-shaped") one of humankind's earliest writing systems, consisting of wedge-shaped marks

impressed into clay by means of a reed stylus

dolmen a stone tomb formed by two posts capped by a lintel

hieroglyph (Greek, "sacred sign") the pictographic script of ancient Egypt

hominid any of a family of bipedal primate mammals, including modern humans and their ancestors, the earliest of which is *Australopithecus*

lost wax (also French, *cire-perdu*) a method of metal-

casting in which a figure is modeled in wax, then enclosed in a clay mold that is fired; the wax melts, and molten metal is poured in to replace it; finally, the clay mold is removed and the solid metal form is polished (see Figure 0.18)

megalith a large, roughly shaped stone, often used in ancient architectural construction

pictograph a pictorial symbol used in humankind's earliest

systems of writing

polychrome having many or various colors

post-and-lintel the simplest form of architectural construction, consisting of vertical members (posts) and supporting horizontals (lintels); see Figure 0.9

prehistory the study of history before written records

stele an upright stone slab or pillar

PART ONE

The first
civilizations

The first chapters in the history of human life are often regarded as the most exciting. They present us with a gigantic puzzle that requires the piecing together of numerous fragments of information, most of which, like buried treasure, have been dug out of the earth. Reassembled, these fragments reveal the progress of humankind from its Bronze Age beginnings through the cultural history of ancient civilizations in Africa, Southwest Asia, India, and China. In the opening chapters of this book, history's four earliest civilizations are presented geographically and chronologically. It is not, however, the detailed histories of these individual civilizations that are our major concern. Rather, each of these chapters pursues three principle *themes*: the formulation of belief systems providing bonds between the secular and spiritual realms; the establishment of rulership within the earliest urban communities; and finally, the nature and development of the social order as revealed in law and other forms of cultural expression. These three themes address concerns that are universal; inevitably, they dominate the visual and literary works of humankind's earliest civilizations.

Common to all of the civilizations of the ancient world was the belief that the forces of nature were greater and more powerful than those of mere humans. The sun that nourishes a bountiful harvest, the winds that may sweep away whole villages, the rains that cause rivers to flood the land – all of these natural forces affect daily life even in our own time. Among our early ancestors, however, those for whom survival was a day-to-day struggle, such forces, or the gods that represented them, assumed positions of primary importance. Belief systems and religious practices differed dramatically from one ancient civilization to another; but all systems and practices reflect the human effort to come to terms with the unknown: to understand the origins of life, the workings of nature, the meaning of death, and the destiny and purpose of humankind.

Throughout the ancient world, the survival of the community depended on strong leadership and communal cooperation. In Egypt, as in Mesopotamia, India, and China, rulership and the authority of law provided security and protection. The success of each civilization depended on a shared view of the earthly order as god-given or as immutably fixed in nature; as these civilizations matured, the bonds between the divine and secular realms gave shape to both social and moral life. In the arts—the astonishingly rich legacy of these four ancient civilizations—we discover a wealth of resources for an understanding of the dynamic interaction between the gods, the rulers, and the people who constituted the social order. In looking at the material evidence of the first civilizations, we come to understand not simply what happened in the ancient past, but how and why our forebears arrived at strategies and values that, in many instances, have influenced our own.

(opposite) Throne with Tutankhamen and Queen, detail of the back, late Amarna period, New Kingdom, Eighteenth Dynasty, ca. 1360 B.C.E. Wood, plated with gold and silver, inlays of glass paste, approx. 12 × 12 in. Egyptian Museum, Cairo. Photo: Andrea Jemolo, Rome.

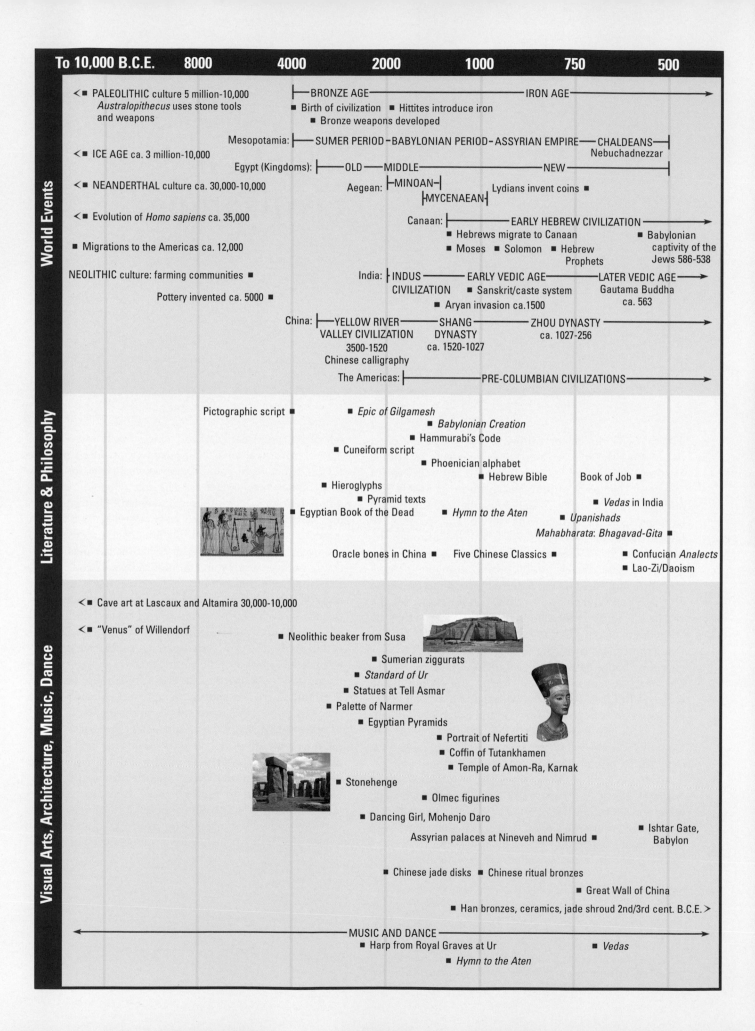

| To 10,000 B.C.E. | 8000 | 4000 | 2000 | 1000 | 750 | 500 |

World Events

◄ ■ PALEOLITHIC culture 5 million-10,000 *Australopithecus* uses stone tools and weapons

├─BRONZE AGE─────────IRON AGE────────►
■ Birth of civilization ■ Hittites introduce iron
■ Bronze weapons developed

◄ ■ ICE AGE ca. 3 million-10,000

Mesopotamia: ├─SUMER PERIOD─BABYLONIAN PERIOD─ASSYRIAN EMPIRE──CHALDEANS─┤
Nebuchadnezzar

Egypt (Kingdoms): ├─OLD─MIDDLE──────────NEW────────┤

◄ ■ NEANDERTHAL culture ca. 30,000-10,000

Aegean: ├MINOAN─┤   Lydians invent coins ■
├MYCENAEAN─┤

◄ ■ Evolution of *Homo sapiens* ca. 35,000

Canaan: ├──────EARLY HEBREW CIVILIZATION────────►
■ Hebrews migrate to Canaan   ■ Babylonian
captivity of the
■ Migrations to the Americas ca. 12,000   ■ Moses ■ Solomon ■ Hebrew   Jews 586-538
Prophets

NEOLITHIC culture: farming communities ■

India: ├INDUS──────EARLY VEDIC AGE────────LATER VEDIC AGE──►
CIVILIZATION ■ Sanskrit/caste system   Gautama Buddha
Pottery invented ca. 5000 ■   ■ Aryan invasion ca.1500   ca. 563

China: ├──YELLOW RIVER──────SHANG──────ZHOU DYNASTY──────►
VALLEY CIVILIZATION   DYNASTY   ca. 1027-256
3500-1520   ca. 1520-1027
Chinese calligraphy

The Americas: ├────────PRE-COLUMBIAN CIVILIZATIONS────────►

Literature & Philosophy

Pictographic script ■   ■ *Epic of Gilgamesh*
■ *Babylonian Creation*
■ Hammurabi's Code
■ Cuneiform script
■ Phoenician alphabet
■ Hebrew Bible   Book of Job ■
■ Hieroglyphs
■ Pyramid texts   ■ *Vedas* in India
■ Egyptian Book of the Dead   ■ *Hymn to the Aten*   ■ *Upanishads*
Mahabharata: Bhagavad-Gita ■

Oracle bones in China ■   Five Chinese Classics ■   ■ Confucian *Analects*
■ Lao-Zi/Daoism

Visual Arts, Architecture, Music, Dance

◄ ■ Cave art at Lascaux and Altamira 30,000-10,000

◄ ■ "Venus" of Willendorf

■ Neolithic beaker from Susa
■ Sumerian ziggurats
■ *Standard of Ur*
■ Statues at Tell Asmar
■ Palette of Narmer
■ Egyptian Pyramids
■ Portrait of Nefertiti
■ Coffin of Tutankhamen
■ Temple of Amon-Ra, Karnak
■ Stonehenge
■ Olmec figurines
■ Dancing Girl, Mohenjo Daro   ■ Ishtar Gate,
Assyrian palaces at Nineveh and Nimrud ■   Babylon

■ Chinese jade disks ■ Chinese ritual bronzes
■ Great Wall of China
■ Han bronzes, ceramics, jade shroud 2nd/3rd cent. B.C.E. ►

◄────MUSIC AND DANCE────►
■ Harp from Royal Graves at Ur   ■ *Vedas*
■ *Hymn to the Aten*

CHAPTER ONE

Egypt: gods, rulers, and the social order

"The barges sail upstream and downstream too, for every way is open at your rising."
The Hymn to the Aten

Ancient Egyptian civilization emerged along the banks of the Nile River in northeast Africa. From the heart of Africa, the thin blue thread of the Nile flowed some 4,000 miles to its fan-shaped delta at the Mediterranean Sea. Along this river, agricultural villages thrived, coming under the rule of a sole ruler around 3150 B.C.E. Surrounded by sea and desert, Egypt was relatively invulnerable to foreign invasion (Map **1.1**), a condition that lent stability to Egyptian history. Unlike Mesopotamia, home to many different civilizations, ancient Egypt enjoyed a fairly uniform religious, political, and cultural life that lasted for almost 3,000 years. Its population shared a common language and a common world view. Although emerging slightly later than the first civilization in Mesopotamia, ancient Egypt thus provides a more accessible model for our understanding of the dynamics of the first civilizations.

The Gods of Ancient Egypt

Geography, climate, and the realities of the natural environment worked to shape the world views and religious beliefs of all ancient peoples. In the hot, arid climate of Northeast Africa, where ample sunlight made possible the cultivation of crops, the sun god held the place of honor. Variously called Amon, Re (Ra), or Aten, this god was considered greater than any other deity in the Egyptian pantheon. His cult dominated the **polytheistic** belief system of ancient Egypt for three millenia. Equally important to Egyptian life was the Nile, the world's longest river. Egypt, called by the Greek historian Herodotus "the gift of the Nile," depended on the annual overflow of Nile, which left fertile layers of rich silt along its banks. The 365-day cycle of the river's inundation became the basis of the solar calendar and the primary source of Egypt's deep sense of order. In the regularity of the sun's daily cycle and the Nile's annual deluge, ancient Egyptians found security. From the natural elements—the sun, the Nile, and the mountainless topography of North Africa—they also con-

structed their **cosmology**, that is, their theory of the origin and structure of the universe. With graphic immediacy, they described the earth as a flat platter floating on the waters of the underworld. According to Egyptian mythology, at the beginning of time, the Nile's primordial waters brought forth a mound of silt, out of which emerged the self-generating sun god; from that god, the rest of Egypt's gods were born.

Ancient Egyptians viewed the sun's daily ascent in the east as symbolic of the god's "rebirth"; his daily resurrection signified the victory of the forces of day, light, purity, goodness, and life over those of night, darkness, ignorance, evil, and death. In the cyclical regularity of nature evidenced by the daily rising and setting of the sun, the ancient Egyptians perceived both the inevitability of death and the promise of birth. "The Hymn to the Aten", a song of praise with numerous Egyptian antecedents, probably accompanied fertility rituals and celebrations honoring Egypt's pharaoh, the divinely appointed representative of the sun god (Figure **1.1**). Depictions of such rituals on the walls of Egyptian temples and tombs show the pharaoh receiving from Amon the gift of immortality in the form of the *ankh*, the hieroglyphic symbol meaning "life." In both the visual arts and in poetry, the sun is exalted as the source of light and heat, but also as the proactive life force, the "creator of seed." The optimism and sense of security that pervades this hymn typifies ancient Egyptian culture.

READING 1.3 From "The Hymn to the Aten",
(ca. 1352–1336)

You rise in perfection on the horizon of the sky   1
    living Aten,[1] who started life.
Whenever you are risen upon the eastern horizon
    you fill every land with your perfection.

---
[1] The sun disk.

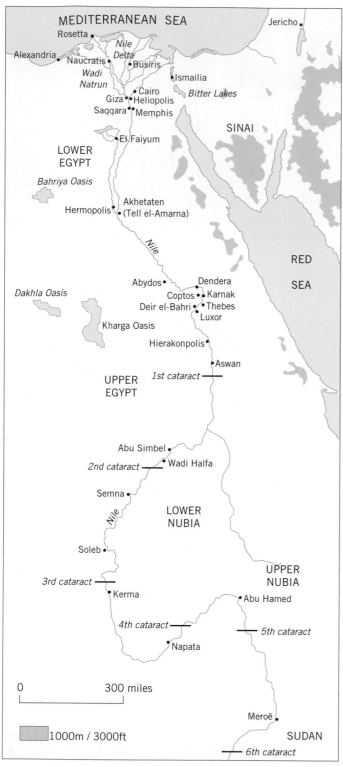

Map 1.1 Ancient Egypt.

Map labels:
MEDITERRANEAN SEA
Rosetta
Alexandria • Naucratis
Nile Delta
• Busiris
Jericho •
Wadi Natrun
Ismailia
• Cairo
Giza • • Heliopolis
Saqqara • • Memphis
Bitter Lakes
SINAI
• El Faiyum
LOWER EGYPT
Bahriya Oasis
Akhetaten (Tell el-Amarna)
Hermopolis •
Nile
RED SEA
Dakhla Oasis
Abydos •
Dendera
Coptos • • Karnak
Deir el-Bahri • • Thebes
• Luxor
Kharga Oasis
Hierakonpolis •
• Aswan
1st cataract
UPPER EGYPT
Abu Simbel •
2nd cataract • Wadi Halfa
Semna •
Nile
LOWER NUBIA
Soleb •
UPPER NUBIA
3rd cataract
• Kerma
• Abu Hamed
4th cataract
5th cataract
• Napata
0   300 miles
Meroë •
1000m / 3000ft
SUDAN
6th cataract

You are appealing, great, sparkling, high over every land;   5
    your rays hold together the lands as far as everything
        you have made.
Since you are Re,[2] you reach as far as they do,
    and you curb them for your beloved son.
Although you are far away, your rays are upon the land;
    you are in their faces, yet your departure is not observed.   10

Whenever you set on the western horizon,
    the land is in darkness in the manner of death.
They sleep in a bedroom with heads under the covers,
    and one eye does not see another.
    If all their possessions which are under their heads were
        stolen,   15
    they would not know it.
Every lion who comes out of his cave
    and all the serpents bite,
    for darkness is a blanket.
The land is silent now, because he who made them   20
    is at rest on his horizon

But when day breaks you are risen upon the horizon,
    and you shine as the Aten in the daytime.
When you dispel darkness and you give forth your rays
    the two lands[3] are in festival,   25
    alert and standing on their feet,
    now that you have raised them up.
Their bodies are clean,
    and their clothes have been put on;
    their arms are [lifted] in praise at your rising.   30
The entire land performs its work:
    all the cattle are content with their fodder,
    trees and plants grow,
    birds fly up to their nests,
    their wings [extended] in praise for your Ka.[4]   35
All the Kine[5] prance on their feet;
    everything which flies up and alights,
    they live when you
    have risen for them.
The barges sail upstream and downstream too,   40
    for every way is open at your rising.
The fishes in the river leap before your face
    when your rays are in the sea.

You who have placed seed in woman
    and have made sperm into man,   45
    who feeds the son in the womb of his mother,
    who quiets him with something to stop his crying;
    you are the nurse in the womb,
    giving breath to nourish all that has been begotten.

    . . . .

Second only to the sun as the major natural force in Egyptian life was the Nile River. Ancient Egyptians identified the Nile with Osiris, ruler of the underworld and god of the dead. According to Egyptian myth, Osiris was slain by his evil brother, Set, who chopped his body into pieces

---

[2] Another name for the sun god, associated with his regenerative powers.

[3] The kingdoms of Upper and Lower Egypt, so designated because the Nile flows from the heart of Africa in the south to the Mediterranean Sea in the north. Upper Egypt extended south as far as the first cataract at Syene (Aswan); Lower Egypt comprised the Nile delta north of Memphis; see Map 1.1.
[4] The governing spirit or soul of a person or god.
[5] Cow.

Figure 1.1 *Amon receives Sesostris (Senusret) I*, ca. 1925 B.C.E. Pillar relief, White Chapel, Karnak. photo: Andrea Jemolo, Rome.

Name	Role	Depicted As
Anubis	patron of embalmers, god of cemeteries	jackal
Amon	sun god, creator of heaven and earth	falcon, sun rays
Aten	god of the solar disk	solar disk
Bes	helper of women in childbirth, protector against snakes	lion-faced dwarf
Hapi	god of the Nile	bull
Hathor	mother, wife, and daughter of Ra, sky goddess	cow
Horus	son of Isis and Osiris, sky god	falcon
Isis	wife of Osiris, mother of Horus, fertility goddess	female
Maat	goddess of truth and universal order	head-feather
Osiris	god of the underworld	mummified king
Ptah	creator of humans, patron of craftspeople	mummified man
Set	brother of Osiris, god of storms and violence	pig, ass, hippopotamus
Thoth	inventor of writing, patron of scribes	ibis

Figure 1.2 Principal Egyptian gods.

and threw them into the Nile. But Osiris's loyal wife Isis, Queen of Heaven, gathered the fragments and restored Osiris to life. The union of Isis and the resurrected Osiris produced a son, Horus, who ultimately avenged his father by overthrowing Set and becoming ruler of Egypt. The Osiris myth vividly describes the idea of resurrection that was central to the ancient Egyptian belief system. Though the cult of the sun in his various aspects dominated the official religion of Egypt, local gods and goddesses—more than 2,000 of them—made up the Egyptian pantheon. These deities, most of whom held multiple powers (Figure 1.2), played protective roles in the daily lives of the ancient Egyptians. The following invocation to Isis, however, suggests her central role among the female deities of Egypt:

> Praise to you, Isis, the Great One
> God's Mother, Lady of Heaven,
> Mistress and Queen of the Gods.

The Rulers of Ancient Egypt

Local rulers governed the Neolithic villages along the Nile until roughly 3150 B.C.E., when they were united under the authority of Egypt's first pharaoh, Narmer (also known as Menes). This important political event—the union of Upper and Lower Egypt—is commemorated on a two-foot-high slate object known as the Palette of Narmer (Figures 1.3 and 1.4). The back of the slate palette shows the triumphant Narmer seizing a fallen enemy by the hair.

Below his feet lie the bodies of the vanquished. To his left, a slave (represented smaller in size than Narmer) dutifully carries his master's sandals. At the upper right is the victorious falcon, symbol of the god Horus. Horus/Narmer holds by the leash the now-subdued lands of Lower Egypt, symbolized by a severed head and **papyrus**, the reed-like plants that grow along the Nile. On the front, the top register bears a victory procession flanked by rows of defeated soldiers, who stand with their decapitated heads between their legs. Narmer's conquest initiated Egypt's first **dynasty**. For some 2,500 years to follow, ancient Egypt was ruled by a succession of dynasties, the history of which was divided into chronological periods by an Egyptian priest of the third century B.C.E.:

> Early Dynastic Period ca. 3100–2700 B.C.E.
>   (Dynasties I–II)
> Old Kingdom ca. 2700–2150 B.C.E.
>   (Dynasties III–VI)
> Middle Kingdom ca. 2050–1785 B.C.E.
>   (Dynasties XI–XII)
> New Kingdom ca. 1575–1085 B.C.E.
>   (Dynasties XVIII–XX)

Civil dissent marked the intermediate period between the Old and Middle Kingdoms, while the era between the Middle and New Kingdoms (roughly 1785 to 1575) withstood the invasion of the Hyksos, warlike tribes who introduced the horse and chariot into Egypt. Following the expulsion of Hyksos, New Kingdom pharaohs (the word means "great house" in the sense of "first family") created Egypt's first empire, extending their authority far into Syria, Palestine, and Nubia.

Throughout their long history, ancient Egyptians viewed the land as sacred. It was owned by the gods, ruled by the pharaohs, and farmed by the peasants with the assistance of slaves. By divine decree, the fruits of each harvest were shared according to the needs of the community. This type of *theocratic socialism* provided Egypt with an abundance of food and a surplus that encouraged widespread trade. The land itself, however, passed from generation to generation not through the male but through the female line, that is, from the king's daughter to the man she married. For the pharaoh's son to come to the throne, he would have to marry his own sister or half-sister (hence the numerous brother–sister marriages in Egyptian dynastic history). This tradition, probably related to the practice of tracing parentage to the childbearer, lasted longer in Egypt than anywhere else in the ancient world. In the

−2650	Pharaoh Khufu (or Cheops) orders construction of the Great Pyramid of Gizeh[†]
−1500	Egyptians employ a simple form of the sundial
−1450	the water clock is devised in Egypt
−1400	glass in produced in Egypt and Mesopotamia

[†]All dates in this chapter are approximate;
− (minus) signifies B.C.E.

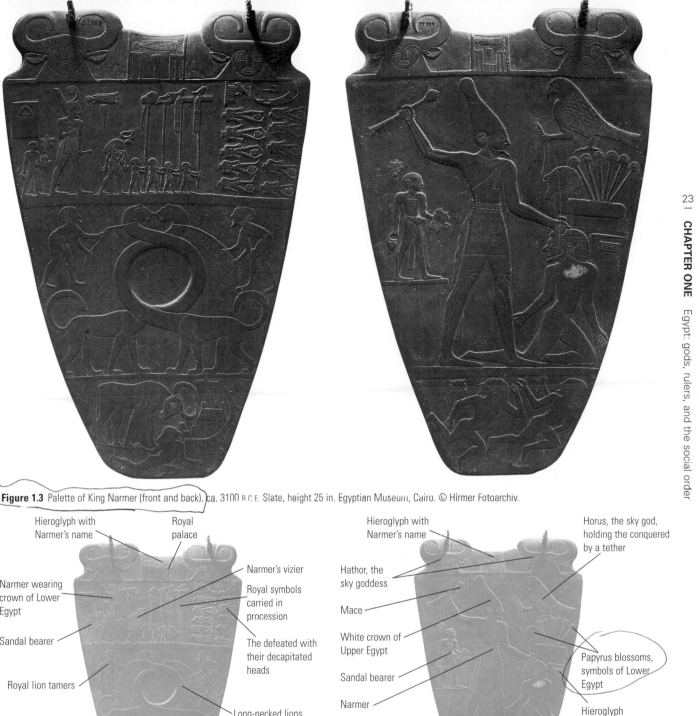

Figure 1.3 Palette of King Narmer (front and back), ca. 3100 B.C.E. Slate, height 25 in. Egyptian Museum, Cairo. © Hirmer Fotoarchiv.

Front labels:
Hieroglyph with Narmer's name
Royal palace
Narmer's vizier
Narmer wearing crown of Lower Egypt
Royal symbols carried in procession
Sandal bearer
The defeated with their decapitated heads
Royal lion tamers
Long-necked lions
Bull symbolizing royal power
City walls
Palace of the defeated city

Figure 1.4 Palette of King Narmer.

Front

Back labels:
Hieroglyph with Narmer's name
Horus, the sky god, holding the conquered by a tether
Hathor, the sky goddess
Mace
White crown of Upper Egypt
Papyrus blossoms, symbols of Lower Egypt
Sandal bearer
Narmer
Hieroglyph identifying Narmer's victim
Defeated enemies

Back

freestanding sculpture of the Old Kingdom pharaoh Mycerinus, the queen stands proudly at his side, one arm around his waist and the other gently touching his arm (Figure 1.5). A sense of shared purpose is conveyed by their lifted chins and confident demeanor. While Egypt's rulers were traditionally male, women came to the throne three times. The most notable of all female pharaohs, Hatshepsut (ca. 1500–1447 B.C.E.), governed Egypt for twenty-two years. She is often pictured in male attire,

wearing the royal wig and false beard, and carrying the crook and the flail—traditional symbols of rulership.

Theocracy and the Cult of the Dead

From earliest times, political power was linked with spiritual power and superhuman might. The Egyptians held that divine power flowed from the gods to their royal agents. In this **theocracy** (rule by god or god's representative), reigning **monarchs** represented heaven's will on

Figure 1.5 Pair Statue of Mycerinus and Queen Kha-merer-nebty II, Gizeh, Mycerinus, Fourth Dynasty, 2599–1571 B.C.E. Slate schist, height 4 ft. 6½ in. (complete statue). Courtesy, Museum of Fine Arts, Boston. Harvard MFA Expedition.

features of powerful animals. Such is the case with the Great Sphinx, the recumbent creature that guards the entrance to the ceremonial complex at Gizeh (Figure 1.6). This haunting figure, antiquity's largest and earliest surviving colossal statue, bears the portrait head of the Old Kingdom pharaoh Khafre and the body of a lion, king of the beasts. As such, it is a hybrid symbol of superhuman power and authority.

Ancient Egyptians venerated the pharaoh as the living representative of the sun god. They believed that on his death, the pharaoh would join with the sun to govern Egypt eternally. His body was prepared for burial by means of a special, ten-week embalming procedure that involved removing all of his internal organs (with the exception of his heart) and filling his body cavity with preservatives. His intestines, stomach, lungs, and liver were all embalmed separately—the brain was removed and discarded. The king's corpse was then wrapped in fine linen and placed in an elaborately ornamented coffin (Figure 1.7), which was floated down the Nile on a royal barge to a burial site located at Gizeh, near the southern tip of the Nile Delta (see Map 1.1). Fourth Dynasty pharaohs of the Old Kingdom built tombs in the shape of a pyramid representing the mound of silt from which the primordial sun god arose.

Constructed between 2600 and 2500 B.C.E., the pyramids are technological wonders, as well as symbols of ancient Egypt's endurance through time (Figure 1.8). A work force of some 50,000 men (divided into gangs of twenty-five) labored almost thirty years to raise the Great Pyramid of Khufu. According to recent DNA analysis of the workers found buried at Gizeh, the pyramid builders were Egyptians, not foreign slaves, as was previously assumed. This native work force quarried, transported, and assembled thousands of mammoth stone blocks, most weighing between 2 and 50 tons. These they lifted from tier to tier by means of levers—though some historians speculate they were slid into place on inclined ramps of sand and rubble (Figure 1.9). Finally, they faced the surfaces of the great tombs with finely polished limestone. All of these feats were achieved with copper saws and chisels, and without pulleys or mortar. The Great Pyramid of Khufu, which stands as part of a large walled burial complex at Gizeh (Figure 1.10), consists of more than two million stone blocks rising to a height of approximately 480 feet and covering a base area of thirteen acres. The royal burial vault, hidden within a series of chambers connected to the exterior by tunnels (Figure 1.11), was prepared as a home for eternity—a tribute to communal faith in the eternal benevolence of the pharaoh. Its chambers were fitted with his most cherished possessions: priceless treasures of jewellery, weapons, and furniture, all of which he might require in the life to come. The chamber walls were painted in **fresco** and carved in **relief** with images recreating the pharaoh's life on earth (Figure 1.13). Hieroglyphs formed an essential component of pictorial illustration, narrating the achievements of Egypt's rulers, listing the grave goods, and offering perpetual prayers for the deceased (see also Figure 1.1). Carved and painted fig-

earth. In ancient Egypt, the pharaoh ruled in the name of the immortal and generative sun god. Egypt's kings were also identified with Horus, the avenging son of Osiris and Isis, symbolized by the falcon. So close was the association between rulers and gods that Egyptian hymns to the pharaoh address him in terms identical with those used in worshiping the gods. In the visual arts, rulers and gods alike were depicted with the attributes and physical

Figure 1.6 Sphinx at Gizeh, Egypt, ca. 2540–2514 B.C.E. Limestone, length 240 ft., height 65 ft. Historical Picture Service, Inc., Chicago.

Figure 1.7 Egyptian Mummy and Coffin, ca. 1000 B.C.E. Reproduced by courtesy of the Trustees of the British Museum, London.

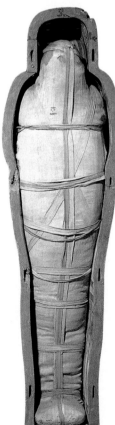

Figure 1.8 Great Pyramids of Gizeh: Menkure, ca. 2575 B.C.E., Khafre, ca. 2600 B.C.E., Khufu, ca. 2650 B.C.E. Top height approx. 480 ft. Zefa Picture Library (UK) Ltd. London.

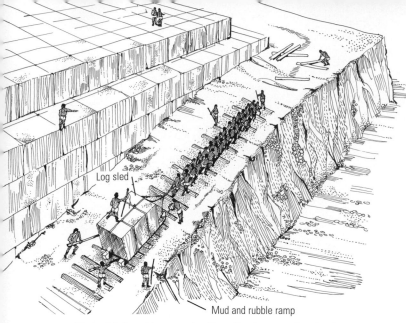

Log sled

Mud and rubble ramp

Figure 1.9 Pyramid construction. Some historians speculate that the vast stone building blocks were hauled into position using log sleds and inclined ramps made of packed sand.

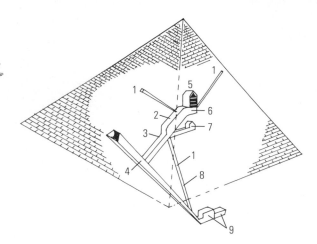

Figure 1.11 Burial chambers within a typical pyramid.

1	air shaft?	**6**	burial chamber
2	gallery to chambers	**7**	abandoned
3	ascending corridor		burial chamber
4	descending corridor	**8**	escape route?
5	weight-relieving chamber	**9**	original burial chambers

ures carrying provisions—loaves of bread, fowl, beer, and fresh linens—accompanied the pharaoh to the afterlife (Figure 1.12). And death masks or "reserve" portrait heads of the pharaoh might be placed in the tomb to provide the king's *ka* (life force or soul) with safe and familiar dwelling places.

Intended primarily as homes for the dead, the pyramids were built to assure the ruler's comfort in the afterlife.

However, in the centuries after their construction, grave robbers greedily despoiled them, and their contents were largely plundered and lost. Middle and Late Kingdom pharaohs turned to other methods of burial, including interment in the rock cliffs along the Nile and in unmarked graves in the Valley of the Kings west of Thebes. In time, these too were pillaged. One of the few royal graves to have escaped vandalism was that of a minor

Figure 1.10 Reconstruction of the Pyramids of Khufu and Khafre at Gizeh, ca. 2650–2600 B.C.E. (after Hoelscher). **1** Khafre, height approx. 470 ft. **2** Mortuary temple **3** Covered causeway **4** Valley temple **5** Great Sphinx **6** Khufu, height approx. 480 ft. **7** Pyramids of the royal family and mastabas of the nobles. From Horst de la Croix and Robert G. Tansey, *Art Through the Ages*, sixth edition, copyright © 1975 Harcourt Brace Jovanovich, Inc., reprinted by permission of the publisher.

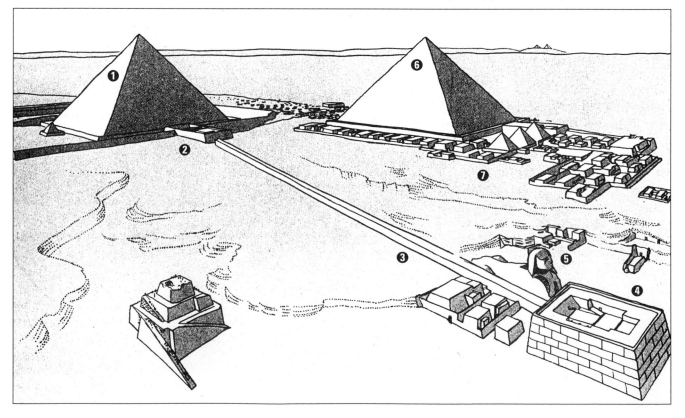

Figure 1.13 Scene of Fowling, from the Tomb of Neb-amon at Thebes, Egypt, ca. 1400 B.C.E. Fragment of a fresco secco, height 32¼ in. Reproduced by courtesy of the Trustees of the British Museum, London.

Figure 1.12 A girl carrying meat in a box and a duck, produce of an estate of Meketre, ca. 2050 B.C.E. Height 44 in. The Metropolitan Museum, New York.

fourteenth-century B.C.E. ruler named Tutankhamen (ca. 1386–1325 B.C.E.). Uncovered by the British archaeologist Howard Carter in 1922, the tomb housed riches of astonishing variety, including the pharaoh's solid gold coffin, inlaid with semi-precious carnelian and lapis lazuli (Figure **1.14**).

The promise of life after death seems to have dominated at all levels of Egyptian culture. The most elaborate homes for the dead were reserved for royalty and members of the aristocracy, but recent excavations of the lower cemetery at Gizeh reveal at least 700 graves of workmen and artisans. In the coffins of ancient Egypt's dead are found papyrus scrolls inscribed with prayers and incantations to guide the soul in the afterlife. *The Book of the Dead*, a collection of funerary prayers originating as far back as 4000 B.C.E., prepared each individual for final judgment. In the presence of the gods Osiris and Isis, the dead souls were expected to recite a lengthy confession attesting to their purity of heart, including:

I have not done iniquity.
I have not robbed with violence.
I have not done violence [to any man].
I have not committed theft.
I have not slain man or woman.
I have not made light the bushel.
I have not acted deceitfully.
I have not uttered falsehood.
I have not defiled the wife of a man.
I have not stirred up strife.
I have not cursed the god.
I have not behaved with insolence.
I have not increased my wealth, except with such things as are my own possessions.*

A painted papyrus scroll from *The Book of the Dead* depicts the last judgment itself: the enthroned Osiris, god of the underworld (far right) and his wife Isis (far left) oversee the ceremony in which the heart of the deceased Princess Entiu-ny is weighed against the figure of Truth (Figure **1.15**). Having made her testimony, the princess watches as the jackal-headed god of death, Anubis, prepares her heart for the ordeal. "Grant thou," reads the prayer to Osiris, "that I may have my being among the living, and that I may sail up and down the river among those

_____

*Adapted from *The Egyptian Book of the Dead*, edited by E. Wallis Budge (Secaucus, New Jersey: University Books, Inc., 1977, pp. 576–577).

Figure 1.14 Egyptian cover of the Coffin of Tutankhamen (portion), from the Valley of the Kings, ca. 1360 B.C.E. Gold with inlay of enamel, carnelian, lapis lazuli, and turquoise. Egyptian Museum, Cairo. Photo: Wim Swann, The Getty Center, Santa Monica.

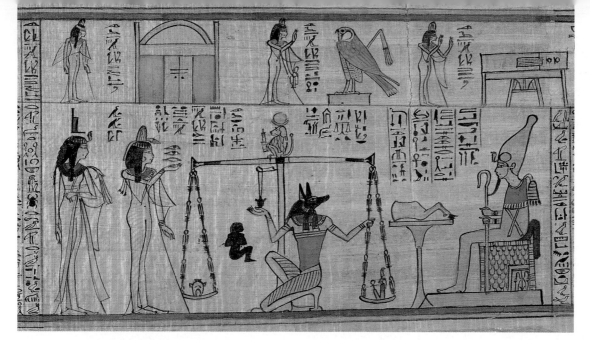

Figure 1.15 Scene from a Funerary Papyrus, Book of the Dead. Princess Entiu-ny stands to the left of a set of scales on which Anubis, the jackal-headed god, weighs her heart against the figure of Truth, while Osiris, Lord of the Dead, judges from his throne. His wife, Isis, stands behind the princess. Height 11¾ in. The Metropolitan Museum of Art, New York, Rogers Fund.

who are in thy following." If the heart is not "found true by trial of the Great Balance," it will be devoured by the monster, Ament, thus meeting a second death. If pure, it might sail with the sun "up and down the river," or flourish in a realm where wheat grows high and the living souls of the dead enjoy feasting and singing. An image of this heavenly domain is depicted on the walls of the tomb of Sennudjem: the "fields of the blessed" are bordered by beneficent gods (top) and flourishing fruit trees (bottom) (Figure 1.16). Here death is a continuation of daily life in a realm that floats eternally on the primordial waters of creation.

Figure 1.16
Illustration of Spell 110 from the Book of the Dead in the burial chamber of Sennudjem, ca. 1279 B.C.E. Photo: Abdel Gaffar Shedid, Munich.

Akhenaten's Reform

Throughout the dynastic history of Egypt, the central authority of the pharaoh was repeatedly contested by local temple priests, each of whom held religious and political authority in their own regions along the Nile. Perhaps in an effort to consolidate his authority against such encroachments, the New Kingdom pharaoh Amenhotep IV (ca. 1353–1336 B.C.E.) defied the tradition of polytheism by elevating Aten (God of the Sun Disk) to a

Figure 1.17 *The royal family under the "Aten with Rays".* Ca. 1345 B.C.E. New Kingdom, Eighteenth Dynasty. Alabaster, height 3 ft. 4 in. Egyptian Museum, Cairo. Photo: Jürgen Liepe, Berlin.

Figure 1.18 Portrait of head of Queen Nefertiti, ca. 1355 B.C.E. New Kingdom, Eighteenth Dynasty. Painted limestone, height 20 in. State Museums, Berlin.

position of supremacy over all other gods. Changing his own name to Akhenaten ("Shining Spirit of Aten"), the pharaoh abandoned the political capital at Memphis and the religious center at Thebes to build a new palace midway between the two at a site called Akhetaten ("Place of the Sun Disk's Power") (see Map 2.1). In a small stone carving from Akhenaten's palace, the pharaoh is seen with his wife Nefertiti and one of their daughters making offerings to Aten (Figure **1.17**). The sun's rays end in human hands, some of which carry the *ankh.* The elongated figures and relaxed contours suggest a conscious departure from traditional (more formal) modes of representation. Akhenaten's chief wife, Queen Nefertiti, along with her mother-in-law, assisted in organizing the affairs of state. The mother of six daughters, Nefertiti is often pictured as

Isis, the goddess from whom all Egyptian queens were said to have descended. Nefertiti's confident beauty inspired numerous sculpted likenesses, some of which are striking in their blend of realism and abstraction (Figure **1.18**). Akhenaten's monotheistic reform lasted only as long as his reign, and in the years following his death, Egypt's conservative priests and nobles returned to the polytheism of their forebears.

Nubia and Ancient Egypt

Throughout its history, ancient Egypt maintained commercial and cultural contact with other African civilizations—Libya in the north, Punt in the east, and Nubia in the south. The most significant of these, the civilization of Nubia was located between the first and sixth cataracts of the Nile (see Map 1.1). Nubia was the first literate urban society to appear in Africa south of the Sahara. Famous for its large quantities of gold, copper, iron, and cattle, it came under Egyptian rule as early as the Middle Kingdom. But during the ninth century B.C.E., the powerful state of Kush in Nubia came to rule all of southern Egypt. The history of Nubia, which dates from at least 2300 B.C.E., reflects the importation of Egyptian religion and culture, but its artifacts testify to a high level of native artistry and technical sophistication. This is especially visible in the area of metal-crafting, as reflected, for instance, in the bronze statue of the Kushan king Shabaqo (Figure **1.19**). In this small, but forceful portrait, Nubia anticipated the birth of an African tradition in portraiture that flowered in the western Sudan as early as 500 B.C.E. and continued to flourish for at least a thousand years (see chapter 18).

Figure 1.19 King Shabaqo, from the area of the ancient Kush, ca. eighth century B.C.E. Solid cast bronze, height 6 in. National Museum, Athens, no. 632. Photo: courtesy National Museum.

Law in Ancient Egypt

In ancient Egypt, long-standing customs and unwritten rules preceded the codification and transcription of civil and criminal law. Indeed, Egyptian law consisted of the unwritten decrees of the pharaoh (passed down orally until they were transcribed during the New Kingdom). An inscription on an Old Kingdom tomb wall sums up this phenomenon as follows: "the law of the land is the mouth of the pharaoh." In Egypt no written laws have been preserved from any period before the fourth century B.C.E. When one considers that toward the end of the thirteenth century B.C.E., the pharaoh Rameses II ruled approximately three million people, it is clear that the oral tradition—the verbal transmission of rules, conventions, and customs—played a vital part in establishing political continuity.

The Social Order

Like all ancient civilizations, Egypt could not have existed without a high level of cooperation among those whose individual tasks—governing, trading, farming, fighting—contributed to communal survival. Powerful families, tribes, and clans, usually those that had proved victorious in battle, established long-standing territorial claims. Such families often claimed descent from, or association with, the gods. Once royal authority was entrenched, it was almost impossible to unseat. The ruling dynasty, in conjunction with a priestly caste that supervised the religious activities of the community, formed an elite group of men and women who regulated the lives of the lower classes: merchants, farmers, herders, artisans, soldiers, and servants. Nevertheless, the class structure in ancient Egypt seems to have been quite flexible. Ambitious individuals of any class were free to rise in status, usually by way of education. The westward migration of sub-Saharan (dark-skinned)* peoples and the thriving commercial activity between Egypt and Nubia produced a multiracial and multicultural population: at all levels, light- and dark-skinned people appear to have held similar social status.

For well over 2,000 years, Egypt was administered by the pharaoh's vast bureaucracy, members of which collected taxes, regulated public works, and mobilized the army. In the social order, these individuals, along with large landowners and priests, constituted the upper classes. As in all ancient societies, power was not uniformly distributed but descended from the top rung of the hierarchy in diminishing degrees of influence. Those closest to the pharaoh participated most fully in his authority and prestige. Other individuals might advance their positions and improve their status through service to the pharaoh.

*Since skin pigmentation varies in accordance with the amount of melanin and keratin particles in the underskin (which regulates the permeation of sun rays), relative distance from the equator determined African skin colors, which differed from the very light brown of Mediterranean types to the very dark brown of black Nubian and sub-Saharan peoples.

At the top of the bureaucratic pyramid stood the vizier. Essential to the administration and the security of the state, the vizier was in charge of appointing members of the royal bureaucracy and dispatching the local officials. He oversaw the mobilization of troops, the irrigation of canals, the taking of inventories, and, with the assistance of official scribes, he handled all litigation for the Egyptian state. Merchants, traders, builders, and scribes made up a prosperous middle class, who ranked in status just below the aristocracy. At the base of the social pyramid, the great masses of peasants constituted the agricultural backbone of ancient Egypt. Aided by slaves, peasant men and women worked side by side to farm the land. Even in the afterlife, husbands and wives shared the tasks of reaping wheat in the fields of the blessed (see Figure 1.16). Class status seems to have extended into the afterlife: in the cemeteries recently uncovered at Gizeh, artisans received separate and more elaborate burials than common laborers.

Slaves constituted a class of unfree men and women. In the ancient world, slaves were victims of military conquest. Enslaving one's enemy captives was a humane alternative to executing them. Other people became slaves as punishment for criminal acts, and still others as a result of falling into debt. Slaves might be sold or traded like any other form of property, but in Egypt and elsewhere in the ancient world, it appears that some slaves were able to acquire sufficient wealth to buy their own or their children's freedom.

Egyptian Women

Possibly because all property was inherited through the female line, Egyptian women seem to have enjoyed a large degree of economic independence, as well as civil rights and privileges. Women who could write and calculate might go into business. Women of the pharaoh's harem oversaw textile production, while others found positions as shop-keepers, midwives, musicians, and dancers (Figure 1.20). Nevertheless, men were wary of powerful women, as is indicated in a Middle Kingdom manual of good conduct, which offers the husband this advice concerning his wife: "Make her happy while you are alive, for she is land profitable to her lord. Neither judge her nor raise her to a position of power . . . her eye is a stormwind when she sees."

The Arts in Ancient Egypt

Literature

Ancient Egypt did not produce any literary masterpieces. Nevertheless, from tomb and temple walls, and from papyrus rolls, come prayers and songs, royal decrees and letters, prose tales, and texts that served to educate the young. One school text, which reflects the fragile rela-

Figure 1.20 Painting from the tomb of Neb-aman, Dra Abu el-Naga, West Thebes, Egypt, Eighteenth Dynasty, ca. 1550–1295 B.C.E. Painted stucco, height 25 in. The upper register shows a banquet. In the lower register two young girls are dancing to the music of the double flute. Reproduced by courtesy of the Trustees of the British Museum, London.

tionship between oral and written traditions, reads, "Man decays, his corpse is dust,/All his kin have perished;/But a book makes him remembered'/Through the mouth of its reciter." The so-called "wisdom literature" of Egypt, which consists of words of advice and instruction, anticipates parts of the Hebrew Bible. From the New Kingdom, however, came a very personal type of poetry that would later be defined as **lyric** (literally, accompanied by the lyre or harp). In the following three poems, two in a male voice and one female, nature and the natural world are freely used as metaphors for sentiments of love and desire.

READING 1.4 Egyptian Poetry

Boy   I will lie down within   1
        and feign to be ill, and then
my neighbors will come to see.
        My sister[1] will enter with them.
She'll put the physicians to shame,   5
        for she will understand
that I am sick for love.

———◆———

Boy   My sister has come to me.   1
        My heart is filled with joy.
I open my arms wide
        that I may embrace her.
My heart is as happy in   5
        my breast as a red fish
swimming in its pond.
        O night, you are mine
forever, since my sister
        has come in love to me.   10

———◆———

Girl   The Voice of the goose sounds forth   1
        as he's caught by the bait. Your love
ensnares me. I can't let it go.
        I shall take home my nets,
but what shall I tell my mother,   5
        to whom I return every day
laden with lovely birds?
        I set no traps today,
ensnared as I was by love.

The Visual Arts

Egyptian art—at least that with which we are most familiar—comes almost exclusively from tombs and graves. Such art was not intended as decoration; rather, it was created to replicate the living world for the benefit of the dead. Stylistically, Egyptian art mirrors the deep sense of order and regularity that dominated ancient Egyptian life. Indeed, for 3,000 years, Egypt followed a set of conventions that dictated the manner in which subjects should be depicted. In representations of everyday life, figures are

[1]Meaning "mistress" or "lady."

usually sized according to a strict hierarchy, or graded order: Upper-class individuals are shown larger than lower-class ones, and males usually outsize females and servants (Figure 1.13). In monumental sculptures of royalty, however, the chief wife of the pharaoh is usually shown the same size as her husband (see Figure 1.5).

Very early in Egyptian history, artists developed a **canon** (or set of rules) by which to represent the human form. The proportions of the human body were determined according to a **module** (or standard of measurement) represented by the width of the clenched fist (Figure **1.21**). More generally, Egyptian artists adhered to a set of guidelines by which they might "capture" the most characteristic and essential aspects of the subject matter: In depicting the human figure the upper torso is shown from the front, while the lower is shown from the side; the head is depicted in profile, while the eye and eyebrow are frontal. This method of representation is *conceptual*—that is, based on ideas—rather than *perceptual*—that is, based on visual evidence. The conceptual approach represents a highly stylized record of reality.

The Egyptian approach to space was also conceptual. Spatial depth is indicated by placing one figure above (rather than behind) the next, often in horizontal registers, or rows. Cast in this timeless matrix, Egyptian figures shared the symbolic resonance of the hieroglyphs by which they are framed (see Figure 1.1). Nowhere else in the ancient world do we see such an intimate and intelligible conjunction of images and words—a union designed to immortalize ideas rather than imitate reality. This is not to say that Egyptian artists ignored the world of the senses.

Figure 1.21 The Egyptian canon of proportion.

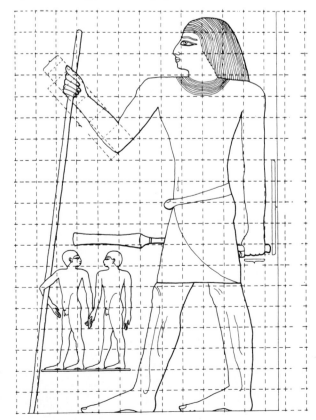

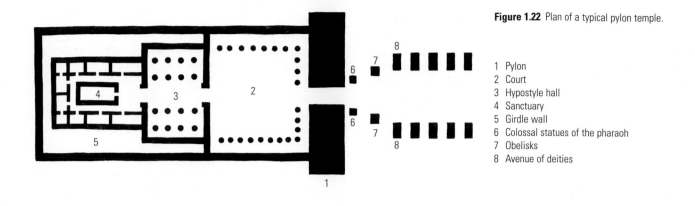

Figure 1.22 Plan of a typical pylon temple.

1 Pylon
2 Court
3 Hypostyle hall
4 Sanctuary
5 Girdle wall
6 Colossal statues of the pharaoh
7 Obelisks
8 Avenue of deities

Their love for realistic detail is evident, for example, in the hunting scene from the tomb of Neb-amon at Thebes, where fish and fowl are depicted with such extraordinary accuracy that individual species of each can be identified (see Figure 1.13). It is in the union of the particular and the general that Egyptian art achieves its defining quality.

New Kingdom Temples

Temples were built by the Egyptians from earliest times, but most of those that have survived date from the New Kingdom. The basic plan of the temple mirrored the central features of the Egyptian cosmos: the **pylons** (two truncated pyramids that made up the gateway) symbolized the mountains that rimmed the edge of the world, while the progress from the open courtyard through the **hypostyle** hall into the dark inner sanctuary housing the cult statue represented the voyage from light to darkness (and back) symbolic of the sun's cyclical journey (Figure **1.22**). Oriented on an east–west axis, the temple received the sun's morning rays, which reached through the sequence

Figure 1.23 Hypostyle Hall, Temple of Amon, Karnak, ca. 1220 B.C.E. Photo: Robert Harding Picture Library, London.

of hallways into the sanctuary. The Great Temple of Amon-Ra at Karnak was the heart of a five-acre religious complex that included a sacred lake, a sphinx-lined causeway, and numerous **obelisks** (commemorative stone pillars). The temple's hypostyle hall is adorned with painted reliefs that cover the walls and the surfaces of its 134 massive columns shaped like budding and flowering papyrus, the plants identified with the marsh of creation (Figure **1.23**). Decorated with stars and other celestial images, the ceiling of the hall symbolized the heavens. Such sacred precincts were not intended for communal assembly—in fact, commoners were forbidden to enter. Rather, Egyptian temples were sanctuaries in which priests performed daily rituals of cosmic renewal on behalf of the pharaoh and the people. Temple rituals were celebrations of the solar cycle, associated not only with the birth of the sun god but with the regeneration of the ruler upon whom cosmic order depended.

Music in Ancient Egypt

Tomb paintings reveal much about ancient Egyptian culture. They are, for example, our main source of information about ancient Egyptian music and dance. It is clear that song and poetry were interchangeable (hymns like that praising Aten were chanted, not spoken). Musical instruments, including harps, flutes, pipes, and sistrums (a type of rattle)—often found buried with the dead—accompanied song and dance. Greek sources indicate that Egyptian music was based in theory; nevertheless, we have no certain knowledge how that music actually sounded. Visual representations confirm, however, that music had a special place in religious rituals, in festive and funeral processions, and in many aspects of secular life (see Figure 1.20).

SUMMARY

Among ancient civilizations, nature and the natural environment influenced the formation of religious attitudes and beliefs. Egypt's relatively secure location, regular climate, and dependable Nile River encouraged a belief in a host of essentially benevolent nature deities, the most important of which were the gods of the sun and the Nile. The representative of the sun on earth, Egypt's theocratic monarch was accorded a burial befitting one who, after death, would work to ensure the well-being of his people. The belief in life after death, an expression of ancient Egypt's positive view of life, is evident in grave goods, tomb paintings, and hieroglyphic inscriptions, all of which manifest the artistic magnificence of ancient Egyptian civilization.

As elsewhere in the ancient world, the survival of the Egyptian community depended on cooperation among individuals with specialized responsibilities and tasks. It also depended on a shared view of the world as animated by the gods. Egypt's hierarchic social structure and its polytheistic belief system contributed to a deep sense of order. In the buoyant optimism of its poetry, the confident

imagery of its tomb paintings, and the cosmic symbolism of its temple architecture, we detect a basic trust in forces that are greater and more powerful than those of perishable humankind.

GLOSSARY

canon a set of rules or standards used to establish proportions

cosmology the theory of the origins, evolution, and structure of the universe

dynasty a sequence of rulers from the same family

fresco (Italian, "fresh") a method of painting on walls or ceilings surfaced with fresh, moist, lime plaster

hypostyle a hall whose roof is supported by columns

lyric literally "accompanied by the lyre," hence, verse that is meant to be sung rather than spoken; usually characterized by individual and personal emotion

module a unit of measurement used to determine proportion

monarch a single or sole ruler

obelisk a tall, four-sided pillar that tapers to a pyramidal apex

papyrus a reed-like plant from which the ancient Egyptians made paper

polytheism the belief in many gods

pylon a massive gateway in the form of a pair of truncated pyramids

relief a sculptural technique in which figures or forms are carved either to project from the background surface (raised relief) or cut away below the background level (sunk relief); the degree of relief is designated as high, low, or sunken

theocracy rule by god or god's representative

SUGGESTIONS FOR READING

Edwards, I. E. S. *The Pyramids of Egypt.* Baltimore: Penguin, 1986.

Frankfort, Henri, et al. *Before Philosophy.* Baltimore: Penguin, 1961.

Hodges, Peter. *How the Pyramids Were Built.* Lonmead: Element Books, 1989.

Johnson, Paul. *The Civilization of Ancient Egypt.* New York: HarperCollins, 1999.

Lehrer, Mark. *The Complete Pyramids.* London: Thames and Hudson, 1998.

Murray, M. S. *The Splendor That Was Egypt.* New York: Praeger, 1972.

Quirke, Stephen. *Ancient Egyptian Religion.* London: British Museum Press, 1992.

Robins, Gay. *Women in Ancient Egypt.* London: British Museum Press, 1993.

Taylor, John N. *Egypt and Nubia.* Cambridge, Mass.: Harvard University Press, 1991.

Tiradritti, Francesco, ed. *Egyptian Treasures from the Egyptian Museum in Cairo.* New York: Abrams, 1998.

Watterson, Barbara. *Women in Ancient Egypt.* New York: St. Martin's Press, 1992.

CHAPTER TWO

Mesopotamia: gods, rulers, and the social order

"From the days of old there is no permanence. The sleeping and the dead, how alike they are, they are like a painted death."
The Epic of Gilgamesh

Mesopotamia, literally "the land between the two rivers," describes the region in southwest Asia* that was the home of many civilizations over a period of 3,000 years. The earliest of these civilizations appeared around 3500 B.C.E. at Sumer, where the Tigris and Euphrates Rivers empty into the Persian Gulf (Map 2.1). Watered by these two rivers, the rich soil at the southeastern end of the Fertile Crescent made agricultural life possible and supported the growth of humankind's first cities—Uruk, Ur, Kish, Nippur, and Lagash. In contrast with the Nile River, which flooded its banks with comfortable regularity, the two rivers essential to food production in Mesopotamia overflowed unpredictably, often devastating whole villages and cities. Unlike Egypt, whose natural boundaries of desert and water worked to protect the civilization from

*Also known by Westerners as the "Near East."

foreign invasion, Mesopotamia's exposed and fertile plains invited the repeated attacks of tribal nomads, who descended from the mountainous regions north of the Fertile Crescent. And while Egypt's climate was regularly hot and dry, that of ancient Mesopotamia suffered fierce changes of weather, including drought, violent rainstorms, flood, wind, and hail. Mesopotamia's unpredictable rivers, vulnerable geographic situation, and erratic climate contributed to the mood of fear and insecurity that is reflected in all forms of Mesopotamian expression.

Mesopotamia was the stage on which many civilizations rose and fell. Some, like the Sumerian, formed small groups of city-states; others, like the Assyrian, founded great empires. And yet others, like the Hebrews, were tribal people who ultimately forged a political state. No one language or single, continuous form of government united these various Mesopotamian civilizations, yet they shared

Map 2.1 Southwest Asia (Near and Middle East)

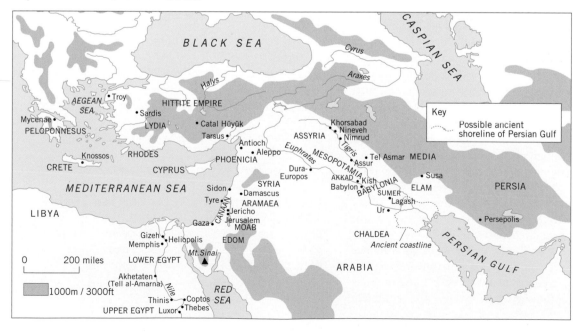

a common world view and—with the exception of the Hebrews—a polytheistic religious outlook.

The Gods of Mesopotamia

As in ancient Egypt, Mesopotamia's gods and goddesses were associated with nature and its forces. However, like the environment of Mesopotamia, its gods were fierce and capricious (Figure **2.1**), its mythology filled with physical and spiritual woe, and its cosmology based in the themes of chaos and conflict. *The Babylonian Creation*, humankind's earliest cosmological myth, illustrates all of these conditions. *The Babylonian Creation* is a Sumerian poem recorded early in the second millennium B.C.E. Recited during the festival of the New Year, it celebrates the birth of the gods and the order of creation. It describes a universe that originated by means of spontaneous generation: At a moment when there was neither heaven nor earth, the sweet and bitter waters "mingled" to produce the first family of gods. As the story unfolds, chaos and discord prevail amid the reign of Tiamat, the great goddess of the primeval waters, until Marduk, hero-god and offspring of Wisdom, takes matters in hand: He destroys the Great Mother and proceeds to establish a new order, bringing to an end the long and ancient tradition of matriarchy. Marduk founds the holy city of Babylon (literally, "home of the gods") and creates human beings, whose purpose it is to serve heaven's squabbling divinities.

READING 1.5 From *The Babylonian Creation*

When there was no heaven,   **1**
no earth, no height, no depth, no name,
   when Apsu[1] was alone,
the sweet water, the first begetter; and Tiamat[2]
   the bitter water, and that   **5**
return to the womb, her Mummu,[3]
   when there were no gods —

When sweet and bitter
mingled together, no reed was plaited, no rushes
   muddied the water,   **10**
the gods were nameless, natureless, futureless, then
   from Apsu and Tiamat
in the waters gods were created, in the waters
   silt precipitated,

Lahmu and Lahamu,[4]   **15**
were named; they were not yet old,
   not yet grown tall

---

[1]The primeval sweet waters.
[2]The primeval bitter waters.
[3]One of the primordial beings of the universe.
[4]Male and female primordial beings.

Name	Role
Adad	storm and rain god
Anu	father of the gods, god of heaven
Apsu	god of the primeval sweet waters
Dumuzi (Tammuz)	god of vegetation, fertility and the underworld; husband of Ishtar
Ea	god of wisdom and patron of the arts
Enlil	god of earth, wind, and air
Ishtar (Innana)	goddess of love, fertility, and war; Queen of Heaven
Ninhursag	mother goddess, creator of vegetation; wife of Enlil
Nisaba	goddess of grain
Shamash	god of the sun; judge and law-giver; god of wisdom
Sin (Nanna)	goddess of the moon

Figure 2.1 Principal Mesopotamian Gods

when Anshar and Kishar[5] overtook them both,
   the lines of sky and earth
stretched where horizons meet to separate   **20**
   cloud from silt.

Days on days, years
on years passed till Anu,[6] the empty heaven,
   heir and supplanter,
first-born of his father, in his own nature   **25**
   begot of Nudimmud-Ea[7]
intellect, wisdom, wider than heaven's horizon,
   the strongest of all the kindred.

Discord broke out among the gods although they were
brothers, warring and jarring in the belly of Tiamat,   **30**
heaven shook, it reeled with the surge of the dance.
Apsu could not silence the clamour. Their behaviour was
bad, overbearing, and proud. . . .

[Ea kills Apsu; Marduk is born and Tiamat spawns serpents and monsters to make war on the gods.]

When her labour of creation was ended, against her children   **1**
Tiamat began preparations of war. This was the evil she did to requite Apsu, this was the evil news that came to Ea.

When he had learned how matters lay he was stunned, he sat in black silence till rage had worked itself out; then he remembered the gods before him. He went to Anshar, his father's father, and told him how Tiamat plotted,

'She loathes us, father, our mother Tiamat has raised up that Company, she rages in turbulence and all have joined her, all those gods whom you begot,   **10**

---

[5]The horizon of the sky (male) and the horizon of the earth (female).
[6]God of the sky (the offspring of Anshar and Kishar).
[7]Another name for Ea, god of wisdom (the offspring of Anu).

'Together they jostle the ranks to march with Tiamat, day and night furiously they plot, the growling roaring rout, ready for battle, while the Old Hag, the first mother, mothers a new brood. . . .'

[The gods make Marduk Supreme Commander of the wars; he leads the attack on Tiamat.]

Then Marduk made a bow and strung it to be his own weapon, he set the arrow against the bow-string, in his right hand he grasped the mace and lifted it up, bow and quiver hung at his side, lightnings played in front of him, he was altogether an incandescence.   **1**

He netted a net, a snare for Tiamat; the winds from their quarters held it, south wind, north, east wind, west, and no part of Tiamat could escape. . . .

He turned back to where Tiamat lay bound, he straddled the legs and smashed her skull (for the mace was merciless), he severed the arteries and the blood streamed down the north wind to the unknown ends of the world.   **10**

When the gods saw all this they laughed out loud, and they sent him presents. They sent him their thankful tributes.

The lord rested; he gazed at the huge body, pondering how to use it, what to create from the dead carcass. He split it apart like a cockle-shell; with the upper half he constructed the arc of sky, he pulled down the bar and set a watch on the waters, so they should never escape. . . .

[Marduk makes Babylon "the home of the gods" and proceeds to create Man.]   **20**

Now that Marduk has heard what it is the gods are saying, he is moved with desire to create a work of consummate art. He told Ea the deep thought in his heart.

> Blood to blood
> I join,
> blood to bone
> I form
> an original thing,
> its name is MAN,   **30**
> aboriginal man
> is mine in making.
>
> All his occupations
> are faithful service,
> the gods that fell
> have rest,
> I will subtly alter
> their operations,
> divided companies
> equally blest.   **40**

Ea answered with carefully chosen words, completing the plan for the gods' comfort. He said to Marduk,
     "Let one of the kindred be taken; only one need die for the new creation. Bring the gods together in the Great Assembly; there let the guilty die, so the rest may live."

. . . .

The Search for Immortality

The theme of human vulnerability and the search for everlasting life are the central motifs in the *Epic of Gilgamesh*, the world's first epic. An **epic**, that is, a long narrative poem that recounts the deeds of a hero in quest of meaning and identity, embodies the ideals and values of the culture from which it comes. The *Epic of Gilgamesh* was

Figure 2.2 Gilgamesh between Two Human-Headed Bulls (top portion). Soundbox of a Harp, from Ur, Iraq, ca. 2600 B.C.E. Wood with inlaid gold, lapis lazuli, and shell, height approx. 12 in. The University Museum, University of Pennsylvania, Philadelphia (Neg. #T4–109).

recited orally for centuries before it was recorded at Sumer in the late third millennium. As literature, it precedes the Hebrew Bible and all the other major writings of antiquity. Its hero is a semi-historical figure who probably ruled the ancient Sumerian city of Uruk around 2800 B.C.E. Described as two-thirds god and one-third man, Gilgamesh is blessed by the gods with beauty and courage. But when he spurns the affections of the Queen of Heaven, Ishtar (a fertility goddess not unlike the Egyptian Isis), he is punished with the loss of his dearest companion, Enkidu. Despairing over Enkidu's death, Gilgamesh undertakes a long and hazardous quest in search of everlasting life. He meets Utnapishtim, a mortal whom the gods have rewarded with eternal life for having saved humankind from a devastating flood. Utnapishtim helps Gilgamesh locate the plant that miraculously restores lost youth. But ultimately, a serpent snatches the plant, and Gilgamesh is left with the haunting vision of death as "a house of dust" and a place of inescapable sadness. On the soundbox of a harp found in the royal graves at Ur, Gilgamesh is depicted standing between two human-headed bulls, while some of the epic's fantastic characters, such as the Man-Scorpion, appear in the registers below (Figure **2.2**). The Great Harp itself (Figure **2.3**) may have been used to accompany the chanting of this epic.

READING 1.6 From the Epic *of Gilgamesh*

O Gilgamesh, Lord of Kullab,[1] great is thy praise. This was **1** the man to whom all things were known; this was the king who knew the countries of the world. He was wise, he saw mysteries and knew secret things, he brought us a tale of the days before the flood. He went on a long journey, was weary, worn-out with labor, and returning engraved on a stone the whole story.

When the Gods created Gilgamesh they gave him a perfect body. Shamash the glorious sun endowed him with beauty, Adad the god of the storm endowed him with courage, the **10** great gods made his beauty perfect, surpassing all others. Two thirds they made him god and one third man.

In Uruk[2] he built walls, a great rampart, and the temple of blessed Eanna for the god of the firmament Anu, and for Ishtar the goddess of love.[3]

[Gilgamesh and his bosom companion, Enkidu, destroy Humbaba, the guardian of the cedar forest, and perform other heroic deeds. But Gilgamesh spurns the affections of Ishtar, and in revenge, she takes Enkidu's life.]

Bitterly Gilgamesh wept for his friend Enkidu; he wandered over the wilderness as a hunter, he roamed over the plains; in his bitterness he cried, "How can I rest, how can I be at peace? Despair is in my heart. What my brother is now, that

---

[1]Park of Uruk.
[2]A city located in Sumer. Gilgamesh was the fifth ruler in the Dynasty of Uruk after the flood.
[3]Also associated with fertility and war.

Figure 2.3 Lyre (reconstructed) from Ur, ca. 2600 B.C.E. Wood and inlays of gold, lapis lazuli and shell. Height 42 in. British Museum, London.

shall I be when I am dead. Because I am afraid of death I will go as best I can to find Utnapishtim whom they call the Faraway, for he has entered the assembly of the gods." So Gilgamesh traveled over the wilderness, he wandered over the grasslands, a long journey, in search of Utnapishtim, whom the gods took after the deluge; and they set him to live in the land of Dilmun,[4] in the garden of the sun; and to him alone of men they gave everlasting life.

At night when he came to the mountain passes Gilgamesh prayed: "In these mountain passes long ago I saw lions, I was afraid and I lifted my eyes to the moon; I prayed and my prayers went up to the gods, so now, O moon god Sin, protect me." When he had prayed he lay down to sleep, until he was woken from out of a dream. He saw the lions round him glorying in life; then he took his axe in his hand, he drew his sword from his belt, and struck and destroyed and scattered them.

So at length Gilgamesh came to that great mountain whose name is Mashu, the mountain which guards the rising and the setting sun. Its twin peaks are as high as the wall of heaven and its paps reach down to the underworld. At its gate the Scorpions stand guard, half man and half dragon; their glory is terrifying, their stare strikes death into men, their shimmering halo sweeps the mountains that guard the rising sun. When Gilgamesh saw them he shielded his eyes for the length of a moment only; then he took courage and approached. When they saw him so undismayed the Man-Scorpion called to his mate, "This one who comes to us now is flesh of the gods." The mate of the Man-Scorpion answered, "Two thirds is god but one third is man."

Then he called to the man Gilgamesh, he called to the child of the gods: "Why have you come so great a journey; for what have you traveled so far, crossing the dangerous waters; tell me the reason for your coming?" Gilgamesh answered, "For Enkidu; I loved him dearly, together we endured all kinds of hardships; on his account I have come, for the common lot of man has taken him. I have wept for him day and night, I would not give up his body for burial, I thought my friend would come back because of my weeping. Since he went, my life is nothing; that is why I have traveled here in search of Utnapishtim my father; for men say he has entered the assembly of the gods, and has found everlasting life. I have a desire to question him concerning the living and the dead." The Man-Scorpion opened his mouth and said, speaking to Gilgamesh, "No man born of woman has done what you have asked, no mortal man has gone into the mountain; the length of it is twelve leagues[5] of darkness; in it there is no light, but the heart is oppressed with darkness. From the rising of the sun to the setting of the sun there is no light." Gilgamesh said, "Although I should go in sorrow and in pain, with sighing and with weeping, still I must go. Open the gate of the mountain." And the Man-Scorpion said, "Go, Gilgamesh, I permit you to pass through the mountain of Mashu and through the high ranges; may your feet carry you safely home. The gate of the mountain is open."

When Gilgamesh heard this he did as the Man-Scorpion had said, he followed the sun's road to his rising, through the mountain. When he had gone one league the darkness became thick around him, for there was no light, he could see nothing ahead and nothing behind him. After two leagues the darkness was thick and there was no light, he could see nothing ahead and nothing behind him. After three leagues the darkness was thick, and there was no light, he could see nothing ahead and nothing behind him. After four leagues the darkness was thick and there was no light, he could see nothing ahead and nothing behind him. At the end of five leagues the darkness was thick and there was no light, he could see nothing ahead and nothing behind him. At the end of six leagues the darkness was thick and there was no light, he could see nothing ahead and nothing behind him. When he had gone seven leagues the darkness was thick and there was no light, he could see nothing ahead and nothing behind him. When he had gone eight leagues Gilgamesh gave a great cry, for the darkness was thick and he could see nothing ahead and nothing behind him. After nine leagues he felt the north wind on his face, but the darkness was thick and there was no light, he could see nothing ahead and nothing behind him. After ten leagues the end was near. After eleven leagues the dawn light appeared. At the end of twelve leagues the sun streamed out.

There was the garden of the gods; all round him stood bushes bearing gems. Seeing it he went down at once, for there was fruit of carnelian with the vine hanging from it, beautiful to look at; lapis lazuli leaves hung thick with fruit, sweet to see. For thorns and thistles there were hematite and rare stones, agate, and pearls from out of the sea. While Gilgamesh walked in the garden by the edge of the sea Shamash[6] saw him, and he saw that he was dressed in the skins of animals and ate their flesh. He was distressed, and he spoke and said, "No mortal man has gone this way before, nor will, as long as the winds drive over the sea." And to Gilgamesh he said, "You will never find the life for which you are searching." Gilgamesh said to glorious Shamash, "Now that I have toiled and strayed so far over the wilderness, am I to sleep, and let the earth cover my head forever? Let my eyes see the sun until they are dazzled with looking. Although I am no better than a dead man, still let me see the light of the sun."

[Gilgamesh meets Siduri, the maker of wine, who advises him to give up his search and value more highly the good things of the earth. Gilgamesh prepares to cross the Ocean and, with the help of the ferryman Urshanabi, finally reaches Dilmun, the home of Utnapishtim.]

"Oh, father Utnapishtim, you who have entered the assembly of the gods, I wish to question you concerning the living and the dead, how shall I find the life for which I am searching?"

Utnapishtim said, "There is no permanence. Do we build a house to stand for ever, do we seal a contract to hold for all time? Do brothers divide an inheritance to keep for ever, does

---

[4]The Sumerian paradise, a mythical land resembling the Garden of Eden described in the Hebrew Bible.
[5]Approximately 36 miles.

---

[6]The Semitic sun god.

the flood-time of rivers endure? It is only the nymph of the dragon-fly who sheds her larva and sees the sun in his glory. From the days of old there is no permanence. The sleeping and the dead, how alike they are, they are like a painted death. What is there between the master and the servant when both have fulfilled their doom? When the Annunaki, the judges, come together, and Mammetun the mother of destinies, together they decree the fates of men. Life and death they allot but the day of death they do not disclose."

Then Gilgamesh said to Utnapishtim the Faraway, "I look at you now, Utnapishtim, and your appearance is no different from mine; there is nothing strange in your features. I thought I should find you like a hero prepared for battle, but you lie here taking your ease on your back. Tell me truly, how was it that you came to enter the company of the gods and to possess everlasting life?" Utnapishtim said to Gilgamesh, "I will reveal to you a mystery, I will tell you a secret of the gods."

[Utnapishtim relates the story of the flood.]

In those days the world teemed, the people multiplied, the world bellowed like a wild bull, and the great god was aroused by the clamor. Enlil heard the clamor and he said to the gods in council, "The uproar of mankind is intolerable and sleep is no longer possible by reason of the babel." So the gods in their hearts were moved to let loose the deluge; but my lord Ea warned me in a dream. He whispered their words to my house of reeds. . . . "Tear down your house, I say, and build a boat. These are the measurements of the barque as you shall build her: let her beam equal her length, let her deck be roofed like the vault that covers the abyss; then take up into the boat the seed of all living creatures. . . ."

For six days and six nights the winds blew, torrent and tempest and flood overwhelmed the world, tempest and flood raged together like warring hosts. When the seventh day dawned the storm from the south subsided, the sea grew calm, the flood was stilled; I looked at the face of the world and there was silence, all mankind was turned to clay. The surface of the sea stretched as flat as a roof-top; I opened a hatch and the light fell on my face. Then I bowed low, I sat down and I wept, the tears streamed down my face, for on every side was the waste of water.

[Utnapishtim leads Gilgamesh to Urshanabi the Ferryman.]

Then Gilgamesh and Urshanabi launched the boat on to the water and boarded it, and they made ready to sail away; but the wife of Utnapishtim the Faraway said to him, "Gilgamesh came here wearied out, he is worn out; what will you give him to carry him back to his own country?" So Utnapishtim spoke, and Gilgamesh took a pole and brought the boat in to the bank. "Gilgamesh, you came here a man wearied out, you have worn yourself out; what shall I give you to carry you back to your own country? Gilgamesh, I shall reveal a secret thing, it is a mystery of the gods that I am telling you. There is a plant that grows under the water, it has a prickle like a thorn, like a rose; it will wound your hands, but if you succeed in taking it, then your hands will hold that which restores his lost youth to a man."

When Gilgamesh heard this he opened the sluices so that a sweet-water current might carry him out to the deepest channel; he tied heavy stones to his feet and they dragged him down to the water-bed. There he saw the plant growing; although it pricked him he took it in his hands; then he cut the heavy stones from his feet, and the sea carried him and threw him on the shore. Gilgamesh said to Urshanabi the ferryman, "Come here, and see this marvelous plant. By its virtue a man may win back all his former strength. I will take it to Uruk of the strong walls; there I will give it to the old to eat. Its name shall be 'the Old Men are Young Again'; and at last I shall eat it myself and have back all my lost youth." So Gilgamesh returned by the gate through which he had come, Gilgamesh and Urshanabi went together. They traveled their twenty leagues and then they broke their fast; after thirty leagues they stopped for the night.

Gilgamesh saw a well of cool water and he went down and bathed; but deep in the pool there was lying a serpent,[7] and the serpent sensed the sweetness of the flower. It rose out of the water and snatched it away, and immediately it sloughed its skin and returned to the well. Then Gilgamesh sat down and wept, the tears ran down his face, and he took the hand of Urshanabi; "O Urshanabi, was it for this that I toiled with my hands, is it for this I have wrung out my heart's blood? For myself I have gained nothing; not I, but the beast of the earth has joy of it now. Already the stream has carried it twenty leagues back to the channels where I found it. I found a sign and now I have lost it. Let us leave the boat on the bank and go."

. . . .

The *Epic of Gilgamesh* is important not only as the world's first epic poem, but also as the earliest known literary work that tries to come to terms with death, or non-being. It reflects the profound human need for an immortality ideology—a body of beliefs that anticipates the survival of some aspect of the self in a life hereafter. Typical of the mythic hero, Gilgamesh seeks to understand and control the unknown. He is driven to discover his human limits, but his quest for personal immortality is frustrated and his goals remain unfulfilled. In the uncertainty of its conclusions, the *Epic of Gilgamesh* stands in stark contrast with Egyptian writings, which confidently celebrate the promise of life after death.

The Rulers of Mesopotamia

The area collectively known as Sumer was a loosely knit group of city-states, that is, urban centers that governed the neighboring countryside. Here, men and women produced humankind's earliest Bronze Age technology and refined the cuneiform script that became the first written language. In each of the city-states of Sumer, individual priest-kings ruled as agents of one or another of the gods. The priest-king led the army, regulated the supply and

[7]More literally "earth lion" or "chameleon."

distribution of food, and provided political and religious leadership. From the temple at his palace, he conducted the services that were designed to win the favor of the gods.

Disunited and generally rivalrous, the city-states of Sumer were vulnerable to invasion from tribal warriors to the north. Around 2350 B.C.E. a gifted Akkadian warlord named Sargon I (Figure 2.4) conquered the city-states of Sumer and united them under his command. Consolidating a variety of peoples and language groups under his administration, Sargon created the world's first **empire**. By 2000 B.C.E., however, Sargon's empire fell to the attacks of nomadic tribespeople from the north. The invaders—establishing the pattern that dominated all of Mesopotamian history—built on the accomplishments of the very states they conquered. So, theocratic monarchy, religious polytheism, a socialistic economy, and established traditions of trade and barter would prevail from civilization to civilization. The myths and legends, indeed the *Epic of Gilgamesh* itself, would be transmitted from century to century to be transcribed in ever more refined versions of cuneiform script.

The Social Order

In the newly formed civilizations of the ancient world, community life demanded collective effort in matters of production and distribution, as well as in the irrigation of fields and the construction of roads, temples, palaces, and military defenses. As in Egypt, specialization of labor and the demands of urban life encouraged the development of social classes with different kinds of training, different responsibilities, and different types of authority. In early civilizations, the magician-priest who prepared the wine in the ritual vessel, the soldier who protected the city, and the farmer who cultivated the field represented fairly distinct classes of people with unique duties and responsibilities to society as a whole. The social order and division of labor that prevailed in Mesopotamia around 2700 B.C.E. are depicted in the "Standard of Ur," a wooden panel found in the royal tombs excavated at the city of Ur (Figure 2.5). The double-sided panel, executed in shell, mother-of-pearl, and lapis lazuli, appears to commemorate a Sumerian victory. On one side, in the top and middle registers, the ruler and his soldiers are seen taking prisoners after a battle; the bottom register depicts part of the battle itself with horse-drawn chariots trampling the defeated. On the reverse side of the panel, the ruler and six high officials of the Sumerian community lift their goblets at a celebratory banquet where the entertainers include a harpist and his female companion (top register, far right). The two lower registers record the procession of bearers with cows, rams, fish, and tribute in the form of various bundles carried on the backs of foreigners, probably prisoners of war. Although the precise function of this object is unknown, the Standard of Ur provides a mirror of class divisions in Mesopotamia of the third millennium B.C.E.

Law and the Social Order in Babylon

Shortly after 2000 B.C.E., rulers of the city-state of Babylon unified the neighboring territories of Sumer to establish the first Babylonian empire. In an effort to unite these regions politically and provide them with effective leadership, Babylon's sixth ruler, Hammurabi, called for a sys-

Figure 2.4 Head of the Akkadian ruler Sargon I, from Nineveh, Iraq, ca. 2350 B.C.E. Bronze, height 12 in. Iraq Museum, Baghdad. Photo: Scala.

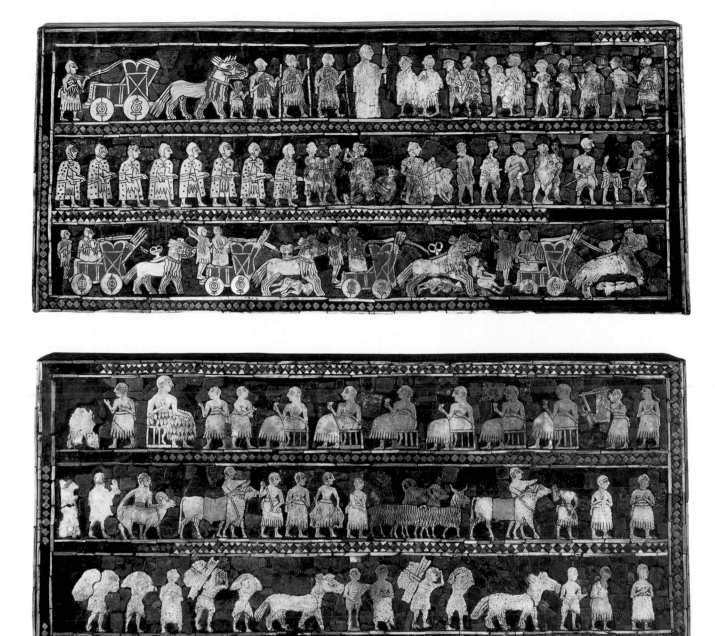

Figure 2.5 The Standard of Ur, ca. 2700 B.C.E. Double-sided panel inlaid with shell, lapis lazuli, and red limestone, approx. 8 x 19 in. Reproduced by courtesy of the Trustees of the British Museum, London.

tematic codification of existing legal practices. He sent out envoys to collect the local statutes and had them consolidated into a single body of law. Hammurabi's Code—a collection of 282 clauses engraved on an 8-foot-high stele—is our most valuable index to life in ancient Mesopotamia (Figure 2.6). The Code is not the first example of recorded law among the Babylonian kings; it is, however, the most extensive and comprehensive set of laws to survive from ancient times. Although Hammurabi's Code addressed primarily secular matters, it bore the force of divine decree. This fact is indicated in the prologue to the Code, where Hammurabi claims descent from the gods. It is also manifested visually in the low-relief carving at the top of the stele: Here, in a scene that calls to mind the story of the biblical Moses on Mount Sinai, Hammurabi is pictured receiving the law (symbolized by a staff) from the

sun god Shamash. Wearing a conical crown topped with bull's horns, and discharging flames from his shoulders, the god sits enthroned atop a sacred mountain, symbolized by triangular markings beneath his feet.

Written law represented a significant advance in the development of human rights in that it protected the individual from the capricious decisions of monarchs. Unwritten law was subject to the hazards of memory and the eccentricities of the powerful. Written law, on the other hand, permitted a more impersonal (if more objective and impartial) kind of justice than did oral law. It replaced the flexibility of the spoken word with the rigidity of the written word. It did not usually recognize exceptions and was not easily or quickly changed. Ultimately, recorded law shifted the burden of judgment from the individual ruler to the legal establishment. Although written

Figure 2.6 Stele of Hammurabi, ca. 1760 B.C.E. Babylonian. Basalt, entire stele approx. 7ft. 4 in. Louvre, Paris. Photo: RMN.

(clauses 162 and 168), professional obligations (clauses 218, 219, 229, and 232), and the individual's responsibilities to the community (clauses 109 and 152). It also documents the fact that under Babylonian law, individuals were not regarded as equals. Human worth was defined in terms of a person's wealth and status in society. Violence committed by one free person upon another was punished reciprocally (clause 196), but the same violence committed upon a lower-class individual drew considerably lighter punishment (clause 198), and penalties were reduced even further if the victim was a slave (clause 199). Similarly, a principle of "pay according to status" was applied in punishing thieves (clause 8): The upper-class thief was more heavily penalized or fined than the lower-class one. A thief who could not pay at all fell into slavery or was put to death. Slaves, whether captives of war or victims of debt, had no civil rights under law and enjoyed only the protection of the household to which they belonged.

In Babylonian society, women were considered intellectually and physically inferior to men and—much like slaves—were regarded as the personal property of the male head of the household. A woman went from her father's house to that of her husband, where she was expected to bear children (clause 138). Nevertheless, as indicated by the Code, women enjoyed commercial freedom (clause 109) and considerable legal protection (clause 134, 138, 209, and 210), their value as childbearers and housekeepers clearly acknowledged. Clause 142 is an astonishingly early example of no-fault divorce: Since a husband's neglect of his spouse was not punishable, neither party to the marriage was legally "at fault."

READING 1.7 From the Code of Hammurabi
(ca. 1750 B.C.E.)

. . . Hammurabi, the shepherd, named by Enlil am I, who increased plenty and abundance. The ancient seed of royalty, the powerful king, the sun of Babylon, who caused light to go forth over the lands of Sumer and Akkad . . . the favorite of Innana [Ishtar] am I. When Marduk sent me to rule the people and to bring help to the land, I established law and justice in the language of the land and promoted the welfare of the people.

Clause 8 If a man has stolen an ox, or sheep or an ass, or a pig or a goat, either from a god or a palace, he shall pay thirty-fold. If he is a plebeian,[1] he shall render ten-fold. If the thief has nothing to pay, he shall be slain.
14 If a man has stolen a man's son under age, he shall be slain.
109 If rebels meet in the house of a wine-seller and she does not seize them and take them to the palace, that wine-seller shall be slain.
129 If the wife of a man is found lying with another male, they shall be bound and thrown into the water; unless the

law necessarily restricted individual freedom, it safe-guarded the basic values of the community.

Hammurabi's Code covers a broad spectrum of moral, social, and commercial obligations. Its civil and criminal statutes specify penalties for murder, theft, incest, adultery, kidnapping, assault and battery, and many other crimes. More important for our understanding of ancient culture, it is a storehouse of information concerning the nature of class divisions, family relations, and human rights. The Code informs us, for instance, on matters of inheritance

---

[1] A member of the lower class, probably a peasant who worked the land for the ruling class.

husband lets his wife live, and the king lets his servant live.

134 If a man has been taken prisoner, and there is no food in his house, and his wife enters the house of another; then that woman bears no blame.

138 If a man divorces his spouse who has not borne him children, he shall give to her all the silver of the bride-price, and restore to her the dowry which she brought from the house of her father; and so he shall divorce her.

141 If a man's wife, dwelling in a man's house, has set her face to leave, has been guilty of dissipation, has wasted her house, and has neglected her husband; then she shall be prosecuted. If her husband says she is divorced, he shall let her go her way; he shall give her nothing for divorce. If her husband says she is not divorced, her husband may espouse another woman, and that woman shall remain a slave in the house of her husband.

142 If a woman hate her husband, and says "Thou shalt not possess me," the reason for her dislike shall be inquired into. If she is careful and has no fault, but her husband takes himself away and neglects her; then that woman is not to blame. She shall take her dowry and go back to her father's house.

143 If she has not been careful, but runs out, wastes her house and neglects her husband; then that woman shall be thrown into the water.

152 If, after that woman has entered the man's house, they incur debt, both of them must satisfy the trader.

154 If a man has known his daughter, that man shall be banished from his city.

157 If a man after his father has lain in the breasts of his mother, both of them shall be burned.

162 If a man has married a wife, and she has borne children, and that woman has gone to her fate; then her father has no claim upon her dowry. The dowry is her children's.

168 If a man has set his face to disown his son, and has said to the judge, "I disown my son," then the judge shall look into his reasons. If the son has not borne a heavy crime which would justify his being disowned from filiation, then the father shall not disown his son from filiation.

195 If a son has struck his father, his hand shall be cut off.

196 If a man has destroyed the eye of a free man,[2] his own eye shall be destroyed.

198 If he has destroyed the eye of a plebeian, or broken the bone of a plebeian, he shall pay one mina[3] of silver.

199 If he has destroyed the eye of a man's slave, or broken the bone of a man's slave, he shall pay half his value.

209 If a man strike the daughter of a free man, and causes her foetus to fall; he shall pay ten shekels[4] of silver for her foetus.

210 If that woman die, his daughter shall be slain.

213 If he has struck the slave of a man, and made her foetus fall; he shall pay two shekels of silver.

214 If that slave die, he shall pay a third of a mina of silver.

---

[2]Above the lower-class peasant, the free man who rented land owed only a percentage of the produce to the ruling class.

[3]A monetary unit equal to approximately one pound of silver.

[4]60 shekels = 1 mina.

—**1800** multiplication tables are devised in Babylon

—**1750** mathematicians in Babylon develop quadratic equations, square roots, cube roots, and an approximate value of *pi*

—**1700** windmills are employed for irrigation in Babylon

All dates in this chapter are approximate; — (minus) signifies B.C.E.

218 If a doctor has treated a man with a metal knife for a severe wound, and has caused the man to die, or has opened a man's tumor with a metal knife, and destroyed the man's eye; his hands shall be cut off.

219 If a doctor has treated a slave of a plebeian with a metal knife for a severe wound, and caused him to die he shall render slave for slave.

229 If a builder has built a house for a man, and his work is not strong, and if the house he has built falls in and kills the householder, that builder shall be slain.

232 If goods have been destroyed, he shall replace all that has been destroyed; and because the house that he built was not made strong, and it has fallen in, he shall restore the fallen house out of his own personal property.

282 If a slave shall say to his master, "Thou are not my master," he shall be prosecuted as a slave, and his owner shall cut off his ear.

The Arts in Mesopotamia

Although not as elaborate as the tombs of the Egyptians, the royal graves found at Ur and elsewhere in Mesopotamia have yielded artifacts of great beauty. Jewelry, weapons, household goods, and musical instruments testify to the wealth of Mesopotamia's princely rulers (see Figures 2.2 and 2.3). Rather than building elaborate homes for the dead, however, the inhabitants of Sumer and Babylon raised structures that might bring them closer to heaven. The **ziggurat**—a massive terraced tower made of rubble and brick—symbolized the sacred mountain linking the realms of heaven and earth (Figure 2.7). Ascended by a steep stairway, it provided a platform for sanctuaries dedicated to local deities and tended by priests and priestesses. Unlike the Egyptian pyramid, which functioned as a tomb, the ziggurat served as a shrine and temple. Hence, it formed the spiritual center of the city-state. Striking similarities exist between the ziggurats of Mesopotamia and the stepped platform pyramids of ancient Mexico, built somewhat later (Figure 2.8). Erected atop rubble mounds much like the Mesopotamian ziggurat, the temples of Meso-America functioned as solar observatories, religious sanctuaries, and gravesites. Whether or not any historical link exists between these Mesopotamian and the structurally similar Native American monuments remains among the many mysteries of ancient history.

In the shrine rooms located some 250 feet atop the ziggurat, local priests stored clay tablets inscribed with

Figure 2.7 Ziggurat at Ur (partially reconstructed), Third Dynasty of Ur, Iraq, ca. 2150–2050 B.C.E. © Hirmer Fotoarchiv.

cuneiform records of the city's economic activities, its religious customs, and its rites. The shrine room of the ziggurat at Tell Asmar in Sumer also housed a remarkable group of statues representing men and women of various sizes, with large, staring eyes and hands clasped across their chests (Figure **2.9**). Carved out of soft stone, these cult images may represent the gods, but it is more likely that they are votive (devotional) figures that represent the townspeople of Tell Asmar in the act of worshipping their local deities. The larger figures may be priests, and the smaller figures, laypersons. Rigid and attentive, they stand as if in perpetual prayer. Their enlarged eyes, inlaid with shell and black limestone convey the impression of dread and awe, visual testimony to the sense of human apprehension in the face of divine power. These images do not share the buoyant confident of the Egyptians; rather,

they convey the insecurities of a people whose vulnerability was an ever-present fact of life.

The Hebrews

While the civilizations of the Fertile Crescent established the cultural roots of the ancient world, a small group of Mesopotamians known as the Hebrews formulated a lasting contribution to the humanistic tradition in the form of ethical monotheism. Almost everything we know about the Hebrew people comes from the Bible—the word derives from the Greek *biblia*, meaning "books." Nevertheless, the archeology of the Near East offers considerable information by which we may reconstruct the history of the Hebrews before the formation of their first political state around 1000 B.C.E. The tribal people called by their neighbors "Hebrews" originated in Sumer. Some time after 2000 B.C.E., under the leadership of Abraham of Ur, they migrated westward across the Fertile Crescent and settled in Canaan along the Mediterranean Sea (see Map 2.1). In Canaan, according to the Book of Genesis, Abraham received God's word that his descendants would return to that land and become a "great nation." God's promise to Abraham established the Hebrew claim to the land of Canaan (modern-day Israel). At the same time, a special bond between God and the Hebrews ("I will be your God; you will be my people," Genesis 17:7–8) marked the beginning of the Hebrew belief that they were God's Chosen (or Holy) People.

Some time after 1700 B.C.E., the Hebrews migrated into Egypt, but falling subject to pharaohic efforts to rid Egypt of the Hyksos, they were reduced to the status of state slaves. Around 1300 B.C.E., under a dynamic leader named Moses, they departed Egypt and headed back toward Canaan.

Figure 2.8 Pyramid of the Magician, Uxmal, Yucatan, late classic Maya, ca. 550–900 C.E. Photo: Werner Forman, London.

Figure 2.9 Statuettes from the Abu Temple, Tell Asmar, Iraq, ca. 2900–2600 B.C.E. Marble, tallest figure ca. 30 in. The Iraq Museum, Baghdad, and The Oriental Institute, University of Chicago.

This event became the basis for Exodus (literally, "going out"), the second book of the Hebrew Bible. Since Canaan was now occupied by local tribes with sizable military strength, the Hebrews settled briefly in an arid region near the Dead Sea. During a forty-year period—which archeologists place sometime between 1300 and 1150 B.C.E.—the Hebrews forged the fundamentals of their faith: **monotheism** (the belief in one and only one god); a set of ethical and spiritual obligations; and a **covenant** (or contract) that bound the Hebrew community to God in return for God's protection. The covenant rested in a set of ten laws (the Decalogue), which defined the proper relationship between God and the faithful, as well as between and among all members of the Hebrew community. The "Ten Commandments," like the testimonials of the Egyptian *Book of the Dead*, are framed in the negative. The consequence for the violation of each law is unspecified. The Hebrew god provides no prophecy of hell and damnation and no heavenly reward for obedience; only the terrible warning (Exodus 20:5) to those who do not "keep the commandments:" Their children will suffer "to the third and fourth generation."

Hebrew monotheism focused on devotion to a single Supreme Being, the god that came to be called Yahweh*

(in Latin, Jehovah). The idea of a single creator-god appeared as well in Egypt around 1350 B.C.E., when the pharaoh Amenhotep IV (Akhenaten) made the sun god Aten the sole deity of Egypt (see chapter 1). Like other ancient gods and goddesses, Aten was an arbitrary force associated with a specific natural phenomenon: the sun. The Hebrew deity, on the other hand, transcended nature and all natural phenomena. As Supreme Creator, the Hebrew god preceded the physical universe. Whereas in Babylonian myth the universe is spontaneously generated and initially chaotic, the Hebrew Creation describes a universe that is systematically planned and invested with a preconceived moral order; it is the miraculous feat of a single benevolent, all-knowing Being. In contrast to the Babylonian universe, where squabbling gods require human beings as their servants, the Hebrew universe is the gift given by God, its creator, to God's supreme creation: humankind. Hebrew monotheism stands apart from other ancient conceptions of divine power (including that of Akhenaten's Aten) in yet another essential dimension: its ethical charge. The veneration of Yahweh as the source of

---

*An acronym based on four Hebrew letters used to represent the Divine Name.

and guide for an ethical life was unique to the Hebrew faith. Ethical monotheism, the belief in a moral system that derives from a sole, omnipotent God, became the most lasting of the Hebrew contributions to world culture.

The excerpts below belong to the Hebrew Bible, a collection of stories and songs passed down orally for hundreds of years. The first five books of the Bible, known as the **Torah** (literally "instruction"), were assembled from four main sources some time during the tenth century B.C.E. Parts of Genesis, the first book of the Torah, belong to a common pool of traditions rooted in Mesopotamia, where the Hebrews originated; so the story of the Flood, for instance, appears in both Genesis and the *Epic of Gilgamesh* (as well as in other Mesopotamian texts). Two groups of laws are represented below: the first, whose penalties are unspecified, constitute the unconditional law of the Decalogue. The second, which belongs to a much larger body of Hebrew laws, resemble those of Hammurabi. Unlike the Ten Commandments, the latter, which deal primarily with social obligations, prescribe specific consequences for their violation. Some so closely parallel the laws of the First Babylonian Empire that scholars think both may look back to a common source. The Bible—like the *Epic of Gilgamesh*—conflates centuries of legend and fact, and its significance as great literature is unquestionable; but its value as an historical document has been hotly debated for well over a century. It is exalted by many as the revelation of divine authority, and it is regarded as sacred scripture by three world religions: Judaism, Christianity, and Islam. Even as it expounds a message of faith and moral instruction, it narrates the saga of a people who came to view all history as divinely directed.

READING 1.8a From the Hebrew Bible (Genesis 1, 2)

The Creation

Chapter 1

²⁶God said, "Let us make man in our own image, in the likeness of ourselves, and let them be masters of the fish of the sea, the birds of heaven, the cattle, all the wild animals and all the creatures that creep along the ground."

²⁷God created man in the image of himself,
in the image of God he created him,
male and female he created them.

²⁸God blessed them, saying to them, "Be fruitful, multiply, fill the earth and subdue it. Be masters of the fish of the sea, the birds of heaven and all the living creatures that move on earth." ²⁹God also said, "Look, to you I give all the seed-bearing plants everywhere on the surface of the earth, and all the trees with seed-bearing fruit; this will be your food. ³⁰And to all the wild animals, all the birds of heaven and all the living creatures that creep along the ground, I give all the foliage of the plants as their food." And so it was. ³¹God saw all he had made, and indeed it was very good. Evening came and morning came: the sixth day.

Chapter 2

¹Thus heaven and earth were completed with all their array. ²On the seventh day God had completed the work he had been doing. He rested on the seventh day after all the work he had been doing. ³God blessed the seventh day and made it holy, because on that day he rested after all his work of creating.

⁴Such was the story of heaven and earth as they were created.

Paradise, and the test of free will

At the time when Yahweh God made earth and heaven ⁵there was as yet no wild bush on the earth nor had any wild plant yet sprung up, for Yahweh God had not sent rain on the earth, nor was there any man to till the soil. ⁶Instead, water flowed out of the ground and watered all the surface of the soil. ⁷Yahweh God shaped man from the soil of the ground and blew the breath of life into his nostrils, and man became a living being.

⁸Yahweh God planted a garden in Eden, which is in the east, and there he put the man he had fashioned. ⁹From the soil, Yahweh God caused to grow every kind of tree, enticing to look at and good to eat, with the tree of life in the middle of the garden, and the tree of the knowledge of good and evil.

¹⁰A river flowed from Eden to water the garden, and from there it divided to make four streams. ¹¹The first is named the Pishon, and this winds all through the land of Havilah where there is gold. ¹²The gold of this country is pure; bdellium* and cornelian** stone are found there. ¹³The second river is named the Gihon, and this winds all through the land of Cush. ¹⁴The third river is named the Tigris, and this flows to the east of Ashur. The fourth river is the Euphrates.

¹⁵Yahweh God took the man and settled him in the garden of Eden to cultivate and take care of it. ¹⁶Then Yahweh God gave the man this command, "You are free to eat of all the trees in the garden. ¹⁷But of the tree of the knowledge of good and evil you are not to eat; for, the day you eat of that, you are doomed to die."

¹⁸Yahweh God said, "It is not right that the man should be alone. I shall make him a helper." ¹⁹So from the soil Yahweh God fashioned all the wild animals and all the birds of heaven. These he brought to the man to see what he would call them; each one was to bear the name the man would give it. ²⁰The man gave names to all the cattle, all the birds of heaven and all the wild animals. But no helper suitable for the man was found for him. ²¹Then, Yahweh God made the man fall into a deep sleep. And, while he was asleep, he took one of his ribs and closed the flesh up again forthwith. ²²Yahweh God fashioned the rib he had taken from the man into a woman, and brought her to the man. ²³And the man said:

This one at last is bone of my bones
    and flesh of my flesh!
She is to be called Woman,
    because she was taken from Man.

²⁴This is why a man leaves his father and mother and becomes attached to his wife, and they become one flesh.

²⁵Now, both of them were naked, the man and his wife, but they felt no shame before each other.

---

*Variously interpreted as a deep-red gem or a pearl.
**A semi-precious red stone (carnelian).

READING 1.8b From the Hebrew Bible

(Exodus 20:1–20; 21:1–2, 18–27, 37; 23:1–9)

The Decalogue (Ten Commandments)

[1]Then God spoke all these words. He said, [2]"I am Yahweh your God who brought you out of Egypt, where you lived as slaves.

[3]"You shall have no other gods to rival me.

[4]"You shall not make yourself a carved image or any likeness of anything in heaven above or on earth beneath or in the waters under the earth.

[5]"You shall not bow down to them or serve them. For I, Yahweh your God, am a jealous God and I punish a parent's fault in the children, the grandchildren, and the great grandchildren among those who hate me; [6]but I act with faithful love towards thousands of those who love me and keep my commandments.

[7]"You shall not misuse the name of Yahweh your God, for Yahweh will not leave unpunished anyone who misuses his name.

[8]"Remember the Sabbath day and keep it holy. [9]For six days you shall labour and do all your work, [10]but the seventh day is a Sabbath for Yahweh your God. You shall do no work that day, neither you nor your son nor your daughter nor your servants, men or women, nor your animals nor the alien living with you. [11]For in six days Yahweh made the heavens, earth and sea and all that these contain, but on the seventh day he rested; that is why Yahweh has blessed the Sabbath day and made it sacred.

[12]Honour your father and your mother so that you may live long in the land that Yahweh your God is giving you.

[13]"You shall not kill.

[14]"You shall not commit adultery.

[15]"You shall not steal.

[16]"You shall not give false evidence against your neighbour.

[17]"You shall not set your heart on your neighbour's house. You shall not set your heart on your neighbour's spouse, or servant, man or woman, or ox, or donkey, or any of your neighbour's possessions."

[18]Seeing the thunder pealing, the lightning flashing, the trumpet blasting and the mountain smoking, the people were all terrified and kept their distance. [19]"Speak to us yourself," they said to Moses, "and we will obey; but do not let God speak to us, or we shall die." [20]Moses said to the people, "Do not be afraid; God has come to test you, so that your fear of him, being always in your mind, may keep you from sinning." [21]So the people kept their distance while Moses approached the dark cloud where God was.

Laws Concerning Slaves

[1]"These are the laws you must give them: [2]When you buy a Hebrew slave, his service will last for six years. In the seventh year he will leave a free man without paying compensation."

Blows and Wounds

[18]"If people quarrel and one strikes the other a blow with stone or fist so that the injured party, though not dead, is confined to bed,[19] but later recovers and can go about, even

with a stick, the one who struck the blow will have no liability, other than to compensate the injured party for the enforced inactivity and to take care of the injured party until the cure is complete.

[20]"If someone beats his slave, male or female, and the slave dies at his hands, he must pay the penalty. [21]But should the slave survive for one or two days, he will pay no penalty because the slave is his by right of purchase.

[22]"If people, when brawling, hurt a pregnant woman and she suffers a miscarriage but no further harm is done, the person responsible will pay compensation as fixed by the woman's master, paying as much as the judges decide. [23]If further harm is done, however, you will award life for life, [24]eye for eye, tooth for tooth, hand for hand, foot for foot, [25]burn for burn, wound for wound, stroke for stroke.

[26]"If anyone strikes the eye of his slave, male or female, and destroys the use of it, he will give the slave his freedom to compensate for the eye. [27]If he knocks out the tooth of his slave, male or female, he will give the slave his freedom to compensate for the tooth."

Theft of Animals

[37]"If anyone steals an ox or a sheep and slaughters or sells it, he will pay back five beasts from the herd for the ox, and four animals from the flock for the sheep."

Justice. Duties towards Enemies

[1]"You will not spread false rumours. You will not lend support to the wicked by giving untrue evidence. [2]You will not be led into wrong-doing by the majority nor, when giving evidence in a lawsuit, side with the majority to pervert the course of justice; [3]nor will you show partiality to the poor in a lawsuit. [4]"If you come on your enemy's ox or donkey straying, you will take it back to him. [5]If you see the donkey of someone who hates you fallen under its load, do not stand back; you must go and help him with it.

[6]"You will not cheat the poor among you of their rights at law. [7]Keep clear of fraud. Do not cause the death of the innocent or upright, and do not acquit the guilty. [8]You will accept no bribes, for a bribe blinds the clear-sighted and is the ruin of the cause of the upright.

[9]"You will not oppress the alien; you know how an alien feels, for you yourselves were once aliens in Egypt. . . ."

It is worth noting that there is a major difference between the laws of the Hebrews and those of Babylon: Among the Hebrews, punishment was not levied according to social class. This is not to say that class distinctions did not exist in Hebrew society, but rather that the law was meant to apply equally to all classes, with the exception of slaves. The humanitarian bias of the Hebrew laws is best reflected in God's frequent reminder to the Hebrews that since they themselves were once aliens and slaves, they must treat even the lowest members of the social order as worthy human beings. If Babylonian law prized economic prosperity and political stability, it was the unity of religious and moral life that lay at the heart of the Hebrew laws.

Figure 2.10 The Ark of the Covenant and sanctuary implements, Hammath near Tiberias, fourth century. Mosaic. Israel Antiquities Authority, Jerusalem. Photo: Zev Rodovan, Jerusalem.

The Hebrew State and the Social Order

By the beginning of the first millennium B.C.E., the Hebrews had reestablished themselves in Palestine—as ancient Canaan came to be called following its occupation by powerful tribes of Philistines in the twelfth century B.C.E. Under the rule of the Hebrew kings, Saul (ca. 1040–1000 B.C.E.), David (ca. 1000–960 B.C.E.), and Solomon (ca. 960–920 B.C.E.), Canaan became a powerful state defended by armies equipped with iron war chariots. In the city of Jerusalem (see Map 2.1), King Solomon constructed a royal palace and a magnificent temple (no longer standing) to enshrine the Ark of the Covenant. The curtained Ark that sheltered the Torah, along with the **menorah** (a seven-branched candelabrum) and other sacramental objects (Figure 2.10) took the place of pictorial representations of Yahweh in Hebrew houses of worship.

The social order of the Hebrews was shaped by biblical precepts. Between Hebrew kings and their people, there existed a covenant—protection in exchange for loyalty and obedience—similar to that which characterized the relationship between God and the Hebrews. This same patriarchal bond also prevailed between Jewish fathers and their families. Hebrew kings were considered the divinely appointed representatives of God; and Hebrew wives and children came under the direct control of the male head of the household and were listed among his possessions. In

short, the covenant between God and the Hebrews, as expressed in the laws, established the model for both secular and familial authority.

In the course of his reign, Solomon divided the Hebrew state into two administrative divisions: a northern portion called Israel, and a southern portion called Judah (hence the name "Jews"). While commercial pursuits of the young Hebrew nation generated wealth and material comforts, the cults of the Canaanite fertility gods and goddesses— "carved images" of which gave them tangible presence on earth—seduced many Hebrews to stray from their rigorous and wholly abstract monotheistic faith. By the eighth century B.C.E., as signs of moral laxity increased, a group of zealous teachers worked to renew the ancient covenant: Known as *prophets* (literally "those who speak for another"), Amos, Hosea, and Isaiah voiced urgent pleas for spiritual reform. They warned that violations of the covenant and the laws would result in divine punishment. A century after the fall of Israel to the Assyrians in 722 B.C.E., the prophet Jeremiah explained the event as an expression of divine chastisement. He warned the people of Judah to shun local religious cults and urged them to reaffirm the covenant or again feel God's wrath. The Hebrew concept of destiny as divinely governed is confirmed in Jeremiah's message: God rewards and punishes not in a life hereafter, but here on earth.

READING 1.8c From the Hebrew Bible

(Jeremiah 11: 1–14)

Jeremiah and the Observance of the Covenant

¹The word that came to Jeremiah from Yahweh, ²"Hear the terms of this covenant; tell them to the people of Judah and to the inhabitants of Jerusalem. ³Tell them, 'Yahweh, God of Israel, says this: Cursed be anyone who will not listen to the terms of this covenant ⁴which I ordained for your ancestors when I brought them out of Egypt, out of that iron-foundry. Listen to my voice, I told them, carry out all my orders, then you will be my people and I shall be your God, ⁵so that I may fulfil the oath I swore to your ancestors, that I may give them a country flowing with milk and honey, as is the case today.'" I replied, "So be it, Yahweh!" ⁶Then Yahweh said to me, "Proclaim all these terms in the towns of Judah and in the streets of Jerusalem, saying, 'Listen to the terms of this covenant and obey them. ⁷For when I brought your ancestors out of Egypt, I solemnly warned them, and have persistently warned them until today, saying: Listen to my voice. ⁸But they did not listen, did not pay attention; instead, each followed his own stubborn and wicked inclinations. And against them, in consequence, I put into action the words of this covenant which I had ordered them to obey and which they had not obeyed.'"

⁹Yahweh said to me, "Plainly there is conspiracy among the people of Judah and the citizens of Jerusalem. ¹⁰They have reverted to the sins of their ancestors who refused to listen to my words: they too are following other gods and serving them. The House of Israel and the House of Judah have broken my covenant which I made with their ancestors. ¹¹And so, Yahweh says this, 'I shall now bring a disaster on them which they cannot escape; they will call to me for help, but I shall not listen to them. ¹²The towns of Judah and the citizens of Jerusalem will then go and call for help to the gods to whom they burn incense, but these will be no help at all to them in their time of distress!

¹³'For you have as many gods
as you have towns, Judah!
You have built as many altars to Shame,
as many incense altars to Baal,
as Jerusalem has streets!

¹⁴'You, for your part, must not intercede for this people, nor raise either plea or prayer on their behalf, for I will not listen when their distress forces them to call to me for help.'"

. . . .

The Babylonian Captivity and the Book of Job

In 586 B.C.E., Judah fell to Chaldean armies led by the mighty King Nebuchadnezzar (ca. 630–562 B.C.E.). Nebuchadnezzar burned the city, raided the Temple, and took the inhabitants of Jerusalem into captivity. In the newly restored city of Babylon, with its glazed brick portals (Figure 2.11), its resplendent "hanging" gardens, its towering ziggurat—the model for the Tower of Babel described in Genesis—the Hebrews experienced almost fifty years of exile (586–538 B.C.E.). Their despair and doubt in the absolute goodness of God are voiced in the Book of Job, probably written in the years after the Babylonian Captivity. The finest example of wisdom literature in the Hebrew Bible, the Book of Job raises the question of unjustified suffering in a universe governed by a merciful god. The "blameless and upright" Job has obeyed the Commandments and has been a devoted servant of God throughout his life. Yet he is tested unmercifully by the loss of his possessions, his family, and his health. His wife begs him to renounce God, and his friends encourage him to acknowledge his sinfulness. But Job defiantly protests that he has given God no cause for anger. Job asks a universal question: "If there is no heaven (and thus no justice after death), how can a good man's suffering be justified?" or simply phrased, "Why do bad things happen to good people?"

Figure 2.11 A drawing of Babylon as it might have looked in the sixth century B.C.E. The Ishtar Gate stands at the center, with the palace of Nebuchadnezzar II and the Hanging Gardens behind and to its right. On the horizon and the east bank of the Euphrates looms the Marduk Ziggurat. The Oriental Institute of the University of Chicago.

The Book of Job

Chapter 1

¹There was once a man in the land of Uz called Job: a sound and honest man who feared God and shunned evil. ²Seven sons and three daughters were born to him.. ³And he owned seven thousand sheep, three thousand camels, five hundred yoke of oxen and five hundred she-donkeys, and many servants besides. This man was the most prosperous of all the Sons of the East. ⁴It was the custom of his sons to hold banquets in one another's houses in turn, and to invite their three sisters to eat and drink with them. ⁵Once each series of banquets was over, Job would send for them to come and be purified, and at dawn on the following day he would make a burnt offering for each of them. "Perhaps," Job would say, "my sons have sinned and in their heart blasphemed." So that was what Job used to do each time.

⁶One day when the sons of God came to attend on Yahweh, among them came Satan. *⁷So Yahweh said to Satan, "Where have you been?" "Prowling about on earth," he answered, "roaming around there." ⁸So Yahweh asked him, "Did you pay any attention to my servant Job? There is no one like him on the earth: a sound and honest man who fears God and shuns evil." ⁹"Yes," Satan said, "but Job is not God-fearing for nothing, is he? ¹⁰Have you not put a wall round him and his house and all his domain? You have blessed all he undertakes, and his flocks throng the countryside. ¹¹But stretch out your hand and lay a finger on his possessions: then, I warrant you, he will curse you to your face." ¹²"Very well," Yahweh said to Satan, "all he has is in your power. But keep your hands off his person." So Satan left the presence of Yahweh.

¹³On the day when Job's sons and daughters were eating and drinking in their eldest brother's house, ¹⁴a messenger came to Job. "Your oxen," he said, "were at the plough, with the donkeys grazing at their side, ¹⁵when the Sabaeans swept down on them and carried them off, and put the servants to the sword: I alone have escaped to tell you." ¹⁶He had not finished speaking when another messenger arrived. "The fire of God," he said, "has fallen from heaven and burnt the sheep and shepherds to ashes: I alone have escaped to tell you." ¹⁷He had not finished speaking when another messenger arrived. "The Chaldeans," he said, "three bands of them, have raided the camels and made off with them, and put the servants to the sword: I alone have escaped to tell you." ¹⁸He had not finished speaking when another messenger arrived. "Your sons and daughters," he said, "were eating and drinking at their eldest brother's house,¹⁹ when suddenly from the desert a gale sprang up, and it battered all four corners of the house which fell in on the young people. They are dead: I alone have escaped to tell you."

²⁰Then Job stood up, tore his robe and shaved his head. Then, falling to the ground, he prostrated himself ²¹ and said:

Naked I came from my mother's womb,
naked I shall return again.

---

*Literally, "adversary."

Yahweh gave, Yahweh has taken back.
Blessed be the name of Yahweh!

²²In all this misfortune Job committed no sin, and he did not reproach God. . . .

Chapter 2

¹Another day, the sons of God came to attend on Yahweh and Satan came with them too. ²So Yahweh said to Satan, "Where have you been?" "Prowling about on earth," he answered, "roaming around there." ³So Yahweh asked him, "Did you pay any attention to my servant Job? There is no one like him on the earth: a sound and honest man who fears God and shuns evil. He persists in his integrity still; you achieved nothing by provoking me to ruin him." ⁴"Skin after skin!" Satan replied. "Someone will give away all he has to save his life. ⁵But stretch out your hand and lay a finger on his bone and flesh; I warrant you, he will curse you to your face." ⁶"Very well," Yahweh said to Satan, "he is in your power. But spare his life." ⁷So Satan left the presence of Yahweh.

He struck Job down with malignant ulcers from the sole of his foot to the top of his head. ⁸Job took a piece of pot to scrape himself, and went and sat among the ashes. ⁹Then his wife said to him, "Why persist in this integrity of yours? Curse God and die." ¹⁰"That is how a fool of a woman talks," Job replied. "If we take happiness from God's hand, must we not take sorrow too?" And in all this misfortune Job uttered no sinful word.

¹¹The news of all the disasters that had fallen on Job came to the ears of three of his friends. Each of them set out from home—Eliphaz of Teman, Bildad of Shuah and Zophar of Naamath—and by common consent they decided to go and offer him sympathy and consolation. ¹²Looking at him from a distance, they could not recognise him; they wept aloud and tore their robes and threw dust over their heads. ¹³They sat there on the ground beside him for seven days and seven nights. To Job they spoke never a word, for they saw how much he was suffering.

Chapter 3: Job Curses the Day of his Birth

¹In the end it was Job who broke his silence and cursed the day of his birth. ²This is what he said:

³Perish the day on which I was born
and the night that told of a boy conceived.
⁴May that day be darkness,
may God on high have no thought for it,
may no light shine on it.
⁵May murk and shadow dark as death claim it for their own,
clouds hang over it,
eclipse swoop down on it.

. . . .

¹⁷What are human beings that you should take them so seriously,
subjecting them to your scrutiny,
¹⁸that morning after morning you should examine them
and at every instant test them?
¹⁹Will you never take your eyes off me
long enough for me to swallow my spittle?
²⁰Suppose I have sinned, what have I done to you,

you tireless watcher of humanity?
Why do you choose me as your target?
    Why should I be a burden to you?
²¹Can you not tolerate my sin,
    not overlook my fault?
For soon I shall be lying in the dust,
    you will look for me and I shall be no more.

Chapter 14
¹A human being, born of woman,
    [his] life is short but full of trouble.
²Like a flower, such a one blossoms and withers,
    fleeting as a shadow, transient.
³And this is the creature on whom you fix your gaze,
    and bring to judgement before you!
⁴But will anyone produce the pure from what is impure?
    No one can!
⁵Since his days are measured out,
    since his tale of months depends on you,
    since you assign him bounds he cannot pass,
⁶turn your eyes from him, leave him alone,
    like a hired labourer, to finish his day in peace.
⁷There is always hope for a tree:
    when felled, it can start its life again;
    its shoots continue to sprout.
⁸Its roots may have grown old in the earth,
    its stump rotting in the ground,
⁹but let it scent the water, and it buds,
    and puts out branches like a plant newly set.
¹⁰But a human being? He dies, and dead he remains,
    breathes his last, and then where is he?
¹¹The waters of the sea will vanish,
    the rivers stop flowing and run dry:
¹²a human being, once laid to rest, will never rise again,
    the heavens will wear out before he wakes up,
    or before he is roused from his sleep.
¹³Will no one hide me in Sheol,
    and shelter me there till your anger is past,
    fixing a certain day for calling me to mind—
¹⁴can the dead come back to life?—
        day after day of my service, I should be waiting
        for my relief to come.
¹⁵Then you would call, and I should answer,
    you would want to see once more what you have made.
¹⁶Whereas now you count every step I take,
    you would then stop spying on my sin;
¹⁷you would seal up my crime in a bag,
    and put a cover over my fault.
¹⁸Alas! Just as, eventually, the mountain falls down,
    the rock moves from its place,
¹⁹water wears away the stones,
    the cloudburst erodes the soil;
    so you destroy whatever hope a person has.
²⁰You crush him once for all, and he is gone;
    first you disfigure him, then you dismiss him.
²¹His children may rise to honours—he does not know it;
    they may come down in the world—he does not care.
²²He feels no pangs, except for his own body,
    makes no lament, except for his own self.

Chapter 38: Job Must Bow to the Creator's Wisdom
¹Then from the heart of the tempest Yahweh gave Job his
answer. He said:

²Who is this, obscuring my intentions
    with his ignorant words?
³Brace yourself like a fighter;
    I am going to ask the questions, and you are to inform me!
⁴Where were you when I laid the earth's foundations?
    Tell me, since you arc so well-informed!
⁵Who decided its dimensions, do you know?
    Or who stretched the measuring line across it?
⁶What supports its pillars at their bases?
    Who laid its cornerstone
⁷to the joyful concert of the morning stars
    and the unanimous acclaim of the sons of God?
⁸Who pent up the sea behind closed doors
    when it leapt tumultuous from the womb,
⁹when I wrapped it in a robe of mist
    and made black clouds its swaddling bands;
¹⁰when I cut out the place I had decreed for it
    and imposed gates and a bolt?
¹¹"Come so far," I said, "and no further;
    here your proud waves must break!"
¹²Have you ever in your life given orders to the morning
    or sent the dawn to its post,
¹³to grasp the earth by its edges
    and shake the wicked out of it?
¹⁴She turns it as red as a clay seal,
    she tints it as though it were a dress,
¹⁵stealing the light from evil-doers
    and breaking the arm raised to strike.
¹⁶Have you been right down to the sources of the sea
    and walked about at the bottom of the Abyss?
¹⁷Have you been shown the gates of Death,
    have you seen the janitors of the Shadow dark as death?
¹⁸Have you an inkling of the extent of the earth?
    Tell me all about it if you have!

Chapter 42: Job's Final Answer
¹This was the answer Job gave to Yahweh:

²I know that you are all-powerful:
    what you conceive, you can perform.
³I was the man who misrepresented your intentions
    with my ignorant words.
You have told me about great works that I cannot understand,
about marvels which are beyond me, of which I know
    nothing.
⁴(Listen, please, and let me speak:
I am going to ask the questions, and you are to inform me.)
⁵Before, I knew you only by hearsay
    but now, having seen you with my own eyes,
⁶I retract what I have said,
    and repent in dust and ashes.

God's answer to Job is an eloquent vindication of unques-
tioned faith: God's power is immense and human beings
cannot expect rational explanations of the divine will;

indeed, they have no business demanding such. Proclaiming the magnitude of divine power and the fragility of humankind, the Book of Job confirms the pivotal role of human faith (the belief and trust in God) that sustains the Hebrew covenant. The anxious sense of human vulnerability that pervades the Book of Job recalls the *Epic of Gilgamesh*. Indeed, the two works bear comparison. Both heroes, Job and Gilgamesh, are tested by superhuman forces, and both come to realize that misfortune and suffering are typical of the human condition. Gilgamesh seeks but fails to secure personal immortality; Job solicits God's promise of heavenly reward but fails to secure assurance that once dead, he might return to life. Just as Utnapishtim tells Gilgamesh, "There is no permanence," so Job laments that man born of woman "Like a flower, such a one blossoms and withers, . . . He dies and dead he remains." Such pessimism was not uncommon in Mesopotamia, the area in which both the *Epic of Gilgamesh* and the Hebrew Bible originated. The notion of life after death (so prominent in Egyptian religious thought) is as elusive a concept in Hebraic literature as it is in Mesopotamian myth. Nevertheless, following the Babylonian Captivity, Jews speculated on the idea of an afterlife. Job anticipates a final departure to an underworld, an abode of the dead known among the Hebrews as *Sheol* or Shadowland. Yet, even without the promise of reward, Job remains stubbornly faithful to the covenant. His tragic vision involves the gradual but dignified acceptance of his place in a divinely governed universe.

The Hebrew Bible played a major role in shaping the humanistic tradition in the West. It provided the religious and ethical foundations for Judaism, and, almost 2,000 years after the death of Abraham, for Christianity and Islam. Biblical teachings, including the belief in a single, personal, caring god who intervenes on behalf of a faithful people, have become fundamental to Western thought. And Bible stories—from Genesis to Job—have inspired some of humankind's greatest works of art, music, and literature.

The Iron Age

While the first kings of Israel administered the laws of the young Hebrew nation, all of Mesopotamia felt the effects of a new technology: Iron was introduced into Asia Minor by the Hittites, a nomadic tribe that entered the area before 2000 B.C.E. Cheaper to produce and more durable than bronze, iron represented new, superior technology. In addition to their iron weapons, the Hittites made active use of horse-drawn war chariots, which provided increased speed and mobility in battle. The combination of war chariots and iron weapons gave the Hittites clear military superiority over all of Mesopotamia.

As iron technology spread slowly throughout the Near East, it transformed the ancient world. Iron tools contributed to increased agricultural production, which in turn supported an increased population. In the wake of the Iron Age, numerous small states came to flower, bringing with them major cultural innovations. By 1500 B.C.E., for instance, the Phoenicians, an energetic, seafaring people

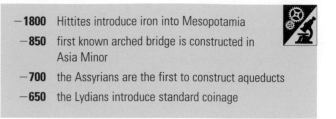

- **1800** Hittites introduce iron into Mesopotamia
- **850** first known arched bridge is constructed in Asia Minor
- **700** the Assyrians are the first to construct aqueducts
- **650** the Lydians introduce standard coinage

located on the Mediterranean Sea (see Map 2.1), had developed an alphabet of twenty-two signs. These signs eventually replaced earlier forms of script and became the basis of all Western alphabets. In Asia Minor, the Lydians, successors to the Hittites, began the practice of minting coins. Cheaper and stronger weapons also meant larger, more efficient armies. By the first millennium B.C.E., war was no longer the monopoly of the elite. Iron technology encouraged the rapid rise of large and powerful empires: Equipped with iron weapons, the Assyrians (ca. 750–600 B.C.E.), the Chaldeans (ca. 600–540 B.C.E.), and the Persians (ca. 550–330 B.C.E.) followed one another in conquering vast portions of Mesopotamia. Each of these empires grew in size and authority by imposing military control over territories outside their own natural boundaries—a practice known as *imperialism*.

The Assyrian Empire

The first of the great empire-builders, the Assyrians earned a reputation as the most militant civilization of ancient Mesopotamia. Held together by a powerful army that systematically combined engineering and fighting techniques, the Assyrians turned their iron weapons against most of Mesopotamia. In 721 B.C.E., they conquered Israel and dispersed its population. By the middle of the seventh century B.C.E. they had swallowed up most of the land between the Persian Gulf and the Nile valley. Assyrian power is reflected in the imposing walled citadel of Khorsabad, located some 10 miles from Nineveh (see Map 2.1). Covering 25 acres, this walled complex featured a ziggurat and an elaborate palace with more than 200 rooms: a maze of courtyards, harem quarters, treasuries, and state apartments (Figure **2.12**). The palace walls were adorned with low-relief scenes of war and pillage and with cuneiform inscriptions that celebrate Assyrian military victories. One seventh-century B.C.E. relief shows the imperial armies of King Ashurbanipal (668–627 B.C.E.) storming the battlements of an African city (Figure **2.13**). In the lower left, male captives (their chieftains still wearing the feathers of authority) are led away, followed in procession by women, children, and the spoils of war.

Flanking the scenes of military conquest on the palace walls at Nineveh and Nimrud are depictions of the royal lion hunt. Hunting and war, two closely related enterprises, were ideal vehicles by which to display the ruler's courage and physical might. In Assyrian reliefs, the lion, a traditional symbol of power throughout the ancient world (see Figure 1.6) is depicted as the adversary of the king. Ceremonial lion hunts celebrated the invincibility of the monarch, who, in earlier times, might have proved his prowess by combating wild animals in the field—in the

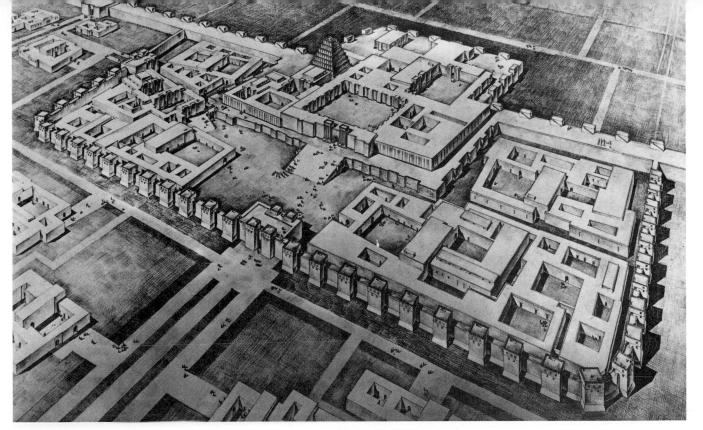

Figure 2.12 The citadel of Sargon II, Khorsabad, Iraq, ca. 720 B.C.E.,reconstruction drawing. Artist: Charles Altman. Institute of Archeology Library, University of London.

Figure 2.13 Ashurbanipal besieging an Egyptian city, 667 B.C.E. Alabaster relief. Reproduced by courtesy of the Trustees of the British Museum, London.

manner of the legendary Gilgamesh (see Figure 2.2). One dramatic scene from Nimrud depicts a wounded lion fiercely pursuing the royal chariot as it speeds away, while another beast lies dying before the wheels of the king's chariot (Figure 2.14). Spatial depth is indicated by superimposing the chariot wheels over the rear lion's legs. Yet the heads and legs of the horses are shown on a single plane, and clarity of design dictates that the second wounded lion, crouching in pain, fit precisely within the space between the front and rear legs of the prancing steeds. The balance between figures (positive shapes) and ground (negative or "empty" space) results in a brilliant formal

design. The Assyrian reliefs—housed in large numbers at the British Museum in London—are superb examples of the artist's ability to infuse violent subject matter with narrative grandeur. If the lion hunt reliefs made implicit reference to the ruler's invincibility, colossal sculpture clearly manifested his superhuman status. Ten-foot-tall hybrid beasts guarded the gateways of Assyrian palaces (Figure 2.15), much in the way the sphinx guarded the royal tombs of Egypt. Bearing the facial features of the monarch, these colossi united the physical attributes of the bull (virility), the lion (physical strength), and the eagle (predatory agility). The winged, human-headed bulls from the citadel at Khorsabad were power-symbols designed to inspire awe and fear among those who passed beneath their impassive gaze. The art of Assyria was a form of visual propaganda, designed not simply to celebrate Assyrian rulership, but to intimidate its enemies.

The Persian Empire

The Persian Empire, the last and the largest of the empires of Mesopotamia, was brought to its peak by Cyrus II (ca. 585–ca. 529 B.C.E.), called "the Great" for his conquests over territories ranging from the frontiers of India to the Mediterranean Sea. Persia's monarchs, aided by efficient administrators, oversaw a network of roads connecting the major cities of the Near East. Persian message-bearers traveled swiftly throughout the empire. Described by the Greek historian Herodotus as men unhindered "by snow, or rain, or heat, or by the darkness of night," they provided a model and a motto for the United States Postal Service.

The Persians devised a monotheistic religion based on the teachings of the prophet Zoroaster (ca. 628–ca. 551 B.C.E.). Denying the nature gods of earlier times, Zoroaster exalted the sole god Ahura-Mazda ("Wise Lord"), who demanded good thoughts, good works, and good deeds from his followers. Zoroaster taught that life was a battlefield on which the opposing forces of light and darkness contended for supremacy. Human beings took part in this cosmic struggle by way of their freedom to choose between good and evil, the consequences of which would determine their fate at the end of time. According to Zoroaster, a Last Judgment would consign the wicked to everlasting darkness, while the good would live eternally in an abode of luxury and light—the Persian *pairidaeza*, from which the English word "paradise" derives. Zoroastrianism came to influence the moral teachings of three great world religions: Judaism, Christianity, and Islam (see chapters 8 and 10).

At the Persian capital of Persepolis (in modern-day Iran), artists perpetuated the architectural and sculptural traditions of Assyria. The Persians also brought to perfection the art of metalworking that had flourished in Mesopotamia since the beginning of the Bronze Age. Utensils, vessels, and jewellery produced by Persian craftspeople, display some of the most intricate and sophisticat-

Figure 2.15 Winged human-headed bull from Khorsabad, Iraq, ca. 720 B.C.E. Limestone, approx. height 13 ft. 10 in. Louvre, Paris.

Figure 2.16 Achaemenid (Persian) gold vessel, fifth to third century B.C.E. Archaeological Museum, Teheran.

ed techniques of gold-working known to the history of that medium (Figure **2.16**). Many of these techniques would be practiced for centuries to come (see chapter 11).

SUMMARY

Mesopotamia's vulnerable geographic location contributed to the rise and fall of many different civilizations. Despite the differences in languages and ethnicity, the civilizations of this region, beginning with Sumer and ending with the Persian Empire, shared elements of a common culture. Unstable climate and the irregular overflow of the Tigris and Euphrates Rivers contributed to the formulation of a pantheon of fierce and capricious Mesopotamian deities and the evolution of a generally pessimistic world view. The world's first major literary work, the *Epic of Gilgamesh*, describes the futility of the human search for immortal life. Neither the Sumerians nor the Hebrews inhabiting the region developed the deep sense of order that characterized ancient Egyptian culture; nor did any of the civilizations of the Near East (with the exception of Persia) produce a clearly defined picture of life after death comparable to that of the Egyptians. Among the Hebrews, the covenant with a single, personal and transcendent god formed the basis for a religion that emphasized unswerving faith and high moral conduct. The Hebraic emphasis on ethical monotheism strongly influenced Western religious thought.

Mesopotamian rulers acted as agents of the gods. Within the civilizations of the Fertile Crescent, "divine-right monarchs" from Sargon to Cyrus the Great brought law and order to their societies. The close association between secular authority and spiritual power fostered the concept of law as a form of divine justice. From Mesopotamia came the world's first system of recorded law: Under the Babylonian ruler Hammurabi, laws were recorded and codified. Unlike the Hebrews, whose laws applied equally to all classes, the Babylonians punished violators according to their status in society. Iron technology made possible the establishment of large armies and ushered in centuries of imperialism. Yet the empires of the Near East perpetuated cultural traditions that reached back to Sumer: Civilization after civilization honored the gods with ziggurats, copied and recopied the *Epic of Gilgamesh*, and passed on the technology of metalworking. Yet it may be on Assyria's palace walls, inscribed with violent scenes of warfare, that the turbulent history of Mesopotamia is most vividly recorded. The arts of Mesopotamia reflect the lives of people for whom survival was a day-to-day struggle. These artworks proclaim the power of the ruler, the omnipotence of the gods, and the frailties of human beings as they try to understand the workings of nature, the meaning of death, and the destiny and purpose of humankind.

GLOSSARY

covenant contract; the bond between the Hebrew people and their God

epic a long narrative poem that recounts the deeds of a legendary or historical hero in his quest for meaning or identity

empire a state achieved militarily by the unification of territories under a single sovereign power

menorah a seven-branched candelabrum

monotheism the belief in one and only one god

Torah (Hebrew, "instruction," "law," or "teaching") the first five books of the Hebrew Bible: Genesis, Exodus, Leviticus, Numbers, and Deuteronomy

ziggurat a terraced tower of rubble and brick that served ancient Mesopotamians as a temple-shrine

SUGGESTIONS FOR READING

Anderson, Bernhard. *Understanding the Old Testament*, 4th ed. Englewood Cliffs, N.J.: Prentice-Hall, 1986.

Collon, Dominique. *Ancient Near Eastern Art*. Berkeley: University of California Press, 1993.

Cotterell, Arthur, ed. *The Penguin Book of Ancient Civilization*. London: Penguin, 1980.

Gabel, John B., and C. B. Wheeler. *The Bible as Literature: An Introduction*, 2nd ed. New York: Oxford University Press, 1990.

Gorden, Cyrus H. And Gary Rendsburg. *The Bible and the Ancient Near East.*, 4th edition. New York: Norton, 1997.

Holbrook, Clyde A. *The Iconoclastic Deity: Biblical Images of God*. Lewisburg, Pa.: Bucknell University Press, 1984.

Kramer, S. N. *History Begins at Sumer*, 3rd ed. Philadelphia: University of Pennsylvania Press, 1981.

Mellaart, Henry. *The Earliest Civilizations of the Near East*. London: Thames and Hudson, 1965.

Saggs, H. W. F. *The Babylonians*. Norman: University of Oklahoma, 1995.

———— *The Might That Was Assyria*. Salem, N.H.: Merrimack, 1984.

CHAPTER THREE

India and China: gods, rulers, and the social order

"He knows peace who has forgotten desire.
He lives without craving:
Free from ego, free from pride."
The *Bhagavad-Gita*

India and China, two of the oldest continuous civilizations in world history, emerged somewhat later than the civilizations of Egypt and Mesopotamia. These ancient Asian cultures nevertheless contributed significantly to the humanistic tradition, producing literature, philosophy, art, and music that ranks with that of the other great civilizations. But the Asian world view differs somewhat from that of the Western cultures we have examined. In India, for example, the fundamentals of spirituality were grounded in **pantheism**, the belief that all things in the universe are pervaded by an ineffable divine spirit. For the ancient Chinese, the natural order of the universe was central to all aspects of material and spiritual existence. In both of these cultures, all aspects of reality, whether human or divine, were thought to belong to the larger organic whole. This holistic outlook contributed to the evolution of rulership and the formation of the social order.

Ancient India

Indus Valley Civilization (ca. 2700–1500 B.C.E.)

India's earliest known civilization was located in the lower Indus valley, in an area called Sind—from which the words "India" and "Hindu" derive (Map **3.1**).

At Mohenjo-daro (part of modern-day Pakistan) and other urban centers, a sophisticated Bronze Age culture flourished before 2500 B.C.E. India's first cities were planned communities: their streets, lined with fired-brick houses were laid out in a grid pattern, and their covered sewage systems were unmatched in other parts of the civilized world. Bronze Age India also claimed a form of written language, although the 400 pictographic signs that constitute their earliest script are still undeciphered. There is little evidence of temple or tomb architecture, but a vigorous sculptural tradition is evident in both bronze and stone. The lively female dancer pictured in Figure **3.2** is one of many objects (see also Figure 0.19)

that reflect India's mastery of the lost-wax method of working bronze. In the medium of stone, the powerful portrait of a bearded man (possibly a priest or ruler) distinguished by an introspective expression, anticipates the meditative images of India's later religious art (Figure **3.1**).

Figure 3.1 *Bearded Man*, Mohenjo-daro, Indus valley, ca. 2000 B.C.E. Limestone, height 7 in. Karachi Museum. Photo: Robert Harding, London.

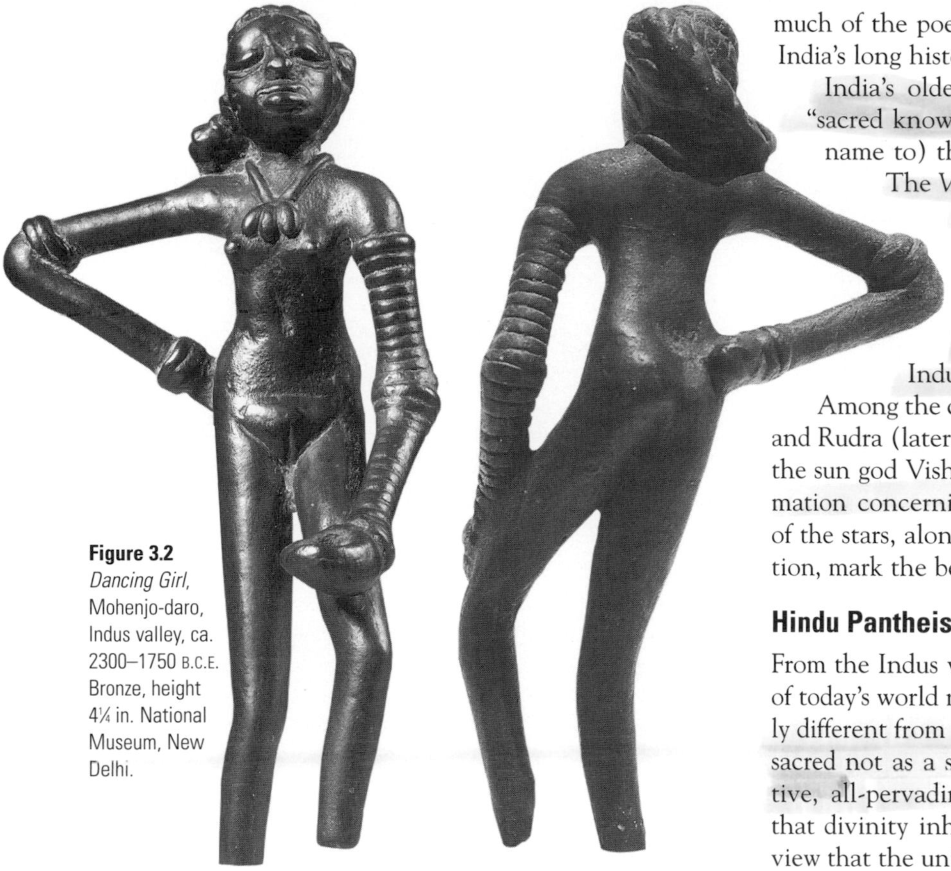

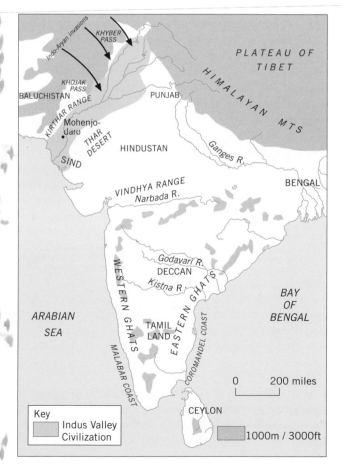

Figure 3.2
Dancing Girl, Mohenjo-daro, Indus valley, ca. 2300–1750 B.C.E. Bronze, height 4¼ in. National Museum, New Delhi.

much of the poetry, drama, and art produced throughout India's long history.

India's oldest devotional texts, the *Vedas* (literally, "sacred knowledge"), also originate in (and give their name to) the thousand-year period after 1500 B.C.E. The *Vedas* are a collection of prayers, sacrificial formulae, and hymns, one example of which appears in Reading 1.2 in the Introduction. Transmitted orally for centuries, the *Vedas* reflect the blending of the native folk traditions of the Indus valley and that of the invading Aryans. Among the chief Vedic deities were the sky gods Indra and Rudra (later known as Shiva), the fire god Agni, and the sun god Vishnu. The *Vedas* provide a wealth of information concerning astronomical phenomena. The study of the stars, along with the practice of surgery and dissection, mark the beginnings of scientific inquiry in India.

Hindu Pantheism

From the Indus valley civilization came the most ancient of today's world religions: Hinduism. Hinduism is markedly different from the religions of the West. It identifies the sacred not as a superhuman personality, but as an objective, all-pervading cosmic Spirit. Pantheism, the belief that divinity inheres in all things, is basic to the Hindu view that the universe itself is sacred. While neither polytheistic nor monotheistic in the traditional sense, Hinduism venerates all forms and manifestations of the

The Vedic Era (ca. 1500–322 B.C.E.)

Some time after 1500 B.C.E., warring, semi-nomadic tribes known as Aryans ("lords" or "nobles") invaded the Indus valley. These light-skinned peoples enslaved or removed the dark-skinned populations of Sind and established a set of societal divisions that anticipated the **caste system**. While a hierarchical order marked the social systems of all ancient civilizations, India developed the most rigid kind of class stratification, which prevailed until modern times. By 1000 B.C.E., four principal castes existed: priests and scholars, rulers and warriors, artisans and merchants, and unskilled workers. Slowly, these castes began to subdivide according to occupation. At the very bottom of the social order, or, more accurately, outside it, lay those who held the most menial and degrading occupations. They became known as Untouchables.

It was the Aryans who introduced Sanskrit, which would become the classic language of India. The bards of India recounted stories of the bitter tribal wars between competing Aryan families. These stories were the basis for India's two great epics—the *Mahabharata* (*Great Deeds of the Bharata Clan*) and the *Ramayana* (*Song of Prince Rama*), transmitted orally for generations but not recorded until the eighth century B.C.E. The *Mahabharata*—the world's longest folk epic—recreates the ten-year-long struggle for control of the Ganges valley occurring around the year 1000 B.C.E. Along with the *Ramayana*, this epic assumed a role in the cultural history of India not unlike that of the *Iliad* and the *Odyssey* in Hellenic history. Indeed, the two epics have been treasured resources for

Map 3.1 Ancient India.

all-pervasive Spirit. Hence, Hinduism embraces all of the Vedic gods, who themselves take countless forms. Hindus believe in the oneness of Spirit, but worship that Spirit by way of a multitude of deities, who are perceived as emanations of the divine. In the words of the *Rig Veda*, "Truth is one, but the wise call it by many names."

Hinduism is best understood by way of the religious texts known as the *Upanishads*, some 250 prose commentaries on the *Vedas*. Like the *Vedas* themselves, the *Upanishads* were orally transmitted and recorded in Sanskrit between the eighth and sixth centuries B.C.E. While the *Vedas* teach worship through prayer and sacrifice, the *Upanishads* teach enlightenment through meditation. They predicate the concept of the single, all-pervading cosmic force called **Brahman**. Unlike the nature deities of Egypt and Mesopotamia, Brahman is infinite, formless, and ultimately unknowable. Unlike the Hebrew Yahweh, Brahman assumes no personal and contractual relationship with humankind. Brahman is the Uncaused Cause and the Ultimate Reality. In every human being, there resides the individual manifestation of Brahman: the Self, or **Atman**, which, according to the *Upanishads*, is "soundless, formless, intangible, undying, tasteless, odorless, without beginning, without end, eternal, immutable, [and] beyond nature." Although housed in the material prison of the human body, the Self (Atman) seeks to be one with the Absolute Spirit (Brahman). The (re)union of Brahman and Atman—a condition known as **nirvana**—is the goal of the Hindu. This blissful reabsorption of the Self into Absolute Spirit must be preceded by one's gradual rejection of the material world, that is, the world of illusion and ignorance, and by the mastery of the techniques of meditation. On reaching nirvana, however, the Hindu is released from the endless cycle of death and rebirth.

Essentially a literature of humility, the *Upanishads* offer no guidelines for worship, no moral laws, and no religious dogma. They neither exalt divine power, nor do they interpret it. They do, however, instruct the individual Hindu on the subject of death and rebirth. The Hindu anticipates a succession of lives: that is, the successive return of the Atman in various physical forms. The physical form, whether animal or human and of whatever species or class, is determined by the level of spiritual purity that Hindu has achieved by the time of his or her death. The Law of **Karma** holds that the collective spiritual energy gained from accumulated deeds determines one's physical state in the next life. Reincarnation, or the Wheel of Rebirth, is the fate of Hindus until they achieve nirvana. In this ultimate state, the enlightened Atman is both liberated and absorbed—a process that may be likened to the dissolution of a grain of salt in the vast waters of the ocean.

The *Bhagavad-Gita*

The fundamental teachings of Hinduism are lyrically expressed in one of India's most popular religious poems: the *Bhagavad-Gita (Song of God)*, which constitutes one episode from the *Mahabharata*. In this most famous part of the poem, a dialogue takes place between Arjuna, the warrior-hero, and Krishna, the incarnation of the god Vishnu

and a divine manifestation of Brahman. Facing the prospect of shedding the blood of his own kinsmen in the battle to come, Arjuna seeks to reconcile his material obligations with his spiritual quest for selflessness. Krishna's answer to Arjuna—a classic statement of resignation—represents the essence of Hindu thought as distilled from the *Upanishads*. Although probably in existence earlier, the *Bhagavad-Gita* was not recorded until sometime between the fifth and second centuries B.C.E.

READING 1.9 From the *Bhagavad-Gita*

He [who] knows bliss in the Atman   1
And wants nothing else.
Cravings torment the heart:
He renounces cravings.
I call him illumined.   5
Not shaken by adversity,
Not hankering after happiness:
Free from fear, free from anger,
Free from the things of desire,
I call him a seer, and illumined.   10
The bonds of his flesh are broken.
He is lucky, and does not rejoice:
He is unlucky, and does not weep.
I call him illumined.

. . . .

Thinking about sense-objects   15
Will attach you to sense-objects;
Grow attached, and you become addicted;
Thwart your addiction, it turns to anger;
Be angry, and you confuse your mind;
Confuse your mind, you forget the lesson of experience;   20
Forget experience, you lose discrimination;
Lose discrimination, and you miss life's only purpose.
When he has no lust, no hatred,
A man walks safely among the things of lust and hatred.
To obey the Atman   25
Is his peaceful joy:
Sorrow melts
Into that clear peace;
His quiet mind
Is soon established in peace.   30

The uncontrolled mind
Does not guess that the Atman is present:
How can it meditate?
Without meditation, where is peace?
Without peace, where is happiness?   35

The wind turns a ship
From its course upon the waters:
The wandering winds of the senses
Cast man's mind adrift
And turn his better judgment from its course.   40
When a man can still the senses

I call him illumined.
The recollected mind is awake
In the knowledge of the Atman
Which is dark night to the ignorant: 45
The ignorant are awake in their sense-life
Which they think is daylight:
To the seer it is darkness.
Water flows continually into the ocean
But the ocean is never disturbed: 50
Desire flows into the mind of the seer
But he is never disturbed.
The seer knows peace:
The man who stirs up his own lusts
Can never know peace.   55
He knows peace who has forgotten desire.
He lives without craving:
Free from ego, free from pride.

This is the state of enlightenment in Brahman:
A man who does not fall back from it   60
Into delusion.
Even at the moment of death
He is alive in that enlightenment:
Brahman and he are one. . . .

Figure 3.3 Ritual disc, Zhou Dynasty, fifth to third century B.C.E. Jade, diameter 6½ in. Nelson Atkins Museum, Kansas City, Missouri. 33–81.

The Hindu view of the relationship between people and gods differs significantly from the religious views of ancient Egyptians and Mesopotamians. While the latter held human beings as separate from the gods, Hindus, guided by the *Upanishads* and the *Bhagavad-Gita*, asserted the oneness of matter and spirit. Where Western religions emphasized the imperishability of individual consciousness, Hinduism aspired to its sublimation, or rather, its reabsorption into the spiritual infinite. Although Hinduism still embraces the vast pantheon of Vedic gods and goddesses, it has remained relatively unaffected by the religious precepts of Western Judaism and Christianity. Unlike the latter, Hinduism has no institutional forms of worship and no doctrinal laws. On the other hand, since the nineteenth century, Hinduism's holistic view of nature has increasingly influenced Western thought and belief. And since the last decades of the twentieth century, Hindu techniques of deep meditation have made a notable impact on the disciplines of religion, philosophy, and medical science.

Ancient China

Ancient Chinese civilization emerged in the fertile valleys of two great waterways: the Yellow and the Yangzi* Rivers (Map **3.2**). As early as 3500 B.C.E., the Neolithic villages of China were producing silk, a commodity that would bring wealth and fame to Chinese culture, but the hallmarks of civilization—urban centers, metallurgy, and writing—did not appear until the second millennium B.C.E. By 1750 B.C.E., the Chinese had developed a script that employed some 4,500 characters (each character representing an individual word), some of which are still used today. A combination of pictographic and phonetic elements, Chinese characters became the basis for writing throughout East Asia. Although it is likely that China's first dynasties flourished for some three centuries before the appearance of writing, China's Bronze Age urban culture coincided with the rise of a warrior tribe known as the Shang.

The Shang Dynasty
(ca. 1520–1027 B.C.E.)

Shang rulers were hereditary kings who were regarded as intermediaries between the people and the spirit world. Limited in power by councils consisting of China's landholding nobility, they claimed their authority from the Lord on High (Shang-ti). Hence, as in Egypt, they ruled by divine right. Royal authority was symbolized by the dragon, a hybrid beast that stood for strength, fertility and life-giving water (Figure **3.3**). Occupants of the "dragon

*All transcriptions of Chinese names appear in the system known as Hanyu Pinyin.

flourished between 2000 and 1400 B.C.E., when it seems to have been absorbed or destroyed by the Mycenaeans.

Minoan Civilization (ca. 2000–1400 B.C.E.)

Centered in the Palace of Minos at Knossos on the island of Crete (Figure **4.1**), Minoan culture was prosperous and seafaring. The absence of protective walls around the palace complex suggests that the Minoans enjoyed a sense of security. The three-story palace at Knossos was a labyrinthine masonry structure with dozens of rooms and corridors built around a central courtyard. The interior walls of the palace bear magnificent frescoes illustrating natural and marine motifs (Figure **4.2**), ceremonial processions, and other aspects of Cretan life. The most famous of the palace frescoes, the so-called "bull-leaping" fresco, shows two women and a man, the latter vigorously somersaulting over the back of a bull (Figure **4.3**). Probably associated with the cult of the bull—ancient symbol of virility (see Figures 1.3 and 2.15)—the ritual game prefigures the modern bullfight, the "rules" of which were codified in Roman times by Julius Caesar. Since 1979, when modern archeologists uncovered the evidence of human sacrifice in Minoan Crete, historians have speculated on the meaning of ancient bull-vaulting (a sport still practiced in Portugal), and its possible relationship to rituals of blood sacrifice. Nevertheless, the significance

of the representation lies in the authority it bestows upon the players: Human beings are pictured here not as pawns in a divine game, but, rather, as challengers in a contest of wit and physical agility. Other Minoan artifacts suggest the persistence of ancient fertility cults honoring gods traditionally associated with procreation: The small statue of a bare-breasted female brandishing snakes may represent a popular fertility goddess; or it may depict a priestess performing specific cult rites, such as those accompanying ancient Greek dances that featured live snakes (Figure **4.4**). Minoan writing (known as "Linear A") has not yet been deciphered, but a later version of the script ("Linear B") found on mainland Greece appears to be an early form of Greek. Modern archeologists were not the first to prize Minoan culture; the Greeks immortalized the Minoans in myth and legend. The most famous of these legends describes a Minotaur—a monstrous half-man, half-bull hybrid born of the union of Minos' queen and a sacred white bull. According to the story, the clever Athenian hero Theseus, aided by the king's daughter Ariadne, threaded his way through the Minotaur's labyrinthine lair to kill the monster, thus freeing Athens from its ancient bondage to the Minoans. Around 1700 B.C.E., some three centuries before mainland Greece absorbed Crete, an earthquake brought devastation to Minoan civilization.

Figure 4.1 Palace of Minos, Knossos, Crete, ca. 1500 B.C.E. Photo: Gloria K. Fiero.

Figure 4.2 The Queen's Quarters, Palace of Minos, Knossos, Crete, ca. 1450 B.C.E. Ancient Art and Architecture Collection, Middlesex.

Figure 4.3 Bull-leaping fresco from the Palace of Minos, Knossos, Crete, ca. 1500 B.C.E. Height 32 in. Archeological Museum, Heraklion, Crete. Scala, Florence.

abroad to foreign shores, to a wealthy, noble host,
and a sense of marvel runs through all who see him—
so Achilles marveled, beholding majestic Priam.
His men marveled too, trading startled glances.
But Priam prayed his heart out to Achilles: 185
"Remember your own father, great godlike Achilles—
as old as / am, past the threshold of deadly old age!
No doubt the countrymen round about him plague him now,
with no one there to defend him, beat away disaster.
No one—but at least he hears you're still alive   190
and his old heart rejoices, hopes rising, day by day,
to see his beloved son come sailing home from Troy.
But I—dear god, my life so cursed by fate . . .
I fathered hero sons in the wide realm of Troy
and now not a single one is left, I tell you.   195
Fifty sons I had when the sons of Achaea came,
nineteen born to me from a single mother's womb
and the rest by other women in the palace. Many,
most of them violent Ares cut the knees from under.
But one, one was left me, to guard my walls, my people— 200
the one you killed the other day, defending his fatherland,
my Hector! It's all for him I've come to the ships now,
to win him back from you—I bring a priceless ransom.
Revere the gods, Achilles! Pity me in my own right,
remember your own father! I deserve more pity...   205
I have endured what no one on earth has ever done before—
I put to my lips the hands of the man who killed my son."

Those words stirred within Achilles a deep desire
to grieve for his own father. Taking the old man's hand
he gently moved him back. And overpowered by memory   210
both men gave way to grief. Priam wept freely
for man-killing Hector, throbbing, crouching
before Achilles' feet as Achilles wept himself,
now for his father, now for Patroclus once again,
and their sobbing rose and fell throughout the house.   215
Then, when brilliant Achilles had his fill of tears
and the longing for it had left his mind and body,
he rose from his seat, raised the old man by the hand
and filled with pity now for his gray head and gray beard,
he spoke out winging words, flying straight to the heart: 220
"Poor man, how much you've borne—pain to break the spirit!
What daring brought you down to the ships, all alone,
to face the glance of the man who killed your sons,
so many fine brave boys? You have a heart of iron.
Come, please, sit down on this chair here...   225
Let us put our griefs to rest in our own hearts,
rake them up no more, raw as we are with mourning.
What good's to be won from tears that chill the spirit?
So the immortals spun our lives that we, we wretched men
live on to bear such torments—the gods live free of sorrows. 230
There are two great jars that stand on the floor of Zeus's halls
and hold his gifts, our miseries one, the other blessings.
When Zeus who loves the lightning mixes gifts for a man,
now he meets with misfortune, now good times in turn.
When Zeus dispenses gifts from the jar of sorrows only,   235
he makes a man an outcast—brutal, ravenous hunger
drives him down the face of the shining earth,
stalking far and wide, cursed by gods and men.

So with my father, Peleus. What glittering gifts
the gods rained down from the day that he was born!   240
He excelled all men in wealth and pride of place,
he lorded the Myrmidons, and mortal that he was,
they gave the man an immortal goddess for a wife.
Yes, but even on him the Father piled hardships,
no powerful race of princes born in his royal halls,   245
only a single son he fathered, doomed at birth,
cut off in the spring of life—
and I, I give the man no care as he grows old
since here I sit in Troy, far from my fatherland,
a grief to you, a grief to all your children.   250
And you too, old man, we hear you prospered once:
as far as Lesbos, Macar's kingdom, bounds to seaward,
Phrygia east and upland, the Hellespont vast and north—
that entire realm, they say, you lorded over once,
you excelled all men, old king, in sons and wealth.   255
But then the gods of heaven brought this agony on you—
ceaseless battles round your walls, your armies slaughtered.
You must bear up now. Enough of endless tears,
the pain that breaks the spirit.
Grief for your son will do no good at all.   260
You will never bring him back to life—
sooner you must suffer something worse."

But the old and noble Priam protested strongly:
"Don't make me sit on a chair, Achilles, Prince,
not while Hector lies uncared-for in your camp!   265
Give him back to me, now, no more delay—
I must see my son with my own eyes.
Accept the ransom I bring you, a king's ransom!
Enjoy it, all of it—return to your own native land,
safe and sound . . . since now you've spared my life."   270
A dark glance—and the headstrong runner answered,
"No more, old man, don't tempt my wrath, not now!
My own mind's made up to give you back your son.
A messenger brought me word from Zeus—my mother,
Thetis who bore me, the Old Man of the Sea's daughter.   275
And what's more, I can see through you, Priam—
no hiding the fact from me: one of the gods
has led you down to Achaea's fast ships.
No man alive, not even a rugged young fighter,
would dare to venture into our camp. Never—   280
how could he slip past the sentries unchallenged?
Or shoot back the bolt of my gates with so much ease?
So don't anger me now. Don't stir my raging heart still more.
Or under my own roof I may not spare your life, old man—
suppliant that you are—may break the laws of Zeus!"   285

The old man was terrified. He obeyed the order.
But Achilles bounded out of doors like a lion—
not alone but flanked by his two aides-in-arms,
veteran Automedon and Alcimus, steady comrades,
Achilles' favorites next to the dead Patroclus.   290
They loosed from harness the horses and the mules,
they led the herald in, the old king's crier,
and sat him down on a bench. From the polished wagon
they lifted the priceless ransom brought for Hector's corpse
but they left behind two capes and a finely-woven shirt   295

to shroud the body well when Priam bore him home.
Then Achilles called the serving-women out:
"Bathe and anoint the body—
bear it aside first. Priam must not see his son."
He feared that, overwhelmed by the sight of Hector,   **300**
wild with grief, Priam might let his anger flare
and Achilles might fly into fresh rage himself,
cut the old man down and break the laws of Zeus.
So when the maids had bathed and anointed the body
sleek with olive oil and wrapped it round and round   **305**
in a braided battle-shirt and handsome battle-cape,
then Achilles lifted Hector up in his own arms
and laid him down on a bier, and comrades helped him
raise the bier and body onto the sturdy wagon . . .
Then with a groan he called his dear friend by name: **310**
"Feel no anger at me, Patroclus, if you learn—
even there in the House of Death—I let his father
have Prince Hector back. He gave me worthy ransom
and you shall have your share from me, as always,
your fitting, lordly share."

               So he vowed   **315**
and brilliant Achilles strode back to his shelter,
sat down on the well-carved chair that he had left,
at the far wall of the room, leaned toward Priam
and firmly spoke the words the king had come to hear:
"Your son is now set free, old man, as you requested.   **320**
Hector lies in state. With the first light of day
you will see for yourself as you convey him home.
Now, at last, let us turn our thoughts to supper."

. . . .

The Greek Gods

The ancient Greeks envisioned their gods as a family of immortals who intervened in the lives of human beings. Originating in the cultures of Crete and Mycenae, the Greek pantheon exalted Zeus, the powerful sky god, and his wife, Hera, as the ruling deities. Among the lesser gods were Poseidon, god of the sea; Apollo, god of light, medicine, and music; Dionysus, god of wine and vegetation; Athena, goddess of wisdom and war; and Aphrodite, goddess of love and procreation. Around these and other deities (Figure **4.8**) there emerged an elaborate mythology.

Many Greek myths look back to the common pool of legends and tales that traveled throughout the Mediterranean and the Near East. In the *Theogony* (*The Birth of the Gods*), a poem recounting the history and genealogy of the gods, Homer's contemporary Hesiod (fl. 700 B.C.E.) describes the origins of the universe in a manner reminiscent of *The Babylonian Creation*:

> First of all, the Void came into being, next broad-bosomed Earth, the solid and eternal home of all, and Eros [Desire], the most beautiful of the immortal gods, who in every man and every god softens the sinews and overpowers the prudent purpose of the mind. Out of Void came Darkness and black Night, and out of Night came Light and day, her children conceived after union in love with Darkness. Earth first produced starry Sky, equal in size with herself . . .*

The Greeks also had their own version of the Isis/Osiris myth. When Hades, god of the underworld, abducts the beautiful Persephone, her mother, Demeter, rescues her; tricked by Hades, however, this goddess of vegetation is forced to return annually to the underworld, leaving the earth above barren and desolate. Cults based in myths of death and rebirth offered their devotees the hope for personal regeneration.

The Greeks traced their origins to events related to the fury of Zeus: Angered by human evil, Zeus decided to destroy humankind by sending a flood. Deucalion, the Greek Noah, built a boat for himself and his wife and obeyed an oracle that commanded them to throw the "bones" of Mother Earth overboard. From these stones sprang up human beings, the first of whom was Hellen, the legendary ancestor of the Greeks, or "Hellenes."

Although immortal, the Greek gods were much like the human beings who worshipped them: They were amorous, capricious, and quarrelsome. They lived not in some remote heaven, but (conveniently enough) atop a mountain in northern Greece—that is, among the Greeks themselves. From their home on Mount Olympus, the gods might take sides in human combat (as they regularly do in the *Iliad*), seduce mortal women, and meddle in the lives of ordinary people. The Greek gods were not always benevolent or just. Unlike the Hebrew God, they set forth

---

*Hesiod, *Theogony*, translated by Norman O. Brown (New York: Bobbs-Merrill, 1953), 56.

Figure 4.8 The Principal Greek Gods.

Greek Name	Roman Name	Represents
Aphrodite	Venus	Love, beauty
Apollo	Phoebus	Solar light, medicine, music
Artemis	Diana	Hunting, wildlife, the moon
Athena	Minerva	War, wisdom
Demeter	Ceres	Agriculture, grain
Dionysus	Bacchus	Wine, vegetation
Eros	Amor/Cupid	Erotic love, desire
Hades	Pluto	Underworld
Helios	Phoebus	Sun
Hephaestus	Vulcan	Fire, metallurgy
Hera	Juno	Queen of the gods
Heracles	Hercules	Strength, courage
Hestia	Vesta	Hearth, domestic life
Hermes	Mercury	Male messenger of the gods
Nike		Victory
Persephone	Prosperina	Underworld
Poseidon	Neptune	Sea
Selene	Diana	Moon
Zeus	Jupiter	King of the gods, sky

no clear principles of moral conduct and no guidelines for religious worship. Priests and priestesses tended the temples and shrines and oversaw rituals, including human and animal sacrifices performed to win the favor of the gods. Popular Greek religion produced no sacred scripture and no doctrines—circumstances that may have contributed to the freedom of intellectual inquiry for which the Greeks became famous. Equally famous, at least in ancient times, was the ancient oracle at Delphi, the shrine of Apollo and the site that marked for the Greeks the center of the universe and the "navel" of the earth. Here the priestess of Apollo sat on a tripod over a fissure in the rock, and, in a state of ecstasy (which recent archeologists attribute to hallucinogenic fumes from narcotic gases in two geologic faults below), uttered inscrutable replies to the questions of suppliants from near and far. The oracle at Delphi remained the supreme source of prophecy and mystical wisdom until the temple-shrine was destroyed in late Roman times.

The Greek City-State and the Persian Wars (ca. 750–480 B.C.E.)

Toward the end of the Homeric Age, the Greeks formed small rural colonies that gradually grew into urban communities, mainly through maritime trade. Geographic conditions—a rocky terrain interrupted by mountains, valleys, and narrow rivers—made overland travel and trade difficult. At the same time, Greek geography (see Map 4.1) encouraged the evolution of the independent city-state (in Greek, *polis*). Ancient Greece consisted of a constellation of some 200 city-states, a few as large as 400 square miles and others as tiny as 2 square miles. Many of these (Athens, for instance) were small enough that a person might walk around their walls in only a few hours. Although all of the Greek city-states shared the same language, traditions, and religion, each *polis* governed itself, issued its own coinage, and provided its own military defenses. The autonomy of the Greek city-states—so unlike the monolithic Egyptian state—fostered fierce competition and commercial rivalry. However, like the squabbling members of a family who are suddenly menaced by aggressive neighbors, the Greek city-states, confronted by the rising power of Persia, united in self-defense.

By the sixth century B.C.E., the Persian Empire had conquered most of the territories between the western frontier of India and Asia Minor. Advancing westward, Persia annexed Ionia, the Greek region on the coast of Asia Minor (see Map 4.1), a move that clearly threatened mainland Greece. Thus, when in 499 B.C.E. the Ionian cities revolted against Persian rule, their Greek neighbors came to their aid. In retaliation, the Persians sent military expeditions to punish the rebel cities of the Greek mainland. In 490 B.C.E., on the plain of Marathon, 25 miles from Athens, a Greek force of 11,000 men met a Persian army with twice its numbers and defeated them, losing only 192 men. Persian casualties exceeded 6,000. The Greek warrior who brought news of the victory at Marathon to Athens died upon completing the 26-mile run. (Hence the word "marathon" has come to designate a long-distance endurance contest.) But the Greeks soon realized that without a strong navy even the combined land forces of all the city-states could not hope to oust the Persians. They thus proceeded to build a fleet of warships, which, in 480 B.C.E., ultimately defeated the Persian armada at Salamis in one of the final battles of the Persian Wars.

The story of the Persian Wars intrigued the world's first known historian, Herodotus (ca. 485–425 B.C.E), "the father of history." Writing not as an eye-witness to the wars, but a half-century later, Herodotus nevertheless brought keen critical judgment to sources that included hearsay as well as record. His sprawling narrative is filled with fascinating anecdotes and colorful digressions, including a "travelogue" of his visits to Egypt and Asia— accounts that remain among our most detailed sources of information about ancient African and West Asian life. The chapters on Africa, filled with numerous comparisons between Greek and Egyptian social practices and religious beliefs, show Herodotus as an early investigator of what would today be called "comparative culture." By presenting various (and often contradictory) pieces of evidence and weighing them before arriving at a conclusion, Herodotus laid the basis for the historical method. His procedures and his writings established a boundary between myth and history. *The Persian Wars*, which followed the Homeric poems by some 300 years, remains significant as the Western world's first major work in prose.

Athens and the Greek Golden Age (ca. 480–430 B.C.E.)

Although all of the city-states had contributed to expelling the Persians, it was Athens that claimed the crown of victory. Indeed, in the wake of the Persian Wars, Athens assumed political dominion among the city-states, as well as commercial supremacy in the Aegean Sea. The defeat of Persia inspired a mood of confidence and a spirit of vigorous chauvinism. This spirit ushered in a Golden Age of drama, philosophy, music, art, and architecture. In fact, the period between 480 and 430 B.C.E., often called a Golden Age, was one of the most creative in the history of the world. In Athens, it was as if the heroic idealism of the *Iliad* had bloomed into civic patriotism.

Athens, the most cosmopolitan of the city-states, was unique among the Greek communities, for the democratic government that came to prevail there was the exception rather than the rule in ancient Greece. In its early history, Athens—like most of the other Greek city-states—was an **oligarchy**, that is, a government controlled by an elite minority. But a series of enlightened rulers who governed Athens between roughly 600 and 500 B.C.E. introduced reforms that placed increasing authority in the hands of its citizens. The Athenian statesman, poet, and legislator Solon (ca. 638–558 B.C.E) fixed the democratic course of Athenian history by abolishing the custom of debt slavery and encouraging members of the lower classes to serve in public office. By broadening the civic responsibilities of Athenians, Solon educated citizens of all classes in the activities of government. By 550 B.C.E., the Popular Assembly of Citizens (made up of all citizens) was operating alongside the Council of Five Hundred (made up of aristocrats who handled routine state business) and the Board of Ten Generals (an annually elected executive body). When, at last, in the year 508 B.C.E., the Popular Assembly acquired the right to make laws, Athens became the first direct democracy in world history.

The word **"democracy"** derives from Greek words describing a government in which the people (*demos*) hold power (*kratos*). In the democracy of ancient Athens, Athenian citizens exercised political power directly, thus—unlike the United States, where power rests in the hands of representatives of the people—the citizens of Athens themselves held the authority to make the laws and approve state policy. Athenian democracy was, however, highly exclusive. Its citizenry included only landowning males over the age of eighteen. Of an estimated population of 250,000, this probably constituted some 40,000 people. Women, children, resident aliens, and slaves—approximately 150,000 individuals—did not qualify as citizens. (Slaves, as in earlier civilizations, arrived at their unfree condition as a result of warfare or debt, not race or skin color.) Clearly, in the mind of the Athenian, Hellenes were superior to non-Greeks (or outsiders, whom the Greeks called *barbaros*, from which comes the English word "barbarians"), Athenians were superior to non-Athenians, Athenian males were superior to Athenian females, and all classes of free men and women were superior to slaves.

Fundamental to Athenian democracy was a commitment to the legal equality of its participants: One citizen's vote weighed as heavily as the next. Equally important to Athenian (as to any) democracy was the hypothesis that individuals who had the right to vote would do so, and, moreover, were willing to take responsible action in the interest of the common good. (Such ideals are still highly valued in many parts of the modern world.) The small size of Athens probably contributed to the success of its unique form of government. Although probably no more than 5,000 Athenians attended the Assembly that met four times a month to make laws in the open-air marketplace (the Agora) located at the foot of the Acropolis, these men were the proponents of a brave new enterprise in governing.

Golden Age Athens stands in vivid contrast to those ancient civilizations whose rulers—the incarnate representatives of the gods—held absolute power while its citizens held none. Athens also stands in contrast to its rival, Sparta, the largest *polis* on the Peloponnesus (see Map 4.1). In Sparta, an oligarchy of five officials, elected annually, held tight reins on a society whose male citizens (from the age of seven on) were trained as soldiers. All physical labor fell to a class of unfree workers called *helots*, the captives of Sparta's frequent local wars. Spartan soldiers were renowned for their bravery; their women, expected to live

up to the ideas of a warrior culture, enjoyed a measure of freedom that was unknown in Athens. Yet, the history of Sparta would be one in which a strict social order left little room for creativity, in government or in the arts.

Pericles' Glorification of Athens

The leading proponent of Athenian democracy was the statesman Pericles (ca. 495–429 B.C.E.) (Figure **4.9**), who dominated the Board of Ten Generals for more than thirty years until his death. An aristocrat by birth, Pericles was a democrat at heart. In the interest of broadening the democratic system, he initiated some of Athens' most sweeping domestic reforms, such as payment for holding public office and a system of public audit in which the finances of outgoing magistrates were subject to critical scrutiny. In Pericles' time many public offices were filled by lottery—a procedure that invited all citizens to seek governmental office, and one so egalitarian as to be unthinkable today. Pericles' foreign policy was even more ambitious than his domestic policies. In the wake of the Persian Wars, he encouraged the Greek city-states to form a defensive alliance against future invaders. At the outset, the league's collective funds were kept in a treasury on the sacred island of Delos (hence the name "Delian League"). But, in a bold display of chauvinism, Pericles moved the fund to Athens and expropriated its monies to rebuild the Athenian temples that had been burned by the Persians.

Figure 4.9 Marble bust from Tivoli inscribed with the name of Pericles. Roman copy after a bronze original of 450–425 B.C.E. Reproduced by courtesy of the Trustees of the British Museum, London.

unwillingly, making a short road long. But at last I got up courage to come to you, and though there is little to my story, I will tell it; for I have got a good grip on one thought—that I can suffer nothing but what is my fate.

Creon: Well, and what is it that makes you so upset?

Guard: First let me tell you that I did not do the deed and I did not see it done, so it would not be just to make me suffer for it.   190

Creon: You have a good care for your own skin, and armor yourself well against blame. I take it that you have news to tell?

Guard: Yes, that I have, but bad news is nothing to be in a hurry about.

Creon: Tell it, man, will you?—tell it and be off.

Guard: Well, this is it. The corpse—someone has done it funeral honors—sprinkled dust upon it, and other pious rites.

Creon: What—what do you say? What man has dared this deed?   200

Guard: That I cannot tell you. There was no sign of a pick being used, no earth torn up the way it is by a mattock. The ground was hard and dry, there was no track of wheels. Whoever did it left no trace; when the first day-watchman showed it to us, we were struck dumb. You couldn't see the dead man at all; not that he was in any grave, but dry dust was strewn that thick all over him. It was the hand of someone warding off a curse did that. There was no sign that any dog or wild beast had been at the body.   210

Then there were loud words, and hard words, among us of the guard, everyone accusing someone else, 'til we nearly came to blows, and it's a wonder we didn't. Everyone was accused and no one was convicted, and each man stuck to it that he knew nothing about it. We were ready to take red-hot iron in our hands—to walk through fire—to swear by the gods that we did not do the deed and were not in the secret of whoever did it.

At last, when all our disputing got us nowhere, one of the men spoke up in a way that made us look down at the ground   220 in silence and fear; for we could not see how to gainsay him, nor how to escape trouble if we heeded him. What he said was, that this must be reported to you, it was no use hiding it. There was no doubt of it, he was right; so we cast lots, and it was my bad luck to win the prize. Here I am, then, as unwelcome as unwilling, I know; for no man likes the bearer of bad news.

Chorus: O King, my thoughts have been whispering, could this deed perhaps have been the work of gods?

Creon: Silence, before your words fill me with anger, and   230 you prove yourself as foolish as you are old! You say what is not to be borne, that the gods would concern themselves with this corpse. What!—did they cover his nakedness to reward the reverence he paid them, coming to burn their pillared shrines and sacred treasures, to harry their land, to put scorn upon their laws? Do you think it is the way of the gods to honor the wicked? No! From the first there were some in this city who muttered against me, chafing at this edict, wagging their heads in secret; they would not bow to the yoke, not they, like men contented with my rule.   240

I know well enough, it is such malcontents who have bribed and beguiled these guards to do this deed or let it be done.

Nothing so evil as money ever arose among men. It lays cities low, drives peoples from their homes, warps honest souls 'til they give themselves to works of shame; it teaches men to practice villainies and grow familiar with impious deeds.

But the men who did this thing for hire, sooner or later they shall pay the price. Now, as Zeus still has my reverence, know this—I tell you on my oath: Unless you find the very man whose hand strewed dust upon that body, and bring him here   250 before mine eyes, death alone shall not be enough for you, but you shall first be hung up alive until you reveal the truth about this outrage; that henceforth you may have a better idea about how to get money, and learn that it is not wise to grasp at it from any source. I will teach you that ill-gotten gains bring more men to ruin than to prosperity.

Guard: May I speak? Or shall I turn and go?

Creon: Can you not see that your voice offends me?

Guard: Are your ears troubled, or your soul?

Creon: And why should you try to fix the seat of my pain?   260

Guard: The doer of the deed inflames your mind, but I, only your ears.

Creon: Bah, you are a babbler born!

Guard: I may be that, but I never did this deed.

Creon: You did, for silver; but you shall pay with your life.

Guard: It is bad when a judge misjudges.

Creon: Prate about "judgment" all you like; but unless you show me the culprit in this crime, you will admit before long that guilty wages were better never earned.

(Creon goes into his house.)

Guard: Well, may the guilty man be found, that's all I ask.   270 But whether he's found or not—fate will decide that—you will not see me here again. I have escaped better than I ever hoped or thought—I owe the gods much thanks.

(The Guard departs, going toward the plain.)

Chorus: Wonders are many in the world, and the
    wonder of all is man.
With his bit in the teeth of the storm and his faith in a
    fragile prow,
Far he sails, where the waves leap white-fanged, wroth at
    his plan.
And he has his will of the earth by the strength of his
    hand on the plough.

The birds, the clan of the light heart, he snares with his
    woven cord,
And the beasts with wary eyes, and the stealthy fish in
    the sea;
That shaggy freedom-lover, the horse, obeys his word,   280
And the sullen bull must serve him, for cunning of wit is
    he.

Against all ills providing, he tempers the dark and the
    light,
The creeping siege of the frost and the arrows of sleet
    and rain,
The grievous wounds of the daytime and the fever that
    steals in the night;
Only against Death man arms himself in vain.

With speech and wind-swift thought he builds the State
  to his mood,
Prospering while he honors the gods and the laws of the
  land.
Yet in his rashness often he scorns the ways that are
  good—
May such as walk with evil be far from my hearth and
  hand!

(The Guard reappears leading Antigone.)

Chorus: But what is this?—what portent from the gods is 290
this? I am bewildered, for surely this maiden is Antigone; I
know her well. O luckless daughter of a luckless father, child
of Oedipus, what does this mean? Why have they made you
prisoner? Surely they did not take you in the folly of breaking
the King's laws?

Guard: Here she is, the doer of the deed! We caught this
girl burying him. But where is Creon?

Chorus: Look, he is coming from the house now.

(Creon comes from the house.)

Creon: What is it? What has happened that makes my
coming timely? 300

Guard: Sire, a man should never say positively "I will do
this" or "I won't do that," for things happen to change the
mind. I vowed I would not soon come here again, after the
way you scared me, lashing me with your threats. But there's
nothing so pleasant as a happy turn when we've given up
hope, so I have broken my sworn oath to hurry back here with
this girl, who was taken showing grace to the dead. This time
there was no casting of lots; no, this is my good luck, no one
else's. And now, Sire, take her yourself, question her, examine
her, all you please; but I have a right to free and final 310
quittance of this trouble.

Creon: Stay!—this prisoner—how and where did you take
her?

Guard: She was burying the man; that's all there is to tell
you.

Creon: Do you mean what you say? Are you telling the
truth?

Guard: I saw her burying the corpse that you had forbidden
to bury. Is that plain and clear?

Creon: What did you see? Did you take her in the act? 320

Guard: It happened this way. When we came to the place
where he lay, worrying over your threats, we swept away all
the dirt, leaving the rotting corpse bare. Then we sat us down
on the brow of the hill to windward, so that the smell from
him would not strike us. We kept wide awake frightening
each other with what you would do to us if we didn't carry out
your command. So it went until the sun was bright in the top
of the sky, and the heat began to burn. Then suddenly a
whirlwind came roaring down, making the sky all black, hiding
the plain under clouds of choking dust and leaves torn from 330
the trees. We closed our eyes and bore this plague from the
gods.

And when, after a long while, the storm had passed, we
saw this girl, and she crying aloud with the sharp cry of a bird
in its grief; the way a bird will cry when it sees the nest bare
and the nestlings gone, it was that way she lifted up her voice

when she saw the corpse uncovered; and she called down
dreadful curses on those that did it. Then straightway she
scooped up dust in her hands, and she had a shapely ewer of
bronze, and she held that high while she honored the dead 340
with three drink-offerings.

We rushed forward at this and closed on our quarry, who
was not at all frightened at us. Then we charged her with the
past and present offences, and she denied nothing—I was
both happy and sorry for that. It is good to escape danger
one's self, but hard to bring trouble to one's friends. However,
nothing counts with me so much as my own safety.

Creon: You, then—you whose face is bent to the earth—
do you confess or do you deny the deed?

Antigone: I did it; I make no denial. 350

Creon *(to Guard)*: You may go your way, wherever you will,
free and clear of a grave charge. *(To Antigone)*: Now tell me—
not in many words, but briefly—did you know of the edict that
forbade what you did?

Antigone: I knew it. How could I help knowing?—it was
public.

Creon: And you had the boldness to transgress that law?

Antigone: Yes, for it was not Zeus made such a law; such
is not the Justice of the gods. Nor did I think that your decrees
had so much force, that a mortal could override the unwritten 360
and unchanging statutes of heaven. For their authority is not
of today nor yesterday, but from all time, and no man knows
when they were first put forth.

Not through dread or any human power could I answer to
the gods for breaking these. That I must die I knew without
your edict. But if I am to die before my time, I count that a
gain; for who, living as I do in the midst of many woes, would
not call death a friend?

It saddens me little, therefore, to come to my end. If I had
let my mother's son lie in death an unburied corpse, that 370
would have saddened me, but for myself I do not grieve. And if
my acts are foolish in your eyes, it may be that a foolish judge
condemns my folly.

Chorus: The maiden shows herself the passionate daughter
of a passionate father, she does not know how to bend the
neck.

Creon: Let me remind you that those who are too stiff and
stubborn are most often humbled; it is the iron baked too hard
in the furnace you will oftenest see snapped and splintered.
But I have seen horses that show temper brought to order by 380
a little curb. Too much pride is out of place in one who lives
subject to another. This girl was already versed in insolence
when she transgressed the law that had been published; and
now, behold, a second insult—to boast about it, to exult in her
misdeed!

But I am no man, she is the man, if she can carry this off
unpunished. No! She is my sister's child, but if she were
nearer to me in blood than any who worships Zeus at the altar
of my house, she should not escape a dreadful doom—nor her
sister either, for indeed I charge her too with plotting this 390
burial.

And summon that sister—for I saw her just now within,
raving and out of her wits. That is the way minds plotting evil
in the dark give away their secret and convict themselves even
before they are found out. But the most intolerable thing is

thought. They asked not simply "*What* do we know (about nature)?" but "*How* do we know what we know?" The transition from the examination of matter to the exploration of mind established the humanistic direction of Greek philosophy for at least two centuries (Figure **4.13**).

The first humanist philosophers were a group of traveling scholar-teachers called Sophists. Masters of formal debate, the Sophists were concerned with defining the limits of human knowledge. The Thracian Sophist Protagoras (ca. 485–410 B.C.E.) believed that knowledge could not exceed human opinion, a position summed up in his memorable dictum: "Man is the measure of all things." His contemporary Gorgias (ca. 483–ca. 376 B.C.E.) tried to prove that reality is incomprehensible and that even if one could comprehend it, one could not describe the real to others. Such skepticism was common to the Sophists, who argued that truth and justice were relative: What might be considered just and true for one individual or situation might not be just and true for another.

Socrates and the Quest for Virtue

Athens' foremost philosopher, Socrates (ca. 470–399 B.C.E.), vigorously opposed the views of the Sophists. Insisting on the absolute nature of truth and justice, he described the ethical life as belonging to a larger set of universal truths and an unchanging moral order. For Socrates, virtue was not discovered by means of clever but misleading argumentation—a kind of reasoning that would come to be called (after the Sophists) *sophistry*, nor was it relative to individual circumstances. Rather, virtue was a condition of the *psyche**, the seat of both the moral and intellectual faculties of the individual. Hence, understanding the true meaning of virtue was preliminary to acting virtuously: To know good was to do good.

The question of right conduct was central to Socrates' life and teachings. A stonemason by profession, Socrates preferred to roam the streets of Athens and engage his fellow-citizens in conversation and debate (Figure **4.14**). Insisting that the unexamined life was not worth living, he challenged his peers on matters of public and private virtue, constantly posing the question, "What is the great-

Figure 4.14 Portrait bust of Socrates. Roman marble copy of an original bronze supposedly created by Lysippos, ca. 350 B.C.E. © Hirmer Fotoarchiv.

est good?" In this pursuit, Socrates employed a rigorous question-and-answer technique known as the **dialectical method**. Unlike the Sophists, he refused to charge fees for teaching: he argued that wealth did not produce excellence; rather, wealth derived *from* excellence. Socrates described himself as a large horsefly, alighting upon and pestering the well-bred but rather sluggish horse—that is, Athens. So Socrates "alighted" on the citizens of Athens, arousing, persuading, and reproaching them and—most important—demanding that they give rational justification for their actions. His style of intellectual cross-examination, the question-and-answer method, proceeded from his first principle of inquiry, "Know thyself," while the progress of his analysis moved from specific examples to general principles, and from particular to universal truths, a type of reasoning known as *inductive*. The inductive method demands a process of abstraction: a shift of focus from the individual thing (the city) to all things (cities) and from the individual action (just or unjust) to the idea of justice. Central to Socratic inquiry was discourse. The notion that talk itself humanizes the individual is typically Greek and even more typically Socratic. Indeed, the art of conversation—the dialectical exchange of ideas—united the citizens of the *polis* (Figure **4.14**).

As gadfly, Socrates won as many enemies as he won friends. The great masses of Greek citizens found comfort in the traditional Greek gods and goddesses. They had little use for Socrates' religious skepticism and stringent

---

*Often translated as "soul," but more accurately understood as representing one's individual personality.

methods of self-examination. Outspoken in his commitment to free inquiry, Socrates fell into disfavor with the reactionary regime that governed Athens after its defeat in the Peloponnesian Wars. Although he had fought bravely in the wars, he vigorously opposed the new regime and the moral chaos of post-war Athens. In the year 399 B.C.E., when he was over seventy years old, he was brought to trial for subversive behavior, impiety, and atheism. The Athenian jury found him guilty by a narrow margin of votes and sentenced him to death by drinking hemlock, a poisonous herb.

In his lifetime, Socrates wrote no books or letters: What we know of him comes mainly from the writings of his students. The dialogue called *Crito* (written by Plato) narrates the last events of Socrates' life: Crito, Socrates' friend and pupil, urges him to escape from prison, but the old philosopher refuses. He explains that to run away would be to subvert the laws by which he has lived. His escape would represent an implicit criticism of the democratic system and the city-state that he had defended throughout his life. For Socrates, the loyalty of the citizen to the *polis*, like that of the child to its parents, is a primary obligation. To violate the will of the community to which he belongs would constitute dishonor. Like Antigone, Socrates prefers death to dishonor. In the excerpt from *Crito*, Socrates explains why right action is crucial to the destiny of both the individual and the community. These words reaffirm the Hellenic view that immortality is achieved through human deeds, which outlast human lives.

READING 1.15 From Plato's *Crito* (ca. 390 B.C.E.)

Crito: . . . O my good Socrates, I beg you for the last time 1
to listen to me and save yourself. For to me your death will be more than a single disaster: not only shall I lose a friend the like of whom I shall never find again, but many persons who do not know you and me well will think that I might have saved you if I had been willing to spend money, but that I neglected to do so. And what reputation could be more disgraceful than the reputation of caring more for money than for one's friends? The public will never believe that we were anxious to save you, but that you yourself refused to escape. 10

Socrates: But, my dear Crito, why should we care so much about public opinion? Reasonable men, of whose opinion it is worth our while to think, will believe that we acted as we really did.

Crito: But you see, Socrates, that it is necessary to care about public opinion, too. This very thing that has happened to you proves that the multitude can do a man not the least, but almost the greatest harm, if he is falsely accused to them.

Socrates: I wish that the multitude were able to do a man the greatest harm, Crito, for then they would be able to do 20
him the greatest good, too. That would have been fine. But, as it is, they can do neither. They cannot make a man either wise or foolish: they act wholly at random . . . . Consider it in this way. Suppose the laws and the commonwealth were to come and appear to me as I was preparing to run away (if that is the right phrase to describe my escape) and were to ask, "Tell us, Socrates, what have you in your mind to do? What do you mean by trying to escape but to destroy us, the laws, and the whole state, so far as you are able? Do you think that a state can exist and not be overthrown, in which the decisions of 30
law are of no force, and are disregarded and undermined by private individuals?" How shall we answer questions like that, Crito? Much might be said, especially by an orator, in defense of the law which makes judicial decisions supreme. Shall I reply, "But the state has injured me by judging my case unjustly." Shall we say that?

Crito: Certainly we will, Socrates.

Socrates: And suppose the laws were to reply, "Was that our agreement? Or was it that you would abide by whatever judgments the state should pronounce?" And if we were 40
surprised by their words, perhaps they would say, "Socrates, don't be surprised by our words, but answer us; you yourself are accustomed to ask questions and to answer them. What complaint have you against us and the state, that you are trying to destroy us? Are we not, first of all, your parents? Through us your father took your mother and brought you into the world. Tell us, have you any fault to find with those of us that are the laws of marriage?" "I have none," I should reply. "Or have you any fault to find with those of us that regulate the raising of the child and the education which you, like 50
others, received? Did we not do well in telling your father to educate you in music and athletics?" "You did," I should say. "Well, then, since you were brought into the world and raised and educated by us, how, in the first place, can you deny that you are our child and our slave, as your fathers were before you? And if this be so, do you think that your rights are on a level with ours? Do you think that you have a right to retaliate if we should try to do anything to you? You had not the same rights that your father had, or that your master would have had if you had been a slave. You had no right to retaliate if 60
they ill-treated you, or to answer them if they scolded you, or to strike them back if they struck you, or to repay them evil with evil in any way. And do you think that you may retaliate in the case of your country and its laws? If we try to destroy you, because we think it just, will you in return do all that you can to destroy us, the laws, and your country, and say that in so doing you are acting justly—you, the man who really thinks so much of excellence? Or are you too wise to see that your country is worthier, more to be revered, more sacred, and held in higher honor both by the gods and by all men of 70
understanding, than your father and your mother and all your ancestors; and that you ought to reverence it, and to submit to it, and to approach it more humbly when it is angry with you than you would approach your father; and either to do whatever it tells you to do or to persuade it to excuse you; and to obey in silence if it orders you to endure flogging or imprisonment, or if it sends you to battle to be wounded or die? That is just. You must not give way, nor retreat, nor desert your station. In war, and in the court of justice, and everywhere, you must do whatever your state and your 80
country tell you to do, or you must persuade them that their commands are unjust. But it is impious to use violence against your father or your mother; and much more impious to use violence against your country." What answer shall we make,

Crito? Shall we say that the laws speak the truth, or not?

Crito: I think that they do.

Socrates: "Then consider, Socrates," perhaps they would say, "if we are right in saying that by attempting to escape you are attempting an injustice. We brought you into the world, we raised you, we educated you, we gave you and every other citizen a share of all the good things we could. Yet we proclaim that if any man of the Athenians is dissatisfied with us, he may take his goods and go away wherever he pleases; we give that privilege to every man who chooses to avail himself of it, so soon as he has reached manhood, and sees us, the laws, and the administration of our state. No one of us stands in his way or forbids him to take his goods and go wherever he likes, whether it be to an Athenian colony, or to any foreign country, if he is dissatisfied with us and with the state. But we say that every man of you who remains here, seeing how we administer justice, and how we govern the state in other matters, has agreed, by the very fact of remaining here, to do whatsoever we tell him. And, we say, he who disobeys us acts unjustly on three counts: he disobeys us who are his parents, and he disobeys us who reared him, and he disobeys us after he has agreed to obey us, without persuading us that we are wrong. Yet we did not tell him sternly to do whatever we told him. We offered him an alternative; we gave him his choice either to obey us or to convince us that we were wrong; but he does neither. "These are the charges, Socrates, to which we say that you will expose yourself if you do what you intend; and you are more exposed to these charges than other Athenians." And if I were to ask, "Why?" they might retort with justice that I have bound myself by the agreement with them more than other Athenians. They would say, "Socrates, we have very strong evidence that you were satisfied with us and with the state. You would not have been content to stay at home in it more than other Athenians unless you had been satisfied with it more than they. You never went away from Athens to the festivals, nor elsewhere except on military service; you never made other journeys like other men; you had no desire to see other states or other laws; you were contented with us and our state; so strongly did you prefer us, and agree to be governed by us. And what is more, you had children in this city, you found it so satisfactory. Besides, if you had wished, you might at your trial have offered to go into exile. At that time you could have done with the state's consent what you are trying now to do without it. But then you gloried in being willing to die. You said that you preferred death to exile. And now you do not honor those words: you do not respect us, the laws, for you are trying to destroy us; and you are acting just as a miserable slave would act, trying to run away, and breaking the contracts and agreement which you made to live as our citizen. First, therefore, answer this question. Are we right, or are we wrong, in saying that you have agreed not in mere words, but in your actions, to live under our government?" What are we to say, Crito? Must we not admit that it is true?

Crito: We must, Socrates. . . .

. . . .

Plato and the Theory of Forms

Socrates' teachings were an inspiration to his pupil Plato (ca. 428–ca. 347 B.C.E.). Born in Athens during the Peloponnesian Wars, Plato reaped the benefits of Golden Age culture along with the insecurities of the post-war era. In 387 B.C.E, more than a decade after the death of his master, he founded the world's first school of philosophy, the Academy. Plato wrote some two dozen treatises, most of which were cast in the dialogue or dialectical format that Socrates had made famous. Some of the dialogues may be precise transcriptions of actual conversations, whereas others are clearly fictional, but the major philosophical arguments in almost all of Plato's treatises are put into the mouth of Socrates. Since Socrates himself wrote nothing, it is almost impossible to distinguish between the ideas of Plato and those of his teacher Socrates.

Plato's most famous treatise, the *Republic*, asks two central questions: "What is the meaning of justice?" and "What is the nature of a just society?" In trying to answer these questions, Plato introduces a theory of knowledge that is both visionary and dogmatic. It asserts the existence of a two-level reality, one consisting of constantly changing particulars available to our senses, the other consisting of unchanging eternal truths understood by way of the intellect. According to Plato, the higher reality of eternal truths, which he calls Forms, is distinct from the imperfect and transient objects of sensory experience, which are mere copies of Forms. Plato's Theory of Forms proposes that all sensory objects are imitations of the Forms, which, like the simplest mathematical equations, are imperishable and forever true. For example, the circle and its three-dimensional counterpart, the sphere, exist independent of any *particular* circle and sphere. They have always existed and will always exist. But the beach ball I toss in the air, an imperfect copy of the sphere, is transitory. Indeed, if all of the particular beach balls in the world were destroyed, the Universal Form—Sphere—would still exist. Similarly, suggests Plato, Justice, Love, and Beauty (along with other Forms) stand as unchanging and eternal models for the many individual and particular instances of each in the sensory world.

According to Plato, Forms descend from an ultimate Form, the Form of the Good. Plato never located or defined the Ultimate Good, except by analogy with the sun. Like the sun, the Form of the Good illuminates all that is intelligible and makes possible the mind's perception of Forms as objects of thought. The Ultimate Good, knowledge of which is the goal of dialectical inquiry, is the most difficult to reach.

In the *Republic*, Plato uses a literary device known as **allegory** to illustrate the dilemma facing the *psyche* in its ascent to knowledge of the imperishable and unchanging Forms. By way of allegory, the device by which the literal meaning of the text implies a figurative or "hidden" meaning, Plato describes a group of ordinary mortals chained within an underground chamber (the *psyche* imprisoned within the human body); their woeful position permits them to see only the shadows on the walls of the cave (the imperfect and perishable imitations of the

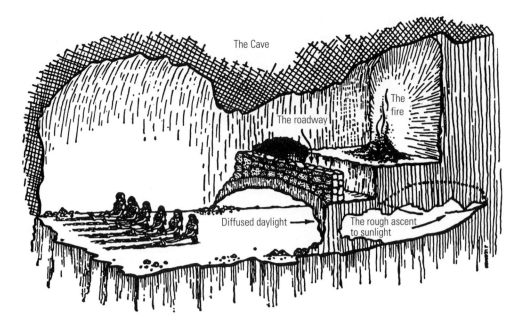

The Cave

The roadway

The fire

Diffused daylight →

The rough ascent to sunlight

Figure 4.15 "Allegory of the Cave" from *The Great Dialogues of Plato*, translated by W.H.D. Rouse, translation copyright © 1956, renewed 1984 by J.C.G. Rouse. Used by permission of Dutton Signet, a division of Penguin Books USA Inc.

Forms that occupy the world of the senses), which the prisoners, in their ignorance, believe to be real (Figure **4.15**). Only when one of the prisoners (the philosopher-hero) ascends to the domain of light (true knowledge, or knowledge of the Forms) does it become clear that what the cave-dwellers perceive as truth is nothing more than shadows of Reality. This intriguing parable is presented as a dialogue between Socrates and Plato's older brother, Glaucon.

READING 1.16 The "Allegory of the Cave" from Plato's *Republic* (ca. 375 B.C.E.)

Next, said [Socrates], here is a parable to illustrate the degrees in which our nature may be enlightened or unenlightened. Imagine the condition of men living in a sort of cavernous chamber underground, with an entrance open to the light and a long passage all down the cave. Here they have been from childhood, chained by the leg and also by the neck, so that they cannot move and can see only what is in front of them, because the chains will not let them turn their heads. At some distance higher up is the light of a fire burning behind them; and between the prisoners and the fire is a track[1] with a parapet built along it, like the screen at a puppet-show, which hides the performers while they show their puppets over the top.   10

I see, said he.

Now behind this parapet imagine persons carrying along various artificial objects, including figures of men and animals in wood or stone or other materials, which project above the parapet. Naturally, some of these persons will be talking, others silent.[2]

It is a strange picture, he said, and a strange sort of   20
prisoners.

Like ourselves, I replied; for in the first place prisoners so

confined would have seen nothing of themselves or of one another, except the shadows thrown by the fire-light on the wall of the Cave facing them, would they?

Not if all their lives they had been prevented from moving their heads.

And they would have seen as little of the objects carried past.

Of course.   30

Now, if they could talk to one another, would they not suppose that their words referred only to those passing shadows which they saw?

Necessarily.

And suppose their prison had an echo from the wall facing them? When one of the people crossing behind them spoke, they could only suppose that the sound came from the shadow passing before their eyes.

No doubt.

In every way, then, such prisoners would recognize as   40
reality nothing but the shadows of those artificial objects.

Inevitably.

Now consider what would happen if their release from the chains and the healing of their unwisdom should come about in this way. Suppose one of them were set free and forced suddenly to stand up, turn his head, and walk with eyes lifted to the light; all these movements would be painful, and he would be too dazzled to make out the objects whose shadows he had been used to see. What do you think he would say, if someone told him that what he had formerly seen was   50
meaningless illusion, but now, being somewhat nearer to

---

[1]The track crosses the passage into the cave at right angles and is above the parapet built along it.

[2]A modern Plato would compare his Cave to an underground cinema, where the audience watch the play of shadows thrown by the film passing before a light at their backs. The film itself is only an image of "real" things and events in the world outside the cinema. For the film Plato has to substitute the clumsier apparatus of a procession of artificial objects carried on their heads by persons who are merely part of the machinery, providing for the movement of the objects and the sound whose echo the prisoners hear. The parapet prevents these persons' shadows from being cast on the wall of the Cave.

reality and turned towards more real objects, he was getting a truer view? Suppose further that he were shown the various objects being carried by and were made to say, in reply to questions, what each of them was. Would he not be perplexed and believe the objects now shown him to be not so real as what he formerly saw?

Yes, not nearly so real.

And if he were forced to look at the fire-light itself, would not his eyes ache, so that he would try to escape and turn back to the things which he could see distinctly, convinced that they really were clearer than these other objects now being shown to him?

Yes.

And suppose someone were to drag him away forcibly up the steep and rugged ascent and not let him go until he had hauled him out into the sunlight, would he not suffer pain and vexation at such treatment, and, when he had come out into the light, find his eyes so full of its radiance that he could not see a single one of the things that he was now told were real?

Certainly he would not see them all at once.

He would need, then, to grow accustomed before he could see things in that upper world. At first it would be easiest to make out shadows, and then the images of men and things reflected in water, and later on the things themselves. After that, it would be easier to watch the heavenly bodies and the sky itself by night, looking at the light of the moon and stars rather than the Sun and the Sun's light in the day-time.

Yes, surely.

Last of all, he would be able to look at the Sun and contemplate its nature, not as it appears when reflected in water or any alien medium, but as it is in itself in its own domain.

No doubt.

And now he would begin to draw the conclusion that it is the Sun that produces the seasons and the course of the year and controls everything in the visible world, and moreover is in a way the cause of all that he and his companions used to see.

Clearly he would come at last to that conclusion.

Then if he called to mind his fellow prisoners and what passed for wisdom in his former dwelling-place, he would surely think himself happy in the change and be sorry for them. They may have had a practice of honoring and commending one another, with prizes for the man who had the keenest eye for the passing shadows and the best memory for the order in which they followed or accompanied one another, so that he could make a good guess as to which was going to come next. Would our released prisoner be likely to covet those prizes or to envy the men exalted to honor and power in the Cave? Would he not feel like Homer's Achilles, that he would far sooner "be on earth as a hired servant in the house of a landless man"[3] or endure anything rather than go back to his old beliefs and live in the old way?

Yes, he would prefer any fate to such a life.

Now imagine what would happen if he went down again to take his former seat in the Cave. Coming suddenly out of the sunlight, his eyes would be filled with darkness. He might be required once more to deliver his opinion on those shadows, in competition with the prisoners who had never been released, while his eyesight was still dim and unsteady; and it might take some time to become used to the darkness. They would laugh at him and say that he had gone up only to come back with his sight ruined; it was worth no one's while even to attempt the ascent. If they could lay hands on the man who was trying to set them free and lead them up, they would kill him.[4]

Yes, they would.

Every feature in this parable, my dear Glaucon, is meant to fit our earlier analysis. The prison dwelling corresponds to the region revealed to us through the sense of sight, and the fire-light within it to the power of the Sun. The ascent to see the things in the upper world you may take as standing for the upward journey of the soul into the region of the intelligible; then you will be in possession of what I surmise, since that is what you wish to be told. Heaven knows whether it is true; but this, at any rate, is how it appears to me. In the world of knowledge, the last thing to be perceived and only with great difficulty is the essential Form of Goodness. Once it is perceived, the conclusion must follow that, for all things, this is the cause of whatever is right and good; in the visible world it gives birth to light and to the lord of light, while it is itself sovereign in the intelligible world and the parent of intelligence and truth. Without having had a vision of this Form no one can act with wisdom, either in his own life or in matters of state.

So far as I can understand, I share your belief.

Then you may also agree that it is no wonder if those who have reached this height are reluctant to manage the affairs of men. Their souls long to spend all their time in that upper world—naturally enough, if here once more our parable holds true. Nor, again, is it at all strange that one who comes from the contemplation of divine things to the miseries of human life should appear awkward and ridiculous when, with eyes still dazed and not yet accustomed to the darkness, he is compelled, in a law-court or elsewhere, to dispute about the shadows of justice or the images that cast those shadows, and to wrangle over the notions of what is right in the minds of men who have never beheld Justice itself.

It is not at all strange.

No; a sensible man will remember that the eyes may be confused in two ways—by a change from light to darkness or from darkness to light; and he will recognize that the same thing happens to the soul. When he sees it troubled and unable to discern anything clearly, instead of laughing thoughtlessly, he will ask whether, coming from a brighter existence, its unaccustomed vision is obscured by the darkness, in which case he will think its condition enviable and its life a happy one; or whether, emerging from the depths of ignorance, it is dazzled by excess of light. If so, he will rather feel sorry for it; or, if he were inclined to laugh, that would be less ridiculous than to laugh at the soul which has

---

[3]This verse, spoken by the ghost of Achilles, suggests that the Cave is comparable with Hades, the Greek underworld.

[4]An allusion to the fate of Socrates.

come down from the light.

That is a fair statement.

If this is true, then, we must conclude that education is not what it is said to be by some, who profess to put knowledge into a soul which does not possess it, as if they could put sight into blind eyes. On the contrary, our own account signifies that the soul of every man does possess the power of learning the truth and the organ to see it with; and that, just as one might have to turn the whole body round in order that the eye should see light instead of darkness, so the entire soul must be turned away from this changing world, until its eye can bear to contemplate reality and that supreme splendor which we have called the Good. Hence there may well be an art whose aim would be to effect this very thing, the conversion of the soul, in the readiest way; not to put the power of sight into the soul's eye, which already has it, but to ensure that, instead of looking in the wrong direction, it is turned the way it ought to be.

Yes, it may well be so.

It looks, then, as though wisdom were different from those ordinary virtues, as they are called, which are not far removed from bodily qualities, in that they can be produced by habituation and exercise in a soul which has not possessed them from the first. Wisdom, it seems, is certainly the virtue of some diviner faculty, which never loses its power, though its use for good or harm depends on the direction towards which it is turned. You must have noticed in dishonest men with a reputation for sagacity the shrewd glance of a narrow intelligence piercing the objects to which it is directed. There is nothing wrong with their power of vision, but it has been forced into the service of evil, so that the keener its sight, the more harm it works.

Quite true.

And yet if the growth of a nature like this had been pruned from earliest childhood, cleared of those clinging overgrowths which come of gluttony and all luxurious pleasure and, like leaden weights charged with affinity to this mortal world, hang upon the soul, bending its vision downwards; if, freed from these, the soul were turned round towards true reality, then this same power in these very men would see the truth as keenly as the objects it is turned to now.

Yes, very likely.

Is it not also likely, or indeed certain after what has been said, that a state can never be properly governed either by the uneducated who know nothing of truth or by men who are allowed to spend all their days in the pursuit of culture? The ignorant have no single mark before their eyes at which they must aim in all the conduct of their own lives and of affairs of state; and the others will not engage in action if they can help it, dreaming that, while still alive, they have been translated to the Island of the Blest.

Quite true.

It is for us, then, as founders of a commonwealth, to bring compulsion to bear on the noblest natures. They must be made to climb the ascent to the vision of Goodness, which we called the highest object of knowledge; and, when they have looked upon it long enough, they must not be allowed, as they now are, to remain on the heights, refusing to come down again to the prisoners or to take any part in their labors

and rewards, however much or little these may be worth.

Shall we not be doing them an injustice, if we force on them a worse life than they might have?

You have forgotten again, my friend, that the law is not concerned to make any one class specially happy, but to ensure the welfare of the commonwealth as a whole. By persuasion or constraint it will unite the citizens in harmony, making them share whatever benefits each class can contribute to the common good; and its purpose in forming men of that spirit was not that each should be left to go his own way, but that they should be instrumental in binding the community into one.

True, I had forgotten.

You will see, then, Glaucon, that there will be no real injustice in compelling our philosophers to watch over and care for the other citizens. We can fairly tell them that their compeers in other states may quite reasonably refuse to collaborate: there they have sprung up, like a self-sown plant, in despite of their country's institutions; no one has fostered their growth, and they cannot be expected to show gratitude for a care they have never received. "But," we shall say, "it is not so with you. We have brought you into existence for your country's sake as well as for your own, to be like leaders and king-bees in a hive; you have been better and more thoroughly educated than those others and hence you are more capable of playing your part both as men of thought and as men of action. You must go down, then, each in his turn, to live with the rest and let your eyes grow accustomed to the darkness. You will then see a thousand times better than those who live there always; you will recognize every image for what it is and know what it represents, because you have seen justice, beauty, and goodness in their reality; and so you and we shall find life in our commonwealth no mere dream, as it is in most existing states, where men live fighting one another about shadows and quarreling for power, as if that were a great prize; whereas in truth government can be at its best and free from dissension only where the destined rulers are least desirous of holding office."

Quite true.

Then will our pupils refuse to listen and to take their turns at sharing in the work of the community, though they may live together for most of their time in a purer air?

No; it is a fair demand, and they are fair-minded men. No doubt, unlike any ruler of the present day, they will think of holding power as an unavoidable necessity.

Yes, my friend; for the truth is that you can have a well-governed society only if you can discover for your future rulers a better way of life than being in office; then only will power be in the hands of men who are rich, not in gold, but in the wealth that brings happiness, a good and wise life. All goes wrong when, starved for lack of anything good in their own lives, men turn to public affairs hoping to snatch from thence the happiness they hunger for. They set about fighting for power, and this internecine conflict ruins them and their country. The life of true philosophy is the only one that looks down upon offices of state; and access to power must be confined to men who are not in love with it; otherwise rivals will start fighting. So whom else can you compel to undertake the guardianship of the commonwealth, if not those who, besides understanding best the principles of government, enjoy a nobler life than the politician's and look for rewards of a different kind?

There is indeed no other choice. . . .

The "Allegory of the Cave" illustrates some key theories in the teachings of Plato. The first of these is **idealism**, the theory that holds that reality lies in the realm of unchanging, immaterial ideas, rather than in material objects. Platonic idealism implies a dualistic (spirit-and-matter or mind-and-body) model of the universe: The *psyche* belongs to the world of the eternal Forms, while the *soma* belongs to the sensory or material world. Imprisoned in the body, the mind forgets its once-perfect knowledge of the Forms. It is, nevertheless, capable of recovering its prenatal intelligence. The business of philosophy is to educate the *psyche*, to draw it out of its material prison so that it can regain perfect awareness.

Plato's concept of an unchanging force behind the flux of our perceptions looks back to the theories of Heraclitus, while his description of the Forms resembles Pythagorean assertions of the unchanging reality of number. It is not without significance that Plato's Theory of Forms has been hailed in modern physics: The celebrated twentieth-century German physicist Werner Heisenberg argued that the smallest units of matter are not physical objects in the ordinary sense; rather, he asserted, they are "forms," or ideas that can be expressed unambiguously only in mathematical language. In constructing the Theory of Forms, Plato may also have been influenced by Asian religious thought. The spiritual "spark" with which humans are born, according to Plato, and which must be kindled and cultivated, resembles the Hindu Atman (see chapter 3). And Plato's distinction between the realm of the senses and the ultimate, all-embracing Form recalls the Hindu belief that the illusory world of matter stands apart from Ultimate Being or Brahman. In contrast with Hinduism, however, Plato's teachings do not advocate enlightenment as escape from the material world. Rather, Plato perceives the mind's ascent to knowledge as a prerequisite of individual well-being and the attainment of the good life here on earth. Such enlightenment is essential to achieving a just state and a healthy society. Unlike the Hindu philosophers, whose mystical ascent to enlightenment is accomplished through withdrawal from the world, meditation, and self-denial, Plato defends a practical system of education by which individuals might arrive at knowledge of the Good. That educational system is expounded in the *Republic*.

Plato's utopian community permitted no private property and little family life, but exalted education as fundamental to society. While all people (male and female) would be educated equally, the ability of each would determine that person's place within society. Thus the roles of all citizens—laborers, soldiers, or governors—would be consistent with their mental and physical abilities. Plato had little use for democracy of the kind practiced in Athens. Governing, according to Plato, should fall to those who are the most intellectually able, that is, those who have most fully recovered a knowledge of the Forms, are obliged to act as "king-bees" in the communal hive. (Plato might have been surprised to discover that the ruling bee in a beehive is female.) The life of contemplation carried with it heavy responsibilities, for in the hands of the philosopher-kings lay "the welfare of the commonwealth as a whole." Plato's views on the ideal state were remarkably compatible with the ancient Chinese belief that a natural hierarchy determined who was intellectually fit to govern (see chapter 3).

Aristotle and the Life of Reason

Among Plato's students at the Academy was a young Macedonian named Aristotle, whose contributions to philosophy ultimately rivaled those of his teacher. After a period of travel in the eastern Mediterranean and a brief career as tutor to the young prince of Macedonia (the future Alexander the Great), Aristotle returned to Athens and founded a school known as the Lyceum. Aristotle's habit of walking up and down as he lectured gave him the nickname the "peripatetic philosopher." His teachings, which exist only in the form of lecture notes compiled by his students, cover a wider and more practical range of subjects than those of Plato. Aristotle did not accept the Theory of Forms. Insisting that mind and matter could not exist independently of each other, he rejected Plato's notion of an eternal *psyche*. Nevertheless, he theorized that a portion of the soul identified with reason (and with the impersonal force he called the Unmoved Mover) might be immortal.

Aristotle's interests spanned many fields, including those of biology, physics, politics, poetry, drama, logic, and ethics. The son of a physician, Aristotle's formative education inspired him to gather specimens of plant and animal life and classify them according to their physical similarities and differences. Over five hundred different animals, some of which Aristotle himself dissected, are mentioned in his zoological treatises. Though he did little in the way of modern scientific experimentation, Aristotle's practice of basing conclusions on very careful observation advanced the **empirical method**—a method of inquiry dependent on direct experience. Indeed, whereas Plato was the traditional rationalist, Aristotle pursued the path of the empiricist. He brought to his analysis of political life, literature, and human conduct the same principles he employed in classifying plants and animals: objectivity, clarity, and consistency. Before writing the *Politics*, he examined the constitutions of more than 150 Greek city-states. And in the *Poetics* he defined the various genres of literary expression (see chapter 5). In the fields of biology, astronomy, and physics, Aristotle's conclusions (including many that were incorrect) remained unchallenged for centuries. For instance, Aristotle theorized that in sexual union, the male was the "generator" and the female the "receptacle," since procreation involved the imposition of life-giving form (the male) on chaotic matter (the female). In short, Aristotle's views on female biology and sexuality led centuries of scholars to regard woman as an imperfect and incomplete version of man.

Aristotle's application of scientific principles to the reasoning process was the basis for the science of logic. Aristotelian logic requires the division of an argument into individual terms, followed—in Socratic fashion—by an examination of the meaning of those terms. Aristotle formulated the **syllogism**, a deductive scheme that presents two premises from which a conclusion may be drawn (Figure **4.16**). As a procedure for reasoned thought without reference to specific content, the syllogism is a system of notation that is similar to mathematics. Not the least of Aristotle's contributions was that which he made to **ethics**, that branch of philosophy that sets forth the principles of human conduct. Proceeding from an examination of human values, Aristotle hypothesizes that happiness or "the good life" (the Greek word *eudaimonia* means both) is the only human value that might be considered a final goal or end (*telos*) in itself, rather than a means to any other end. Is not happiness the one goal to which all human beings aspire? If so, then how does one achieve it? The answer, says Aristotle, lies in fulfilling one's unique function. The function of any thing is that by which it is defined: The function of the eye is to see; the function of the racehorse is to run fast; the function of a knife is to cut, and so on. How well a thing performs is synonymous with its excellence or virtue (in Greek, the word *arete* denotes both): The excellence of the eye, then, lies in seeing well; the excellence of a racehorse lies in how fast it runs; the excellence of a knife depends on how sharp it cuts, and so on. The unique function of the human being, observes Aristotle, is the ability to reason; hence, the excellence of any human creature lies in the exercise of reason.

In the *Ethics*, edited by Aristotle's son Nicomachus, Aristotle examines the Theory of the Good Life and the Nature of Happiness. He explains that action in accordance with reason is necessary for the acquisition of excellence, or virtue. Ideal conduct, suggests Aristotle, lies in the Golden Mean, the middle ground between any two extremes of behavior. Between cowardice and recklessness, for instance, one should seek the middle ground: courage. Between boastfulness and timidity, one should cultivate modesty. The Doctrine of the Mean rationalized the classical search for moderation and balance. In contrast with the divinely ordained moral texts of other ancient cultures, Aristotle's teachings required individuals to reason their way to ethical conduct.

THE SYLLOGISM
All men are mortal.
a:b
Socrates is a man.
c:a
Therefore, Socrates
is mortal.
∴ c = b

Figure 4.16 The Syllogism.

READING 1.17 From Aristotle's Nicomachean Ethics (ca. 340 B.C.E.)

Every art and every scientific inquiry, and similarly every action and purpose, may be said to aim at some good. Hence the good has been well defined as that at which all things aim. But it is clear that there is a difference in the ends; for the ends are sometimes activities, and sometimes results beyond the mere activities. Also, where there are certain ends beyond the actions, the results are naturally superior to the activities. . . .   1

If it is true that in the sphere of action there is an end which we wish for its own sake, and for the sake of which we wish for everything else, and that we do not desire all things for the sake of something else (for, if that is so, the process will go on *ad infinitum*, and our desire will be idle and futile) it is clear that this will be the good or the supreme good. Does it not follow then that the knowledge of this supreme good is of great importance for the conduct of life, and that, if we know it, we shall be like archers who have a mark at which to aim, we shall have a better chance of attaining what we want? But, if this is the case, we must endeavor to comprehend, at least in outline, its nature, and the science or faculty to which it belongs. . . .   10   20

It seems not unreasonable that people should derive their conception of the good or of happiness from men's lives. Thus ordinary or vulgar people conceive it to be pleasure, and accordingly approve a life of enjoyment. For there are practically three prominent lives, the sensual, the political, and, thirdly, the speculative. Now the mass of men present an absolutely slavish appearance, as choosing the life of brute beasts, but they meet with consideration because so many persons in authority share the tastes of Sardanapalus.[1] Cultivated and practical people, on the other hand, identify happiness with honor, as honor is the general end of political life. But this appears too superficial for our present purpose; for honor seems to depend more upon the people who pay it than upon the person to whom it is paid, and we have an intuitive feeling that the good is something which is proper to a man himself and cannot easily be taken away from him. It seems too that the reason why men seek honor is that they may be confident of their own goodness. Accordingly they seek it at the hands of the wise and of those who know them well, and they seek it on the ground of virtue; hence it is clear that in their judgment at any rate virtue is superior to honor. . . .   30   40

We speak of that which is sought after for its own sake as more final than that which is sought after as a means to something else; we speak of that which is never desired as a means to something else as more final than the things which are desired both in themselves and as means to something else; and we speak of a thing as absolutely final, if it is always desired in itself and never as a means to something else.   50

It seems that happiness preeminently answers to this description, as we always desire happiness for its own sake and never as a means to something else, whereas we desire

[1]The legendary king of Assyria, known for his sensuality.

honor, pleasure, intellect, and every virtue, partly for their own sakes (for we should desire them independently of what might result from them) but partly also as being means to happiness, because we suppose they will prove the instruments of happiness. Happiness, on the other hand, nobody desires for the sake of these things, nor indeed as a means to anything else at all. . . .

Perhaps, however, it seems a truth which is generally admitted, that happiness is the supreme good; what is wanted is to define its nature a little more clearly. The best way of arriving at such a definition will probably be to ascertain the function of Man. For, as with a flute- player, a statuary, or any artisan, or in fact anybody who has a definite function and action, his goodness, or excellence seems to lie in his function, so it would seem to be with Man, if indeed he has a definite function. Can it be said then that, while a carpenter and a cobbler have definite functions and actions, Man, unlike them, is naturally functionless? The reasonable view is that, as the eye, the hand, the foot, and similarly each . . . part of the body has a definite function, so Man may be regarded as having a definite function apart from all these. What then, can this function be? It is not life; for life is apparently something which man shares with the plants; and it is something peculiar to him that we are looking for. We must exclude therefore the life of nutrition and increase. There is next what may be called the life of sensation. But this too, is apparently shared by Man with horses, cattle, and all other animals. There remains what I may call the practical life of the rational part of *Man's being*. But the rational part is twofold; it is rational partly in the sense of being obedient to reason, and partly in the sense of possessing reason and intelligence. The practical life too may be conceived of in two ways, viz., *either as a moral state, or as a moral activity*: but we must understand by it the life of activity, as this seems to be the truer form of the conception.

The function of Man then is an activity of soul in accordance with reason, or not independently of reason. . . .

Our present study is not, like other studies, purely speculative in its intention; for the object of our inquiry is not to know the nature of virtue but to become ourselves virtuous, as that is the sole benefit which it conveys. It is necessary therefore to consider the right way of performing actions, for it is actions as we have said that determine the character of the resulting moral states. . . .

The first point to be observed then is that in such matters as we are considering[,] deficiency and excess are equally fatal. It is so, as we observe, in regard to health and strength; for we must judge of what we cannot see by the evidence of what we do see. Excess or deficiency of gymnastic exercise is fatal to strength. Similarly an excess or deficiency of meat and drink is fatal to health, whereas a suitable amount produces, augments and sustains it. It is the same then with temperance, courage, and the other virtues. A person who avoids and is afraid of everything and faces nothing becomes a coward; a person who is not afraid of anything but is ready to face everything becomes foolhardy. Similarly he who enjoys every pleasure and never abstains from any pleasure is licentious; he who eschews all pleasures like a boor is an insensible sort of person. For temperance and courage are destroyed by excess and deficiency but preserved by the mean state. . . .

The nature of virtue has been now generically described. But it is not enough to state merely that virtue is a moral state, we must also describe the character of that moral state.

It must be laid down then that every virtue or excellence has the effect of producing a good condition of that of which it is a virtue or excellence, and of enabling it to perform its function well. Thus the excellence of the eye makes the eye good and its function good, as it is by the excellence of the eye that we see well. Similarly, the excellence of the horse makes a horse excellent and good at racing, at carrying its rider and at facing the enemy. If then this is universally true, the virtue or excellence of man will be such a moral state as makes a man good and able to perform his proper function well. We have already explained how this will be the case, but another way of making it clear will be to study the nature or character of this virtue.

Now in everything, whether it be continuous or discrete, it is possible to take a greater, a smaller, or an equal amount, and this either absolutely or in relation to ourselves, the equal being a mean between excess and deficiency. By the mean in respect of the thing itself, or the absolute mean, I understand that which is equally distinct from both extremes; and this is one and the same thing for everybody. By the mean considered relatively to ourselves I understand that which is neither too much nor too little; but this is not one thing, nor is it the same for everybody. Thus if 10 be too much and 2 too little we take 6 as a mean in respect of the thing itself; for 6 is as much greater than 2 as it is less than 10, and this is a mean in arithmetical proportion. But the mean considered relatively to ourselves must not be ascertained in this way. It does not follow that if 10 pounds of *meat* be too much and 2 be too little for a man to eat, a trainer will order him 6 pounds, as this may itself be too much or too little for the person who is to take it; it will be too little [for instance] for Milo,[2] but too much for a beginner in gymnastics. It will be the same with running and wrestling; *the right amount will vary with the individual.* This being so, everybody who understands his business avoids alike excess and deficiency; he seeks and chooses the mean, not the absolute mean, but the mean considered relatively to ourselves.

60

70

80

90

100

110

120

130

140

150

-390 Plato coins the term "elements" to describe four primary substances: earth, air, fire, and water (earlier introduced by Empedocles)

-350 Aristotle posits a spherical earth based on observations of a lunar eclipse

-340 Eudemus of Rhodes writes the *History of Mathematics*

-330 Aristotle's *Historia Animalium* classifies animals and records details of animal life; other of his writings advance the study of medicine, biology, and physics

[2]A famous athlete from the Greek city-state of Crotona in southern Italy. As a teenager, he began lifting a calf each day, until, as both his strength and the calf grew, he could lift a full-grown bullock.

Every science then performs its function well, if it regards the mean and refers the works which it produces to the mean. This is the reason why it is usually said of successful works that it is impossible to take anything from them or to add anything to them, which implies that excess or deficiency is fatal to excellence but that the mean state ensures it. Good **160** artists too, as we say, have an eye to the mean in their works. But virtue, like Nature herself, is more accurate and better than any art; virtue therefore will aim at the mean;—I speak of moral virtue, as it is moral virtue which is concerned with emotions and actions, and it is these which admit of excess and deficiency and the mean. Thus it is possible to go too far, or not to go far enough, in respect of fear, courage, desire, anger, pity, and pleasure and pain generally, and the excess and the deficiency are alike wrong; but to experience these emotions at the right times and on the right occasions and **170** towards the right persons and for the right causes and in the right manner is the mean or the supreme good, which is characteristic of virtue. Similarly there may be excess, deficiency, or the mean, in regard to actions. But virtue is concerned with emotions and actions, and here excess is an error and deficiency a fault, whereas the mean is successful and laudable, and success and merit are both characteristics of virtue.

Virtue then is a state of deliberate moral purpose consisting in a mean that is relative to ourselves, the mean being **180** determined by reason, or as a prudent man would determine it. . . .

Aristotle and the State

While the Golden Mean gave every individual a method for determining right action, Aristotle was uncertain that citizens would put it to efficient use in governing themselves. Like Plato, he questioned the viability of the democratic state. Political privilege, argued Aristotle, was the logical consequence of the fact that some human beings were naturally superior to others: From the hour of their birth some were marked out for subjection and others for rule. Aristotle also insisted that governments must function in the interest of the state, not in the interest of any single individual or group. He criticized democracy because, at least in theory, it put power in the hands of great masses of poor people who might rule in their own interests. He also pointed out that Athenian demagogues were capable of persuading the Assembly to pass less-than-worthy laws. In his *Politics*, the first treatise on political theory produced in the West, Aristotle concluded that the best type of government was a constitutional one ruled by the middle class. Aristotle defined the human being as a *polis*-person (the term from which we derive the word "political"). Humans are, in other words, political creatures, who can reach their full potential only within the political framework of the state. Only beasts and gods, he noted, have no need for the state—he gracefully excluded women from such considerations. Aristotle resolved the relationship between the individual and the state as follows:

[The] state is by nature clearly prior to the family and to the individual, since the whole is of necessity prior to the part. . . . The proof that the state is a creation of nature and prior to the individual is that the individual, when isolated, is not self-sufficing; and therefore he is like a part in relation to the whole. But he who is unable to live in society, or who has no need because he is sufficient for himself, must be either a beast or a god: he is no part of a state. A social instinct is implanted in all men by nature, and yet he who first founded the state was the greatest of benefactors.

For man, when perfected, is the best of animals, but, when separated from law and justice, he is the worst of all; since armed injustice is the more dangerous, and he is equipped at birth with arms, meant to be used by intelligence and virtue, he is the most unholy and the most savage of animals, and the most full of lust and gluttony. But justice is the bond of men in states, for the administration of justice, which is the determination of what is just, is the principle of order in political society.

SUMMARY

The Aegean civilizations of Crete and Mycenae laid the foundations for much of Greek life and legend. Based in these pre-Greek cultures, the Homeric epics describe an aggressive and warlike people who balance vigorous individualism against a deep devotion to the tribal community. The heroes of the *Iliad*, unlike those of other ancient civilizations, do not place themselves at the mercy of the gods; rather, they determine their own destinies.

This spirit of individualism also shaped the values of the emerging Greek city-states. It contributed to the creation of Athenian democracy—the world's first and only direct democracy—and to the Golden Age in cultural productivity that followed the Persian Wars. In Pericles' Funeral Speech the heroic ideal assumes a civic context. In Sophocles' *Antigone* individual choice challenges the inflexible demands of the state. These works confirm the humanistic thrust of Greek culture. In them, we encounter the Hellenic claim that freedom was no gift of heaven, but rather, a human enterprise involving the active engagement of the individual in the life of the community. The literary achievements of the ancient Greeks in epic poetry, historical narrative, and drama are memorable for the majesty of their language and the profundity of their insights into the human condition. They convey the enduring belief that the good life is within the grasp of mortals.

The ancient Greeks made the speculative leap from belief to reason and from supernatural to natural explanations of the universe. The naturalist philosophers tried to determine the material basis of the universe: Democritus advanced the atomic theory of matter, and Pythagoras held that proportion based on number constituted the underlying cosmic order. The Sophists and the humanist philosophers Socrates, Plato, and Aristotle moved "beyond physics" to probe the limits of human knowledge and the nature of moral action. The Sophists argued that knowledge and virtue were relative, while their critic Socrates pursued absolute standards for moral conduct. Induction and the dialectical method served Socrates in his quest for virtue. Plato's Theory of Forms laid the basis for philosophical idealism and for the separation of mind and matter. In the *Republic*, Plato explained how virtue might be cultivated for the mutual benefit of the individual and the community. The more practical Aristotle investigated a wide variety of subjects ranging from logic and zoology to the art of poetry and the science of statecraft. In his *Ethics*, Aristotle asserted that the good life was identical with the life of reason, a life guided by the Golden Mean. The writings of Plato and Aristotle are the fountainhead of Western philosophic thought. They explore methods of critical thinking that lie at the heart of Western rationalism. As such, they have made an immeasurable contribution to the humanistic tradition.

SUGGESTIONS FOR READING

Blundell, Sue. *Women in Ancient Greece*. Cambridge, Mass.: Harvard University Press, 1995.

Cartledge, Paul. *The Greeks: A Portrait of Self and Others*. New York: Oxford University Press, 1993.

Dover, K. J. *Greek Popular Morality in the Time of Plato and Aristotle*. Berkeley, Calif.: University of California Press, 1980.

Finley, M. I., ed. *The Legacy of Greece: A New Appraisal*. Oxford: Oxford University Press, 1981.

Green, Richard and Eric Handley. *Images of the Greek Theater*. Austin: University of Texas Press, 1995.

Lear, Jonathan. *Aristotle: The Desire to Understand*. New York: Oxford University Press, 1993.

Loraux, Nicole. *The Children of Athena: Athenian Ideas about Citizenship and the Division Between the Sexes*, trans. by C. Levine. Princeton, N.J.: Princeton University Press, 1993.

Martin, Thomas R. *Ancient Greece: From Prehistoric to Hellenistic Times*. New Haven, Conn.: Yale University Press, 1996.

Miller, Dean A. *The Epic Hero*. Baltimore, Md.: Johns Hopkins Press, 2000.

Morgan, Michael L. *Platonic Piety: Philosophy and Ritual in Fourth-Century Athens*. New Haven, Conn.: Yale University Press, 1990.

Reeder, Ellen D., ed. *Pandora: Women in Classical Greece*. Princeton: Princeton University Press, 1996.

Sinn, Ulrich. *Olympia: Cult, Sport, and Ancient Festival*. Princeton: Markus Weiner, 2000.

Stone, I. F. *The Trial of Socrates*. New York: Doubleday, 1989.

Vlastos, Gregory. *Socrates, Ironist and Moral Philosopher*. Ithaca, N.Y.: Cornell University Press, 1991.

GLOSSARY

allegory a literary device in which objects, persons, or actions are equated with secondary, figurative meanings that underlie their literal meaning

antagonist the character that directly opposes the protagonist in drama or fiction

catalog a list of people, things, or attributes, characteristic of biblical and Homeric literature

democracy a government in which supreme power is vested in the people

dialectical method a question-and-answer style of inquiry made famous by Socrates

empirical method a method of inquiry dependent on direct experience or observation

epithet a characterizing word or phrase; in Homeric verse, a compound adjective used to identify a person or thing

ethics that branch of philosophy that sets forth the principles of human conduct

idealism (Platonic) the theory that holds that things in the material world are manifestations of an independent realm of unchanging, immaterial ideas of forms (see also Kantian idealism, chapter 25)

oligarchy a government in which power lies in the hands of an elite minority

protagonist the leading character in a play or story

simile a figure of speech comparing two essentially unlike things, often introduced by "like" or "as"

syllogism a deductive scheme of formal argument, consisting of two premises from which a conclusion may be drawn

The classical style

"Men are day-bound. What is a man? What is he not? Man is a shadow's dream. But when divine advantage comes, men gain a radiance and a richer life."
Pindar

The words "classic" or "classical" are commonly used to mean "first-rate" and "enduring"; but they also describe the unique style that dominated the arts during the Greek Golden Age, that is, the period that followed the Persian Wars. The classical style embraced principles of clarity, harmony, and proportioned order in the visual arts, as well as in literature and music. At its height (ca. 480–400 B.C.E.) the so-called High Classical style provided a standard of beauty and excellence that was imitated for centuries, but most immediately by the civilizations that came to prominence after the collapse of Hellenic power. During the fourth century B.C.E., Alexander the Great carried Greek language and culture into North Africa and Central Asia, thus "Hellenizing" a vast part of the civilized world. Thereafter, the Romans absorbed Greek culture and, by imitation and adaptation, ensured the survival of classicism. In music and literature, as in the visual arts, the Greeks provided models that the Romans ultimately transmitted to the West.* Most of the freestanding sculptures of the Greek masters survive only in Roman replicas, and what remains is a fraction of what once existed. The balance fell to the ravages of time and barbarian peoples, who pulverized marble statues to make mortar and melted down bronze pieces to mint coins and cast cannons.

Despite these losses, the classical conception of beauty has had a profound influence on Western cultural expression. Its mark is most visible in the numerous neoclassical ("new classical") revivals that have flourished over the centuries, beginning with the Renaissance in Italy (see chapters 16–17). Some analysis of the defining features of the classical style is essential to an appreciation (and an understanding) of how and why that style became the touchstone by which creative expression was to be judged for centuries.

---

*The Roman contribution to the classical style is discussed in chapter 6.

Key Features of the Classical Style

Order and Proportion

The search for a natural order was the driving force behind the evolution of the classical style, even as it was the impetus for the rise of Greek philosophy. In chapter 4, it became clear that the quest to identify the natural order—the fundamental order underlying the chaos of human perception—preoccupied the early Greek philosophers. Pythagoras, for example, tried to show that the order of the universe could be understood by observing proportion (both geometric and numerical) in nature: He produced a taut string that, when plucked, sounded a specific pitch; by pinching that string in the middle and plucking either half he generated a sound exactly consonant with (and one octave higher than) the first pitch. Pythagoras claimed that relationships between musical sounds obeyed a natural symmetry that might be expressed numerically and geometrically. If music was governed by proportion, was not the universe as a whole subject to similar laws? And, if indeed nature itself obeyed laws of harmony and proportion, then should not artists work to imitate them?

Among Greek artists and architects, such ideas generated the search for a canon, or set of rules for determining physical proportion. To arrive at a canon, the artist fixed on a module, or standard of measurement, that governed the relationships beween all parts of the work of art and the whole. The size of the module was not absolute, but varied according to the subject matter. In the human body, for instance, the distance between the chin to the top of the forehead, representing one-tenth of the whole body height, constituted a module by which body measurements might be calculated. Unlike the Egyptian canon (see Figure 1.21), the Greek canon was flexible: It did not employ a grid on which the human form was mapped, with fixed positions for parts of the body. Nevertheless, the

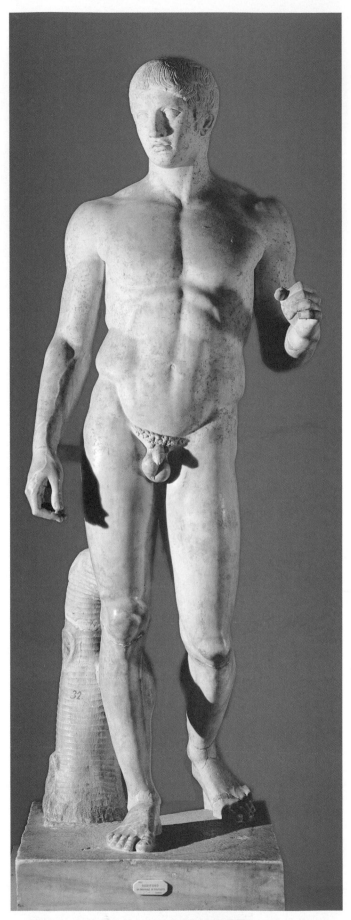

Figure 5.1 Polycleitus, *Doryphorus (Spear-Bearer)*, Roman marble copy after a bronze Greek original of ca. 450–440 B.C.E. Height 6 ft. 11 in. National Museum, Naples. Photo: Fotografica Foglia, Naples.

Greek canon made active use of that principle of proportion known as *symmetry*, that is, correspondence of opposite parts in size, shape, or position, as is evident in the human body.

Although little survives in the way of Greek literary evidence, Roman sources preserve information that helps us to understand the canon which, after three centuries of experimentation, artists of the Greek Golden Age put into practice. Among these sources, the best is the *Ten Books on Architecture* written by the Roman architect and engineer, Vitruvius Pollio (?–26 B.C.E.). Vitruvius recorded many of the aesthetic principles and structural techniques used by the ancient Greeks. In defining the classical canon, Vitruvius advised that the construction of a building and the relationship between its parts must imitate the proportions of the human body. Without proportion, that is, the correspondence between the various parts of the whole, there can be no design, argued Vitruvius. And without design, there can be no art. The eminent Golden Age Greek sculptor Polycleitus, himself the author of a manual on proportion (no longer in existence), is believed to have employed the canon Vitruvius describes (Figure **5.1**). But it was the Vitruvian model itself that, thanks to the efforts of the Renaissance artist/scientist Leonardo da Vinci (see chapter 17), became a symbol for the centrality of the ideally proportioned human being in an ideally proportioned universe (Figure **5.2**).

Figure 5.2 Leonardo da Vinci, *Proportional Study of a Man in the Manner of Vitruvius*, ca. 1487. Pen and ink, 13½ × 9⅝ in. Galleria dell'Accademia, Venice.

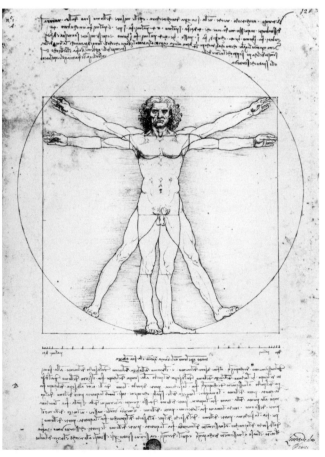

READING 1.18 From Vitruvius' Principles of Symmetry (ca. 46–30 b.c.e.)

On Symmetry: In Temples and in the Human Body

1 The Design of a temple depends on symmetry, the principles of which must be most carefully observed by the architect. They are due to proportion. . . . Proportion is a correspondence among the measures of the members of an entire work, and of the whole to a certain part selected as standard. From this result the principles of symmetry. Without symmetry and proportion there can be no principles in the design of any temple; that is, if there is no precise relation between its members, as in the case of those of a well shaped man.

2 For the human body is so designed by nature that the face, from the chin to the top of the forehead and lowest roots of the hair, is a tenth part of the whole height; the open hand from the wrist to the tip of the middle finger is just the same; the head from the chin to the crown is an eighth, and with the neck and shoulder from the top of the breast to the lowest roots of the hair is a sixth; from the middle of the breast to the summit of the crown is a fourth. If we take the height of the face itself, the distance from the bottom of the chin to the under side of the nostrils is one third of it; the nose from the underside of the nostrils to a line between the eyebrows is the same; from there to the lowest roots of the hair is also a third, comprising the forehead. The length of the foot is one sixth of the height of the body; of the forearm, one fourth; and the breadth of the breast is also one fourth. The other members, too, have their own symmetrical proportions, and it was by employing them that famous painters and sculptors of antiquity attained to great and endless renown.

3 Similarly, in the members of a temple there ought to be the greatest harmony in the symmetrical relations of the different parts to the general magnitude of the whole. Then again, in the human body the central point is naturally the navel. For if a man be placed flat on his back, with hands and feet extended, and a pair of compasses centered at his navel, the fingers and toes of his two hands and feet will touch the circumference of a circle described therefrom. And just as the human body yields a circular outline, so too a square figure may be found from it [see Figure 5.2]. For if we measure the distance from the soles of the feet to the top of the head, and then apply that measure to the outstretched arms, the breadth will be found to be the same as the height, as in the case of plane surfaces which are perfectly square.

4 Therefore, since nature has designed the human body so that its members are duly proportioned to the frame as a whole, it appears that the ancients had good reason for their rule, that in perfect buildings the different members must be in exact symmetrical relations to the whole general scheme. Hence, while transmitting to us the proper arrangements for buildings of all kinds, they are particularly careful to do so in the case of temples of the gods, buildings in which merits and faults usually last forever. . . .

Humanism, Realism, and Idealism

While proportion and order are two guiding principles of the classical style, other features informed Greek art from earliest times: One of these is *humanism*. Greek art is said to be humanistic not only because it observes fundamental laws derived from the human physique, but because it focuses so consistently on the actions of human beings. Greek art is fundamentally *realistic*, that is, faithful to nature; but it refines nature in a process of *idealization*, that is, the effort to achieve a perfection that surpasses nature. Humanism, realism, and idealism are hallmarks of Greek art.

Because almost all evidence of Greek wall-painting has disappeared, decorated vases are our main source of information about Greek painting. During the first three hundred years of Greek art—the *Geometric Period* (ca. 1200–700 B.C.E)—artists painted their ceramic wares with angular figures and complex geometric patterns organized according to the shape of the vessel (Figure **5.3**). By the *Archaic Period* (ca. 700–480 B.C.E.), figures painted in black or brown, and scenes from mythology, literature, and everyday life, came to dominate the central zone of the vase (Figure **5.4**; see also Figures 4.7 and 4.10). Water jars, wine jugs, storage vessels, drinking cups, and bowls all reflect the keen enjoyment of everyday activities among the Greeks: working, dancing, feasting, fighting, and gaming. In these compositions, little if any physical setting is

Figure 5.3 Krater with "Geometric" decoration, ca. 750 B.C.E. Terra-cotta, height 3 ft. 4½ in. The Metropolitan Museum of Art, New York..

5.5). They continued to position figures and objects so that they would complement the shape of the vessel (see also Figures 4.13 and 5.4). However, the red-figured style allowed artists to delineate physical details on the buff-colored surface, thereby making the human form appear more lifelike. Although still flattened and aligned side by side, figures are posed naturally. *Realism*, that is, fidelity to nature, has overtaken the decorative aspect of the geometric and archaic styles. At the same time, artists of the Classical Period moved toward aesthetic *idealism*. Socrates is noted for having described the idealizing process: He advised the painter Parrhasius that he must reach beyond the flawed world of appearances by selecting and combining the most beautiful details of many different models. To achieve ideal form, the artist must simplify the subject matter, free it of incidental detail, and impose the accepted canon of proportion. Accordingly, the art object will surpass the imperfect and transient objects of sensory experience. Like Plato's Ideal Forms, the artist's imitations of reality are lifelike in appearance, but they improve upon sensory reality in their absolute perfection. Among the Greeks, as among the Egyptians, conception played a large part in the art-making process; with the Greeks, however, the created object was no longer a static sacred sign, but a dynamic, rationalized version of the physical world.

Figure 5.4 Exekias, Black amphora with Achilles and Ajax Playing Dice, ca. 530 B.C.E. Height 24 in. Vatican Museums, Rome.

provided for the action. Indeed, in their decorative simplicity, the figures often resemble the abstract shapes that ornament the rim, handle, and foot of the vessel (see Figure 5.4). The principles of clarity and order so apparent in the Geometric style (see Figure 5.3) remain evident in the decoration of later vases, where a startling clarity of design is produced by the interplay of light and dark areas of figure and ground.

By the *Classical Period* (480–323 B.C.E.), artists had replaced the black-figured style with one in which the human body was left the color of the clay and the ground was painted black (Figure

Figure 5.5 Epictetus, Cup (detail), ca. 510 B.C.E. Terra-cotta, diameter 13 in. Reproduced by courtesy of the Trustees of the British Museum, London.

The Evolution of the Classical Style

Greek Sculpture: The Archaic Period
(ca. 700–480 B.C.E.)

Nowhere is the Greek affection for the natural beauty of the human body so evident as in Hellenic sculpture, where the male nude form assumed major importance as a subject. Freestanding Greek sculptures fulfilled the same purpose as Egyptian and Mesopotamian votive statues: They paid perpetual homage to the gods. They also served as cult statues, funerary monuments, and memorials

Figure 5.7 *Calf-Bearer*, ca. 575–550 B.C.E. Marble, height 5 ft. 6 in. Acropolis Museum, Athens. © Hirmer Fotoarchiv.

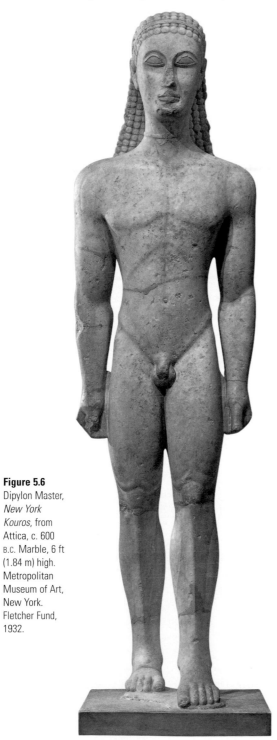

Figure 5.6
Dipylon Master,
*New York
Kouros*, from
Attica, c. 600
B.C. Marble, 6 ft
(1.84 m) high.
Metropolitan
Museum of Art,
New York.
Fletcher Fund,
1932.

designed to honor the victors of the athletic games. Since athletes both trained and competed in the nude, representation of the unclothed body was completely appropriate. Ultimately, however, the centrality of the nude in Greek art reflects the Hellenic regard for the human body as nature's perfect creation. (The fig leaves that cover the genitals of some Greek sculptures are additions dating from the Christian era.)

As in painting, so in sculpture, the quest for realism was offset by the will to idealize form. Achieving the delicate balance between real and ideal was a slow process, one that had its beginnings early in Greek history. During the Archaic phase of Greek sculpture, freestanding representations of the male youth (*kouros*) still resembled the blocklike statuary of ancient Egypt (see Figure 1.5). The kouros from Sounion (ca. 600 B.C.E) is rigidly posed, with arms close to its sides and its body weight distributed equally on both feet (Figure 5.6). Like most Archaic stat-

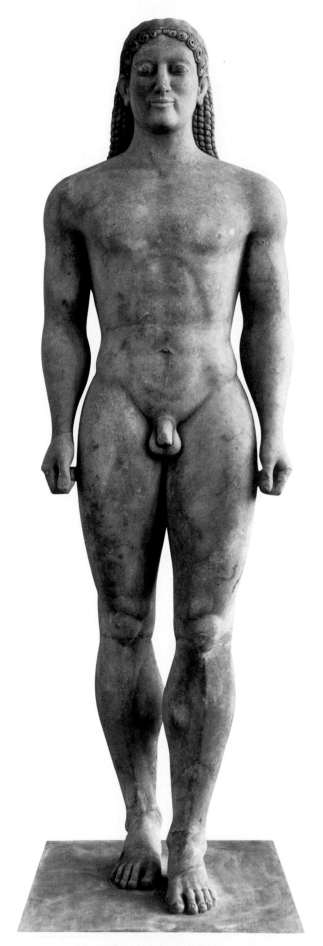

Figure 5.8 Kroisos from Anavyssos, ca. 525 B.C.E. Marble with traces of paint, height 6 ft. 4½ in. National Archeological Museum, Athens. Photo: Alison Frantz.

ues, the figure retains the rigid verticality of tree trunks from which early Greek sculptures were carved.

Produced some fifty years after the Sounion *kouros*, the *Calf-Bearer* (ca. 575–550 B.C.E) is more gently and more realistically modeled—note especially the abdominal muscles and the sensitively carved bull calf (Figure **5.7**). The hollow eyes of the shepherd once held inlays of semi-precious stones (mother-of-pearl, gray agate, and lapis lazuli) that would have given the face a strikingly realistic appearance. Such lifelike effects were enhanced by the brightly colored paint that (now almost gone) enlivened the lips, hair, and other parts of the figure. A quarter of a century later, the robust likeness of a warrior named Kroisos (found marking his grave) shows close anatomical attention to knee and calf muscles. Like his carved predecessors, he strides aggressively forward, but his forearms now turn in toward his body, and his chest, arms, and legs swell with powerful energy (Figure **5.8**). He also bears a blissful smile that, in contrast with the awestruck countenances of Mesopotamian votive statues (see Figure 2.9), reflects the buoyant optimism of the early Greeks.

Greek Sculpture: The Classical Period (480–323 B.C.E.)

By the early fifth century B.C.E., a major transformation occurred in Hellenic art. With the Kritios Boy, the Greek sculptor had arrived at the natural positioning of the human body that would characterize the classical style: The sensuous torso turns on the axis of the spine, and the weight of the body shifts from equal distribution on both legs to greater weight on the left leg—a kind of balanced opposition that is at once natural and graceful (Figure **5.9**). (This counterpositioning would be called ***contrapposto*** by Italian Renaissance artists.) The muscles of the Kritios Boy are no longer geometrically schematized, but protrude subtly at anatomical junctures. And the figure is no longer smiling, but instead, solemn and contemplative. The new poised stance, along with a complete mastery of human anatomy and proportion, are features of the High Classical style that flourished between ca. 480–400 B.C.E. At mid-century, Polycleitus brought that style to perfection with the *Doryphorus* (*Spear-Bearer*; see Figure 5.1). Known today only by way of Roman copies, the *Doryphorus* is held by some as the embodiment of the canon of ideal human proportions (see Reading 1.18). The figure, who once held a spear in his left hand, strides forward in a manner that unites motion and repose, energy and poise, confidence and grace—the qualities of the ideal warrior-athlete.

There is little to distinguish man from god in the bronze statue of Zeus (or Poseidon) hurling a weapon, the work of an unknown sculptor (Figure **5.11**). This nude, which conveys the majesty and physical vitality of a mighty Greek deity, might just as well represent a victor of the Olympic games. The Greeks were the first to employ the lost-wax method of bronze casting (see Figure 0.18) for large-sized artworks, such as the monumental Zeus (or Poseidon) itself. This sophisticated technique allowed artists to depict more vigorous action and to include

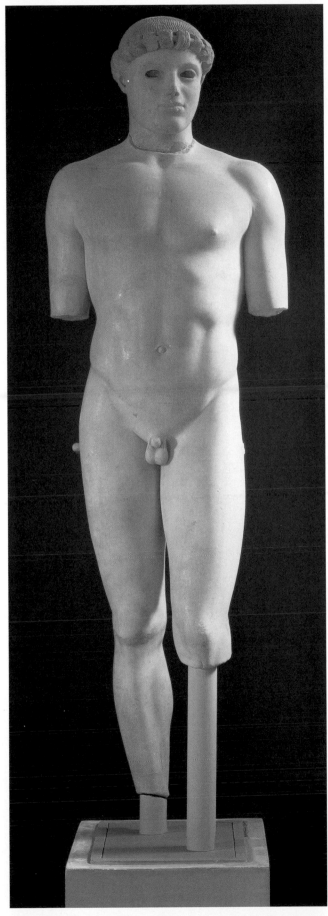

greater detail than was possible in the more restrictive medium of marble. Dynamically posed—the artist has deliberately exaggerated the length of the arms—the god fixes the decisive moment just before the action, when every muscle in the body is tensed, ready to achieve the mark. The sculptor has also idealized the physique in the direction of geometric clarity. Hence the muscles of the stomach are indicated as symmetrical trapezoids, and the strands of his hair and beard assume a distinctive pattern of parallel wavy lines.

Greek and Roman sculptors often made marble copies of popular bronze-cast figures. The *Discobolus (Discus Thrower)*, originally executed in bronze by Myron around 450 B.C.E, but surviving only in various Roman marble copies, is one such example (Figure **5.10**). Like the statue

Figure 5.9 Kritios Boy, ca. 480 B.C.E. Marble, height 34 in. Acropolis Museum, Athens. Photo: Craigo Marie Mauzy, Athens.

Figure 5.10 Myron, *Discobolus (Discus Thrower),* reconstructed Roman marble copy of a bronze Greek original of ca. 450 B.C.E. Height 5 ft. 1 in. Museo Nazionale delle Terme, Rome. Photo: SCALA.

in Figure 5.11, it captures the moment before the action, the ideal moment when intellect guides the physical effort to follow. The male nudes of the High Classical Age seem to fulfill Aristotle's idea of excellence as the exercise of human will dominated by reason.

The evolution of the female figure (*kore*) underwent a somewhat different course from that of the male. Early *korai* were fully clothed and did not appear in the nude until the fourth century B.C.E. Female statues of the Archaic period were ornamental, columnar, and (like their male counterparts) smiling (Figure **5.12**). Not until the Late Classical Age (430–323 B.C.E.) did Greek sculptors arrive at the sensuous female nudes that so inspired Hellenistic, Roman, and (centuries later) Renaissance artists. The *Aphrodite of Knidos* (Figure **5.13**) by Praxiteles established a model for the ideal female form: tall and poised, with small breasts and broad hips. Regarded by the Romans as the finest statue in the world, Praxiteles' goddess of love exhibits a subtle counterposition of shoulders and hips, smooth body curves, and a face that bears a dreamy, melting gaze. She is distinguished by the famous Praxitelean technique of carving that coaxed a translucent

Figure 5.11 Zeus (or Poseidon), ca. 460 B.C.E. Bronze, height 6 ft. 10 in. National Archeological Museum, Athens. Photo: Craig & Marie Mauzy, Athens.

shimmer from the fine white marble. This celebrated nude is a Roman copy of a Greek original, and the bar bracing the hip suggests that the original may have been executed in bronze.

A careful study of Greek statuary from the Archaic through the Late Classical Age (400–323 B.C.E.) reflects increasing refinements in realism and idealism: All imperfections (wrinkles, warts, blemishes) have been purged in favor of a radiant flawlessness. The classical nude is neither very old nor very young, neither very thin nor very fat. He or she is eternally youthful, healthy, and virile—

Figure 5.12 *Kore* from Chios (?), ca. 520 B.C.E. Marble with traces of paint, height approx. 22 in. (lower part missing). Acropolis Museum, Athens. Photo: Studio Kontos Nikos, Athens.

first time goddess shown nude

Figure 5.13 Praxiteles, *Aphrodite of Knidos*, Roman marble copy of marble Greek original of ca. 350 B.C.E. Height 6 ft. 8 in. Vatican Museums, Rome.

serene and dignified, and liberated from all accidents of nature. This synthesis of humanism, realism, and idealism in the representation of the freestanding nude was one of the great achievements of Greek art. Indeed, the Hellenic conception of the nude defined the standard of beauty in Western art for centuries.

Figure 5.14 Ictinus and Kallicrates, West end of the Parthenon, Athens, 448–432 B.C.E. Pentelic marble, height of columns 34 ft. Photo: Sonia Halliday, Weston Turville.

Greek Architecture: The Parthenon

The great monuments of classical architecture were designed to serve the living, not—as in Egypt—the dead. In contrast with the superhuman scale of the Egyptian pyramid, the Greek temple, as Vitruvius observed, was proportioned according to the human body. Greek theaters (see Figure 4.11) celebrated life here on earth rather than the life in the hereafter, while Greek temples served as shrines for the gods and depositories for civic and religious treasures. Both theaters and temples functioned as public meeting places. Much like the Mesopotamian ziggurat, the Greek temple was a communal symbol of reverence for the gods, but, whereas the ziggurat enforced the separation of priesthood and populace, the Greek temple united religious and secular domains.

The outstanding architectural achievement of Golden Age Athens is the Parthenon (Figures **5.14** and **5.15**), a temple dedicated to Athena, the goddess

of war, the patron of the arts and crafts, and the personification of wisdom. The name Parthenon derives from the Greek word *parthenos* ("maiden"), a popular epithet for Athena. Built in glittering Pentelic marble upon the ruins of an earlier temple burned during the Persian Wars, the Parthenon overlooks Athens from the highest point on the Acropolis (Figure **5.16**). Athens' preeminent temple

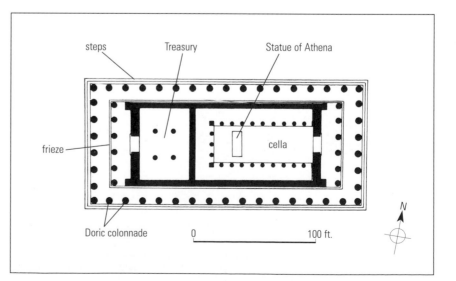

Figure 5.15 Plan of the Parthenon, Athens.

was commissioned by Pericles, designed by the architects Ictinus and Kallicrates, and embellished by the sculptor Phidias (fl. ca. 490–430 B.C.E). Phidias directed and supervised the construction of the temple over a period of more than ten years, from 448 to 432 B.C.E. In the tradition of Egyptian builders, Greek architects used no mortar. Rather, they employed bronze clamps and dowels to fasten the individually cut marble segments.

The Parthenon represents the apex of a long history of post-and-lintel temple building among the Greeks. That history, like the history of Greek painting and sculpture, entailed a search for harmonic proportion, which came to fruition in the Parthenon. The plan of the temple, a rectangle delimited on all four sides by a colonnaded walkway, reflects the typically classical reverence for clarity and symmetry (see Figure 5.15). Freestanding columns (each 34 feet tall) make up the exterior, while two further rows of columns on the east and west ends of the temple provide inner **porticos** (see Figure 5.19). The interior of the Parthenon is divided into two rooms, a central hall (or *cella*), which held the colossal cult statue of Athena, and a smaller room used as a treasury. It was here that the much-disputed Delian League funds were stored. Entirely elevated on a raised platform, the Parthenon invited the individual to move around it, as if it were a piece of monumental sculpture. Indeed, scholars have suggested that the Parthenon was both a shrine to Athena and a victory monument.

The Parthenon makes use of the Doric **order**, one of three programs of architectural design developed by the ancient Greeks (Figure **5.17**). Each of the orders—Doric, Ionic, and (in Hellenistic times) Corinthian—prescribes a fundamental set of structural and decorative parts that stand in fixed relation to each other. Each order differs in details and in the relative proportions of the parts. The Doric order, which originated on the Greek mainland, is simple and severe. In the Parthenon it reached its most refined expression. The Ionic order, originating in Asia Minor and the Aegean Islands, is more delicate and ornamental. Its slender columns terminate in capitals with paired volutes or scrolls. The Ionic order is employed in some of the small temples on the Acropolis (Figure **5.18**). The Corinthian, the most ornate of the orders, is characterized by capitals consisting of acanthus leaves. It is often found on victory monuments, in **tholos** (circular) sanctuaries and shrines, as well as in various Hellenistic and Roman structures (see Figures 6.12 and 6.14).

If an ideal system governed the parts of the Greek building, a similar set of laws determined its proportions. The precise canon of proportion adopted by Phidias for the construction of the Parthenon is still, however, the subject of debate. Most architectural historians agree that a module was used, but whether the module was geometric or numerical, and whether it followed a specific ratio—such as the famous "Golden Section"—has not been resolved. The system of proportions known as the "Golden Section" or "Golden Ratio" is expressed numerically by the ratio of 1.618:1, or approximately 8:5. This ratio, which governs the proportions of the ground plan of the Parthenon and the Vitruvian canon, represents an

Figure 5.16 Model of the classical Acropolis at Athens. American School of Classical Studies at Athens: Agora Excavations.

1 Erechtheion
2 picture gallery
3 Propylaia (entrance gate)
4 Sacred Way
5 Temple of Athena Nike
6 Chalkotheke (armory)
7 Parthenon (Temple of Athena Parthenos)

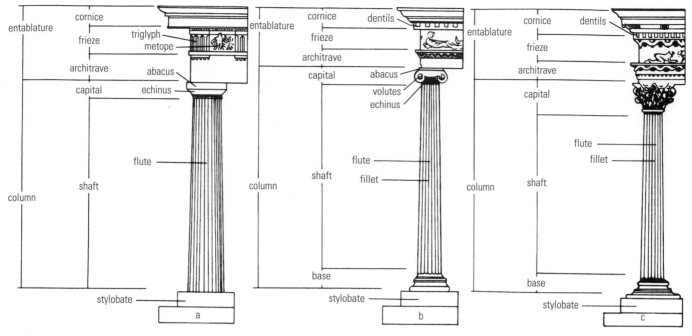

Figure 5.17 The Greek orders: (a) Doric; (b) Ionic; and (c) Corinthian.

Figure 5.18 Kallicrates, Temple of Athena Nike, Acropolis, Athens, ca. 427–424 B.C.E. Pentelic marble, 17 ft. 9 in. × 26 ft. 10 in. Photo: Alison Frantz.

aesthetic ideal found in nature and in the human anatomy. The question of the Parthenon's construction is further complicated by the fact that there are virtually no straight lines in the entire building. Its Doric columns, for instance, swell out near the center to counter the optical effect of thinning that occurs when the normal eye views an uninterrupted set of parallel lines. All columns tilt slightly inward. Corner columns are thicker than the others to compensate for the attenuating effect produced by the bright light of the sky against which the columns are viewed, and also to ensure their ability to bear the weight of the terminal segments of the superstructure. The top step of the platform on which the columns rest is not parallel to the ground, but rises four and a quarter inches at the center, allowing for rainwater to run off the convex surface even as it corrects the optical impression of sagging along the extended length of the platform. Consistently, the architects of the Parthenon corrected negative optical illusions produced by strict conformity to geometric regularity. Avoiding rigid systems of proportion, they took as their primary consideration the aesthetic and functional integrity of the building. Today the Parthenon stands as a noble ruin, the victim of an accidental gunpowder explosion in the seventeenth century, followed by centuries of vandalism, air pollution, and unrelenting tourist traffic.

The Sculpture of the Parthenon

Between 438 and 432 B.C.E. Phidias and the members of his workshop executed the sculptures that would appear in three main locations on the Parthenon: in the **pediments** of the roof **gables**, on the **metopes** or square panels between the beam ends under the roof, and in the area along the outer wall of the *cella* (Figure **5.19**). Brightly painted, as were some of the decorative portions of the building, the Parthenon sculptures relieved the stark angularity of the post-and-lintel structure. In subject matter, the temple sculptures paid homage to the patron deity of Athens: The east pediment narrates the birth of Athena with gods and goddesses in attendance (Figures **5.20** and **5.21**). The west pediment shows the contest between Poseidon and Athena for domination of Athens. The ninety-two metopes that occupy the **frieze** (see Figure 5.20) illustrate scenes of combat between the Greeks (the bearers of civilization) and Giants, Amazons, and Centaurs (the forces of barbarism; Figure **5.22**). Carved in high relief, each metope is a masterful depic-

Figure 5.19 Sculptural and architectural detail of the Parthenon. **Frieze**, a decorative band along the top of a wall; **metopes**, segmented spaces on a frieze; **pediment**, a gable.

tion of two contestants, one human and the other bestial. Appropriate to a temple honoring the Goddess of Wisdom, the sculptural program of the Parthenon celebrates the victory of intellect over barbarism.

Completing Phidias' program of architectural decoration for the Parthenon is the continuous frieze that winds around the outer wall of the *cella* where that wall meets the roofline. The 524-foot-long sculptured band is thought to depict the Panathenaic Festival, a celebration held every four years in honor of the goddess Athena. Hundreds of figures—a cavalcade of horsemen (Figure **5.23**), water bearers, musicians, and votaries—are shown filing in calm procession toward an assembled group of gods and goddesses (Figure **5.24**). The figures move with graceful rhythms, in tempos that could well be translated into music. Once brightly painted and ornamented with

Figure 5.20 Drawing of a reconstruction of the east pediment of the Parthenon, central section. Acropolis Museum, Athens.

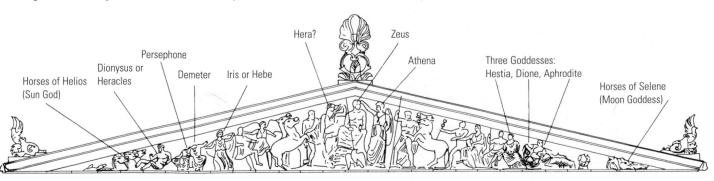

Figure 5.21 Three Goddesses: Hestia, Dione, Aphrodite, from east pediment of the Parthenon, Athens, ca. 437–432 B.C.E. Marble, over life-size. Reproduced by courtesy of the Trustees of the British Museum, London.

Figure 5.22 Lapith Overcoming a Centaur, south metope 27, Parthenon, Athens, 447–438 B.C.E. Marble relief, height 4 ft. 5 in. Reproduced by courtesy of the Trustees of the British Museum, London.

Figure 5.23 A Group of Young Horsemen, from the north frieze of the Parthenon, Athens, 447–438 B.C.E. Marble, height 3 ft. 7 in. Reproduced by courtesy of the Trustees of the British Museum, London.

Figure 5.24 East frieze of the Parthenon, Athens, ca. 437–432 B.C.E. Marble. © TAP Services, Greece.

metal details, the final effect must have been impressively lifelike. To increase this effect and satisfy a viewpoint from below, Phidias graded the relief, cutting the marble more deeply at the top than at the bottom. Housed today in the British Museum in London, where it is hung at approximately eye level, the Parthenon frieze loses much of its illusionistic subtlety. Nevertheless, this masterpiece of the Greek Golden Age reveals the harmonious reconciliation of humanism, realism, and idealism that is the hallmark of the classical style.

The Gold of Greece

The famous statue of Athena that stood in the *cella* of the Parthenon disappeared many centuries ago. However, images of the goddess abound in Hellenic art. One of the most spectacular appears in the form of a gold pendant disk that shows the head of Athena wearing a helmet bearing a sphinx, deer and griffin heads, and an elaborate triple crest (Figure 5.25). From Athena's shoulders snakes spring forth, and by her head stands an owl (the symbol of wisdom)—both motifs recalling the powers of the Minoan priestess (see Figure 4.4). Rosettes of gold filigree and enamel-colored buds ornament the complex of looped chains that hang from the disk.

The Greeks gained international acclaim for their goldworking techniques, many of which had been inher-

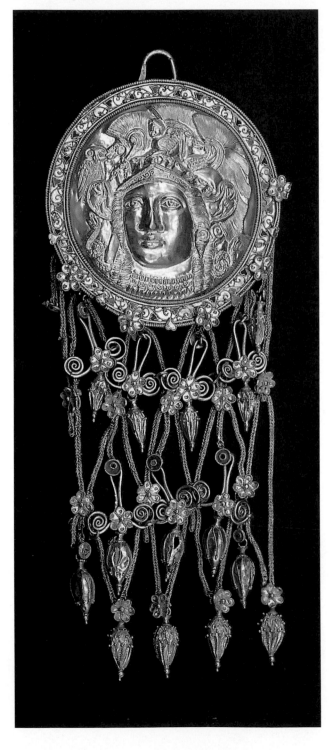

Figure 5.25 Gold pendant disk with the head of Athena (one of a pair), from Kul Oba, ca. 400–350 B.C.E. Height 3.95 in., diameter of disk 1.53 in. Photo: Hermitage KO 5. NOVOSTI, London.

ited from Persia and from the nomadic Scythians of northern Asia. Gold-rich mining areas of northern Greece provided craftspeople with materials for the manufacture of jewelry. Particularly popular were pendants, earrings, and headpieces in the form of miniature sculptures, some of which (like the pendant of Athena) reproduced familiar images of the gods. Much like today, gold jewelry was a mark of wealth that also bore sentimental and religious value. In Greece and especially in the cities of Asia Minor, men as well as women adorned themselves with stylish earrings and bracelets.

The Classical Style in Poetry

In classical Greece, as in other parts of the ancient world, distinctions between various forms of artistic expression were neither clear-cut nor definitive. A combination of the arts prevailed in most forms of religious ritual and in public and private entertainment. In *Antigone*, for instance, choric pantomime and dance complemented dramatic poetry. And in processions and festivals, music, poetry, and the visual arts all served a common purpose. The intimate relationship between music and poetry is revealed in the fact that many of the words we use to describe lyric forms, such as the **ode** and the **hymn**, are also musical terms. The word lyric, meaning "accompanied by the lyre," describes verse that was meant to be sung, not read silently. Lyric poetry was designed to give voice to deep emotions.

Hellenic culture produced an impressive group of lyric poets, the greatest of whom was Sappho (ca. 610–ca. 580 B.C.E.). Her personal life remains a mystery. Born into an aristocratic family, she seems to have married, mothered a daughter, and produced some nine books of poetry, of which only fragments remain. She settled on the island of Lesbos, where she led a group of young women dedicated to the cult of Aphrodite. At Lesbos, Sappho trained women in the production of love poetry and music. Her own highly self-conscious poems, many of which come to us only as fragments, are filled with passion and tenderness. They offer a glimpse of a body of poetry that inspired Sappho's contemporaries to regard her as "the female Homer." Ancient and modern poets alike admired Sappho for her powerful economy of expression and her inventive combinations of sense and sound—features that are extremely difficult to convey in translation. The first of the five poems reproduced below gives lyric voice to Sappho's homoerotic attachment to the women of the Lesbian cult. That bisexual and homosexual relationships were common among the ancient Greeks is given ample evidence in Hellenic literature and art. The scene on the elegant drinking cup by Douris (see Figure 4.14), for instance, is generally interpreted as depicting an older man propositioning a younger one. The last of the selections, a terse and pensive poem, reflects the intense spirit of this-worldliness and the generally negative view of death that typified Sappho's verse and ancient Greek expression in general.

READING 1.19 Sappho's Poems (ca. 590 B.C.E.)

He is more than a hero   1
He is a god in my eyes
the man who is allowed
to sit beside you—he

who listens intimately   5
to the sweet murmur of
your voice, the enticing

laughter that makes my own
heart beat fast. If I meet
you suddenly, I can't   10

speak—my tongue is broken;
a thin flame runs under
my skin; seeing nothing,

hearing only my own ears
drumming, I drip with sweat;   15
trembling shakes my body

and I turn paler than
dry grass. At such times
death isn't far from me

——◆——

With his venom   1
Irresistible
and bittersweet
that loosener
of limbs, Love   5
reptile-like
strikes me down

——◆——

I took my lyre and said: 1
Come now, my heavenly
tortoise shell; become
a speaking instrument

——◆——

Although they are   1
Only breath, words
which I command
are immortal

——◆——

We know this much   1
Death is an evil;
we have the gods'
word for it; they too
would die if death   5
were a good thing

While lyric poetry often conveyed deeply personal feelings, certain types of lyrics, namely odes, served as public eulogies or songs of praise. Odes honoring Greek athletes bear strong similarities to songs of divine praise, such as the Egyptian "Hymn to the Aten" (see chapter 1), the Hebrew Psalms, and Greek invocations. But the sentiments conveyed in the odes of the noted Greek poet Pindar (ca. 522–438 B.C.E.) are firmly planted in the secular world. They celebrate the achievements of the athletes who competed at the games held at the great sanctuaries of Olympia, Delphi, Nemea, and elsewhere (see Figure 4.10). Perpetuating the heroic idealism of the *Iliad*, Pindar's odes make the claim that prowess, not chance, leads to victory, which in turn renders the victor immortal. The first lines of his *Nemean Ode VI* honoring Alcimidas of Aegina (winner in the boys' division of wrestling) assert that gods and men share a common origin. The closest human beings can come to achieving godlike immortality, however, lies in the exercise of "greatness of mind/Or of body." The ode thus narrows the gap between hero-athletes and their divine prototypes. In his *Pythian Ode VIII* (dedicated to yet another victorious wrestler), Pindar develops a more modest balance of opposites: He sets the glories of youth against the adversities of aging and mortality itself. Although mortal limitations separate human beings from the ageless and undying gods, "manly action" secures the "richer life."

READING 1.20 From Pindar's Odes (ca. 420 B.C.E.)

From *Nemean Ode VI*

Single is the race, single   1
Of men and of gods,
From a single mother we both draw breath.
But a difference of power in everything
Keeps us apart;   5
For the one is as nothing, but the brazen sky
Stays a fixed habitation for ever.
Yet we can in greatness of mind
Or of body be like the Immortals,
Though we know not to what goal   10
By day or in the nights
Fate has written that we shall run.

. . . .

From *Pythian Ode VIII*

. . . .

In the Pythian games   1
you pinned four wrestlers
unrelentingly, and sent
them home in losers' gloom;
no pleasant laughter cheered them as they reached   5
their mothers' sides; shunning ridicule,
they took to alleys, licking losers' wounds.

And he, who in his youth
secures a fine advantage
gathers hope and flies   10
on wings of manly action,
disdaining cost. Men's happiness is early-
ripened fruit that falls to earth

from shakings of adversity.
Men are day-bound. What *is* a man? What is
he *not*? Man is a shadow's dream. But when divine
advantage comes, men gain a radiance and a richer life...

−500 steel is first produced in India; the corpus of
Indian geometry is summarized in the Sulvasutras
("Rules of the Cord")[†]

−400 Hellenistic Greeks invent the catapult for use as an
artillery weapon

−300 Euclid completes his *Elements*, a compilation of
mathematics that includes geometry and number
theory

−300 a school of medicine is established in Alexandria

−290 Theophrastus, a student of Plato, writes the detailed
History of Plants

The Classical Style in Music and Dance

The English word *music* derives from *muse*, the Greek word describing any of the nine mythological daughters of Zeus and the Goddess of Memory. According to Greek mythology, the muses presided over the arts and the sciences. Pythagoras observed that music was governed by mathematical ratios and therefore constituted both a science and an art. As was true of the other arts, music played a major role in Greek life. However, we know almost as little about how Greek music sounded as we do in the cases of Egyptian or Sumerian music. The ancient Greeks did not invent a system of notation with which to record instrumental or vocal sounds. Apart from written and visual descriptions of musical performances, there exist only a few fourth-century-B.C.E. treatises on music theory and some primitively notated musical works. The only complete piece of ancient Greek music that has survived

Figure 5.26 The Berlin painter, ca. 490 B.C.E. Terra-cotta, height of vase 16⅜ in. The Metropolitan Museum of Art, New York. Fletcher Fund, 1956.

is an ancient song found chiselled on a first-century B.C.E. gravestone. ♪ It reads: "So long as you live, be radiant, and do not grieve at all. Life's span is short and time exacts the final reckoning." Both vocal and instrumental music were commonplace, and contests between musicians, like those between playwrights, were a regular part of public life. Vase paintings reveal that the principal musical instruments of ancient Greece were the **lyre**, the **cithara**—both belonging to the harp family and differing only in shape, size, and number of strings (Figure **5.26**)—and the **aulos**, a flute or reed pipe (see Figure 5.5). Along with percussion devices often used to accompany dancing, these string and wind instruments were probably inherited from Egypt.

The Greeks devised a system of **modes**, or types of **scales** characterized by fixed patterns of pitch and tempo within the octave. (The sound of the ancient Greek Dorian mode is approximated by playing the eight white keys of the piano beginning with the white key two notes above middle C.) Modified variously in Christian times, the modes were preserved in Gregorian Chant and Byzantine church hymnology (see chapter 9). Although the modes themselves may have been inspired by the music of ancient India, the diatonic scale (familiar to Westerners as the series of notes C, D, E, F, G, A, B, C) originated in Greece. Greek music lacked harmony as we know it. It was thus **monophonic**, that is, confined to a single, unaccompanied line of melody. The strong association between poetry and music suggests that the human voice had a significant influence in both melody and rhythm.

From earliest times, music was believed to hold magical powers and therefore exercise great spiritual influence. Greek and Roman mythology describes gods and heroes who used music to heal or destroy. Following Pythagoras, who equated musical ratios with the unchanging cosmic order, many believed that music might put one "in tune with" the universe. The planets, which Pythagoras described as a series of spheres moving at varying speeds in concentric orbits around the earth, were said to produce a special harmony, the so-called *music of the spheres*. The Greeks believed, moreover, that music had a moral influence. This argument, often referred to as the "Doctrine of Ethos," held that some modes strengthened the will, whereas others undermined it and thus damaged the development of moral character. In the *Republic*, Plato encouraged the use of the Dorian mode, which settled the temper and inspired courage, but he condemned the Lydian mode, which aroused sensuality. Because of music's potential for affecting character and mood, both Plato and Aristotle recommended that the types of music used in the education of young children be regulated by law. As with other forms of classical expression, music was deemed inseparable from its role in the advancement of the individual and the well-being of the community.

Dance was also prized for its moral value, as well as for its ability to give pleasure and induce good health (see Figure 5.5). For Plato the uneducated man was a "danceless" man. Both Plato and Aristotle advised that children be instructed at an early age in music and dancing. However, both men distinguished noble dances from ignoble ones—Dionysian and comic dances, for instance. These they considered unfit for Athenian citizens and therefore inappropriate to the educational curriculum. Nevertheless, the dancing *maenad*, a cult follower of Dionysus, was a favorite image of revelry and intoxication in ancient Greece (Figure **5.27**).

Figure 5.27 A *maenad* leaning on a thyrsos, Roman copy of Greek original, ca. 420–410 B.C.E. Marble relief. The Metropolitan Museum of Art, New York. Fletcher Fund, 1935.

The Diffusion of the Classical Style: The Hellenistic Age (323–30 B.C.E.)

The fourth century B.C.E. was a turbulent era marked by rivalry and warfare among the Greek city-states. Ironically, however, the failure of the Greek city-states to live in peace would lead to the spread of Hellenic culture throughout the civilized world. Manipulating the shifting confederacies and internecine strife to his advantage, Philip of Macedonia eventually defeated the Greeks in 338 B.C.E. When he was assassinated two years later, his twenty-year-old son Alexander (356–323 B.C.E.) assumed the Macedonian throne (Figure **5.28**). A student of Aristotle, Alexander brought to his role as ruler the same kind of far-reaching ambition and imagination that his teacher had exercised in the intellectual realm. Alexander was a military genius: Within twelve years, he created an empire that stretched from Greece to the borders of modern India (Map **5.1**). To all parts of his empire, but especially to the cities he founded—many of which he named after himself—Alexander carried Greek language and culture. Greek art and literature made a major impact on civilizations as far east as India, where it influenced Buddhist art and Sanskrit literature (see chapter 9).

Alexander carved out his empire with the help of an army of 35,000 Greeks and Macedonians equipped with weapons that were superior to any in the ancient world. Siege machines such as catapults and battering rams were used to destroy the walls of the best-defended cities of Asia Minor, Egypt, Syria, and Persia. Finally, in northwest India, facing the prospect of confronting the formidable army of the King of Ganges and his force of five thousand elephants, Alexander's troops refused to go any further. Shortly thereafter, the thirty-two-year-old general died (probably of malaria), and his empire split into three segments: Egypt governed by the Ptolemy dynasty, Persia under the leadership of the Seleucid rulers, and Macedonia-Greece governed by the family of Antigonus the One-Eyed (see Map 5.1).

The era that followed, called Hellenistic ("Greek-like"), lasted from 323 to 30 B.C.E. The defining features of the Hellenistic Age were cosmopolitanism, urbanism, and the blending of Greek, African, and Asian cultures. Trade routes linked Arabia, east Africa, and central Asia, bringing great wealth to the cities of Alexandria, Antioch, Pergamon, and Rhodes. Alexandria, which replaced Athens as a

Figure 5.28 Head of Alexander, from Pergamum, Hellenistic portrait, ca. 200 B.C.E. Marble, height 16 in. Archeological Museum, Istanbul.

cultural center, boasted a population of more than one million people and a library of half a million books (the collection was destroyed by fire when Julius Caesar besieged the city in 47 B.C.E.). The Great Library, part of the cultural complex known as the Temple of the Muses (or "Museum"), was an ancient "think tank" that housed both scholars and books. At the rival library of Pergamon (with some 200,000 books), scribes prepared sheepskin to produce "pergamene paper," that is, parchment, the medium that would be used for centuries of manuscript production prior to the widespread dissemination of paper. The Hellenistic Age made important advances in geography, astronomy, and mathematics. Euclid, who lived in Alexandria during the late fourth century B.C.E., produced a textbook of existing geometric learning that systematized the theorems of plane and solid geometry. Archimedes of Syracuse, who flourished a century later,

calculated the value of *pi* (the ratio of the circumference of a circle to its diameter). An engineer as well as a mathematician, he invented the compound pulley, a windlass for moving heavy weights, and many other mechanical devices. "Give me a place to stand," he is said to have boasted, "and I shall move the earth." Legend describes Archimedes as the typical absent-minded scientist, who often forgot to eat; upon realizing that the water he displaced in his bathtub explained the law of specific gravity, he is said to have jumped out of the bathtub and run naked through the streets of Syracuse, shouting "*Eureka*" ("I have found it!").

Hellenistic Philosophic Thought

The Hellenistic world was considerably different from the world of the Greek city-states. In the latter, citizens identified with their community, which was itself the state; but in Alexander's vast empire, communal loyalties were unsteady and—especially in sprawling urban centers—impersonal. The intellectuals of the Hellenistic Age did not formulate rational methods of investigation in the style of Plato and Aristotle; rather they espoused

Map 5.1 The Hellenistic World.

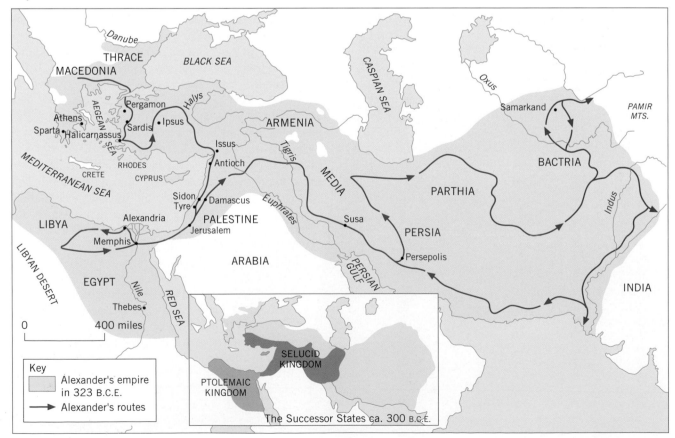

philosophic schools of thought that guided everyday existence: Skepticism, Cynicism, Epicureanism, and Stoicism. The Skeptics—much like the Sophists of Socrates' time—denied the possibility of knowing anything with certainty: They argued for the suspension of all intellectual judgment. The Cynics held that spiritual satisfaction was only possible if one renounced societal values, conventions, and material wealth. The Epicureans, followers of the Greek thinker Epicurus (341–270 B.C.E.), taught that happiness depended on avoiding all forms of physical excess; they valued plain living and the perfect union of body and mind. Epicurus held that the gods played no part in human life, and that death was nothing more than the rearrangement of atoms of which the body and all of nature consisted. Finally, the Stoics found tranquility of mind in a doctrine of detachment that allowed them to accept even the worst of life's circumstances. The aim of the Stoic was to bring the individual will into complete harmony with the will of nature, which they believed was governed by an impersonal intelligence. The Stoics also advanced the notion of universal equality. All four of these schools of thought placed the personal needs and emotions of the individual over and above the good of the community at large; in this, they constituted a practical and radical departure from the Hellenic quest for universal truth.

Hellenistic Art

The shift from city-state to empire that accompanied the advent of the Hellenistic Era was reflected in larger, more monumental forms of architecture and in the construction of utilitarian structures, such as lighthouses, theaters, and libraries. Circular sanctuaries and colossal Corinthian temples with triumphant decorative friezes were particu-

- **−280** the lighthouse at Pharos, north of Alexandria, is the tallest tower in existence
- **−260** Archimedes establishes the law of specific gravity, invents the compound pulley, studies the mechanical properties of the lever, and lays the foundations for calculus.
- **−240** Aristarchus of Samos proposes that the earth and all the planets rotate on their axes and revolve around the sun (the heliocentric theory)
- **−230** Eratosthenes of Cyrene calculates the circumference of the earth with near accuracy
- **−220** Herophilus of Alexandria discovers the human nervous system; he proposes that the arteries carry blood (not air, as previously believed) from the heart
- **−150** Hipparchus of Nicea invents trigonometry; he catalogs 805 fixed stars

larly popular in the fourth century B.C.E. and thereafter. At Pergamon (see Map 5.1) stood the largest sculptural complex in the ancient world: the Altar of Zeus (see Figure **5.29**). Erected around 180 B.C.E. to celebrate the victory of the minor kingdom of Pergamon over the invading tribal Gauls achieved some fifty years earlier, the altar stands atop a 20-foot high platform enclosed by an Ionic colonnade. A massive stairway reaches upward to the shrine. Around the base of the platform runs a 300-foot long sculptured frieze depicting the mythological battle between the Olympic gods and the race of giants known as Titans. The subject matter, symbolizing the victory of

Figure 5.29 The Altar of Zeus (reconstructed), Pergamon, ca. 175 B.C.E. Marble. Pergamonmuseum, Berlin.

The monument that best mirrors the classical style is the Parthenon, the Greek temple built atop the Acropolis to honor Athens' patron goddess of wisdom and war. In its application of the Doric order, the integration of technical refinements, and the intelligent application of architectural decoration, the Parthenon stands as one of the most noble buildings in the history of architecture.

The Hellenic synthesis of humanism and idealism, harnessed to an impassioned quest for order and proportion, also characterized literature and music. The lyric poetry of Sappho and Pindar makes the human being the measure of earthly experience. In Greek music, where the clarity of the single line of melody prevails, modal patterns of pitch and tempo were held to influence the moral condition of the listener.

During the fourth century B.C.E. Alexander the Great spread Greek language and culture throughout a vast, though short-lived, empire that extended from Macedonia to India. During the Hellenistic Age, metaphysics gave way to science and practical philosophy, and the classical style moved further toward realism and melodramatic expressiveness. Nevertheless, the Hellenistic (and thereafter, the Roman) era perpetuated the fundamental features of classicism. Indeed, for centuries to come, Western artists—like newly liberated prisoners from Plato's mythical cave—would try to throw off the chains that bound them to the imperfect world of the senses in pursuit of the classical ideal.

SUGGESTIONS FOR READING

Boardman, John. *The Diffusion of Classical Art in Antiquity*. Princeton: Princeton University Press, 1994.

——— and David Finn. *The Parthenon and its Sculptures*. Austin, Tex.: University of Texas Press, 1985.

Cook, R. M. *Greek Art*. Baltimore, Md.: Penguin, 1976.

Carpenter, Rhys. *The Architecture of the Parthenon*. Baltimore: Penguin, 1972.

Francis, E. D. *Image and Idea in Fifth Century Greece: Art and Literature after the Persian Wars*. New York: Routledge, 1990.

Fullerton, Mark D. *Greek Art*. New York: Cambridge University Press, 2000.

Havelock, Christine M. *Hellenistic Art: The Art of the Classical World from the Death of Alexander the Great to the Battle of Actium*, 2nd ed. New York: Norton, 1981.

Pedley, John G. *Greek Art and Archeology*. Englewood Cliffs, N.J.: Prentice-Hall, 1993.

Pollit, J. J. *Art and Experience in Classical Greece*. Cambridge: Cambridge University Press, 1971.

Spivey, Nigel. *Understanding Greek Sculpture: Ancient Meanings, Modern Readings*. London: Thames and Hudson, 1996.

Stewart, Andrew. *Greek Sculpture: An Exploration*. 2 vols. New Haven: Yale University Press, 1990.

Walbank, F. W. *The Hellenistic World*, rev. ed. Cambridge, Mass.: Harvard University Press, 1993.

MUSIC LISTENING SELECTION

CD One Selection 1 Anonymous, "Seikolos Song." Greek, ca. 50 C.E.

GLOSSARY

aulos a wind instrument used in ancient Greece; it had a double reed (held inside the mouth) and a number of finger holes and was always played in pairs, that is, with the performer holding one in each hand; a leather band was often tied around the head to support the cheeks, thus enabling the player to blow harder (see Figure 6.5)

cithara a large version of the lyre (having seven to eleven strings) and the principal instrument of ancient Greek music

contrapposto (Italian, "counterpoised") a position assumed by the human body in which one part is turned in opposition to another part

frieze in architecture, a sculptured or ornamented band

gable the triangular section of a wall at the end of a pitched roof

hymn a lyric poem offering divine praise or glorification

kouros (Greek, "youth"; pl. *kouroi*) a youthful male figure, usually depicted nude in ancient Greek sculpture; the female counterpart is the *kore* (Greek, "maiden"; pl. *korai*)

lyre any one of a group of plucked stringed instruments; in ancient Greece usually made of tortoise shell or horn and therefore light in weight

metope the square panel between the beam ends under the roof of a structure (see Figure 5.19)

mode a type of musical scale characterized by a fixed pattern of pitch and tempo within the octave; because the Greeks associated each of the modes with a different emotional state, it is likely that the mode involved something more than a particular musical scale, perhaps a set of rhythms and melodic turns associated with each scale pattern

monophony (Greek, "one voice") a musical texture consisting of a single, unaccompanied line of melody

Nike the Greek goddess of victory

octave the series of eight tones forming any major or minor scale

ode a lyric poem expressing exalted emotion in honor of a person or special occasion

order in classical architecture, the parts of a building that stand in fixed and constant relation to each other; the three classical orders are the Doric, the Ionic, and the Corinthian (see Figure 5.17)

pediment the triangular space forming the gable of a two-pitched roof in classical architecture; any similar triangular form found over a portico, door, or window

portico a porch with a roof supported by columns

scale (Latin, *scala*, "ladder") a series of tones arranged in ascending or descending consecutive order; the *diatonic* scale, characteristic of Western music, consists of the eight tones (or series of notes C, D, E, F, G, A, B, C) of the twelve-tone octave; the *chromatic* scale consists of all twelve tones (represented by the twelve piano keys, seven white and five black) of the octave, each a semitone apart

tholos a circular structure, generally in classical Greek style and probably derived from early tombs

CHAPTER SIX

Rome: the rise to empire

". . . remember, Roman,
To rule the people under law, to establish
The way of peace, to battle down the haughty,
To spare the meek. Our fine arts, these forever."
Virgil

At either end of the Eurasian landmass, two great empires—Rome and China—rose to power after the fourth century B.C.E. While imperial Rome and Han China traded through Asian intermediaries across a vast overland route, neither reflects the direct influence of the other. Nevertheless, the two have much in common: Both brought political stability and cultural unity to vast stretches of territory, by virtue of which achievement each created a flourishing empire. Both were profoundly secular in their approach to the world and to the conduct of human beings. Han China and imperial Rome each inherited age-old forms and practices in religion, law, literature, and the arts, which they self-consciously preserved and transmitted to future generations. The classical legacies of China and Rome would come to shape the respective histories of the East and the West.

The Roman Rise to Empire

Rome's Early History

Rome's origins are to be found among tribes of Iron Age folk called Latins, who invaded the Italian peninsula just after the beginning of the first millennium B.C.E. By the mid-eighth century B.C.E., these people had founded the city of Rome in the lower valley of the Tiber River, a spot strategically located for control of the Italian peninsula and for convenient access to the Mediterranean Sea (Map 6.1). While central Italy became the domain of the Latins, the rest of the peninsula received a continuous infusion of eastern Mediterranean people: Etruscans, Greeks, and Phoenicians, who brought with them cultures richer and more complex than that of the Latins. The Etruscans, whose origins are unknown (and whose language remains undeciphered), established themselves in northwest Italy. A sophisticated, Hellenized people with commercial contacts throughout the Mediterranean, they were experts in the arts of metallurgy, town building, and city planning. The Greeks, who colonized the tip of the Italian peninsula and Sicily, were masters of philosophy and the arts. And

the Phoenicians, who settled on the northern coast of Africa, brought westward their alphabet and their commercial and maritime skills. From all of these people, but especially from the first two groups, the Latins borrowed elements that would enhance their own history. From the Etruscans, the Romans absorbed the fundamentals of urban planning, chariot racing, the toga, bronze and gold crafting, and the most ingenious structural principle of Mesopotamian architecture—the arch. The Etruscans provided their dead with tombs designed to resemble the lavish dwelling places of the deceased. On the lids of the **sarcophagi** (stone coffins) that held their cremated remains, Etruscan artists carved portraits of the dead, depicting husbands and wives relaxing and socializing on their dining couch, as if still enjoying a family banquet (Figure **6.1**).

From the Greeks, the Romans borrowed a pantheon of gods and goddesses, linguistic and literary principles, and the aesthetics of the classical style. As the Latins absorbed Etruscan and Greek culture, so they drew these and other peoples into what would become the most powerful world-state in ancient history.

The Roman Republic (509–133 B.C.E.)

For three centuries, Etruscan kings ruled the Latin population, but in 509 B.C.E. the Latins overthrew the Etruscans. Over the next two hundred years, monarchy slowly gave way to a government "of the people" (*res publica*). The agricultural population of ancient Rome consisted of a powerful class of large landowners, the *patricians*, and a more populous class of small farmers called *plebeians*. The plebeians constituted the membership of a Popular Assembly. Although this body conferred civil and military authority (the **imperium**) upon two elected magistrates (called *consuls*), its lower-class members had little voice in government. The wealthy patricians—life members of the Roman Senate—controlled the lawmaking process. But step by step, the plebeians gained increasing political influence. Using as leverage their service as soldiers in the Roman army and their power to veto laws initiated by the

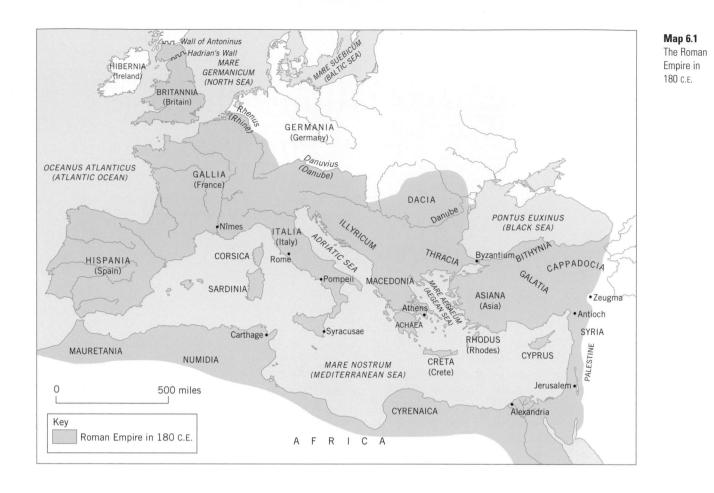

Map 6.1
The Roman Empire in 180 C.E.

Senate, the plebeians—through their leaders, the *tribunes*—made themselves heard. Eventually, they won the freedom to intermarry with the patricians, the right to hold executive office, and, finally, in 287 B.C.E., the privilege of making laws. The stern and independent population of Roman farmers had arrived at a *res publica* by peaceful means. But no sooner had Rome become a Republic than it adopted an expansionist course that would erode these democratic achievements.

Obedience to the Roman state and service in its powerful army were essential to the life of the early Republic. Both contributed to the rise of Roman imperialism, which proceeded by means of long wars of conquest similar to those that had marked the history of earlier empires. After expelling the last of the Etruscan kings, Rome extended its power over all parts of the Italian peninsula. By the middle of the third century B.C.E., having united all of Italy by force or negotiation, Rome stood poised to rule the Mediterranean. A long-standing distrust of the

Phoenicians, and rivalry with the city of Carthage, Phoenicia's commercial stronghold in northeastern Africa, led Rome into the Punic (Latin for "Phoenician") Wars—a 150-year-period of intermittent violence that ended with the destruction of Carthage in 147 B.C.E.

Figure 6.1 Sarcophagus from Cerveteri, ca. 520 B.C.E. Painted terra-cotta, length 6 ft. 7 in. Museo Nazionale di Villa Giulia, Rome

With the defeat of Carthage, Rome assumed naval and commercial leadership in the western Mediterranean, the sea they would come to call *mare nostrum* ("our sea"). But the ambitions of army generals and the impetus of a century of warfare fueled the fire of Roman imperialism. Rome seized every opportunity for conquest, and by the end of the first century B.C.E., the Empire included most of North Africa, the Iberian peninsula, Greece, Egypt, much of Southwest Asia, and the territories constituting present-day Europe as far as the Rhine River (see Map 6.1).

Despite the difficulties presented by the task of governing such far-flung territories, the Romans proved to be efficient administrators. They demanded from their foreign provinces taxes, soldiers to serve in the Roman army, tribute, and slaves. Roman governors, appointed by the Senate from among the higher ranks of the military, ruled within the conquered provinces. Usually, local customs and even local governments were permitted to continue unmodified, for the Romans considered tolerance of provincial customs politically practical. The Romans introduced the Latin language and Roman law in the provinces. They built paved roads, freshwater aqueducts, bridges, and eventually granted the people of their conquered territories Roman citizenship.

Rome's highly disciplined army was the backbone of the Empire. During the Republic, the army consisted of citizens who served two-year terms, but by the first century C.E., the military had become a profession to which all free men might devote twenty-five years (or more) of their lives. Since serving for this length of time allowed a non-Roman to gain Roman citizenship for himself and his children, military service acted as a means of Romanizing foreigners. The Roman army was the object of fear and admiration among those familiar with Rome's rise to power. Josephus (ca. 37–100 C.E.), a Jewish historian who witnessed the Roman destruction of Jerusalem in 70 C.E., described the superiority of the Roman military machine, which he estimated to include more than three hundred thousand armed men. According to Josephus, Roman soldiers performed as though they "had been born with weapons in their hands." The efficiency of the army, reported Josephus, was the consequence of superior organization and discipline. The following description of a Roman military camp reflects the admiration and awe with which non-Romans viewed Roman might. It also describes the nature of that "perfect discipline" and dedication to duty that characterized the Roman ethos and Roman culture in general.

READING 1.21 Josephus' *Description of the Roman Army* (ca. 70 C.E.)

. . . one cannot but admire the forethought shown in this particular by the Romans, in making their servant class useful to them not only for the ministrations of ordinary life but also for war. If one goes on to study the organization of their army as a whole, it will be seen that this vast empire of theirs has come to them as the prize of valor, and not as a gift of fortune. **1**

For their nation does not wait for the outbreak of war to give men their first lesson on arms; they do not sit with folded hands in peace time only to put them in motion in the hour of need. On the contrary, as though they had been born with weapons in hand, they never have a truce from training, never wait for emergencies to arise. Moreover, their peace maneuvers are no less strenuous than veritable warfare; each soldier daily throws all his energy into his drill, as though he were in action. Hence that perfect ease with which they sustain the shock of battle: no confusion breaks their customary formation, no panic paralyzes, no fatigue exhausts them; and as their opponents cannot match these qualities, victory is the invariable and certain consequence. Indeed, it would not be wrong to describe their maneuvers as bloodless combats and combats as sanguinary maneuvers. **10** **20**

The Romans never lay themselves open to a surprise attack; for, whatever hostile territory they may invade, they engage in no battle until they have fortified their camp. This camp is not erected at random or unevenly; they do not all work at once or in disorderly parties; if the ground is uneven, it is first leveled; a site for the camp is then measured out in the form of a square. For this purpose the army is accompanied by a multitude of workmen and of tools for building.

The interior of the camp is divided into rows of tents. The exterior circuit presents the appearance of a wall and is furnished with towers at regular intervals; and on the spaces between the towers are placed "quick-firers," catapults, "stone-throwers," and every variety of artillery engines, all ready for use. In this surrounding wall are set four gates, one on each side, spacious enough for beasts of burden to enter without difficulty and wide enough for sallies of troops in emergencies. The camp is intersected by streets symmetrically laid out; in the middle are the tents of the officers, and precisely in the center the headquarters of the commander-in-chief, resembling a small temple. Thus, as it were, an improvised city springs up, with its market-place, its artisan quarter, its seats of judgment, where captains and colonels adjudicate upon any differences which may arise. . . . **30** **40**

Once entrenched, the soldiers take up their quarters in their tents by companies, quietly and in good order. All their fatigue duties are performed with the same discipline, the same regard for security; the procuring of wood, food-supplies, and water, as required—each party has its allotted task. . . . The same precision is maintained on the battle-field: the troops wheel smartly round in the requisite direction, and, whether advancing to the attack or retreating, all move as a unit at the word of command. **50**

When the camp is to be broken up, the trumpet sounds a first call; at that none remain idle: instantly, at this signal, they strike the tents and make all ready for departure. The trumpets sound a second call to prepare for the march: at once they pile their baggage on the mules and other beasts of burden and stand ready to start, like runners breasting the cord on the race-course. They then set fire to the encampment, both because they can easily construct another [on the spot], and to prevent the enemy from ever making use of it. . . . **60**

Then they advance, all marching in silence and in good order, each man keeping his place in the ranks, as if in face of the enemy. . . . By their military exercises the Romans instil into their soldiers fortitude not only of body but also of soul; fear, too, plays its part in their training. For they have laws which punish with death not merely desertion of the ranks, but even a slight neglect of duty; and their generals are held in even greater awe than the laws. For the high honors with which they reward the brave prevent the offenders whom they punish from regarding themselves as treated cruelly.

This perfect discipline makes the army an ornament of peace-time and in war welds the whole into a single body; so compact are their ranks, so alert their movements in wheeling to right or left, so quick their ears for orders, their eyes for signals, their hands to act upon them. Prompt as they consequently ever are in action, none are slower than they in succumbing to suffering, and never have they been known in any predicament to be beaten by numbers, by ruse, by difficulties of ground, or even by fortune; for they have more assurance of victory than of fortune. Where counsel thus precedes active operations, where the leaders' plan of campaign is followed up by so efficient an army, no wonder that the Empire has extended its boundaries on the east to the Euphrates, on the west to the ocean,[1] on the south to the most fertile tracts of Libya, on the north to the Ister[2] and the Rhine. One might say without exaggeration that, great as are their possessions, the people that won them are greater still. . . .

The Collapse of the Republic (133–30 B.C.E.)

By the beginning of the first millennium C.E., Rome had become the watchdog of the ancient world. Roman imperialism, however, worked to effect changes within the Republic itself. By its authority to handle all military matters, the Senate became increasingly powerful, as did a new class of men, wealthy Roman entrepreneurs (known as *equestrians*), who filled the jobs of provincial administration. The army, by its domination of Rome's overseas provinces, also became more powerful. Precious metals, booty, and slaves from foreign conquests brought enormous wealth to army generals and influential patricians; corruption became widespread. Captives of war were shipped back to Rome and auctioned off to the highest bidders, usually patrician landowners, whose farms soon became large-scale plantations (*latifundia*) worked by slaves. The increased agricultural productivity of the *latifundia* gave economic advantage to large landowners who easily undersold the lesser landowners and drove them out of business. Increasingly, the small farmers were forced to sell their farms to neighboring

patricians in return for the right to remain on the land. Or, they simply moved to the city to join, by the end of the first century B.C.E., a growing unemployed population. The disappearance of the small farmer signaled the decline of the Republic.

As Rome's rich citizens grew richer and its poor citizens poorer, the patricians fiercely resisted efforts to redistribute wealth more equally. But reform measures failed and political rivalries increased. Ultimately, Rome fell victim to the ambitions of army generals, who, having conquered in the name of Rome, now turned to conquering Rome itself. The first century B.C.E. was an age of military dictators, whose competing claims to power fueled a spate of civil wars. As bloody confrontations replaced reasoned compromises, the Republic crumbled.

In 46 B.C.E., an extraordinary army commander named Gaius Julius Caesar (Figure **6.2**) triumphantly entered the city of Rome and established a dictatorship. Caesar, who had spent nine years conquering Gaul (present-day France and Belgium), was as shrewd in politics as he was brilliant in war. These campaigns are described in his prose *Commentaries on the Gallic War*. His brief but successful campaigns in Syria, Asia Minor, and Egypt— where his union with the Egyptian Queen Cleopatra (69–30 B.C.E.) produced a son–inspired his famous boast: *Veni, vidi, vici* ("I came, I saw, I conquered"). A superb organizer, Caesar took strong measures to restabilize Rome: He codified the laws, regulated taxation, reduced debts, sent large numbers of the unemployed proletariat to overseas colonies, and inaugurated public works projects. He also granted citizenship to non-Italians and reformed the Western calendar to comprise 365 days and twelve months (one of which—July—he named after himself). Threatened by Caesar's populist reforms and his contempt for republican institutions, a group of his senatorial opponents, led by Marcus Junius Brutus, assassinated him in 44 B.C.E. Despite Caesar's inglorious death, the name *Caesar* would be used as an honorific title by all his imperial successors well into the second century C.E., as well as by many modern-day dictators.

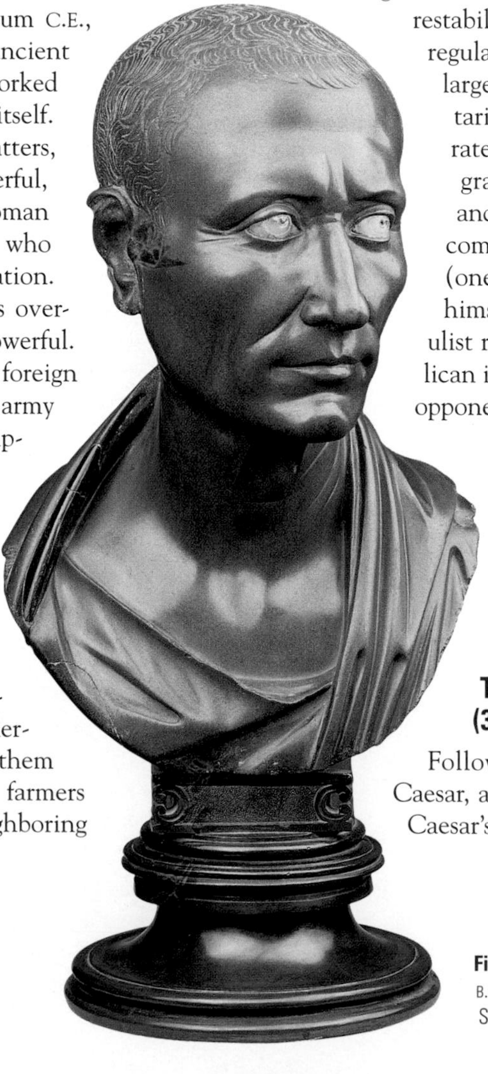

The Roman Empire (30 B.C.E.–180 C.E.)

Following the assassination of Julius Caesar, a struggle for power ensued between Caesar's first lieutenant, Mark Anthony

Figure 6.2 Bust of Julius Caesar, first century B.C.E. Marble, height 1 ft. 4⅛ in. Photo: The Staatliche Museum, Berlin.

[1]The Atlantic.
[2]The Roman name for the Danube River.

(ca. 80–30 B.C.E.) and his grandnephew (and adopted son) Octavian (63 B.C.E.–14 C.E.). The contest between the two was resolved at Actium in 31 B.C.E., when Octavian's navy routed the combined forces of Mark Anthony and Queen Cleopatra. The alliance between Anthony and Cleopatra, like that between Cleopatra and Julius Caesar, advanced the political ambitions of Egypt's most seductive queen, who sought not only to unite the eastern and western portions of Rome's great empire, but to reign over the Roman world state. That destiny, however, would fall to Octavian. In 43 B.C.E., Octavian usurped the consulship and gained the approval of the Senate to rule for life. Although he called himself "first citizen" (*princeps*), his title of Emperor betrayed the reality that he was first and foremost Rome's army general (*imperator*). The Senate, however, bestowed on him the title *Augustus* ("the Revered One"). Augustus shared legislative power with the Senate, but retained the right to veto legislation. Thus, for all intents and purposes, the Republic was defunct. The destiny of Rome lay once again in the hands of a military dictator. It is in this guise that Augustus appears in Roman sculpture (Figure **6.3**). In this freestanding, larger-than-life marble statue from Primaporta, Octavian raises his arm in a gesture of leadership and imperial authority. He wears a breastplate celebrating his victory over the Parthians in 20 B.C.E. At his feet appear Cupid and a dolphin, reminders of his alleged divine descent from Venus—the mother of Aeneas, Rome's legendary founder. Octavian's stance and physical proportions are modeled on the *Doryphorus* by Polykleitus (see Figure 5.1). His handsome face and tall, muscular physique serve to complete the heroic image. In reality, however, the emperor was only 5 feet 4 inches tall—the average height of the Roman male.

Augustus' reign ushered in an era of peace and stability, a *Pax Romana*: From 30 B.C.E. to 180 C.E. the Roman peace prevailed throughout the Empire, and Rome enjoyed active commercial contact with all parts of the civilized world, including India and China. Augustus tried to arrest the tide of moral decay that had swept into Rome: In an effort to restore family values and the begetting of legitimate children, he passed laws (which ultimately failed in their pur-

Figure 6.3 Augustus of Primaporta, early first century C.E., after a bronze of ca. 20 B.C.E. Marble, height 6 ft. 8 in. Vatican Museums, Rome. Photo: E.T. Archive, London.

The Julio-Claudian Dynasty

27 B.C.E.–14 C.E.	Augustus
14–37	Tiberius
37–41	Gaius Caligula
41–54	Claudius
54–68	Nero

The Flavian Dynasty

68–79	Vespasian
79–81	Titus
81–96	Domitian

The "Good Emperors"

96–98	Nerva
97–117	Trajan
117–138	Hadrian
138–161	Antoninus Pius
161–180	Marcus Aurelius

Beginning of Decline

180–192	Commodus

The Severan Dynasty

193–211	Septimius Severus
211–217	Caracalla
222–235	Alexander Severus
235–284	Anarchy
284–305	Diocletian
306–337	Constantine I

Figure 6.4 Principal Roman Emperors.

pose) to curb adultery and to prevent bachelors from receiving inheritances. The *Pax Romana* was also a time of artistic and literary productivity. An enthusiastic patron of the arts, Augustus commissioned literature, sculpture, and architecture. He boasted that he had come to power when Rome was a city of brick and would leave it a city of marble. In most cases, this meant a veneer of marble that was, by standard Roman building practices, laid over the brick surface. In a city blighted by crime, noise, poor hygiene, and a frequent scarcity of food and water, Augustus initiated many new public works (including three new aqueducts and some 500 fountains) and such civic services as a police force and a fire department. The reign of Octavian also witnessed the rise of a new religion, Christianity, which, in later centuries, would spread throughout the Empire (see chapters 8 and 9).

Augustus put an end to the civil wars of the preceding century, but he revived neither the political nor the social equilibrium of the early Republic. Following his death, Rome continued to be ruled by military officials. Since there was no machinery for succession to the imperial throne, Rome's rulers held office until they either died or were assassinated (figure **6.4**). Of the twenty-six emperors who governed Rome during the fifty-year period between 335 and 385 C.E., only one died a natural death. Government by and for the people had been the hallmark of Rome's early history, but the enterprise of imperialism ultimately overtook these lofty republican ideals.

Roman Law

Against this backdrop of conquest and dominion, it is no surprise that Rome's contributions to the humanistic tradition were practical rather than theoretical. The sheer size of the Roman Empire inspired engineering programs, such as bridge and road building, that united all regions under Roman rule. Law—a less tangible means of unification—was equally important in this regard. The development of a system of law was one of Rome's most original and influential achievements.

Roman law (the Latin *jus* means both "law" and "justice") evolved out of the practical need to rule a world-state, rather than—as with the ancient Greeks—as a dialectic on the role of the citizen within the *polis*. Inspired by the laws of Solon, the Romans published their first civil code, the Twelve Tables of Law, in 450 B.C.E. They placed these laws on view in the Forum, the public meeting area for the civic, religious, and commercial activities of Rome. The Twelve Tables of Law provided Rome's basic legal code for almost a thousand years. To this body of law were added the acts of the Assembly and the Senate, and public decrees of the emperors. For some five hundred years, *praetors* (magistrates who administered justice) and *jurisconsults* (experts in the law) interpreted the laws, bringing commonsense resolutions to private disputes. Their interpretations constituted a body of "case law." In giving consideration to individual needs, these magistrates cultivated the concept of equity, which puts the spirit of the law above the letter of the law. The decisions of Roman jurists became precedents that established comprehensive guidelines for future judgments. Thus, Roman law was not fixed, but was an evolving body of opinions on the nature and dispensation of justice.

Early in Roman history, the law of the land (*jus civile*) applied only to Roman citizens, but as Roman citizenship was extended to the provinces, so too was the law. Law that embraced a wider range of peoples and customs, the law of the people (*jus gentium*), assumed an international quality that acknowledged compromises between conflicting customs and traditions. The law of the people was, in effect, a law based on universal principles, that is, the law of nature (*jus naturale*). The full body of Roman law came to incorporate the decisions of the jurists, the acts passed by Roman legislative assemblies, and the edicts of Roman emperors. In the sixth century C.E., two hundred years after the division of the Empire into eastern and western portions and a hundred years after the collapse of Rome, the Byzantine (East Roman) Emperor Justinian would codify this huge body of law, thereafter known as the *Corpus Juris Civilis*. The Roman system of law influenced the development of codified law in all European countries with the exception of England.

The Roman Contribution to Literature

Roman Philosophic Thought

Roman contributions to law were numerous, but such was not the case with philosophy. More a practical than a speculative people, they produced no systems of philosophic thought comparable to those of Plato and Aristotle. Yet they respected and preserved the writings of Hellenic and Hellenistic thinkers. Educated Romans admired Aristotle and absorbed the works of the Epicureans and the Stoics. The Latin poet Lucretius (ca. 95–ca. 55 B.C.E.) popularized the materialist theories of Democritus and Leucippus, which described the world in purely physical terms and denied the existence of the gods and other supernatural beings. Since all of reality, including the human soul, consists of atoms, he argued in his only work, *On the Nature of Things*, there is no reason to fear death: "We shall not feel because we shall not be."

In the vast, impersonal world of the Empire, many Romans cultivated the attitude of rational detachment popular among the Stoics. Like their third-century-B.C.E. forebears, Roman Stoics believed that an impersonal force (Providence or Divine Reason) governed the world, and that happiness lay in one's ability to accept one's fate (see chapter 5). Stoics rejected any emotional attachments that might enslave them. The ideal spiritual condition and the one most conducive to contentment, according to the Stoic point of view, depended on the subjugation of the emotions to reason.

The commonsense tenets of Stoicism encouraged the Roman sense of duty. At the same time, the Stoic belief in the equality of all people had a humanizing effect on Roman jurisprudence and anticipated the all-embracing outlook of early Christian thought (see chapter 8). Stoicism was especially popular among such intellectuals as the noted playwright and essayist Lucius Annaeus Seneca (ca. 4 B.C.E.–65 C.E.) and the Emperor Marcus Aurelius (121–180 C.E.), both of whom wrote stimulating treatises on the subject. Seneca's *On Tranquility of Mind*, an excerpt from which follows, argues that one may achieve peace of mind by avoiding burdensome responsibilities, gloomy companions, and excessive wealth. Stoicism offered a reasoned retreat from psychic pain and moral despair, as well as a practical set of solutions to the daily strife between the self and society.

−312	Consul Appius Claudius orders construction of the "Appian Way," the first in a strategic network of Roman roads†	
−101	the Romans use water power for milling grain	
246	Caesar inaugurates the "Julian Calendar" on which the modern calendar is based	
77	Pliny the Elder completes a 37-volume encyclopedia called *Natural History*, which summarized information about astronomy, geography, and zoology	
79	Pliny the Younger writes a detailed account of the eruption of Mount Vesuvius	

†Minus (−) signifies B.C.E.

READING 1.22 From Seneca's *On Tranquility of Mind* (ca. 40 C.E.)

. . . our question, then, is how the mind can maintain a consistent and advantageous course, be kind to itself and take pleasure in its attributes, never interrupt this satisfaction but abide in its serenity, without excitement or depression. This amounts to tranquility. We shall inquire how it may be attained. . . . [1]

A correct estimate of self is prerequisite, for we are generally inclined to overrate our capacities. One man is tripped by confidence in his eloquence, another makes greater demands upon his estate than it can stand, another burdens a [10] frail body with an exhausting office. Some are too bashful for politics, which require aggressiveness; some are too headstrong for court; some do not control their temper and break into unguarded language at the slightest provocation; some cannot restrain their wit or resist making risky jokes. For all such people retirement is better than a career; an assertive and intolerant temperament should avoid incitements to outspokenness that will prove harmful.

Next we must appraise the career and compare our strength with the task we shall attempt. The worker must be stronger [20] than his project; loads larger than the bearer must necessarily crush him. Certain careers, moreover, are not so demanding in themselves as they are prolific in begetting a mass of other activities. Enterprises which give rise to new and multifarious activities should be avoided; you must not commit yourself to a task from which there is no free egress. Put your hand to one you can finish or at least hope to finish; leave alone those that expand as you work at them and do not stop where you intend they should.

In our choice of men we should be particularly careful to [30] see whether they are worth spending part of our life on and whether they will appreciate our loss of time; some people think we are in their debt if we do them a service. Athenadorus said he would not even go to dine with a man who would not feel indebted for his coming. Much less would he dine with people, as I suppose you understand, who discharge indebtedness for services rendered by giving a dinner and count the courses as favors, as if their lavishness was a mark of honor to others. Take away witnesses and spectators and they will take no pleasure in secret [40] gormandizing.

But nothing can equal the pleasures of faithful and congenial friendship. How good it is to have willing hearts as safe repositories for your every secret, whose privity you fear less than your own, whose conversation allays your anxiety, whose counsel promotes your plans, whose cheerfulness dissipates your gloom, whose very appearance gives you joy! But we must choose friends who are, so far as possible, free from passions. Vices are contagious; they light upon whoever is nearest and infect by contact. During a plague we must be [50] careful not to sit near people caught in the throes and burning with fever, because we would be courting danger and drawing poison in with our breath; just so in choosing friends we must pay attention to character and take those least tainted. To mingle the healthy with the sick is the beginning of disease. But I would not prescribe that you become attached to or attract no one who is not a sage. Where would you find him? We have been searching for him for centuries. Call the least bad man the best. You could not have a more opulent choice, if you were looking for good men, than among the Platos and Xenophons[1] and the famous Socratic brood, or if you had at your disposal the age of Cato,[2] which produced many characters worthy to be his contemporaries (just as it produced many unprecedentedly bad, who engineered monstrous crimes. Both kinds were necessary to make Cato's quality understood: he needed bad men against whom he could make his strength effective and good men to appreciate his effectiveness). But now there is a great dearth of good men, and your choice cannot be fastidious. But gloomy people who deplore everything and find reason to complain you must take pains to avoid. With all his loyalty and good will, a grumbling and touchy companion militates against tranquility. 70

We pass now to property, the greatest source of affliction to humanity. If you balance all our other troubles—deaths, diseases, fears, longings, subjection to labor and pain—with the miseries in which our money involves us, the latter will far outweigh the former. Reflect, then, how much less a grief it is not to have money than to lose it, and then you will realize that poverty has less to torment us with in the degree that it has less to lose. If you suppose that rich men take their losses 80 with greater equanimity you are mistaken; a wound hurts a big man as much as it does a little. Bion[3] put it smartly: a bald man is as bothered when his hair is plucked as a man with a full head. The same applies to rich and poor, you may be sure; in either case the money is glued on and cannot be torn away without a twinge, so that both suffer alike. It is less distressing, as I have said, and easier not to acquire money than to lose it, and you will therefore notice that people upon whom Fortune never has smiled are more cheerful than those she has deserted. . . . 90

All life is bondage. Man must therefore habituate himself to his condition, complain of it as little as possible, and grasp whatever good lies within his reach. No situation is so harsh that a dispassionate mind cannot find some consolation in it. If a man lays even a very small area out skillfully it will provide ample space for many uses, and even a foothold can be made livable by deft arrangement. Apply good sense to your problems; the hard can be softened, the narrow widened, and the heavy made lighter by the skillful bearer. . . .

Latin Prose Literature

Roman literature reveals a masterful use of Latin prose for the purposes of entertainment, instruction, and record-keeping. Ever applying their resources to practical ends,

---

[1]A Greek historian and biographer who lived ca. 428–354 B.C.E.
[2]Marcus Porcius Cato (234–149 B.C.E.), known as "the Censor," a Roman champion of austerity and simplicity.
[3]A Greek poet who lived around 100 B.C.E.

---

the Romans found prose the ideal vehicle for compiling and transmitting information. Rome gave the West its first geographies and encyclopedias, as well as some of its finest biographies, histories, and manuals of instruction. In the writing of history, in particular, the Romans demonstrated their talent for the collection and analysis of factual evidence. Although Roman historians tended to glorify Rome and its leadership, their attention to detail often surpassed that of the Greek historians. One of Rome's greatest historians, Titus Livius ("Livy," ca. 59 B.C.E.–17 C.E.), wrote a history of Rome from the eighth century B.C.E. to his own day. Although only a small portion of Livy's original 142 books survive, this monumental work—commissioned by Octavian himself—constitutes our most reliable account of political and social life in the days of the Roman Republic.

The Romans were masters, as well, in **oratory**, that is, the art of public speaking, and in the writing of **epistles** (letters). In both of these genres, the statesman Marcus Tullius Cicero (106–43 B.C.E.) excelled. A contemporary of Julius Caesar, Cicero produced more than 900 letters—sometimes writing three a day to the same person—and more than one hundred speeches and essays. Clarity and eloquence are the hallmarks of Cicero's prose style, which Renaissance humanists hailed as the model for literary excellence (see chapter 16). While Cicero was familiar with the theoretical works of Aristotle and the Stoics, his letters reflect a profound concern for the political realities of his own day. In his lifetime, Cicero served Rome as consul, statesman, and orator; his carefully reasoned speeches helped to shape public opinion. While he praised Julius Caesar's literary style, he openly opposed his patron's dictatorship. (Caesar congenially confessed to Cicero, "It is nobler to enlarge the boundaries of human intelligence than those of the Roman Empire.") As we see in the following excerpt from his essay *On Duty*, Cicero considered public service the noblest of human activities—one that demanded the exercise of personal courage equal to that required in military combat.

READING 1.23 From Cicero's *On Duty* (44 B.C.E.)

. . . that moral goodness which we look for in a lofty, high-minded spirit is secured, of course, by moral, not by physical, strength. And yet the body must be trained and so disciplined that it can obey the dictates of judgment and reason in attending to business and in enduring toil. But that moral goodness which is our theme depends wholly upon the thought and attention given to it by the mind. And, in this way, the men who in a civil capacity direct the affairs of the nation render no less important service than they who conduct its wars: by their statesmanship oftentimes wars are either 10 averted or terminated; sometimes also they are declared. Upon Marcus Cato's[1] counsel, for example, the Third Punic War was undertaken, and in its conduct his influence was

---

[1]Known as "the Censor," the Roman senator Cato (234–149 B.C.E.) repeatedly demanded the total destruction of Carthage.

dominant, even after he was dead. And so diplomacy in the friendly settlement of controversies is more desirable than courage in settling them on the battlefield; but we must be careful not to take that course merely for the sake of avoiding war rather than for the sake of public expediency. War, however, should be undertaken in such a way as to make it evident that it has no other object than to secure peace. **20**

But it takes a brave and resolute spirit not to be disconcerted in times of difficulty or ruffled and thrown off one's feet, as the saying is, but to keep one's presence of mind and one's self-possession and not to swerve from the path of reason.

Now all this requires great personal courage; but it calls also for great intellectual ability by reflection to anticipate the future, to discover some time in advance what may happen whether for good or for ill, and what must be done in any possible event, and never to be reduced to having to say **30** "I had not thought of that."

These are the activities that mark a spirit strong, high, and self-reliant in its prudence and wisdom. But to mix rashly in the fray and to fight hand to hand with the enemy is but a barbarous and brutish kind of business. Yet when the stress of circumstances demands it, we must gird on the sword and prefer death to slavery and disgrace.

As to destroying and plundering cities, let me say that great care should be taken that nothing be done in reckless cruelty or wantonness. And it is a great man's duty in troublous times **40** to single out the guilty for punishment, to spare the many, and in every turn of fortune to hold to a true and honorable course. For whereas there are many, as I have said before, who place the achievements of war above those of peace, so one may find many to whom adventurous, hot-headed counsels seem more brilliant and more impressive than calm and well-considered measures.

We must, of course, never be guilty of seeming cowardly and craven in our avoidance of danger; but we must also beware of exposing ourselves to danger needlessly. Nothing **50** can be more foolhardy than that. Accordingly, in encountering danger we should do as doctors do in their practice: in light cases of illness they give mild treatment; in cases of dangerous sickness they are compelled to apply hazardous and even desperate remedies. It is, therefore, only a madman who, in a calm, would pray for a storm; a wise man's way is, when the storm does come, to withstand it with all the means at his command, and especially when the advantages to be expected in case of a successful issue are greater than the hazards of the struggle. **60**

The dangers attending great affairs of state fall sometimes upon those who undertake them, sometimes upon the state. In carrying out such enterprises, some run the risk of losing their lives, others their reputation and the good-will of their fellow-citizens. It is our duty, then, to be more ready to endanger our own than the public welfare and to hazard honor and glory more readily than other advantages. . . .

As Cicero indicates, Roman education emphasized civic duty. It aimed at training the young for active roles in civic life. For careers in law and political administration, the art of public speaking was essential. Indeed, in the provinces, where people of many languages mingled, oratory was the ultimate form of political influence. Since the art of public speaking was the distinctive mark of the educated Roman, the practical skills of grammar and rhetoric held an important place in Roman education. One of the greatest spokesmen for the significance of oratory in public affairs was the Roman historian and politician, P. Cornelius Tacitus (ca. 56–120 C.E.). Tacitus' *Dialogue on Oratory* describes the role of public speaking in ancient Roman life. It bemoans the passing of a time when "eloquence led not only to great rewards, but was also a sheer necessity."

READING 1.24 From Tacitus' *Dialogue on Oratory* (ca. 100–105 C.E.)

. . . great oratory is like a flame: it needs fuel to feed it, **1** movement to fan it, and it brightens as it burns.

At Rome too the eloquence of our forefathers owed its development to [special] conditions. For although the orators of today have also succeeded in obtaining all the influence that it would be proper to allow them under settled, peaceable, and prosperous political conditions, yet their predecessors in those days of unrest and unrestraint thought they could accomplish more when, in the general ferment and without the strong hand of a single ruler, a speaker's political **10** wisdom was measured by his power of carrying conviction to the unstable populace. This was the source of the constant succession of measures put forward by champions of the people's rights, of the harangues of state officials who almost spent the night on the hustings,[1] of the impeachments of powerful criminals and hereditary feuds between whole families, of schisms among the aristocracy and never-ending struggles between the senate and the commons.[2] All this tore the commonwealth in pieces, but it provided a sphere for the oratory of those days and heaped on it what one saw were **20** vast rewards. The more influence a man could wield by his powers of speech, the more readily did he attain to high office, the further did he, when in office, outstrip his colleagues in the race for precedence, the more did he gain favor with the great, authority with the senate, and name and fame with the common people. These were the men who had whole nations of foreigners under their protection, several at a time; the men to whom state officials presented their humble duty on the eve of their departure to take up the government of a province, and to whom they paid their respects on their **30** return; the men who, without any effort on their own part, seemed to have praetorships and consulates at their beck and call; the men who even when out of office were in power, seeing that by their advice and authority they could bend both the senate and the people to their will. With them, moreover, it was a conviction that without eloquence it was impossible for anyone either to attain to a position of distinction and prominence in the community, or to maintain it; and no wonder

---

[1]The speaker's platform.
[2]The Popular Assembly.

they cherished this conviction, when they were called on to appear in public even when they would rather not, when it was not enough to move a brief resolution in the senate, unless one made good one's opinion in an able speech, when persons who had in some way or other incurred odium, or else were definitely charged with some offence, had to put in an appearance in person, when, moreover, evidence in criminal trials had to be given not indirectly or by affidavit, but personally and by word of mouth. So it was that eloquence not only led to great rewards, but was also a sheer necessity; and just as it was considered great and glorious to have the reputation of being a good speaker, so, on the other hand, it was accounted discreditable to be inarticulate and incapable of utterance. . . . **40** **50**

Roman Epic Poetry

While the Romans excelled in didactic prose, they also produced some of the world's finest verse. Under the patronage of Octavian, Rome enjoyed a Golden Age of Latin literature whose most notable representative was Virgil (Publius Vergilius Maro, 70–19 B.C.E.). Rome's foremost poet-publicist, Virgil wrote the semilegendary epic that immortalized Rome's destiny as world ruler. The *Aeneid* was not the product of an oral tradition, as were the Homeric epics; rather, it was a literary epic, undertaken as a work that might rival the epics of Homer. The hero of Virgil's poem is Rome's mythical founder, the Trojan-born Aeneas. As the typical epic hero, Aeneas undertakes a long journey and undergoes a series of adventures that test his prowess. The first six books of the *Aeneid* recount the hero's journey from Troy to Italy and his love affair with the beautiful Carthaginian princess, Dido. The second six books describe the Trojan conquest of Latium and the establishment of the Roman state. No summary of the *Aeneid* can represent adequately the monumental impact of a work that was to become the foundation for education in the Latin language. Yet, the following two excerpts capture the spirit of Virgil's vision. In the first, Aeneas, pressed to fulfill his divine mission, prepares to take leave of the passionate Dido. Here, his Stoic sense of duty overcomes his desire for personal fulfillment. The second passage, selected from the lengthy monologue spoken by the ghost of Aeneas' father, Anchises, eloquently sums up the meaning and purpose of Rome's historic mission.

READING 1.25 From Virgil's *Aeneid* (Books Four and Six) (ca. 20 B.C.E.)

[Mercury, the divine herald, urges Aeneas to leave Carthage and proceed to Italy.]

Mercury wastes no time:—"What are you doing, **1**
Forgetful of your kingdom and your fortunes,
Building for Carthage? Woman-crazy fellow,
The ruler of the Gods, the great compeller
Of heaven and earth, has sent me from Olympus **5**
With no more word than this: what are you doing,
With what ambition wasting time in Libya?
If your own fame and fortune count as nothing,
Think of Ascanius[1] at least, whose kingdom
In Italy, whose Roman land, are waiting **10**
As promise justly due." He spoke, and vanished
Into thin air. Apalled, amazed, Aeneas
Is stricken dumb; his hair stands up in terror,
His voice sticks in his throat. He is more than eager
To flee that pleasant land, awed by the warning **15**
Of the divine command. But how to do it?
How get around that passionate queen?[2] What opening
Try first? His mind runs out in all directions,
Shifting and veering. Finally, he has it,
Or thinks he has: he calls his comrades to him, **20**
The leaders, bids them quietly prepare
The fleet for voyage, meanwhile saying nothing
About the new activity; since Dido
Is unaware, has no idea that passion
As strong as theirs is on the verge of breaking, **25**
He will see what he can do, find the right moment
To let her know, all in good time. Rejoicing,
The captains move to carry out the orders.

Who can deceive a woman in love? The queen
Anticipates each move, is fearful even **30**
While everything is safe, foresees this cunning,
And the same trouble-making goddess, Rumor,
Tells her the fleet is being armed, made ready
For voyaging. She rages through the city
Like a woman mad, or drunk, the way the Maenads[3] **35**
Go howling through the night-time on Cithaeron[4]
When Bacchus' cymbals summon with their clashing.
She waits no explanation from Aeneas;
She is the first to speak: "And so, betrayer,
You hoped to hide your wickedness, go sneaking **40**
Out of my land without a word? Our love
Means nothing to you, our exchange of vows,
And even the death of Dido could not hold you.
The season is dead of winter, and you labor
Over the fleet; the northern gales are nothing— **45**
You must be cruel, must you not? Why, even,
If ancient Troy remained, and you were seeking
Not unknown homes and lands, but Troy again,
Would you be venturing Troyward in this weather?
I am the one you flee from: true? I beg you **50**
By my own tears, and your right hand—(I have nothing
Else left my wretchedness)—by the beginnings
Of marriage, wedlock, what we had, if ever
I served you well, if anything of mine
Was ever sweet to you, I beg you, pity **55**
A falling house; if there is room for pleading
As late as this, I plead, put off that purpose.
You are the reason I am hated; Libyans,
Numidians, Tyrians, hate me; and my honor
Is lost, and the fame I had, that almost brought me **60**

---

[1]Aeneas' son.
[2]Dido, Queen of Carthage.
[3]"Mad women," the votaries of Bacchus (Dionysus).
[4]A mountain range between Attica and Boetia.

High as the stars, is gone. To whom, O guest—
I must not call you husband any longer—
To whom do you leave me? I am a dying woman;
Why do I linger on? Until Pygmalion,
My brother, brings destruction to this city? 65
Until the prince Iarbas leads me captive?
At least if there had been some hope of children
Before your flight, a little Aeneas playing
Around my courts, to bring you back, in feature
At least, I would seem less taken and deserted." 70
    There was nothing he could say. Jove bade him keep
Affection from his eyes, and grief in his heart
With never a sign. At last, he managed something:—
"Never, O Queen, will I deny you merit
Whatever you have strength to claim; I will not 75
Regret remembering Dido, while I have
Breath in my body, or consciousness of spirit.
I have a point or two to make. I did not,
Believe me, hope to hide my flight by cunning;
I did not, ever, claim to be a husband, 80
Made no such vows. If I had fate's permission
To live my life my way, to settle my troubles
At my own will, I would be watching over
The city of Troy, and caring for my people,
Those whom the Greeks had spared, and Priam's palace 85
Would still be standing; for the vanquished people
I would have built the town again. But now
It is Italy I must seek, great Italy,
Apollo orders, and his oracles
Call me to Italy. There is my love, 90
There is my country. If the towers of Carthage,
The Libyan citadels, can please a woman
Who came from Tyre,[5] why must you grudge the Trojans
Ausonian land?[6] It is proper for us also
To seek a foreign kingdom. I am warned 95
Of this in dreams: when the earth is veiled in shadow
And the fiery stars are burning, I see my father,
Anchises, or his ghost, and I am frightened;
I am troubled for the wrong I do my son,
Cheating him out of his kingdom in the west, 100
And lands that fate assigns him. And a herald,
Jove's[7] messenger—I call them both to witness—
Has brought me, through the rush of air, his orders;
I saw the god myself, in the full daylight,
Enter these walls, I heard the words he brought me. 105
Cease to inflame us both with your complainings;
I follow Italy not because I want to."

[In the Underworld described in Book 6, Aeneas
encounters the soul of his father, Anchises, who foretells
the destiny of Rome.]

"Others, no doubt, will better mould the bronze
To the semblance of soft breathing, draw from marble,
The living countenance; and others please 110

With greater eloquence, or learn to measure
Better than we, the pathways of the heavens,
The risings of the stars: remember, Roman,
To rule the people under law, to establish
The way of peace, to battle down the haughty, 115
To spare the meek. Our fine arts, these forever."

Roman Lyric Poetry and Satire

While Virgil is best known for the *Aeneid*, he also wrote
pastoral poems, or **eclogues**, that glorify the natural landscape and its rustic inhabitants. Virgil's *Eclogues* found
inspiration in the pastoral sketches of Theocritus, a third-
century-B.C.E. Sicilian poet. Many classicists besides Virgil
looked to Hellenic prototypes. The poetry of Catullus
(ca. 84–54 B.C.E.), for instance, reflects familiarity with
the art of Sappho, whose lyrics he admired. The greatest of
the Latin lyric poets, Catullus came to Rome from Verona.
A young man of some wealth and charm, he wrote primarily on the subjects that consumed his short but intense
life: friendship, love, and sex. His passionate affair with
Clodias, the adulterous wife of a Roman consul, inspired
some of his finest poems, three of which appear below.
These trace the trajectory from the poet's first fevered
amorous passions to his despair and bitterness at the collapse of the affair. The fourth poem betrays the raw invec-
tive and caustic wit that Catullus brought to many of his
verses, including those with themes of jealousy and possession related to his bisexual liaisons. Candid and deeply
personal, these poems strike us with the immediacy of a
modern, secular voice.

READING 1.26 The Poems of Catullus

(ca. 60 B.C.E.)

Come, Lesbia,[1] let us live and love, 1
nor give a damn what sour old men say.
The sun that sets may rise again
but when our light has sunk into the earth,
it is gone forever. 5
    Give me a thousand kisses,
then a hundred, another thousand,
another hundred
    and in one breath
still kiss another thousand, 10
another hundred.
    O then with lips and bodies joined
many deep thousands;
    confuse
their number, 15
    so that poor fools and cuckolds (envious
even now) shall never
learn our wealth and curse us
with their
evil eyes. 20

—◆—

---

[5]A maritime city of ancient Phoenicia, ruled by Dido's father.
[6]From *Ausones*, the ancient name for the inhabitants of middle and
southern Italy.
[7]Jupiter, the sky god.

[1]The name Catullus gave to Clodias, a reference to Sappho of Lesbos.

"Here in town the sick die from insomnia mostly.
Undigested food, on a stomach burning with ulcers,
Brings on listlessness, but who can sleep in a flophouse?
Who but the rich can afford sleep and a garden
   apartment?   **25**
That's the source of infection. The wheels creak by on
   the narrow
Streets of the wards, the drivers squabble and brawl
   when they're stopped,
More than enough to frustrate the drowsiest son of a sea
   cow.
When his business calls, the crowd makes way, as the
   rich man,
Carried high in his car, rides over them, reading or
   writing,   **30**
Even taking a snooze, perhaps, for the motion's composing.
Still, he gets where he wants before we do; for all of our
   hurry
Traffic gets in our way, in front, around and behind us.
Somebody gives me a shove with an elbow, or two-by-
   four scantling.²
One clunks my head with a beam, another cracks down
   with a beer keg.   **35**
Mud is thick on my shins, I am trampled by somebody's
   big feet.
Now what?—a soldier grinds his hobnails into my toes."

If Juvenal found much to criticize among his peers, he was equally hostile toward foreigners and women. His sixth *Satire*, "Against Women," is one of the most bitter antifemale diatribes in the history of Western literature. Here, the poet laments the disappearance of the chaste Latin woman whose virtues, he submits, have been corrupted by luxury. Though Juvenal's bias against womankind strikes a personal note, it is likely that he was reflecting the public outcry against the licentiousness that was widespread in his own day. Increasingly during the second century, men openly enjoyed concubines, mistresses, and prostitutes. Infidelity among married women was on the rise, and divorce was common, as were second and third marriages for both sexes.

    The women of imperial Rome did not have many more civil rights than did their Golden Age Athenian sisters. They could neither vote nor hold public office. However, they did not occupy separate household quarters from males, they could own property, and they were free to manage their own legal affairs. Roman girls were educated along with boys, and most middle-class women could read and write. Some female aristocrats were active in public life, and the consorts of Rome's rulers often shaped matters of succession and politics by way of their influence on their husbands and sons. Roman records confirm that in addition to the traditional occupations of women in food and textile production and in prostitution, they also held positions as musicians, painters, priestesses, midwives, and gladiators.

²A piece of lumber.

Where, you ask, do they come from, such monsters as
   these? In the old days   **1**
Latin women were chaste by dint of their lowly fortunes.
Toil and short hours for sleep kept cottages free from
   contagion,
Hands were hard from working the wood, and husbands
   were watching,
Standing to arms at the Colline Gate, and the shadow of
   Hannibal's looming.¹   **5**
Now we suffer the evils of long peace. Luxury hatches
Terrors worse than the wars, avenging a world beaten
   down.
Every crime is here, and every lust, as they have been
Since the day, long since, when Roman poverty perished.
Over our seven hills,² from that day on, they came
   pouring.   **10**
The rabble and rout of the East, Sybaris, Rhodes, Miletus,
Yes, and Tarentum³ too, garlanded, drunken, shameless.
Dirty money it was that first imported among us
Foreign vice and our times broke down with
   overindulgence.
Riches are flabby, soft. And what does Venus care for   **15**
When she is drunk? She can't tell one end of a thing
   from another,
Gulping big oysters down at midnight, making the
   unguents
Foam in the unmixed wine, and drinking out of a
   conchhorn
While the walls spin round, and the table starts in
   dancing,
And the glow of the lamps is blurred by double their
   number.   **20**

. . . .

There's nothing a woman won't do, nothing she thinks is
   disgraceful
With the green gems at her neck, or pearls distending
   her ear lobes.
Nothing is worse to endure than your Mrs. Richbitch,
   whose visage
Is padded and plastered with dough, in the most
   ridiculous manner.
Furthermore, she reeks of unguents, so God help her
   husband   **25**
With his wretched face stunk up with these, smeared by
   her lipstick.
To her lovers she comes with her skin washed clean. But
   at home

---

¹In 213 B.C.E. the Carthaginian general, Hannibal, Rome's most formidable enemy, was camped only a few miles outside Rome, poised to attack (see Livy, xxvi:10).
²The hills surrounding the city of Rome.
³Greek cities associated with luxury and vice.

Why does she need to look pretty? Nard[4] is assumed for
  the lover,
For the lover she buys all the Arabian perfumes.
It takes her some time to strip down to her face,
  removing the layers   30
One by one, till at last she is recognizable, almost,
Then she uses a lotion, she-asses' milk; she'd need
  herds
Of these creatures to keep her supplied on her
  northernmost journeys.
But when she's given herself the treatment in full, from
  the ground base
Through the last layer of mud pack, from the first wash
  to a poultice,   35
What lies under all this—a human face, or an ulcer?

. . . .

Roman Drama

Roman tragedies were roughly modeled on those of
Greece. They were moral and didactic in intent, and their
themes were drawn from Greek and Roman history.
Theatrical performances in Rome were not, however, of
religious solemnity as they were in Greece. Rather, they
were a form of entertainment offered along with the public games that marked the major civic festivals known
as *ludi*. Unlike the rituals and athletic contests of the
Greeks, the *ludi* featured displays of gladiatorial combat,
chariot races, animal contests, and a variety of other
violent amusements. The nature of these public spectacles
may explain why many of the tragedies written to compete
with them were bloody and ghoulish in character. The
lurid plays of the Stoic writer Seneca drew crowds in
Roman times and were to inspire—some 1500 years
later—such playwrights as William Shakespeare.

The Romans seem to have enjoyed comedies over
tragedies, for most surviving Roman plays are in the comic
genre. Comic writers employed simple plots and broad
(often obscene) humor. The plays of Plautus (ca. 250–184
B.C.E.) are filled with stock characters, such as the good-
hearted prostitute, the shrewish wife, and the clever servant. The characters engage in farcical schemes of the
kind common to today's television situation comedies. In
the comic theater of the Romans, as in Roman culture in
general, everyday life took precedence over fantasy, and
the real, if imperfect, world was the natural setting for
down-to-earth human beings.

---

[4]Spikenard, a fragrant ointment.

The Arts of the Roman Empire

Roman Architecture

Rome's architecture reflected the practical needs of a
sprawling empire whose urban centers suffered from the
congestion, noise, and filth described by Juvenal. To link
the provinces that ranged from the Atlantic Ocean to the
Euphrates River, Roman engineers built fifty thousand
miles of paved roads, many of which are still in use today.
Roman bridges and tunnels defied natural barriers, while
some eighteen aqueducts brought fresh water to Rome's
major cities. The aqueducts, some of which delivered
well over forty million gallons of water per day to a single
site, were the public works that the Romans considered
their most significant technological achievement. The
need to house, govern, and entertain large numbers of
citizens inspired the construction of tenements, meeting
halls, baths, and amphitheaters. Eight- and nine-story
tenements provided thousands with cheap (if often
rat-infested) housing.

Superb engineers, the Romans employed the structural
advantages of the arch (the knowledge of which they
inherited from the Etruscans) to enclose great volumes of
uninterrupted space (Figure **6.5**). The arch constituted a
clear technical advance over the post-and-lintel construction used by the Greeks in buildings like the Parthenon
(see Figure 5.15). The Romans adapted this structural
principle inventively: They placed arches back to back to
form a barrel **vault**, at right angles to each other to form a
cross or groined vault, and around a central point to form
a dome. These innovations allowed the Romans to contain areas of space that were larger than any previously
known. Roman building techniques reveal a combination
of practicality and innovation: The Romans were the first
to use concrete (an aggregate of sand, lime, brick-and-
stone rubble, and water), a medium that made possible
cheap, large-scale construction. They laid their foundations with concrete, raised structures with brick, rubble,
and stone, and finished exterior surfaces with veneers of
marble, tile, bronze, or plaster.

Roman architecture and engineering were considered
one and the same discipline. Vitruvius' *Ten Books on
Architecture* (see chapter 5), the oldest and most influential work of its kind, includes instructions for hydraulic
systems, city planning, and mechanical devices. For the
Roman architect, the function of a building determined

Figure 6.5 Arch principle and arch construction. (A) Arch consisting of voussoirs, wedge-shaped blocks (a,b,c,); (B) Post-and-lintel; (C) Barrel or tunnel vault; (D and E) Groined vault; (F) Dome.

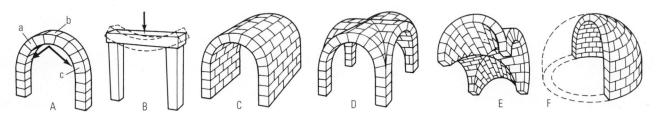

Figure 6.6 Pont du Gard, near Nîmes, France, ca. 20–10 B.C.E. Stone, height 180 ft., length ca. 900 ft. Photo: Paul M.R. Maeyaert, Belgium.

its formal design. The design of villas, theaters, and temples received the same close attention as that given to hospitals, fortresses, and—as Josephus reveals—military camps. One of Rome's most spectacular large-scale engineering projects is the 900-foot-long Pont du Gard, part of a 25-mile-long aqueduct that brought fresh water to the city of Nîmes in southern France (Figure 6.6). Built of six-ton stones and assembled without mortar, the structure reflects the practical function of arches at three levels, the bottom row supporting a bridge and the second row undergirding the top channel through which water ran by gravity to its destination.

Figure 6.7 Reconstruction of fourth-century C.E. Rome by I. Gismondi. Museum of Roman Civilization, Rome.

Figure 6.8 Colosseum, Rome (aerial view), 70–82 C.E. Photo: Fototeca Unione.

crowd. To provide shade from the sun, an awning at the roof level could be extended by means of a system of pulleys. On each level of the exterior, arches were framed by a series of decorative, or engaged, columns displaying the three Greek orders: Doric (at ground level), Ionic, and Corinthian (Figure **6.9**). The ingenious combination of arch and post-and-lintel structural elements in the design of the Colosseum would be widely imitated for centuries, and especially during the Italian Renaissance. More generally, the influence of this Roman amphitheater is apparent in the design of the modern sports arena.

Roman architectural genius may be best illustrated by the Pantheon, a temple whose structural majesty depends on the combination of Roman technical ingenuity and dramatic spatial design. Dedicated to the seven planetary deities, the Pantheon was built in the early second century C.E. Its monumental exterior—once covered with a veneer of white marble and bronze—features a portico with eight Corinthian columns originally elevated by a flight of stairs that now lie

90	a system of aqueducts provide water for the city of Rome
122	in Roman Britain, the emperor Hadrian begins construction of a wall to protect against invasion from the North
140	the Alexandrian astronomer Ptolemy produces the *Almagest*, which posits a geocentric (earth-centered) universe (and becomes the basis for Western astronomy for centuries)
160	Claudius Galen writes over 100 medical treatises (despite errors, they became the basis for Western medical practice for centuries)

Figure 6.9 Outer wall of the Colosseum, Rome, 70–82 C.E. Photo: A F Kersting, London.

The sheer magnitude of such Roman amphitheaters as the Circus Maximus, which seated 200,000 spectators (Figure **6.7**, foreground) and the Colosseum, which covered six acres and accommodated fifty thousand (Figure **6.8**), is a reminder that during the first century C.E., Rome's population exceeded one million people, many of whom were the impoverished recipients of relief in the form of wheat and free entertainment, hence "bread and circuses." The Roman amphitheaters testify to the popular taste for entertainments that included chariot races, mock sea battles, gladiatorial contests, and a variety of violent and brutal blood sports. At the Colosseum, three levels of seating rose above the arena floor. Beneath the floor was a complex of rooms and tunnels from which athletes, gladiators, and wild animals emerged to entertain the cheering

Figure 6.10 Giovanni Paolo Panini, *The Interior of the Pantheon*, ca. 1734–1735. Oil on canvas, 4 ft. 2½ in. × 3 ft. 3 in. National Gallery of Art, Washington, D.C. Samuel H. Kress Collection.

Figure 6.11 The Pantheon, Rome, ca. 118–125 C.E. Photo: R. Liebermann.

Figure 6.13 Thomas Jefferson, The Rotunda, University of Virginia, Charlottesville, Virginia, 1822–1826. Photo: Virginia State Library, Richmond.

buried beneath the city street (Figure **6.11**). One of the few buildings from Classical Antiquity to have remained almost intact, the Pantheon boasts a nineteen-foot-thick rotunda that is capped by a solid dome consisting of five thousand tons of concrete (Figure **6.12**). The interior of the dome, once painted blue and gold to resemble the vault of heaven, is pierced by a 30-foot-wide *oculus*, or "eye," that invites light and air (Figure **6.10**). The proportions of the Pantheon observe the classical principles of symmetry and harmony as described by Vitruvius (see Reading 1.18): The height from the floor to the apex of the dome (143 feet) equals the diameter of the rotunda. The Pantheon has inspired more works of architecture than any other monument in Greco-Roman history. It

Figure 6.12 Plan and section of the Pantheon (after Sir Banister Fletcher). From Horst de la Croix and Richard Tansey, *Art Through the Ages*, sixth edition, © 1975 by Harcourt Brace Jovanovich, Inc., reprinted by permission of the publisher.

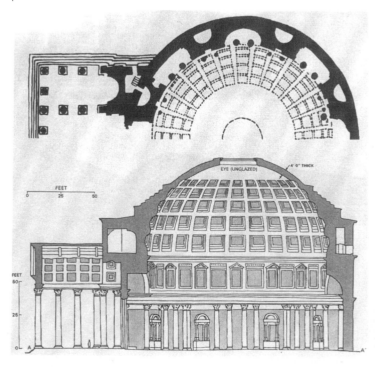

awed and delighted such eminent late eighteenth-century neoclassicists as Thomas Jefferson, who used it as the model for many architectural designs, including that of the Rotunda of the University of Virginia (Figure **6.13**).

The Pantheon is distinctly Roman in spirit; however, other Roman buildings imitated Greek models. The temple in Nîmes, France, for instance, known as the Maison Carrée, stands like a miniature Greek shrine atop a high podium (Figure **6.14**). A stairway and a colonnaded portico accentuate the single entranceway and give the building a frontal "focus" usually lacking in Greek temples. The Corinthian order (see Figure 5.17) appears in the portico, and engaged columns adorn the exterior wall.

The epitome of classical refinement, the Maison Carrée inspired numerous European and American copies. Indeed, the Virginia State Capitol, designed by Thomas Jefferson, offers clear evidence of the use of classical models to convey the dignity, stability, and authority that neoclassicists associated with the world of Greece and Rome.

If temples such as the Pantheon and the Maison Carrée answered the spiritual needs of the Romans, the baths, such as those named for the Emperor Caracalla, satisfied some of their temporal requirements (Figure **6.15**). Elaborate structures fed by natural hot springs (Figure **6.16**), the baths provided a welcome refuge from the noise and grime of the city streets. In addition to rooms in which pools of water were heated to varying degrees, such spas often included steam rooms, exercise rooms, art galleries, shops, cafés, reading rooms, and chambers for physical intimacy. Though most baths had separate women's quarters, many permitted mixed bathing. The popularity of the baths is reflected in the fact that by the third century C.E., there were more than 900 of them in the city of Rome.

Figure 6.14 (above) Maison Carrée, Nîmes, France, ca. 19 B.C.E. Photo: Paul M. R. Maeyaert, Belgium.

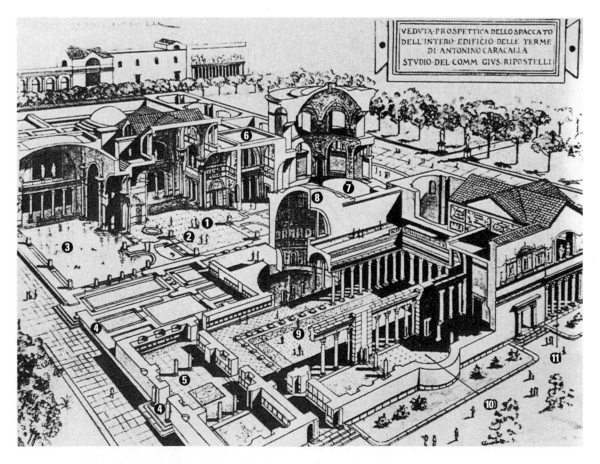

VEDVTA·PROSPETTICA·DELLO·SPACCATO
DELL'INTERO·EDIFICIO·DELLE·TERME
DI·ANTONINO·CARACALLA
STVDIO·DEL·COMM·GIVS·RIPOSTELLI

Figure 6.15
Restoration of the Baths of Caracalla in Rome, 211–217 C.E.

1 Great Hall
2 Oval pools (cool baths)
3 Swimming pool
4 Entrance
5 Vestibule
6 Heated rooms
7 Hot baths
8 Steam baths
9 Colonnaded court
10 Lecture halls
11 Lounges.

Engraving. The Bettmann Archive.

Figure 6.16 Great Bath, Roman bath complex, Bath, England, 54 C.E. Part of the finest group of Roman remains in England, this sumptuous pool is still fed by natural hot springs. Photo: Spectrum Picture Library, London.

The Roman baths centered on a **basilica**, a rectangular colonnaded hall commonly used for public assemblies. The basilica was the ideal structure for courts of law, meeting halls, and marketplaces. The huge meeting hall known as the Basilica of Maxentius consisted of a three-hundred-foot-long central nave, four side aisles, and a semicircular recess called an **apse** (Figure **6.17**). The Roman basilica might be roofed by wooden beams or—as in the case of the Basilica of Maxentius (Figure **6.18**)—by gigantic stone vaults. Completed by the Emperor Constantine in the fourth century C.E., these enormous vaults rested on brick-faced concrete walls some twenty feet thick. In floor plan and construction features, the Roman basilica became the model for the early Christian Church in the West.

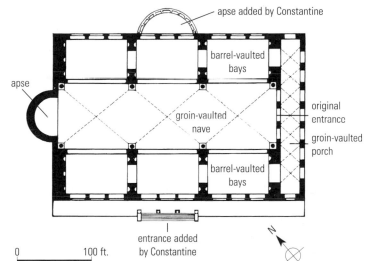

Figure 6.17 (right) Plan of the Basilica of Maxentius and Constantine.

0   100 ft.

Figure 6.18 Basilica of Maxentius, Rome, begun 306–310 C.E., completed by Constantine after 313 C.E. Scala/Art Resource, New York.

(Figure **6.23**). The equestrian portrait of the Roman Emperor Marcus Aurelius depicts the general addressing his troops with the traditional gesture of imperial authority. The body of a conquered warrior once lay under the raised right hoof of the spirited charger, whose veins and muscles seem to burst from beneath his bronze skin.

While the public portrayal of the ruler usually demanded a degree of flattering idealization, images intended for private use invited realistic detail. The Roman taste for realism is perhaps best illustrated in the three-dimensional portraits of Roman men and women, often members of the ruling class or wealthy patricians. In contrast to the idealized portraits of Golden Age Greece (see Figure 4.9), many Roman likenesses reflect obsessive fidelity to nature. So true to life seem some Roman portrait heads that scholars suspect they may have been executed from wax death masks. Roman portrait sculpture tends to reflect the personality and character of the sitter, a fact perhaps related to the ancient custom of honoring the "genius" or in-dwelling spirit of the dead ancestor. The lifelike portrait bust of Julius Caesar, carved in green slate with inset crystal eyes, captures the spirit of resolute determination (see Figure 6.2). It is the record of a particular person at a particular time in his life; as such it conveys a degree of psychological realism absent from most classical Greek portraits. In that portrait sculpture served much as our photographs do today—as physical reminders of favorite relatives and friends—the emphasis on realism is understandable. The balding patrician who carries two portrait busts of his ancestors (Figure **6.24**) reminds us that the Roman family placed extraordinary emphasis on its lineage and honored the father of the family (*paterfamilias*) no

Figure 6.23 Equestrian statue of Marcus Aurelius, ca. 173 C.E. Bronze, height 16 ft. 8 in. Piazza del Campidoglio, Rome. Photo: The Ancient Art and Architecture Collection, London.

less devotedly than did the ancient Chinese. Such intimate sculptured likenesses of the deceased would have been displayed and venerated at special altars and shrines within the Roman home. Finally, the portrait of the square-jawed aristocratic woman, whose wig or hairdo surely required the fastidious application of the curling

Figure 6.24 Roman aristocrat holding portrait busts of his ancestors, late first century B.C.E. Marble, Museo Capitolino, Rome. Photo: Araldo de Luca.

Figure 6.25 Flavian Woman, ca. 89 C.E. Marble, life-size. Museo Capitolino, Rome.

iron, discloses the proud confidence of a Roman matron (Figure **6.25**). Whether cast in bronze, or carved in marble, slate, or terra-cotta, these psychologically penetrating studies are often as unflattering as they are honest. In their lack of idealization and their affection for literal detail, they are representative of Roman sculpture as a record of commonplace reality.

Roman Painting

A similar taste for realism appears in the frescoes with which the Romans decorated their meeting halls, baths, and country villas. Possibly inspired by Greek murals, of which only a few examples survive, Roman artists painted scenes drawn from literature, mythology, and everyday life. Among the finest examples of Roman frescoes are those found in and around Pompeii and Herculaneum, two southern Italian cities that attracted a population of wealthy Romans. But even in the outer reaches of the empire, such as at Zeugma in modern Turkey (uncovered as recently as 1992), the Roman taste for visual representation is evident in magnificently decorated palatial villas, a legacy soon to be submerged in the waters of an urgently needed hydroelectric dam. Pompeii and Herculaneum remain the showcases of Roman suburban life: Both cities were engulfed and destroyed by a mountain of ash from the volcanic eruption of Mount Vesuvius of 79 C.E., but the lava from the disaster preserved many of the area's suburban homes. These residential villas, constructed around an **atrium** (a large central hall open to the sky), are valuable sources of information concerning the lifestyles of upperclass Romans (Figure **6.27**).

At a villa in Boscoreale, about a mile north of Pompeii, floor surfaces display fine, ornamental motifs and scenes illustrated in **mosaic**, a technique by which small pieces of stone or glass are embedded into wet cement surfaces. The walls of many rooms are painted with frescoes designed to give viewers the impression that they are looking out upon gardens and distant buildings (Figure **6.26**). Such illusionism is a kind of visual artifice known by the French phrase *trompe l'oeil* ("fool the eye"). Designed to deceive the eye, they reveal the artist's competence in mastering *empirical perspective*, the technique of achieving a sense of three-dimensional space on a two-dimensional

surface. Other devices, such as light and shade, are also employed to seduce the eye into believing it perceives real objects in deep space: In the extraordinary *Still Life With Eggs and Thrushes*, for instance, one of a series of frescoes celebrating food and found in a villa at Pompeii, light seems to bounce off the metal pitcher, whose shiny surface contrasts with the densely textured towel and the ceramic plate holding ten lifelike eggs (Figure **6.28**). Roman artists integrated illusionistic devices in ways that would not be seen again in Western art for a thousand years (see chapter 23).

The invention of still life as an independent genre (or type) of art confirmed the Roman fondness for the tangible things of the material world. Similarly, their affection for nature led them to pioneer the genre of landscape painting. First-century-B.C.E. frescoes illustrating the adventures of the Greek hero Odysseus feature spacious

Figure 6.26 Bedroom from the Villa of P. Fannius Synistor, Boscoreale, first century B.C.E. Mosaic floor, couch, and footstool come from other Roman villas of later date. Fresco on lime plaster, 8 ft. 8½ in. × 19 ft. 1⅛ in. × 10 ft. 11½ in. The Metropolitan Museum of Art, New York, Rogers Fund, 1903 (03.14.13). Photo: Schecter Lee.

Figure 6.27 Atrium, House of the Silver Wedding, Pompeii, Italy, first century C.E. Alinari/Art Resource, New York.

landscapes filled with rocky plains, feathery trees, animals, and people (Figure **6.29**). Bathed in light and shade, the naturalistically modeled figures cast shadows to indicate their physical presence in atmospheric space. Evident in these Roman landscapes is a deep affection for the countryside and for the pleasures of nature. Arcadia, the mountainous region in the central Peloponnesus inhabited by the peaceloving shepherds and nymphs of ancient Greek legend, provided the model for the classical landscape, which celebrated (as did Greek and Latin **pastoral** poetry) a life of innocence and simplicity. The glorification of bucolic freedom—the "Arcadian Myth"—reflected the Roman disenchantment with city life. The theme was to reappear frequently in the arts of the West, especially during periods of rising urbanization.

Figure 6.28 *Still Life with Eggs and Thrushes*, from the House (or Villa) of Julia Felix, Pompeii, before 79 C.E. Fresco, 35 in. × 48 in. Photo: Fotografic Foglia, Naples.

Figure 6.29 Ulysses in the Land of the Lestrygonians, part of the Odyssey Landscapes, second-style ("architectural") wall-painting from a house in Rome, late first century B.C.E. Height approx. 5 ft. Vatican Library, Rome.

Roman Music

While Roman civilization left abundant visual and literary resources, the absence of surviving examples in music make it almost impossible to evaluate the Roman contribution in this domain. Passages from the writings of Roman historians suggest that Roman music theory was adopted from the Greeks, as were most Roman instruments. In drama, musical interludes replaced the Greek choral odes, a change that suggests the growing distance between drama and its ancient ritual function. Music was, however, essential to most forms of public entertainment and also played an important role in military life; for the latter, the Romans developed brass instruments, such as trumpets and horns, and drums for military processions.

SUMMARY

A genius for practical organization marked all aspects of Roman history. From its Latin beginnings, Rome showed an extraordinary talent for adopting and adapting the best of other cultures: Etruscan and Greek. Although the Roman Republic engaged all citizens in government, power rested largely with the wealthy and influential patri-

cian class. As Rome built an empire and assumed mastery of the civilized world, the Republic fell increasingly into the hands of military dictators, the greatest of whom was Julius Caesar. Caesar's heir, the emperor Octavian, ushered in the *Pax Romana*, a time of peace and high cultural productivity.

The Romans produced no original philosophy but cultivated Hellenistic schools of thought such as Stoicism. Roman literature manifests a practical bias for factual information. The Romans gave the world its first encyclopedias, as well as memorable biographies, essays, speeches, histories, and letters. The high moral tone and lucid prose of Cicero and Tacitus characterize Roman writing at its best. In poetry, Virgil paid homage to the Roman state in the *Aeneid*, Catullus sang of love and loss, while Horace and Juvenal offered a critical view of Roman life in satiric verse, the genre that constitutes Rome's most original contribution to literature.

Rome's most enduring accomplishments lay in the practical areas of law, language, and political life. However, Rome's architectural and engineering projects, which engaged the inventive use of the arch and the techniques of concrete and brick construction, exercised an equally important influence on subsequent civilizations in the West. To the classical style in architecture, the Romans contributed domed and stone-vaulted types of construction that enclosed vast areas of space. Rome borrowed Hellenic models in all of the arts, but the Roman taste for realism dominated narrative relief sculpture, portrait busts, and fresco painting. These genres disclose a love for literal truth that contrasts sharply with the Hellenic effort to generalize and idealize form.

For almost a thousand years, the Romans held together a geographically and ethnically diverse realm, providing a large population with such a high quality of life as to move future generations to envy and praise. The Roman contribution is imprinted on the language, laws, and architecture of the West. By its preservation and transmission of the classical legacy, Rome's influence on the humanistic tradition was felt long after Roman glory and might had faded.

Suggestions for Reading

Bradley, K. R. *Slaves and Masters in the Roman Empire*. Berkeley, Calif.: University of California Press, 1987.

Christ, Karl. *The Romans: An Introduction to Their History and Civilization*. Berkeley, Calif.: University of California Press, 1984.

D'Ambra, Eve. *Roman Painting*. New York: Cambridge University Press, 1999.

Fantham, Elaine. *Roman Literary Culture: From Cicero to Apuleius*. Baltimore, Md.: Johns Hopkins University Press, 1999.

Galinsky, Karl. *Augustan Culture: An Interpretive Introduction*. Princeton: Princeton University Press, 1996.

Hooper, Finley. *Roman Realities*. Detroit: Wayne State University Press, 1980.

Jones, P. V. and K. Sidwell, eds. *The World of Rome: An Introduction to Roman Culture*. New York: Cambridge University Press, 1997.

Kebric, Robert B. *Roman People*. Mountain View, Calif.: Mayfield, 1997.

Kleiner, Diana E. E. *Roman Sculpture*. New Haven, Conn.: Yale University Press, 1992.

Klingaman, William K. *The First Century: Emperors, Gods, and Everyman*. New York: Harper, 1986.

L'Orange, H. P. *The Roman Empire: Art Forms and Civic Life*. New York: Rizzoli, 1985.

Strong, Donald. *Roman Art: The Yale University Press Pelican History of Art*, 3rd edition. New Haven, Conn.: Yale University Press, 1992.

Zanker, Paul. *The Power of Images in the Age of Augustus*. Ann Arbor: University of Michigan Press, 1988.

GLOSSARY

apse a vaulted semicircular recess at one or both ends of a basilica

atrium the inner courtyard of a Roman house, usually colonnaded and open to the sky

attic the superstructure or low upper story above the main order of a facade

basilica a large, colonnaded hall commonly used for public assemblies, law courts, baths, and marketplaces

eclogue a pastoral poem, usually involving shepherds in an idyllic rural setting

epistle a formal letter

equestrian mounted on horseback

imperium (Latin, "command," "empire") the civil and military authority exercised by the rulers of ancient Rome (and the root of the English words "imperialism" and "empire"); symbolized in ancient Rome by an eagle-headed scepter and the *fasces*, an ax bound in a bundle of rods

mosaic a medium by which small pieces of glass or stone are embedded in wet cement on wall and floor surfaces; any picture or pattern made in this manner

oratory the art of public speaking

pastoral pertaining to the country, to shepherds, and the simple rural life; also, any work of art presenting an idealized picture of country life

res publica (Latin, "of the people") a government in which power resides in citizens entitled to vote and is exercised by representatives responsible to them and to a body of law

sarcophagus (plural, **sarcophagi**) a stone coffin

satire a literary genre that ridicules or pokes fun at human vices and follies

trompe l'oeil (French, "fool the eye") a form of illusionistic painting that tries to convince the viewer that the image is real and not painted

vault a roof or ceiling constructed on the arch principle (see Figure 6.5)

Figure 7.3 Terra-cotta army of soldiers, horses, and chariots, tomb of the First Emperor of the Qin Dynasty, 221–207 B.C.E. Spectrum Picture Library, London.

long, would be raised in the early second century in an effort to deter barbarian attacks on Roman Britain's northernmost border. Like Hadrian's Wall, the Great Wall of China would not stop an army on foot, but rather, discouraged mounted men, wagons, and the like from making raids across the borders.

The building of the Great Wall required the labor of some 700,000 people. An equal number of workers is said to have labored for over fifteen years on the Emperor's tomb. The entrance to that tomb, part of a twenty-one-square-mile burial site near the Qin capital at Xian, provides an immortal record of the Qin military machine. It contains almost 8,000 life-sized **terra-cotta** soldiers, most of which are armed with actual swords, spears, and crossbows (Figure 7.3). Standing at strict attention, the huge army of footsoldiers and cavalry guards the tomb itself, which has not yet been opened. These figures may have served to replace the living sacrifices that went to the grave with earlier Chinese kings (see chapter 3). The bodies of the ceramic warriors seem to have been mass-produced from molds, but the faces, no two of which are exactly alike, were individually carved and painted (Figure 7.4). In their lifelike intensity, these images resemble Roman portrait busts (see Figure 6.2). Yet the portraits of Rome were created for the appreciation of the living,

−350	Shin Shen completes a catalogue of some 800 stars
−300	cast iron is produced in China
−250	the crossbow is invented in China
−214	the First Emperor orders the construction of the Great Wall (which is not completed until the seventeenth century)

while those of Qin China were intended for the dead. Nevertheless, the subterranean legions of the First Emperor glorify an armed force that the Romans might have envied.

Legalist theory provided justification for the stringency of the law under the Qin, as well as for the civil and political oppressiveness of imperial authority. The Legalist First Emperor so feared public opposition and the free exercise of thought that he required all privately owned copies of the Confucian classics burned and all who opposed his government beheaded, along with their families. On the other hand, they were loyal students of the *Sun Zi* (*The Art of War*), the world's first treatise on military strategy. This anonymous military classic, dating from the era of the

Figure 7.4 Two terra-cotta soldiers, tomb of the First Emperor of the Qin Dynasty, 221–207 B.C.E. Height 75.5 in. and 48 in. Photo: Dagli Orti, Paris.

Warring States, emphasized the tactical, as well as the strategic and psychological aspects of combat.

The Han Dynasty (206 B.C.E.–220 C.E.)

The Qin dynasty lasted only fifteen years, but under the leadership of succeeding dynasties, China's empire would last more than four centuries. Just as the Roman Empire marked the culmination of classical civilization in the West, so the Han Dynasty represented the high point and the classical phase of Chinese civilization. The intellectual and cultural achievements of the Han, which would remain in place for 2,000 years, made an indelible mark on the history of neighboring Korea, Vietnam, and Japan, whose cultures adopted Chinese methods of writing and the Confucian precepts of filial piety and propriety. The Chinese have long regarded the era of the Han as their classical age, and to this day refer to themselves as the "children of the Han." Han intellectual achievements ranged from the literary and artistic to the domains of **cartography**, medicine, mathematics, and astronomy. The invention of paper, block printing, the seismograph, the

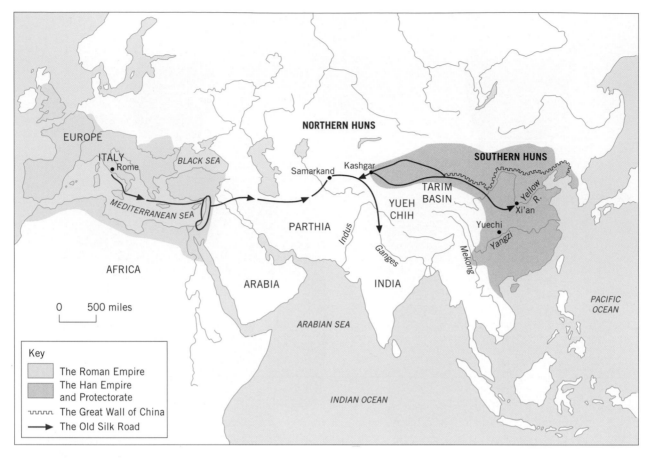

Map 7.1 Han and Roman Empires

horse collar, and the wheelbarrow are but a few of the technological advances of the late Han era.

Han rulers tripled the size of the empire they inherited from the Qin. At its height, the Han empire was roughly equivalent to that of Rome in power and prestige, but larger in actual population—a total of 57 million people, according to the census of 2 C.E. (Map **7.1**) Improvements in farming and advances in technology insured economic prosperity, which in turn stimulated vigorous long-distance trade. In exchange for Western linen, wool, glass, and metalware, the Chinese exported silk, ivory, gems, and spices. Trade proceeded by way of Asian intermediaries, who led camel caravans across the vast "Silk Road" that stretched from Asia Minor to the Pacific Ocean. China traditionally scorned its merchants (whom the Chinese perceived as profiting from the labor of others) and regarded its farmers as honorable. Nevertheless, while Chinese merchants flourished, Chinese peasants failed to reap the benefits of Han prosperity. Conscripted for repeated wars, they fought the nomadic tribes along the bitter cold northern frontier. They also served in the armies that conquered western Korea and northern Vietnam. Heavy taxes levied on Chinese farmers to support the Han machinery of state forced many to sell their lands. Wealthy landowners purchased these lands, on which (in a manner reminiscent of the late Roman republic) bankrupt farmers became tenants or unfree peasants. By the early third century, violent peasant revolts accompanied by "barbarian" incursions, led to the overthrow of the Han dynasty. Like the Roman empire, the great Han empire fell victim to internal and external pressures it could not withstand.

The Literary Contributions of Imperial China

Just as the Romans borrowed the best of the cultural achievements that preceded them, so Han rulers preserved the enduring works of their forebears. These they passed on to future generations as a body of classical learning and thought. Han rulers restored Confucianism to China, and with it came the restoration of Confucian texts and the Confucian scholar/official.

Chinese Prose Literature

As with the Greeks and the Romans, the Chinese placed high value on record-keeping. Hence, the writing of history was one of China's greatest achievements.

−150	iron wheels are designed for shaping jade and reeling silk
−110	the Chinese devise the collar harness (for horses)
−100	the Chinese invent the crank (for turning wheels)
−1	cast iron is used in Chinese suspension bridges

According to tradition, Chinese court historians kept chronicles of events as far back as one thousand years before the Han Era. Unfortunately, many of these chronicles were lost in the wars and notorious "book-burnings" of the Qin era. Beginning with the second century B.C.E., however, palace historians kept a continuous record of rulership. Ancient China's greatest historian Sima Qian (145–90 B.C.E.), the rival of both Thucydides and Livy, produced the monumental *Shih Chi (Records of the Grand Historian)*, a narrative account of Chinese history from earliest times through the lifetime of the author. Sima Qian, himself the son of a palace historian–astronomer, served at the court of the Emperor Wudi, the vigorous ruler who brought Han China to the peak of its power. On Sima's death, China's first woman historian Ban Zhao (45–114) continued his court chronicle. Ban also won fame for her handbook, *Lessons for Women*, which outlined the obligations and duties of the wife to her husband.

The following excerpt from Sima Qian's chapter on "Wealth and Commerce" offers a detailed description of the Han economy, as well as its social and moral life. Whereas economic activity follows the natural order, morals, observes the author, "come as the effects of wealth." In Sima's view, wealth and virtue are interdependent. A flourishing economy will encourage the people to be virtuous, while poverty leads inevitably to moral decay. Stylistically, Sima Qian's *Records* display the economy and vigor of expression that characterizes the finest Han prose.

READING 1.30 From Sima Qian's *Records of the Grand Historian* (ca. 100 B.C.E.)

I do not know about prehistoric times before Shennong,[1] but since [Emperor Yu and the Xia dynasty, after the] twenty-second century B.C.E. during the period discussed by the historical records, human nature has always struggled for good food, dress, amusements, and physical comfort, and has always tended to be proud of wealth and ostentation. No matter how the philosophers may teach otherwise, the people cannot be changed. Therefore, the best of men leave it alone, and next in order come those who try to guide it, then those who moralize about it, and then those who try to make 10 adjustments to it, and lastly come those who get into the scramble themselves. Briefly, Shanxi produces timber, grains, linen, ox hair, and jades. Shandong produces fish, salt, lacquer, silks, and musical instruments. Jiangnan [south of the Yangzi] produces cedar, *zi* [a hard wood for making wood blocks], ginger, cinnamon, gold and tin ores, cinnabar, rhinoceros horn, tortoise shell, pearls, and hides. Longmen produces stone for tablets. The north produces horses, cattle, sheep, furs, and horns. As for copper and iron, they are often found in mountains everywhere, spread out like pawns on a 20 chessboard. These are what the people of China like and what provide the necessities for their living and for ceremonies for

the dead. The farmers produce them, the wholesalers bring them from the country, the artisans work on them, and the merchants trade on them. All this takes place without the intervention of government or of the philosophers. Everybody exerts his best and uses his labor to get what he wants. Therefore prices seek their level, cheap goods going to where they are expensive and higher prices are brought down. People follow their respective professions and do it on their own 30 initiative. It is like flowing water which seeks the lower level day and night without stop. All things are produced by the people themselves without being asked and transported to where they are wanted. Is it not true that these operations happen naturally in accord with their own principles? *The Book of Zhou*[2] says, "Without the farmers, food will not be produced; without the artisans, industry will not develop; without the merchants, the valuable goods will disappear; and without the wholesalers, there will be no capital and the natural resources of lakes and mountains will not be opened 40 up." Our food and our dress come from these four classes, and wealth and poverty vary with the size of these sources. On a larger scale, it benefits a country, and on a smaller scale, it enriches a family. These are the inescapable laws of wealth and poverty. The clever ones have enough and to spare, while the stupid ones have not enough. . . .

Therefore, first the granaries must be full before the people can talk of culture. The people must have sufficient food and good dress before they can talk of honor. The good customs and social amenities come from wealth and disappear when 50 the country is poor. Even as fish thrive in a deep lake and the beasts gravitate toward a deep jungle, so the morals of mankind come as effects of wealth. The rich acquire power and influence, while the poor are unhappy and have no place to turn to. This is even truer of the barbarians. Therefore it is said: "A wealthy man's son does not die in the market place," and it is not an empty saying. It is said:

> The world hustles
> Where money beckons.
> The world jostles 60
> Where profit thickens.

Even kings and dukes and the wealthy gentry worry about poverty. Why wonder that the common people and the slaves do the same?. . .

[Here follows a long section on the economic products and conditions and the people's character and way of living of the different regions.]

Therefore you see the distinguished scholars who argue at courts and temples about policies and talk about honesty and self-sacrifice, and the mountain recluses who achieve a great 70 reputation. Where do they go? They seek after the rich. The honest officials acquire wealth as time goes on, and the honest merchants become wealthier and wealthier. For wealth is something which man seeks instinctively without being taught. You see soldiers rush in front of battle and perform great exploits in a hail of arrows and rocks and against great

---

[1] A legendary cultural hero, inventor of agriculture and commerce, ca. 2737 B.C.E.

[2] The book of documents devoted to the Zhou Dynasty (1111–221 B.C.E.)

dangers, because there is a great reward. You see young men steal and rob and commit violence and dig up tombs for treasures, and even risk the punishments by law, throwing all considerations of their own safety to the winds—all because of money. The courtesans of Zhao and Zheng dress up and play music and wear long sleeves and pointed dancing shoes. They flirt and wink, and do not mind being called to a great distance, irrespective of the age of the men—all are attracted by the rich. The sons of the rich dress up in caps and carry swords and go about with a fleet of carriages just to show off their wealth. The hunters and the fishermen go out at night, in snow and frost, roam in the wooded valleys haunted by wild beasts, because they want to catch game. Others gamble, have cock fights, and match dogs in order to win. Physicians and magicians practice their arts in expectation of compensation for their services. Bureaucrats play hide-and-seek with the law and even commit forgery and falsify seals at the risk of penal sentences because they have received bribes. And so all farmers, artisans, and merchants and cattle raisers try to reach the same goal. Everybody knows this, and one hardly ever hears of one who works and declines pay for it. . . .

80

90

Sima Qian's narrative describes the men and women of the Han Era as practical and this-worldly, in fact, as remarkably similar to Romans. This sensibility, which unites a typically Chinese holism with sober realism, is also visible in the large body of Confucianist essays from the Han period. Of these, only one brief example may be cited, for its similarity to the rationalism of Seneca, Lucretius, and other Roman thinkers is striking. *A Discussion of Death* by Wang Chong (17–100 C.E.), offers a skeptical view of the supernaturalism that attracted the large masses of Chinese people. Wang writes,

> Before a man is born he has no consciousness, so when he dies and returns to this original unconscious state how could he still have consciousness? The reason a man is intelligent and understanding is that he possesses the forces of the five virtues [humanity, righteousness, decorum, wisdom, and faith]. The reason he possesses these is that he has within him the five organs [heart, liver, stomach, lungs, and kidneys]. If these five organs are unimpaired, a man has understanding, but if they are diseased, then he becomes vague and confused and behaves like a fool or an idiot. When a man dies, the five organs rot away and the five virtues no

longer have any place to reside. Both the seat and the faculty of understanding are destroyed. The body must await the vital force [*qi*] before it is complete, and the vital force must await the body before it can have consciousness. Nowhere is there a fire that burns all by itself. How then could there be a spirit with consciousness existing without a body?*

Chinese Poetry

The writing of poetry has a long and rich history in China. While China's earliest poems drew on an ancient oral tradition (see chapter 3), the poems of the Han era originated as written works—a circumstance that may have been encouraged by the Chinese invention of paper. Chinese poetry is striking in its simplicity and its refinement. Humanism and common sense are fundamental to Han poetic expression, and Han verse seems to have played an indispensable part in everyday life. As with Greek and Roman lyrics, Chinese poetry took the form of hymns and ritual songs accompanied by the lute or other stringed instruments. Poems served as entertainments for various occasions, such as banquets, and as expressions of affection that were often exchanged as gifts. In contrast with the Greco-Roman world, however, the Chinese produced neither epics nor heroic poems. Their poetry does not so much glorify individual prowess or valorous achievement as it meditates on human experience. Han poetry, much of which takes the form of the "prose-poem," is personal and intimate rather than moralizing and eulogistic. Even in cases where the poem is the medium for social or political complaint, it is more a mirror of the poet's mood than a vehicle of instruction. Notable too (especially in contrast with Roman poetry) is the large number of female poets among the Chinese. The four poems that appear below (translated by Burton Watson) are drawn from the vast collection of Han poetry. They have been selected not only for their lyric beauty, but as expressions of some of the deepest concerns of Han poets, such as the practice of bestowing women upon neighboring tribes as "conciliatory" gifts and the conscription of laborers for public works projects. The perceptive reader should discover a number of interesting parallels, as well as contrasts, between these poems and those of the Greeks, Sappho and Pindar, and the Romans, Virgil, Horace, and Juvenal.

READING 1.31 A Selection of Han Poems

Song of Sorrow

My family has married me
   in this far corner of the world,
sent me to a strange land,
   to the king of the Wu-sun.
A yurt[1] is my chamber,

1

5

---

*Translated by Burton Watson in *Anthology of Chinese Literature*, edited by Cyril Birch (New York: Grove Press, Inc., 1965), pp. 89–90.
[1]A circular tent of felt and skins on a framework of poles, the common habitation of the nomads of Mongolia.

70	China begins building the Grand Canal (eventually 600 miles long)
90	the Chinese invent a winnowing device that separates grain from the chaff
100	the first insecticide is produced from dried chrysanthemums in China
105	cellulose-based paper is first produced in China
132	Zhang Heng invents the first seismograph

felt is my walls,
flesh my only food,[2]
    kumiss[3] to drink.
My thoughts are all of my homeland,
    my heart aches within.   10
Oh to be the yellow crane
    winging home again!

Liu Xijun, ca. 107 B.C.E.

Song: I Watered My Horse at the Long Wall Caves

I watered my horse at the Long Wall caves,   1
water so cold it hurt his bones;
I went and spoke to the Long Wall boss:
"We're soldiers from Tai-yuan—will you keep us here
    forever?"
"Public works go according to schedule—   5
swing your hammer, pitch your voice in with the rest!"
A man'd be better off to die in battle
than eat his heart out building the Long Wall!
The Long Wall—how it winds and winds,
winds and winds three thousand li;[1]   10
here on the border, so many strong boys;
in the houses back home, so many widows and wives.
I sent a letter to my wife:
"Better remarry than wait any longer—
serve your new mother-in-law with care   15
and sometimes remember the husband you once had."
In answer her letter came to the border:
"What nonsense do you write me now?
Now when you're in the thick of danger,
how could I rest by another man's side?"   20
(HE) If you bear a son, don't bring him up!
    But a daughter—feed her good dried meat.
    Only *you* can't see, here by the Long Wall,
    the bones of the dead men heaped about!
(SHE) I bound up my hair and went to serve you;   25
    constant constant was the care of my heart.
    Too well I know your borderland troubles;
    and I—can I go on like this much longer?

Chen Lin (d. 217)

Two Selections from "Nineteen Old Poems of the Han"

I turn the carriage, yoke and set off,   1
far, far, over the never-ending roads.
In the four directions, broad plain on plain;
east wind shakes the hundred grasses.
Among all I meet, nothing of the past;   5
what can save us from sudden old age?
Fullness and decay, each has its season;
success—I hate it, so late in coming!
Man is not made of metal or stone;
how can he hope to live for long?   10
Swiftly he follows in the wake of change.

---

[2]Meat was a staple of the Mongol diet.
[3]The fermented milk of a horse, mule, or donkey.
[1]A *li* equals approximately one-third of a mile.

A shining name—let that be the prize!

Anonymous, late second century

Man's years fall short of a hundred;   1
a thousand years of worry crowd his heart.
If the day is short and you hate the long night,
why not take the torch and go wandering?
Seek out happiness in season;   5
who can wait for the coming year?
Fools who cling too fondly to gold
earn no more than posterity's jeers.
Prince Qiao,[2] that immortal man—
small hope we have of matching him!   10

Anonymous, late second century

The Visual Arts and Music in Han China

Before the introduction of Buddhism into China late in the Han era (see chapter 9), the Chinese produced no monumental architecture comparable to that of Rome. But because the Chinese built primarily in the impermanent medium of wood, nothing remains of the palaces and temple structures erected during the Han era. Yet some idea of Chinese architecture is provided by the polychromed, ceramic models of the traditional multiroofed buildings—houses and watchtowers—that are found in Chinese tombs (Figure 7.5). Such engineering projects as

---

[2]According to Chinese legend, a prince who became an immortal spirit.

Figure 7.5 Tomb model of a house, Eastern Han Dynasty, first century C.E. Earthenware with unfired pigments, 52 × 33½ × 27 in. The Nelson-Atkins Museum of Art, Kansas City, Missouri (Purchase: Nelson Trust) 33–521.

140 early Chinese compass devised with magnetic silver that always points north–south
190 Chinese mathematicians use powers of 10 to express numbers
200 the double yoke harness is invented in China
220 Chinese make ink from lamp black for early block printing
270 Chinese alchemists create gunpowder
302 the stirrup is depicted for the first time in Chinese art

the Great Wall testify to the high level of Qin and Han building skills. China's royal tombs were replicas of the imperial palace, which was laid out according to a cosmological model: The central building was symmetrical and bisected by a north–south axis. Its foundation was square, symbolizing the earth (*yin*), and its roof was round, symbolizing heaven (*yang*). In its geometric regularity, such designs share the Greco-Roman search for harmony and balanced proportion. However, classical design among the Chinese was less an effort to idealize nature than it was a means of representing the natural order. Cosmological diagrams are frequently inscribed on bronze mirrors found in Han graves (Figure **7.6**). The square and circle, along with stylized dragons and sky symbols, belong to an elaborate diagrammatic description of the prevailing Chinese theory of the universe, which involves the interaction of *yin/yang* forces with the five elements and the forces of nature (see Chapter 3). Similar designs are found on gaming boards on which players pit their human skills against the divine powers.

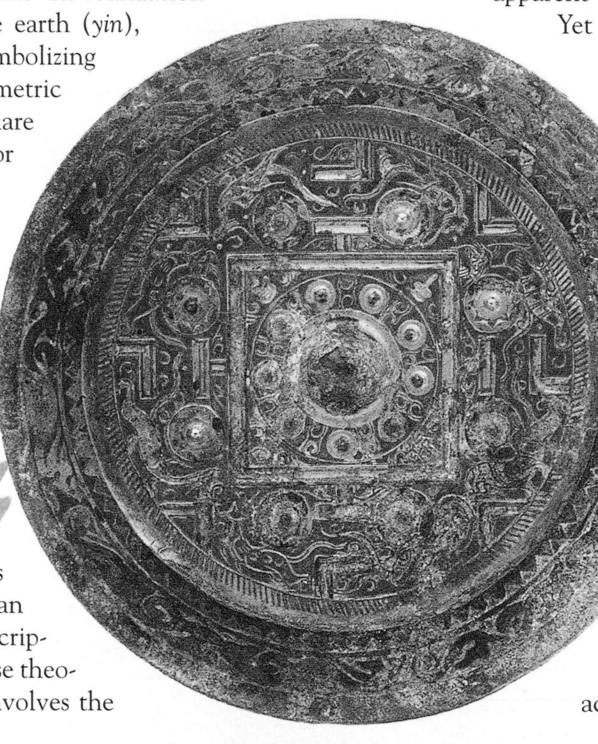

During the Han era, the visual arts flourished. Like their forebears, the Han excelled in bronze casting: Bronze chariots and weapons, mirrors, and jewellery are found in royal burial tombs. Han craftspeople also produced exquisite works in jade and gold, lacquered wood, and silk. But it is in the medium of terra-cotta—glazed for durability—that the Han left a record of daily life almost as detailed as that found in ancient Egyptian tombs. Scenes of threshing, baking, juggling, music-making, game-playing, and other everyday activities appear routinely in three-dimensional polychromed ceramic models recovered from Han funerary chambers (Figure **7.7**). Han art does not consistently demonstrate the high degree of realism that is apparent in Greek and Roman representation. Yet the central place given to figural subject matter in art (as in literature) suggests a similar this-worldly bias. The carved, low reliefs on one Han stone tomb entrance depict an interesting combination of secular and spiritual subjects (Figure **7.9**). The top register of the lintel depicts a lively procession of chariots and horses; beneath are scenes of hunting, while on either side human guardians and winged spirits protect the chamber from evil. On the doors themselves appear fabulous creatures—elegant phoenixes and raging unicorns.

The technical and aesthetic achievement of the Han in the visual

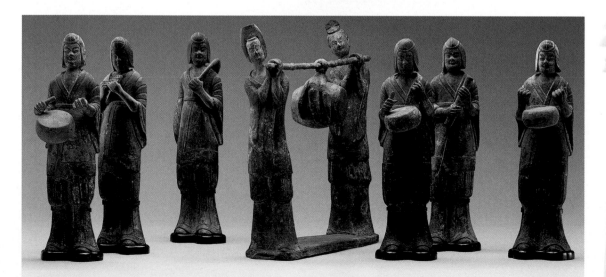

Figure 7.6 Bronze mirror back with cosmic motifs, Han Dynasty, first century C.E. Diameter 14 cm. Barlow Collection, University of Sussex. Photo: Jeff Teasdale.

Figure 7.7 *Musicians*. Chinese, early sixth century mold-pressed clay with traces of unfired pigments. Height 11" each. Northern Wei Dynasty (A.D. 386–534) The Nelson-Atkins Museum of Art, Kansas City, Missouri 32-186/1-7

Figure 7.8
Bronze bells from the tomb of the Marquis Yi of Zeng.

171 | **CHAPTER SEVEN** China: the rise to empire

arts seems to have been matched in music. As early as the Shang era, bronze bells were buried in royal tombs (see Chapter 3), and the tradition of burying sets of royal bells continued for centuries. A set of sixty-five bells, seven large zithers, two panpipes, three transverse flutes, three drums, and other musical instruments accompanied the fifth-century B.C.E. Marquis Yi of Zeng to his grave (Figure 7.8). The instruments (along with the bodies of eight young women and a dog) occupied a subterranean room that replicated the great hall of a palace. Each bell can produce two notes (depending on where the bell is struck) and the name of each note is inscribed in gold on the bell. A set of bells was thus able to range over several octaves, each containing up to ten notes. Whether the bells were used in ceremonial, ritual, or secular events is unclear, but other evidence of other sorts, such as the small ceramic

Figure 7.9 Reliefs of tomb entrance, Eastern Han Dynasty, 25–220 C.E.

orchestra pictured in Figure 7.7 and the bronze buckle with dancers holding cymbals (Figure **7.10**) suggests the Han enjoyed a variety of musical entertainments.

SUMMARY

In a period approximately parallel to the Greco-Roman era, the civilization of China produced many of the definitive and enduring features of its 3,000-year-old culture. During the fifth century B.C.E., Confucius, China's leading thinker, articulated the fundamental rules of proper conduct. Under this influence, the Five Classics came to provide the basis for Chinese education and culture. Confucian thought confirmed ancient Chinese notions of proper behavior and proper rule, which held that the ruler, by his virtuous conduct, exercised the will of heaven on earth.

Figure 7.10 Buckle ornament with dancers, Western Han Dynasty, 206–8 C.E. Gilt bronze 4¾ × 7¼ in. Yunnan Provincial Museum, Kumming, China.

Two centuries after the death of Confucius, the short-lived and militant Qin dynasty created China's first unified empire. Qin emperors embraced the harsh principles of Legalism, rather than the humanistic teachings of Confucius. Like the Romans, the Chinese expanded the empire by way of an aggressive military machine, a detailed record of which survives in the tombs of its emperors. Successors to the Qin, the Han rulers played a vital part in establishing classical Chinese culture. In the 400 years of Han rule, Chinese culture flourished: An educated bureaucracy revived the teachings of Confucius, while a healthy economy encouraged long-distance trade between East and West. As in the Greco-Roman world, the Han produced a body of literature and art that displays a this-worldly affection for nature and a passion for the good life. Han historians and poets assessed the secular world with critical insight and candour. The Han talent for technological invention challenged and even surpassed that of Rome. Nevertheless, it was Han humanism that would come to hold the pivotal place in the classical legacy of East Asia.

Suggestions for Reading

Bodde, Derk. *Chinese Thought, Society, and Science: The Intellectual and Social Background of Science and Technology in Pre-Modern China.* Honolulu: University of Hawaii Press, 1991.

Chang, Kwang-chin. *Art, Myth, and Ritual: The Path to Political Authority in Ancient China.* Cambridge, Mass.: Harvard University Press, 1983.

Fingarette, Herbert. *Confucius: The Secular as Sacred.* New York: Harper & Row, 1972.

Hucker, Charles O. *China's Imperial Past: An Introduction to Chinese History and Culture.* Stanford, CA.: Stanford University Press, 1975.

Loewe, M. *Everyday Life in Early Imperial China.* New York: Dorset Press, 1988.

Miller, Barbara Stoler, ed. *Masterworks of Asian Literature in Comparative Perspective.* Armonk, N.Y.: M.E. Sharpe, 1994.

Needham, Joseph and Robert K. G. Temple. *The Genius of China: 3,000 Years of Science, Discovery, and Invention.* New York: Prion, 1986.

Rawson, Jessica, ed. *The British Museum Book of Chinese Art.* London: Thames and Hudson, 1993.

Schirokauer, Conrad. *A Brief History of Chinese Civilization.* New York: Harcourt, 1991.

Wang, Zhongshu. *Han Civilization*, trans., K. C. Chang. New Haven, Conn.: Yale University Press, 1982.

GLOSSARY

cartography the art of making maps or charts

li (Chinese, "propriety", "ritual", or "arrangement") originally, the proper performance of ritual, but eventually also the natural and moral order, thus, appropriate behavior in all aspects of life

terra-cotta (Italian, "baked earth") a clay medium that may be glazed or painted; also called "earthenware"

Lion Gate, Citadel at Mycenae, ca. 1500–1300 B.C.E. Limestone, height of relief 9 ft. 6 in. © Hirmer Fotoarchiv.

The shaping of the middle ages

Scholars once described the thousand-year period between the fall of Rome and the age of the European Renaissance as a "dark" age whose cultural achievements fell far short of those of ancient Greece and Rome. Our present understanding of the Middle Ages suggests otherwise. As the following chapters indicate, this was one of the most creative periods in the history of Western culture. During the Early Middle Ages—that is, the first seven centuries of the first millennium of the common era—a transition from classical to Christian culture took place in the West. Elsewhere in the world, the same period witnessed the vitalizing effects of two world religions: Buddhism and Islam. So powerful were these religious faiths—Christianity, Buddhism, and Islam—that by the year 1000, the Eastern hemisphere could be described as being divided among them (Map **8.1**).

From the perspective of world history, the transition to the Middle Ages encompassed several significant developments: the decline of classical civilization and the rise of the Christian West, centered in the territories that would come to be called "Europe"; the diffusion of Germanic tribal peoples into the lands of the West Roman Empire; the golden age of Byzantine (or East Roman) civilization, which would outlive the West Roman Empire by a thousand years; the expansion of the teachings of the Buddha from India to China and East Asia; and, finally, the birth and expansion of Islam in Southwest Asia and beyond.

Christianity flowered in the fertile soil of three cultures: Greco-Roman, Hebraic, and West Asian—the area called by Westerners "the Near East." Centering on the teachings of the Hebrew prophet Jesus of Nazareth, the fledgling faith spread westward. In the West the transition from classical to Christian culture was marked by new modes of expression: literary narrative and realistic forms of representation came to be replaced by religious allegory and symbolism. In the East, yet another significant world religion was on the rise. Buddhism, rooted in the Hinduism of ancient India, spread into China and Japan, its religious vocabulary at once absorbing the older traditions of East Asia and projecting a new, more personalized spiritual message.

Before the end of the seventh century, the youngest of the world religions, Islam, had spread from its birthplace in Arabia into the larger world. Islam, the religious faith practiced today by more than a billion people, would play a major role in the shaping of the Middle Ages, not only in terms of the cultural contributions of its artists and scholars but also as the commercial and cultural intermediary between East and the West.

(opposite) San Vitale, Ravenna. Scala/Art Resource, New York.

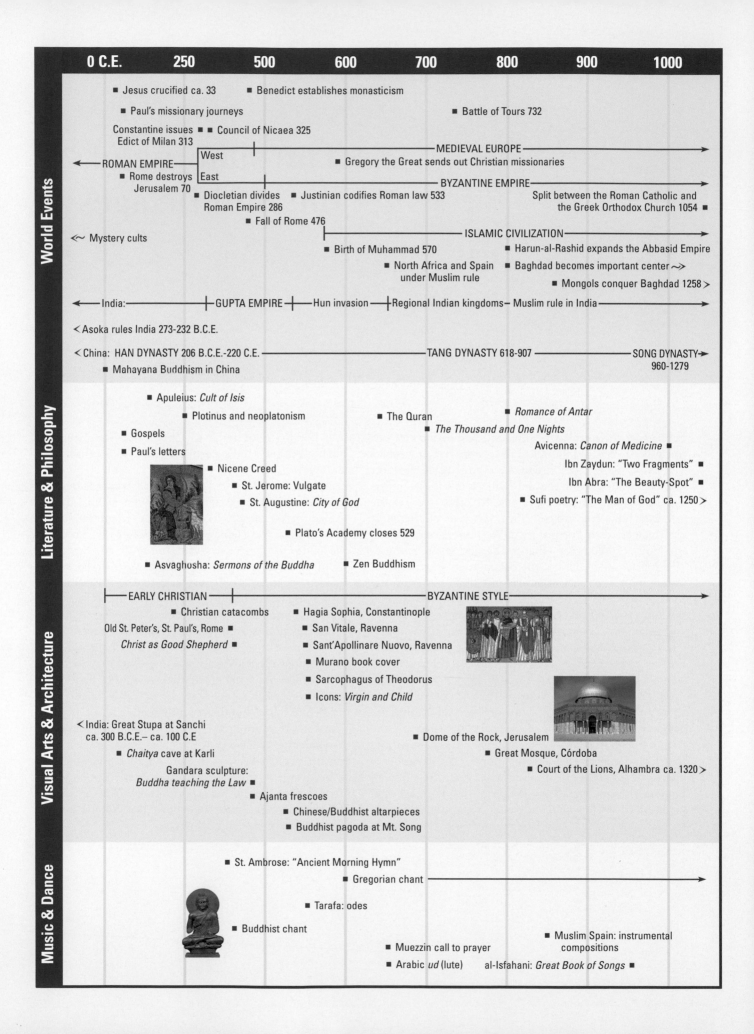

	0 C.E.	250	500	600	700	800	900	1000

World Events

- Jesus crucified ca. 33
- Benedict establishes monasticism
- Paul's missionary journeys
- Battle of Tours 732
- Constantine issues Edict of Milan 313
- Council of Nicaea 325

────────── MEDIEVAL EUROPE ──────────→

←── ROMAN EMPIRE ──── | West |
- Rome destroys Jerusalem 70 | East |
- Gregory the Great sends out Christian missionaries

──────── BYZANTINE EMPIRE ────────→

- Diocletian divides Roman Empire 286
- Justinian codifies Roman law 533
- Split between the Roman Catholic and the Greek Orthodox Church 1054

- Fall of Rome 476

────────── ISLAMIC CIVILIZATION ──────────→

←~ Mystery cults

- Birth of Muhammad 570
- Harun-al-Rashid expands the Abbasid Empire
- North Africa and Spain under Muslim rule
- Baghdad becomes important center ~→
- Mongols conquer Baghdad 1258 >

←── India: ──── | GUPTA EMPIRE | ── Hun invasion ── | Regional Indian kingdoms ── Muslim rule in India ──→

< Asoka rules India 273–232 B.C.E.

< China: HAN DYNASTY 206 B.C.E.–220 C.E. ─────── TANG DYNASTY 618-907 ─────── SONG DYNASTY→ 960-1279

- Mahayana Buddhism in China

Literature & Philosophy

- Apuleius: *Cult of Isis*
- Plotinus and neoplatonism
- The Quran
- *Romance of Antar*
- Gospels
- *The Thousand and One Nights*
- Paul's letters
- Avicenna: *Canon of Medicine* ■
- Nicene Creed
- Ibn Zaydun: "Two Fragments" ■
- St. Jerome: Vulgate
- Ibn Abra: "The Beauty-Spot" ■
- St. Augustine: *City of God*
- Sufi poetry: "The Man of God" ca. 1250 >
- Plato's Academy closes 529
- Asvaghosha: *Sermons of the Buddha*
- Zen Buddhism

Visual Arts & Architecture

|── EARLY CHRISTIAN ────| ──────────── BYZANTINE STYLE ────────────→

- Christian catacombs
- Hagia Sophia, Constantinople
- Old St. Peter's, St. Paul's, Rome ■
- San Vitale, Ravenna
- *Christ as Good Shepherd* ■
- Sant'Apollinare Nuovo, Ravenna
- Murano book cover
- Sarcophagus of Theodorus
- Icons: *Virgin and Child*

< India: Great Stupa at Sanchi ca. 300 B.C.E.– ca. 100 C.E

- Dome of the Rock, Jerusalem
- *Chaitya* cave at Karli
- Great Mosque, Córdoba
- Gandara sculpture: *Buddha teaching the Law* ■
- Court of the Lions, Alhambra ca. 1320 >
- Ajanta frescoes
- Chinese/Buddhist altarpieces
- Buddhist pagoda at Mt. Song

Music & Dance

- St. Ambrose: "Ancient Morning Hymn"
- Gregorian chant ──────────────→
- Tarafa: odes
- Buddhist chant
- Muslim Spain: instrumental compositions
- Muezzin call to prayer
- Arabic *ud* (lute)
- al-Isfahani: *Great Book of Songs* ■

A flowering of faith: Christianity and Buddhism

"Do not imagine that I have come to abolish the Law or the Prophets. I have come not to abolish but to complete them."
Gospel of Matthew

Shortly after the reign of the Roman Emperor Octavian, in the province of Judea (the Roman name for Palestine), an obscure Jewish preacher named Joshua (in Greek, *Jesus*) brought forth a message that became the basis for a new world religion: Christianity. Christianity came to provide an alternative to the secular, rational values associated with classical culture in the West. The pursuit of reason and earthly wisdom gave way to the promise of messianic deliverance and eternal life.

As Christianity began to win converts within the Roman Empire, a somewhat older set of religious teachings was spreading in the East. The message of Siddhartha Gautama, the fifth-century B.C.E.* founder of Buddhism, swept through Asia. By the third century B.C.E., Buddhism had become India's state religion, and by the fifth century C.E.,

---

*Dates are designated as B.C.E., "Before the Christian (or common) era," or C.E., "Christian (or common) era."

Map 8.1 Distribution of Major Religious Faiths, ca. 1000 C.E.

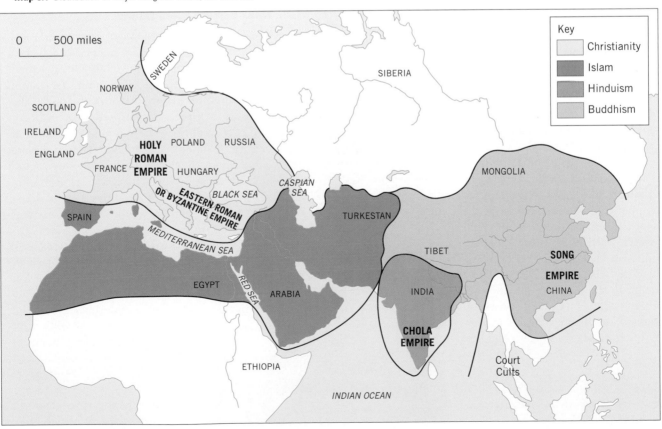

it was the principal religious faith of China. The similarities and differences between Buddhism and Christianity offer valuable insights into the spiritual communities of the East and West. While no in-depth analysis of either religion can be offered here, a brief look at the formative stages of these two world faiths provides some understanding of their significance within the humanistic tradition.

The Background to Christianity

Both as a religious faith and as an historical phenomenon, Christianity emerged out of three distinctly different cultural traditions: Greco-Roman, Near Eastern (West Asian), and Hebraic. All three of these cultures have been examined in the first seven chapters of this book; however, by focusing on the religious life of each at the turn of the first millennium—just prior to the birth of Jesus—we are better able to understand the factors that contributed to the evolution and the rise of the religion that would become the largest of the world's faiths.

The Greco-Roman Background

Roman religion, like Roman culture itself, was a blend of native and borrowed traditions. Ancient pagan religious rituals marked seasonal change and celebrated seedtime and harvest. Augury, the interpretation of omens (a practice borrowed from the Etruscans), was important to Roman religious life as a means of predicting future events. The typically eclectic Romans welcomed the gods of non-Roman peoples and honored them along with the greater and lesser Roman gods. They embraced the Greek gods, who had assumed Latin names (see Table, chapter 4). As with the Greeks, Rome's favorite deities were looked upon as protectors of the household, the marketplace, and the state: Vesta, for instance, guarded the hearth fire, and Mars, god of war, ministered to soldiers. Tolerance for non-Roman cults and creeds contributed to the lack of religious uniformity in the Empire, as well as to wide speculation concerning the possibility of life after death. While Roman poets pictured a shadowy underworld in which the souls of the dead survived (similar to the Greek Hades and the Hebrew Sheol), Roman religion promised neither retribution in the afterlife nor the reward of eternal life.

Figure 8.1 *Isis and Horus Enthroned*, Middle Egyptian, fourth century C.E. Limestone, height 35 in. Staatliche Museen, Berlin.

Rome hosted a wide variety of religious beliefs and practices, along with a number of quasi-religious Hellenistic philosophies (see chapter 6). Of these, Stoicism and neoplatonism were the most influential. Stoicism's ethical view of life and its emphasis on equality among human beings offered an idealized alternative to a social order marked by wide gaps between rich and poor, and between citizens and slaves. Neoplatonism, a school of philosophy developed in Alexandria that took as its inspiration some of the principal ideas in the writings of Plato and his followers, anticipated a mystical union between the individual soul and "the One" or Ultimate Being—comparable with Plato's Form of Goodness. According to Plotinus, a third-century-C.E. Egyptian-born neoplatonist, union with the One could be achieved only by the soul's ascent through a series of levels or degrees of spiritual purification. Neoplatonism's view of the soul as eternal and divine, and its perception of the universe as layered in ascending degrees of perfection, would have a shaping influence on early Christian thought.

Following the decline of the Roman Republic and in the wake of repeated diplomatic contacts with the royal courts of Persia and Egypt (especially that of Cleopatra), Rome absorbed a number of uniquely Eastern traditions. Roman emperors came to be regarded as theocratic monarchs and assumed titles such as *dominus* ("lord") and *deus* ("god"). By the second century, Rome enjoyed a full-blown imperial cult that honored the living emperor as semidivine and deified him after his death. At the same time, widespread social, political, and economic unrest fed a rising distrust of reason and a growing impulse toward mysticism.

The Near Eastern Background

In Greece, Egypt, and throughout Southwest Asia, there had long flourished numerous religious cults whose appeal was less intellectual than that of neoplatonism and far more personal than that of the prevailing Greco-Roman religious philosophies. The promise of personal immortality was the central feature of these cults, called "mystery cults" because their initiation rituals were secret (in Greek, *mysterios*). The cults of Isis in Egypt, Cybele in Phrygia, Dionysus in Greece, and Mithra in Persia, to name but four, had a heritage dating back to Neolithic times. As we have seen in earlier chapters, ancient agricultural societies celebrated seasonal change by means of symbolic performances of the birth, death, and rebirth of gods and goddesses associated with the regeneration of crops. The mystery cults perpetuated these practices. Their initiates participated in symbolic acts of spiritual death and rebirth, including ritual baptism and a communal meal at which they might partake of the flesh or blood of the deity.

The cult of Isis originated in the Egyptian myth of the descent of the goddess Isis into the underworld to find and resurrect her mate Osiris (see chapter 1). Followers of this cult identified Isis as Earth Mother and Queen of Heaven and looked to her to ensure their own salvation (Figure 8.1). Initiation into the cult included formal processions, a ritual meal, purification of the body, and a ten-day period of fasting that culminated in the ecstatic vision of the goddess herself. During the second century C.E., in a Latin novel entitled *The Golden Ass*, or *Metamorphoses*, the Roman writer Lucius Apuleius described the initiation rites of the cult of Isis. At the close of the solemn rites, according to Apuleius, the initiate fell prostrate before the image of the Queen of Heaven and recited the prayer that is reproduced in part in the passage that follows. The ecstatic tone of this prayer—a startling departure from the measured, rational cast of most Greco-Roman literature—reflects the mood of religious longing that characterized the late classical era.

Figure 8.2 Mithraic relief, early third century A.D. Bronze. Metropolitan Museum of Art. Gift of Mr. and Mrs. Klaus G. Perls, 1997. 145.3.

READING 2.1 From Apuleius' *Initiation into the Cult of Isis* (ca. 155)

"O holy and eternal savior of mankind, you who ever [1]
bountifully nurture mortals, you apply the sweet affection of a mother to the misfortunes of the wretched. Neither a day nor a night nor even a tiny moment passes empty of your blessings: you protect men on sea and land, and you drive away the storm-winds of life and stretch forth your rescuing hand, with which you unwind the threads of the Fates even when they are inextricably twisted, you calm the storms of Fortune, and you repress harmful motions of the stars. The spirits above revere you, the spirits below pay you homage. [10]
You rotate the earth, light the sun, rule the universe, and tread Tartarus[1] beneath your heel. The stars obey you, the seasons return at your will, deities rejoice in you, and the elements are your slaves. At your nod breezes breathe, clouds give

nourishment, seeds sprout, and seedlings grow. Your majesty awes the birds traveling the sky, the beasts wandering upon the mountains, the snakes lurking in the ground, and the monsters that swim in the deep. But my talent is too feeble to speak your praises and my inheritance too meager to bring you sacrifices. The fullness of my voice is inadequate to express [20]
what I feel about your majesty; a thousand mouths and as many tongues would not be enough, nor even an endless flow of inexhaustible speech. I shall therefore take care to do the only thing that a devout but poor man can: I shall store your divine countenance and sacred godhead in the secret places of my heart, forever guarding it and picturing it to myself. . . ."

[1]In Greek mythology, a part of the underworld where the wicked are punished.

While the worship of Isis, Dionysus, and Cybele was peculiar to the Mediterranean, Mithraism, the most popular of the mystery cults, originated in Persia. Mithraism looked back to one of the oldest religious philosophies of the ancient world, Zoroastrianism (see chapter 2). Over the centuries, the ancient hero-god Mithra, who had appeared as judge in the Zoroastrian Judgment ceremony, came to play a major part in this Persian belief system. Associated with the forces of Light and the Good, Mithra's slaughter of the Sacred Bull, one of many heroic "labors," was thought to render the earth fertile (Figure 8.2). By their personal attachment to

Figure 8.3 *The Good Shepherd*, ca. 425–450 C.E. Mosaic. Mausoleum of Galla Placidia, Ravenna, Italy. Giraudon, Paris.

Mithra, his devotees looked forward to spiritual well-being and everlasting life. Mithraism featured strict initiation rites, periods of fasting, ritual baptism, and a communal meal of bread and wine. Mithra's followers celebrated his birth on December 25—that is, just after the sun's "rebirth" at the winter solstice. While Mithraism excluded the participation of women, it quickly became the favorite religion of Roman soldiers, who identified with Mithra's physical prowess and heroic self-discipline.

From Persia, Mithraism spread throughout Europe and North Africa, where archeologists have discovered the remains of numerous Mithraic chapels. Indeed, for the first two centuries of the common era, Mithraism was the chief rival of Christianity. The similarities between Mithraism and Christianity—a man-god hero, ritual baptism, a communal meal, and the promise of deliverance from evil—suggest that some of the basic features of Christianity already existed in the religious history of the Roman world prior to the time of Jesus. It is no surprise that many educated Romans considered Christianity to be an imitation of Mithraism.

Although the mystery cults often involved costly and demanding rituals, they were successful in attracting devotees. The Romans readily accommodated the exotic gods and goddesses of these cults as long as their worship did not challenge the authority of the Roman imperial cult or threaten the security of the Roman state.

The Jewish Background

Judaism, the oldest living religion in the Western world, differed from the other religions and religious cults of this period in its strongly ethical bias, its commitment to monotheism, and its exclusivity—that is, its emphasis on a special relationship (or covenant) between God and the Chosen People, the Jews themselves. As discussed in chapter 2, the early history of the Hebrews followed a dramatic narrative of wandering, settlement, and conquest at the hands of foreign powers. Following the sixty years of exile known as the Babylonian Captivity (586–539 B.C.E.), the Hebrews returned to Jerusalem, rebuilt the Temple of Solomon, and renewed their faith in the Torah. Under the influence of the scholar and teacher, Ezra (fl. 428 B.C.E.), the books of the Bible became ever more central in shaping the Hebrew identity. With the eastward expansion of Alexander the Great, the Jews were "hellenized," and by the second century B.C.E., a Greek translation of Hebrew Scriptures appeared. Called the *Septuagint* ("Seventy"), as it was reputed to have been translated by seventy or seventy-two scholars in a period of seventy-two days, this edition is the first known translation of a sacred book into another language.

The homeland of the Jews became the Roman province of Judea in 63 B.C.E., when the Roman general Pompey (106–48 B.C.E.) captured Jerusalem and the neighboring territories. Imperial taxes and loyalty to Rome were among the traditional demands of the conquerors, but Judaism, a monotheistic faith, forbade the worship of Rome's rulers and Rome's gods. Hence the Roman presence in Jerusalem caused mutual animosity and perpetual discord, conditions that would culminate in the Roman destruction of the city in 70 C.E.* (see chapter 6). During the first century B.C.E., however, unrest in Judea was complicated by disunity of opinion and biblical interpretation. Even as a special group of **rabbis** (Jewish teachers) met in 90 C.E. to draw up the authoritative list of thirty-six books that would constitute the canonic Hebrew Bible,** there was no agreement concerning the meaning of many Scriptural references. What, for instance, was the destiny of the Jew in the hereafter? What was the nature and the mission of the figure called by the Hebrew prophets the **Messiah** (the "Anointed One")? The Sadducees, a learned sect of Jewish aristocrats who advocated cultural and religious solidarity among the Jews, envisioned the Messiah as a temporal leader who would consolidate Jewish ideals and lead the Jews to political freedom. They denied that the soul survived the death of the body and accepted only the written law. The Pharisees, the more influential group of Jewish teachers and the principal interpreters of Hebrew law, believed in the advent of a messianic redeemer who, like a shepherd looking after his flock, would lead the righteous to salvation (Figure 8.3). In their view, (one that recognized oral tradition along with Scripture), the human soul was imperishable and the wicked would suffer eternal punishment.

In addition to the Sadducees and the Pharisees, there existed in Judea a minor religious sect called the Essenes, whose members lived in monastic communities near the Dead Sea. The Essenes renounced worldly goods and practiced **asceticism**—strict self-denial and self-discipline. The Essenes believed in the immortality of the soul and its ultimate release and liberation from the body. They anticipated the coming of a teacher of truth who would appear at the end of time. The Dead Sea Scrolls—found in caves near Essene ruins at Qumran—include some of the oldest extant fragments of the Hebrew Bible along with scriptures that forecast a final apocalyptic age. In Judea, where all of these groups along with scores of self-proclaimed miracle workers and preachers competed for an audience, the climate of intense religious expectation was altogether receptive to the appearance of a charismatic leader.

The Message of Jesus

That charismatic leader proved to be a young Jewish rabbi from the city of Nazareth. Since Jesus of Nazareth (d. 33) is not mentioned in non-Christian literature until almost the end of the first century C.E., the historical Jesus is an elusive figure. Our most important sources of information concerning Jesus are the Christian Gospels (literally, "good news"). The oldest, dating from at least forty years after Jesus' death, provides the earliest biographical evidence of the life of Jesus. Yet, since the authors of the Gospels—the evangelists Matthew, Mark, Luke, and John—gave most of their attention to the last months of Jesus' life, these biblical books are not biographies in the true sense of the word. Perhaps because Jesus' followers anticipated his imminent return, they made no effort to keep a careful historical record of their master's life.

Recorded in Greek, the Gospels describe the life and miracles of an eloquent and inspiring teacher. Like all great teachers, Jesus was concerned with ethical matters. His message, cast in simple and direct language and in parables that carried moral lessons, was essentially pacifistic and antimaterialistic. He warned of the perils of riches and the temptations of the temporal world. Jesus' insistence upon the evils of material wealth represented a radically new direction in ancient culture. Despite such exceptions as the Essenes, the neoplatonists, and the Stoics, the classical world was fundamentally materialistic and secular. Jesus preached the renunciation of material goods ("do not lay up for yourselves treasures on earth") not merely as a means of freeing the soul from temporal enslavement, but as a preparation for eternal life.

With a reformer's zeal, Jesus criticized the Judaism of his day, especially its emphasis on strict observance of ritual. He embraced the spirit (rather than the letter) of Hebrew law and proclaimed the primacy of faith over ritual. Asked which of the laws were primary, Jesus cited love of God and love of one's neighbor (Matthew 22:34–40). He pictured God as stern but merciful, loving and protective, rather than chastising (recall Job's Yahweh; see chapter 2) or remote and inaccessible (as with the deities of the mystery cults). Finally, and most importantly, Jesus preached the cultivation of compassion, righteousness, and trust in God, the rewards for which would be reaped in the "kingdom of heaven." For all its simplicity and directness, however, the message of Jesus prescribed an almost impossibly altruistic ideal—an ideal of unconditional love linked to an equally lofty imperative: "You must . . . be perfect, just as your heavenly Father is perfect" (Matthew 5:48). The Sermon on the Mount, as recorded by the apostle Matthew, is probably the most representative of Jesus' sermons. Here Jesus sets forth the basic injunctions of an uncompromising ethic to which moral intention is more important than outward behavior: Love your neighbor; accept persecution with humility; pass no judgment on others; and treat others as you would have them treat you.

READING 2.2 From the Gospel of Matthew (ca. 80–90)

Sermon on the Mount

Chapter 5: The Beatitudes

¹Seeing the crowds, he went onto the mountain. And when he was seated his disciples came to him. ²Then he began to speak. This is what he taught them:

   ³How blessed are the poor in spirit:
   the kingdom of Heaven is theirs.

---

*Hereafter, unless otherwise designated, all dates refer to the Christian (or common) era.

**Following ancient Hebrew tradition, these were grouped into three divisions: the Law (the first five books of instruction, called the *Torah*), the Prophets, and the Writings—that is, wisdom literature (see chapter 2).

⁴Blessed are *the gentle*:
  they shall have the earth as inheritance.
⁵Blessed are those who mourn:
  they shall be comforted.
⁶Blessed are those who hunger and thirst for uprightness:
  they shall have their fill.
⁷Blessed are the merciful:
  they shall have mercy shown them.
⁸Blessed are the pure in heart:
  they shall see God.
⁹Blessed are the peacemakers:
  they shall be recognised as children of God.
¹⁰Blessed are those who are persecuted in the cause of
    uprightness:
  the kingdom of Heaven is theirs.
¹¹"Blessed are you when people abuse you and persecute you and speak all kinds of calumny against you falsely on my account. ¹²Rejoice and be glad, for your reward will be great in heaven; this is how they persecuted the prophets before you.

Salt for the earth and light for the world

¹³"You are salt for the earth. But if salt loses its taste, what can make it salty again? It is good for nothing, and can only be thrown out to be trampled under people's feet.

¹⁴"You are light for the world. A city built on a hill-top cannot be hidden. ¹⁵No one lights a lamp to put it under a tub; they put it on the lamp-stand where it shines for everyone in the house. ¹⁶In the same way your light must shine in people's sight, so that, seeing your good works, they may give praise to your Father in heaven.

The fulfilment of the Law

¹⁷"Do not imagine that I have come to abolish the Law or the Prophets. I have come not to abolish but to complete them. ¹⁸In truth I tell you, till heaven and earth disappear, not one dot, not one little stroke, is to disappear from the Law until all its purpose is achieved. ¹⁹Therefore, anyone who infringes even one of the least of these commandments and teaches others to do the same will be considered the least in the kingdom of Heaven; but the person who keeps them and teaches them will be considered great in the kingdom of Heaven.

The new standard higher than the old

²⁰"For I tell you, if your uprightness does not surpass that of the scribes and Pharisees, you will never get into the kingdom of Heaven.

²¹"You have heard how it was said to our ancestors, *You shall not kill*; and if anyone does kill he must answer for it before the court. ²²But I say this to you, anyone who is angry with a brother will answer for it before the court; anyone who calls a brother 'Fool' will answer for it before the Sanhedrin; and anyone who calls him 'Traitor' will answer for it in hell fire. ²³So then, if you are bringing your offering to the altar and there remember that your brother has something against you, ²⁴leave your offering there before the altar, go and be reconciled with your brother first, and then come back and present your offering. ²⁵Come to terms with your opponent in good time while you are still on the way to the court with him, or he may hand you over to the judge and the judge to the officer, and you will be thrown into prison. ²⁶In truth I tell you, you will not get out till you have paid the last penny.

²⁷"You have heard how it was said, *You shall not commit adultery*. ²⁸But I say this to you, if a man looks at a woman lustfully, he has already committed adultery with her in his heart. ²⁹If your right eye should be your downfall, tear it out and throw it away; for it will do you less harm to lose one part of yourself than to have your whole body thrown into hell. ³⁰And if your right hand should be your downfall, cut it off and throw it away; for it will do you less harm to lose one part of yourself than to have your whole body go to hell.

³¹"It has also been said, *Anyone who divorces his wife must give her a writ of dismissal*. ³²But I say this to you, everyone who divorces his wife, except for the case of an illicit marriage, makes her an adulteress; and anyone who marries a divorced woman commits adultery.

³³"Again, you have heard how it was said to our ancestors, *You must not break your oath, but must fulfil your oaths to the Lord*. ³⁴But I say this to you, do not swear at all, either by *heaven*, since that is *God's throne*; ³⁵or by *earth*, since that is *his footstool*; or by Jerusalem, since that is *the city of the great King*. ³⁶Do not swear by your own head either, since you cannot turn a single hair white or black. ³⁷All you need say is 'Yes' if you mean yes, 'No' if you mean no; anything more than this comes from the Evil One.

³⁸"You have heard how it was said: *Eye for eye and tooth for tooth*. ³⁹But I say this to you: offer no resistance to the wicked. On the contrary, if anyone hits you on the right cheek, offer him the other as well; ⁴⁰if someone wishes to go to law with you to get your tunic, let him have your cloak as well. ⁴¹And if anyone requires you to go one mile, go two miles with him. ⁴²Give to anyone who asks you, and if anyone wants to borrow, do not turn away.

⁴³"You have heard how it was said, *You will love your neighbor* and hate your enemy. ⁴⁴But I say this to you, love your enemies and pray for those who persecute you; ⁴⁵so that you may be children of your Father in heaven, for he causes his sun to rise on the bad as well as the good, and sends down rain to fall on the upright and the wicked alike. ⁴⁶For if you love those who love you, what reward will you get? Do not even the tax collectors do as much? ⁴⁷And if you save your greetings for your brothers, are you doing anything exceptional? ⁴⁸Do not even the gentiles do as much? You must therefore be perfect, just as your heavenly Father is perfect."

Chapter 6: Almsgiving in secret

¹"Be careful not to parade your uprightness in public to attract attention; otherwise you will lose all reward from your Father in heaven. ²So when you give alms, do not have it trumpeted before you; this is what the hypocrites do in the synagogues and in the streets to win human admiration. In truth I tell you, they have had their reward. ³But when you give alms, your left hand must not know what your right is doing; ⁴your almsgiving must be secret, and your Father who sees all that is done in secret will reward you.

Prayer in secret

5"And when you pray, do not imitate the hypocrites; they love to say their prayers standing up in the synagogues and at the street corners for people to see them. In truth I tell you, they have had their reward. 6But when you pray, *go to your private room*, shut yourself in, and so pray to your Father who is in that secret place, and your Father who sees all that is done in secret will reward you.

How to pray. The Lord's Prayer

7"In your prayers do not babble as the gentiles do, for they think that by using many words they will make themselves heard. 8Do not be like them; your Father knows what you need before you ask him. 9So you should pray like this:

> Our Father in heaven,
> may your name be held holy,
> 10your kingdom come,
> your will be done,
> on earth as in heaven.
> 11Give us today our daily bread.
> 12And forgive us our debts,
> as we have forgiven those who are in debt to us.
> 13And do not put us to the test,
> but save us from the Evil One.

14"Yes, if you forgive others their failings, your heavenly Father will forgive you yours; 15but if you do not forgive others, your Father will not forgive your failings either.

Fasting in secret

16"When you are fasting, do not put on a gloomy look as the hypocrites do: they go about looking unsightly to let people know they are fasting. In truth I tell you, they have had their reward. 17But when you fast, put scent on your head and wash your face, 18so that no one will know you are fasting except your Father who sees all that is done in secret; and your Father who sees all that is done in secret will reward you.

True treasures

19"Do not store up treasures for yourselves on earth, where moth and woodworm destroy them and thieves can break in and steal. 20But store up treasures for yourselves in heaven, where neither moth nor woodworm destroys them and thieves cannot break in and steal. 21For wherever your treasure is, there will your heart be too."

Chapter 7: Do not judge

1"Do not judge, and you will not be judged; 2because the judgements you give are the judgements you will get, and the standard you use will be the standard used for you. 3Why do you observe the splinter in your brother's eye and never notice the great log in your own? 4And how dare you say to your brother, 'Let me take that splinter out of your eye,' when, look, there is a great log in your own? 5Hypocrite! Take the log out of your own eye first, and then you will see clearly enough to take the splinter out of your brother's eye.

Do not profane sacred things

6"Do not give dogs what is holy; and do not throw your pearls in front of pigs, or they may trample them and then turn on you and tear you to pieces.

Effective prayer

7"Ask, and it will be given to you; search, and you will find; knock, and the door will be opened to you. 8Everyone who asks receives; everyone who searches finds; everyone who knocks will have the door opened. 9Is there anyone among you who would hand his son a stone when he asked for bread? 10Or would hand him a snake when he asked for a fish? 11If you, then, evil as you are, know how to give your children what is good, how much more will your Father in heaven give good things to those who ask him!

The golden rule

12"So always treat others as you would like them to treat you; that is the Law and the Prophets.

The two ways

13"Enter by the narrow gate, since the road that leads to destruction is wide and spacious, and many take it; 14but it is a narrow gate and a hard road that leads to life, and only a few find it."

The Teachings of Paul

Jesus' urgent and prophetic words, along with the stories of his miraculous acts, spread like wildfire throughout Judea; but his message won few converts from among the Jewish population. Both the Pharisees and the Sadducees opposed Jesus and accused him of violating Jewish law. While the learned community of Judea rejected Jesus as the biblical Messiah, the Romans condemned him as a subversive and a threat to imperial stability. By the authority of the Roman governor, Pontius Pilate, Jesus was put to death by crucifixion (Figure **8.4**), the punishment that the Romans dispensed to thieves and traitors.

Despite the missionary activities of the apostles, the disciples of Jesus, only a small percentage of the population of the Roman Empire—scholarly estimates range from ten to fifteen percent—became Christians in the first hundred years after Jesus' death. And those who did convert came mainly from communities where Jewish tradition was not strong. However, through the efforts of the best-known of the apostles, Paul (d. 65), the message of Jesus gained widespread appeal. A Jewish tentmaker from Tarsus in Asia Minor, Paul had been schooled in both Greek and Hebrew. Though he probably never met Jesus, he became a passionate convert to the teachings of the preacher from Nazareth. Paul is generally believed to have written ten to fourteen of the twenty-seven books of the Christian Scriptures or "New Testament." Paul's most important contributions lie in his having universalized and systematically explained Jesus' message. While Jesus preached only to the Jews, Paul spread the message of Jesus in the non-Jewish communities of Greece, Asia Minor, and Rome, thus earning the title "Apostle to the Gentiles." Preaching among non-Jews, Paul stressed that

from lust; he will desire neither worldly nor heavenly pleasures, and the satisfaction of his natural wants will not defile him. However, let him be moderate, let him eat and drink according to the needs of the body.

"Sensuality is enervating; the self-indulgent man is a slave to his passions, and pleasure-seeking is degrading and vulgar.

"But to satisfy the necessities of life is not evil. To keep the body in good health is a duty, for otherwise we shall not be able to trim the lamp of wisdom, and keep our mind strong and clear. Water surrounds the lotus-flower, but does not wet its petals.

"This is the middle path, O bhikkhus, that keeps aloof from both extremes."

And the Blessed One spoke kindly to his disciples, pitying them for their errors, and pointing out the uselessness of their endeavors, and the ice of ill-will that chilled their hearts melted away under the gentle warmth of the Master's persuasion.

Now the Blessed One set the wheel of the most excellent law[4] rolling, and he began to preach to the five bhikkhus, opening to them the gate of immortality, and showing them the bliss of Nirvāna.

The Buddha said:

"The spokes of the wheel are the rules of pure conduct: justice is the uniformity of their length; wisdom is the tire; modesty and thoughtfulness are the hub in which the immovable axle of truth is fixed.

"He who recognizes the existence of suffering, its cause, its remedy, and its cessation has fathomed the four noble truths. He will walk in the right path.

"Right views will be the torch to light his way. Right aspirations will be his guide. Right speech will be his dwelling-place on the road. His gait will be straight, for it is right behavior. His refreshments will be the right way of earning his livelihood. Right efforts will be his steps: right thoughts his breath; and right contemplation will give him the peace that follows in his footprints.

"Now, this, O bhikkhus, is the noble truth concerning suffering:

"Birth is attended with pain, decay is painful, disease is painful, death is painful. Union with the unpleasant is painful, painful is separation from the pleasant; and any craving that is unsatisfied, that too is painful. In brief, bodily conditions which spring from attachment are painful.

"This, then, O bhikkhus, is the noble truth concerning suffering.

"Now this, O bhikkhus, is the noble truth concerning the origin of suffering:

"Verily, it is that craving which causes the renewal of existence, accompanied by sensual delight, seeking satisfaction now here, now there, the craving for the gratification of the passions, the craving for a future life, and the craving for happiness in this life.

"This, then, O bhikkhus, is the noble truth concerning origin of suffering.

"Now this, O bhikkhus, is the noble truth concerning the destruction of suffering:

"Verily, it is the destruction, in which no passion remains, of this very thirst; it is the laying aside of, the being free from, the dwelling no longer upon this thirst.

"This, then, O bhikkhus, is the noble truth concerning the destruction of suffering.

"Now this, O bhikkhus, is the noble truth concerning the way which leads to the destruction of sorrow. Verily! it is this noble eightfold path; that is to say:

"Right views; right aspirations; right speech; right behavior; right livelihood; right effort; right thoughts; and right contemplation.

"This, then, O bhikkhus, is the noble truth concerning the destruction of sorrow.

"By the practice of loving kindness I have attained liberation of heart, and thus I am assured that I shall never return in renewed births. I have even now attained Nirvāna."

And when the Blessed One had thus set the royal chariot wheel of truth rolling onward, a rapture thrilled through the universes. . . .

READING 2.4b From the Buddha's Sermon on Abuse (recorded ca. 100 B.C.E.)

And the Blessed One observed the ways of society and noticed how much misery came from malignity and foolish offenses done only to gratify vanity and self-seeking pride.

And the Buddha said: "If a man foolishly does me wrong, I will return to him the protection of my ungrudging love; the more evil comes from him, the more good shall go from me; the fragrance of goodness always comes to me, and the harmful air of evil goes to him."

A foolish man learning that the Buddha observed the principle of great love which commends the return of good for evil, came and abused him. The Buddha was silent, pitying his folly.

When the man had finished his abuse, the Buddha asked him, saying: "Son, if a man declined to accept a present made to him, to whom would it belong?" And he answered: "In that case it would belong to the man who offered it."

"My son," said the Buddha, "thou has railed at me, but I decline to accept thy abuse, and request thee to keep it thyself. Will it not be a source of misery to thee? As the echo belongs to the sound, and the shadow to the substance, so misery will overtake the evil-doer without fail."

The abuser made no reply, and the Buddha continued:

"A wicked man who reproaches a virtuous one is like one who looks up and spits at heaven; the spittle soils not the heaven, but comes back and defiles his own person.

"The slanderer is like one who flings dust at another when the wind is contrary; the dust does but return on him who threw it. The virtuous man cannot be hurt and the misery that the other would inflict comes back on himself."

The abuser went away ashamed, but he came again and took refuge in the Buddha, the Dharma,[1] and the Sangha[2]. . . .

---

[4]The Wheel of the Law, or *Dharma*.

[1]The law of Righteousness; the Wheel of the Law.
[2]An assemblage of those who vow to pursue the Buddhist life.

The Spread of Buddhism

During the third century B.C.E. the emperor Asoka (273–232 B.C.E.) made Buddhism the state religion of India. Asoka's active role in spreading Buddhism anticipated Constantine's labors on behalf of Christianity; but Asoka went even further: He sent Buddhist missionaries as far West as Greece and Southeast into Ceylon (present-day Sri Lanka). In spite of Asoka's efforts to give the world a unified faith, the Buddha's teachings generated varying interpretations and numerous factions. By the first century C.E., there were as many as five hundred major and minor Buddhist sects in India alone. In general, however, two principal divisions of Buddhism emerged: Hinayana Buddhism and Mahayana Buddhism. Hinayana Buddhism, which emphasizes the personal pursuit of *nirvana*, remains close to the original teachings of the Buddha. Mahayana Buddhism, on the other hand, elevated the Buddha to the level of a divine being and added a large body of new teachings and legends to the Buddhist canon. Whereas the Buddha had urged his followers to work out their own salvation, Mahayana Buddhists taught that the Buddha was the path to salvation, indeed, that he was a divinity who had come to earth in the form of a man to assist humankind. Other gods, such as the gods of Hinduism, were regarded as incarnations of the Buddha, who himself had appeared in various bodily forms in his previous lives. Moreover, Mahayana Buddhists held that there were many compassionate beings, both before and after the Buddha, who had postponed reaching *nirvana* in order to help suffering humankind. These "Buddhas-to-be," known as **bodhisattvas**, were the heroes of Buddhism; and much like the Christian saints, they became objects of many popular Buddhist cults. The favorite Chinese female *bodhisattva*, Guanyin—originally pictured in Indian art as a mustached male (Figure **8.6**)—was widely regarded as a goddess of mercy and worshiped much in the way that Roman Catholics and Orthodox Christians honor the Virgin Mary. For all the similarities between Christianity and Buddhism, however, one profound difference persists: The concept of human sinfulness, evident in the writings of Paul, is absent from Buddhist thought and belief.

Despite Asoka's vigorous leadership, the Buddha's teachings never gained widespread popularity in India. The strength of the established Hindu tradition in India (like that of Judaism in Judea) and the resistance of the Brahmin caste to Buddhist egalitarianism ultimately hindered the success of Buddhism, and by the seventh century Buddhism was absorbed into Hinduism. In China, however, where Mahayana Buddhism became popular, the faith gained a considerable following. Here, as in many other parts of Asia, the Buddha was regarded not simply as a teacher or reformer, but as a savior whose intercession on one's behalf would free the faithful from physical suffering. Indeed, Chinese Buddhism developed the concept of Heaven in place of the more abstract idea of *nirvana*. Buddhism's tolerance for other religions enhanced its popularity and its universal appeal. Mahayana, the "Great Vehicle" of Buddhism, brought a message of hope and sal-

Figure 8.6 *Standing Bodhisattva*, from the Gandharan region of Northwest Pakistan, late second century C.E. Gray schist, height approx. 3 ft. Courtesy, Museum of Fine Arts, Boston. Helen and Alice Colburn Fund.

vation to millions of people in China, Korea, Japan, and Vietnam, while the more austere Hinayana or "Little Vehicle" of Buddhism became the major faith in Ceylon (Sri Lanka), Burma (Myanmar), Thailand, and Cambodia.

Buddhism entered China during the first century C.E., and rose to prominence during the last turbulent decades of the Han Era. Although comparisons reduce subtle differences to facile analogy, certain similarities between the Roman and Han empires are irrefutable (see chapter 7).

As in Rome, the late Han Era confronted increasing conflicts between wealthy landowners (who deemed themselves exempt from taxation) and impoverished and dissatisfied peasants. The repeated attacks by nomadic tribes along the northern borders of the Han Empire, like those of the Germanic tribes along the frontiers of the Roman Empire, aggravated the prevailing internal disorders and fostered a sense of insecurity. And just as classical humanism gave way to mysticism in the West, the strongly humanistic Confucianism in China felt the challenge of more intuitive forms of religious speculation. During the first century C.E., Buddhist texts were translated into Chinese, and over the following centuries, Buddhism was popularized in China by the writings of the Indian poet Asvaghosha (ca. 80–ca. 150). Asvaghosha's Sanskrit descriptions of the life of the Buddha, which became available in Chinese in the year 420, would become the literary medium for Mahayana Buddhism.

In China, Daoism was easily reconciled with Buddhism, which assumed many different forms. Buddhist "paradise sects" closely resembling the mystery cults of Southwest Asia promised their adherents rebirth in an idyllic, heavenly realm called "the Pure Land of the West." Still another Buddhist sect, strongly influenced by Daoism, emphasized the role of meditation and visionary insight in reaching *nirvana*. Known in China as Chan ("meditation") and in Japan as Zen, this sect held that enlightenment could not be attained by rational means but, rather, through intense concentration that led to a spontaneous awakening of the mind. Among the tools of Zen masters were such mind-sharpening riddles as: "You know the sound of two hands clapping; what, then, is the sound of one hand clapping?" The Zen monk's attention to such queries forced him to move beyond reason. Legend has it that heavily caffeinated tea was introduced from India to China and Japan as an aid to prolonging meditation. In contrast with Christianity, Buddhism (in all its variant forms) extolled the practice of meditation, the act by which the mind is emptied of thoughts, individual identity is obliterated, and total harmony with nature is achieved.

SUMMARY

The world into which Jesus was born was ripe for religious revitalization. Roman religion focused on nature deities and civic gods who provided little in the way of personal spiritual comfort. The mystery cults promised rebirth and resurrection to devotees of fertility gods and goddesses. The province of Judea, beset by religious and political factionalism, sought apocalyptic deliverance from the Roman yoke. The message preached by Jesus demanded an abiding faith in God, compassion for one's fellow human beings, and the renunciation of material wealth. In an age when people were required to serve the state, Jesus asked that they serve God. The apostle Paul universalized Jesus' message by preaching among non-Jews. He explained Jesus' death as atonement for sin and anticipated eternal life for the followers of the *Christos*.

The religion that had begun with the teachings of Siddhartha Gautama in India swept through East Asia in the very centuries that Christianity emerged in the West. Although rooted in different traditions, the two world faiths had much in common, especially in the message of compassion, humility, and right conduct preached by their founders. Christianity and Buddhism had only limited impact in the lands in which their founders were born, but both religions gained popularity in empires that flourished at the same time: Christianity in the Roman world-state, and Buddhism under the late Han dynasty in China. With Pauline Christianity, as with Mahayana Buddhism, the belief in a savior god, the promise of salvation for all human beings, and uncompromising moral goodness provided spiritual alternatives to the prevailing materialism of imperial Rome and Han China. On the soil of these great but declining empires were cast the seeds of two world-historical religions that are still followed by millions of people today.

GLOSSARY

asceticism   strict self-denial and self-discipline

bodhisattva   (Sanskrit, "one whose essence is enlightenment") a being who has postponed his or her own entry into *nirvana* in order to assist others in reaching that goal; worshiped as a deity in Mahayana Buddhism

Messiah   Anointed One, or Savior; in Greek, *Christos*

rabbi   a teacher and master trained in the Jewish law

sutra   (Sanskrit, "thread") an instructional chapter or discourse in any of the sacred books of Buddhism

SUGGESTIONS FOR READING

Brown, Peter. *The World of Late Antiquity, A.D. 150–750*. New York: Norton, 1989.

Crosson, John Dominic. *Jesus: A Revolutionary Biography*. New York: Harper, 1993.

Ferguson, Everett. *Backgrounds of Early Christianity*. Grand Rapids, Mich.: Eerdmans, 1987.

Markus, R.A. *The End of Ancient Christianity*. Cambridge, UK: Cambridge University Press, 1998.

Meeks, W. A. *The First Urban Christians: The Social World of the Apostle Paul*. New Haven: Yale University Press, 1982.

Ross, Nancy W. *Three Ways of Asian Wisdom*. New York: Simon and Schuster, 1966.

Schiffman, Lawrence H. *Reclaiming the Dead Sea Scrolls: The History of Judaism, the Background of Christianity, the Lost Library of Qumran*. Philadelphia: The Jewish Publication Society, 1998.

Singh, Iqbal. *Gautama Buddha*. New York: Oxford University Press, 1997.

Strong, John S. *The Experience of Buddhism: Sources and Interpretations*. Belmont, Calif.: Wadsworth, 1995.

Walsh, Michael. *The Triumph of the Meek: Why Christianity Succeeded*. New York: Harper, 1986.

Wilson, A. N. *Jesus*. New York: Norton, 1992

CHAPTER NINE

The language of faith: symbolism and the arts

"The earthly city loves its own strength as revealed in its men of power, the heavenly city says to its God: 'I will love thee, O Lord, my strength.'"
Augustine of Hippo

Christianity began its rise to world significance amidst an empire beset by increasing domestic difficulties and the assaults of barbarian nomads (see chapter 11). The last great Roman emperors, Diocletian (245–316) and Constantine (ca. 274–337), made valiant efforts to restructure the Empire and reverse military and economic decline. Resolved to govern Rome's sprawling territories more efficiently, Diocletian divided the Empire into western and eastern halves and appointed a coemperor to share the burden of administration and defense. After Diocletian retired, Constantine levied new taxes and made unsuccessful efforts to revive a money economy. By means of the Edict of Milan (313), which proclaimed toleration of all religions (including the fledgling Christianity), Constantine tried to heal Rome's internal divisions. Having failed to breathe new life into the waning Empire, however, in 330 he moved the seat of power from the beleaguered city of Rome to the Eastern capital of the Empire, Byzantium, which he renamed Constantinople.

While the Roman Empire languished in the West, the East Roman or Byzantine Empire—the economic heart of the Roman world—prospered. Located at the crossroads of Europe and Asia, Constantinople was the hub of a vital trade network and the heir to the cultural traditions of Greece, Rome, and Asia. Byzantine emperors formed a firm alliance with Church leaders and worked to create an empire that flourished until the mid-fifteenth century. The Slavic regions of Eastern Europe (including Russia) converted to Orthodox Christianity during the ninth and tenth centuries, thus extending the religious influence of the city that Constantine had designated the "New Rome."

As Christians in Rome and Byzantium worked to formulate an effective language of faith, Buddhists in India, China, and Southeast Asia were developing their own vocabulary of religious expression. Buddhism inspired a glorious outpouring of art, architecture, and music that—like early Christian art in the West—nourished the spiritual needs of millions of people throughout the East.

The Christian Identity

Between the fourth and sixth centuries, Christianity grew from a small, dynamic sect into a full-fledged religion; and its ministerial agent, the Roman Catholic Church, came to replace the Roman Empire as the dominant authority in the West. The history of these developments sheds light on the formation of the Christian identity.

In the first centuries after the death of Jesus, there was little unity of belief and practice among those who called themselves Christians. But after the legalization of the faith in 313, the followers of Jesus moved toward resolving questions of Church hierarchy, **dogma** (prescribed doctrine), and **liturgy** (the rituals for public worship). From Rome, Church leaders in the West borrowed the Latin language, the Roman legal system (which would become the basis for Church, or **canon, law**), and Roman methods of architectural construction. The Church retained Diocletian's administrative divisions, appointing archbishops to oversee the provinces, bishops in the dioceses, and priests in the parishes. As Rome had been the hub of the Western Empire, so it became the administrative center of the new faith, especially as the bishop of Rome rose to prominence within the Church hierarchy. When Church leaders in Constantinople and Antioch contested the administrative primacy of Rome, the bishop of Rome, Leo the Great (ca. 400–461), advanced the "Petrine Doctrine," claiming that Roman pontiffs inherited their position as the successors to Peter, the First Apostle and the principal evangelist of Rome. As Roman emperors had held supreme authority over the state, so Roman Catholic popes—the temporal representatives of Christ—would govern Western Christendom. The new spiritual order in the West was thus patterned after imperial Rome.

While it was essential to the success of the new faith to create a functional administrative hierarchy, it was equally important to formulate a uniform doctrine of belief. As

Figure 9.15 (opposite) Hagia Sophia, Constantinople.

Figure 9.16 (right) Schematic drawing of the dome of Hagia Sophia, showing pendentives.

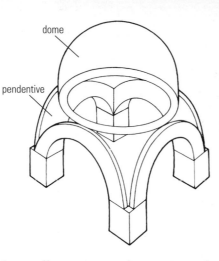

dome

pendentive

Figure 9.17 (above) San Vitale, Ravenna, Italy, ca. 526–547 C.E. Art Archive, London.

Empire (Map **9.1**). In an effort to restore the prestige and power of ancient Rome, he commissioned his legal advisers to revise and codify the extensive body of Roman law. The monumental *Corpus juris civilis* (the *Collected Civil Law*) consisted of four parts: the *Code*, a compilation of Roman laws; the *Digest*, summaries of the opinions of jurists; the *Institutes*, a legal textbook; and the *Novels*, a collection of laws issued after 533. This testament to the primacy of law over imperial authority would have an enormous influence on legal and political history in the West, especially after the eleventh century, when it became the basis for the legal systems in most of the European states. Justinian's leadership was equally important to the Byzantine economy. By directing his ambassadors to smuggle silkworm eggs out of China, Justinian initiated the silk industry that came to compete with Eastern markets. Under Justinian's

leadership an ambitious program of church building was initiated in Constantinople. Of his most notable commission, Hagia Sophia, the emperor is said to have boasted that he had "surpassed" Solomon. Equally ambitious was his effort to embellish Ravenna, the North Italian city that served as his Western imperial outpost.

The sixth-century octagonal domed church of San Vitale in Ravenna is one of the small gems of Byzantine architecture (Figure **9.17**). Its drab exterior hardly pre-

Map 9.1 The Byzantine World Under Justinian, 565 C.E.

CELTS

ANGLO-SAXONS

ATLANTIC OCEAN

FRANKS

BURGUNDIANS

LOMBARDS

SLAVS

Cherson

BLACK SEA

CASPIAN SEA

VISIGOTHS

OSTROGOTHS

Milan

Ravenna

ADRIATIC SEA

Danube

Bosporus

Adrianople

Constantinople

Nicaea

PERSIANS

Rome

Naples

Dara

Tigris

Cartagena

Sea of Marmara

Ephesus

Antioch

Euphrates

VANDALS

Syracuse

Athens

Carthage

Beirut

Damascus

MEDITERRANEAN SEA

Nazareth

Tripoli

0   500 miles

Alexandria

Nile

ARABS

Key

Byzantine Empire under Justinian 1

Figure 9.18 (left) San Vitale, Ravenna. Scala/Art Resource, New York.

Figure 9.19 (below) *Emperor Justinian and His Courtiers*, ca. 547 C.E. Mosaic. San Vitale, Ravenna. © Cameraphoto Arte, Venice.

Figure 9.20 (opposite) *Empress Theodora and Retinue*, ca. 547 C.E. Mosaic. San Vitale, Ravenna. © Cameraphoto Arte, Venice.

pares one for the radiant interior, the walls of which are embellished with polychrome marble, carved alabaster columns, and some of the most magnificent mosaics in the history of world art (Figure **9.18**). The mosaics on either side of the altar show Justinian and his capable consort Theodora, each carrying offerings to Christ (Figures **9.19**, **9.20**). The iconography of the Justinian representation illustrates the bond between Church and state that characterized Byzantine history: Justinian is flanked by twelve companions, an allusion to Christ and the apostles. On his right are his soldiers, the defenders of Christ (note the *chi* and *rho* emblazoned on the shield), while on his left are representatives of the clergy, who bear the instruments of the liturgy: the crucifix, the book, and the incense vessel. Crowned by a solar disc or halo—a device often used in Persian and late Roman art to indicate divine status—Justinian assumes the sacred authority of Christ on earth, thus uniting temporal and spiritual power in the person of the emperor. At the same time, Justinian and his empress reenact the ancient rite of royal donation, a theme underscored by the illustration of the Three Magi on the hem of Theodora's robe (see Figure 9.20).

The style of the mosaic conveys the solemn formality of the event: Justinian and his courtiers stand grave and motionless, as if frozen in ceremonial attention. They are slender, elongated, and rigidly positioned—like the notes of a musical score—against a gold background that works to eliminate spatial depth. Minimally shaded, these "paper cutout" figures with small, flapperlike feet seem to float on the surface of the picture plane, rather than stand anchored in real space. A comparison of this composition with, for instance, any Roman paintings or sculptural reliefs (see chapter 6) underlines the vast differences between the aesthetic aims and purposes of classical and Christian art. Whereas the Romans engaged a realistic narrative style to glorify temporal power, the Christians cultivated an abstract language of line and color to celebrate otherworldly glory.

The sixth-century mosaic of *Jesus Calling the First Apostles, Peter and Andrew* (Figure **9.21**) found in Sant'Apollinare Nuovo in Ravenna—a Christian basilica ornamented by Roman and Byzantine artisans—provides yet another example of the surrender of narrative detail to symbolic abstraction. In the composition, setting is minimal: A gold background shuts out space and provides a supernatural screen against which ritualized action takes place. The figures, stiff and immovable, seem to lack substance. There is almost no sense of muscle and bone beneath the togas of Christ and the apostles. The enlarged eyes and solemn gestures (reminiscent of Mesopotamian votive sculpture; see chapter 2) impart a powerful sense of otherworldly vision and omniscience.

Figure 9.21 *Jesus Calling the First Apostles, Peter and Andrew*, early sixth century C.E. Mosaic. Detail of upper register of north wall, Sant'Apollinare Nuovo, Ravenna. Scala, Florence.

The Byzantine Icon

Although religious imagery was essential to the growing influence of Christianity, a fundamental disagreement concerning the role of icons (images) in divine worship led to conflict between the Roman Catholic and Eastern Orthodox Churches. Most Roman Catholics held that visual representations of God the Father, Jesus, the Virgin, and the saints worked to inspire religious reverence. On the other hand, iconoclasts (those who favored the destruction of icons) held that such images were no better than pagan idols, which were worshiped in and of themselves. During the eighth century, Byzantine iconoclasm resulted in the wholesale destruction of images, while the Iconoclastic Controversy, which remained unresolved until the middle of the ninth century, generated a schism between the Eastern and Western Churches. Nevertheless, for over a thousand years, Byzantine monastics produced solemn portraits of Jesus, Mary, and the saints. The faithful regarded these devotional images as sacred; indeed, some icons were thought to have supernatural and miraculous powers. The idea of the icon as epiphany or "appearance" was linked to the belief that the image (usually that of Mary) was the tangible confirmation of the Blessed Virgin's miraculous appearance. The anonymity of icon painters and the formulaic quality of the image from generation to generation reflects the unique nature of the icon as an archetypal image—one that cannot be altered by the human imagination. Executed in glowing colors and gold paint on small, portable panels, Byzantine icons usually featured the Virgin and Child (alone or surrounded by saints) seated frontally in a formal, stylized manner (Figure **9.22**; compare Figure 9.20). While such representations look back to portrayals of Isis and other East Mediterranean mother cult deities (see Figure 8.1), they also prefigure medieval representations of the Virgin as the seat or throne of wisdom (see Figures 13.28, 13.32).

Following the conversion of Russia to Orthodox Christianity in the tenth century, artists brought new splendor to the art of the icon, often embellishing the painted panel with gold leaf and semiprecious jewels, or enhancing the garments of the saint with thin sheets of hammered gold or silver. To this day, the icon assumes a special importance in the Eastern Orthodox Church and home, where it may be greeted with a kiss, a bow, and the sign of the cross.

Early Christian Music

Early Christians distrusted the sensuous and emotional powers of music, especially instrumental music. Saint Augustine noted the "dangerous pleasure" of music and confessed that on those occasions when he was more "moved by the singing than by what was sung," he felt that he had "sinned criminally." For such reasons, the Early Church was careful to exclude all forms of individual expression from liturgical music. Ancient Jewish religious ritual, especially the practice of chanting daily prayers and singing psalms, directly influenced Church music. Hymns of praise such as those produced by Saint Ambrose were sung by the Christian congregation led by a **cantor** (chief solo singer). But the most important music of Christian antiquity, and that which became central to the liturgy of the Church, was the music of the Mass.

The most sacred rite of the Christian liturgy, the Mass celebrated the sacrifice of Christ's body and blood as enacted at the Last Supper. The service culminated in the sacrament of Holy Communion (or Eucharist), by which Christians symbolically shared the body and blood of their Redeemer. In the West, the service called High Mass featured a series of Latin chants known as either plainsong, plainchant, or Gregorian chant ♪ —the last because Gregory the Great codified and made uniform the many types of religious chant that existed in early Christian times. The invariable or "ordinary" parts of the Mass, that is, those used throughout the year, included "Kyrie eleison" ("Lord have mercy"), "Gloria" ("Glory to God"), "Credo" (the affirmation of the Nicene Creed), "Sanctus" ("Holy, Holy, Holy"), "Benedictus" ("Blessed is He that cometh in the name of the Lord") and "Agnus Dei"

♪ See Music Listening Selections at end of chapter.

("Lamb of God"). Eventually, the "Sanctus" and the "Benedictus" appeared as one chant, making a total of five parts to the ordinary of the Mass.

One of the oldest bodies of liturgical song still in everyday use, Gregorian chant stands among the great treasures of Western music. It is—like early Christian hymnody—monophonic, that is, it consists of a single line of melody. Sung *a cappella* (without instrumental accompaniment), the plainsong of the early Christian era was performed by the clergy and by choirs of monks rather than by members of the congregation. Both the Ambrosian hymns and plainsong could be performed in a **responsorial** style, with the chorus answering the voice of the cantor, or **antiphonally**, with parts of the choir or congregation singing alternating verses. In general, the rhythm of the words dictated the rhythm of the music. Plainsong might

Figure 9.22 *Virgin and Child with Saints and Angels*, second half of sixth century C.E. Icon: encaustic on wood, 27 × 18⅞ in. Monastery of Saint Catherine, Mount Sinai, Egypt.

be **syllabic** (one note to one syllable), or it might involve **melismatic** embellishments (with many notes to one syllable). Since no method for notating music existed before the ninth century, choristers depended on memory and on **neumes**—marks entered above the words of the text to indicate the rise and fall of the voice. The duration and exact pitch of each note, however, had to be committed to memory.

Lacking fixed meter or climax, the free rhythms of Gregorian chant echoed through early Christian churches, whose cavernous interiors enshrined sound and produced effects that were otherworldly and hypnotic. These qualities, conveyed only to a limited degree by modern recordings, are best appreciated when Gregorian chant is performed in large, acoustically resonant basilicas such as the remodeled Saint Peter's in Rome.

The Buddhist Identity

Buddhism, as it spread through India and China, followed a very different path from that of Christianity. Whereas the followers of Jesus established an administrative Church hierarchy, prescribed doctrines, and standardized rituals for public worship, the followers of the Buddha remained divided concerning the real meaning of the Buddha's teachings. Under the leadership of Asoka (see chapter 8), councils of

Buddhist monks met unsuccessfully to organize the Master's teachings into a uniform, official canon. A large body of folklore and legend came to ornament the history of the Buddha's life along with stories of his previous lives, known as *jakatas* ("birth-stories"). The heart of Buddhist scripture, however, is a body of discourses informed by the Master's sermons. There is no Buddhist equivalent of the Nicene Creed, the Mass, or the secular priesthood—in short, no "authority" other than the words of the Buddha. If indeed there is a Buddhist "creed," it calls for adherence to the Law of Righteousness (*Dharma*) and the Eightfold Path. And in its purist (Hinayana) form, it urges Buddhists to work out their own salvation. Among all sects of Buddhism, however, monasteries arose as centers for meditation and instruction. The monastic complex centered on a hall used for teaching and meditation. An adjacent shrine or pagoda might hold relics or ashes of the Buddha.

The Buddhist monk became the model of religious life for a faith that remained aloof from dogma. To this day, religious "services" consist only of the chanting of Buddhist texts (mainly the Buddha's sermons), the recitation of hymns and *mantras* (sacred word and sound formulas), meditation, and confession. Unencumbered by an elaborate liturgy, Buddhism remained grounded in reverence for the Buddha and his teachings. And despite the deification of the Buddha among Mahayana Buddhists and the worship of *bodhisattvas* who might aid humans to achieve *nirvana*, Buddhism never abandoned its profoundly contemplative character.

Figure 9.23 West gateways, the Great Stupa, Sanchi, Central India, Shunga and early Andhra periods, third century B.C.E.—early first century C.E. Shrine height 50 ft.; diameter 105 ft. Scala, Florence.

Figure 9.24
Interior of carved *chaitya* cave, Karli, India, ca. 50 C.E. Government of India, Archeological Survey of India.

Buddhist Art and Architecture in India

Buddhist texts relate that upon his death, the body of the Buddha was cremated and his ashes divided and enshrined in eight burial mounds or **stupas**. When the emperor Asoka made Buddhism the state religion of India in the third century B.C.E., he further divided the ashes, distributing them among some 60,000 shrines. These came to house the relics of the Buddha (and his disciples) and mark the places at which he had taught. The most typical of Buddhist structures, the *stupa* is a beehivelike mound of earth encased by brick or stone. Derived from the prehistoric burial mound, the *stupa* symbolizes at once the World Mountain, the Dome of Heaven, and the hallowed Womb of the Universe. A hemisphere set atop a square base, the shrine is the three-dimensional realization of the cosmic **mandala**—a diagrammatic map of the universe used as a visual aid to meditation and as a ground plan for temple shrines. Separating the shrine from the secular world are stone balustrades. Four gates mark the cardinal points of the compass; both walls and gates are carved with symbols

of the Buddha and his teachings. As they pass through the east gate and circle the *stupa* clockwise, Buddhist pilgrims make the sacred journey that awakens the mind to the rhythms of the universe. While the spiritual journey of the early Christian pilgrim was linear (from narthex to apse), marking the movement from sin to salvation, the Buddhist journey was circular, symbolizing the cycle of regeneration and the quest for *nirvana*.

Begun in the third century B.C.E., the Great Stupa at Sanchi in Central India was one of Asoka's foremost achievements (Figure **9.23**). Elevated on a 20-foot drum and surrounded by a circular stone railing, the shrine is 105 feet in diameter and rises to a height of 50 feet. It is surmounted by a series of **chatras**, umbrellalike shapes that signify the sacred bo tree under which the Buddha reached *nirvana*. The *chatras* also symbolize the levels of human consciousness through which the soul ascends in seeking enlightenment. Occasionally, *stupas* were enclosed in massive, rock-cut caves or placed at the end of arcaded halls adjacent to monastic dwellings (Figures **9.24**, **9.25**).

Figure 9.25 Elevation and ground plan of *chaitya* cave, Karli, ca. 50 C.E.

1 Stupa
2 Column
3 Aisle
4 Main Hall (Nave)
5 Entrance
6 Ambulatory
7 Apse
8 Veranda

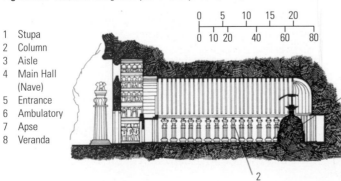

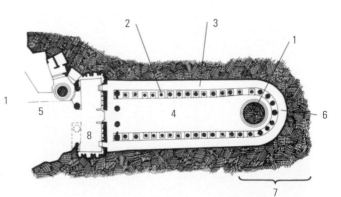

Known as **chaitya** halls, these sacred spaces were not sites for ceremonial worship, as with early Christian churches but, rather, sanctuaries for spiritual retreat. Nevertheless, the *chaitya* hall bore a striking resemblance to the early Christian basilica. Like the basilica, a long colonnaded hall led the devotee from the veranda at the entrance to the semicircular apse in which the *stupa* was situated. The ceilings of both the early Christian church and the *chaitya* hall were made of wood, but the latter was usually barrel vaulted, its curved rafters carrying the eye downward toward an ornate frieze or rows of elephants—symbols of moral and spiritual strength associated with the Buddha.

Buddhism's prohibition of idolatry influenced art in the first centuries after the Master's death, during which time artists avoided portraying the Buddha in human form. Like the early Christians, who devised a body of sacred signs to represent the Christos (see Figure 9.2), Buddhists adopted symbols for the Buddha, such as the fig tree under which he meditated, his footprints, elephants (an ancient symbol of royal authority and spiritual strength), and, most important, the wheel (signifying both the sun and the Wheel of the Law). These symbols, along with sensuous images of nature deities retained from Vedic tradition, make up the densely ornamented surface of the 34-foot-high **toranas** (stone gateways) that mark the entrances to the Great Stupa at Sanchi (Figure **9.26**). Notably different from the

Augustinian antagonism of flesh and spirit evidenced in the *Confessions*, and Christianity's general abhorrence of carnal pleasure, Buddhism (like Hinduism) regarded sexuality and spirituality as variant forms of a single, fundamental cosmic force. Hence, Buddhist art—in contrast with Christian art—did not condemn the representation of the nude body. Indeed, Sanchi's voluptuous fertility goddesses, whose globular breasts and tubelike limbs swell with life, celebrate female sexuality as sensuously as any classically carved Venus (Figure **9.27**).

Mahayana Buddhism, however, glorified the Buddha as a savior, and thus, by the second century C.E., the image of the Buddha himself became important in popular worship. Contacts between Northwest India (Gandhara) and the West influenced the emergence of a distinctly human Buddha icon inspired by Hellenistic and Roman representations of the god Apollo. Gandharan artists created classically draped and idealized freestanding figures of the Buddha and the *bodhisattvas* (see Figures 8.5, 8.6). They also carved elaborate stone reliefs depicting the life of the Buddha. One well-preserved frieze shows four important scenes from this narrative: the birth of the Buddha— shown miraculously emerging from the hip of his mother Queen Maya; the demonic assault on the Buddha as he achieves enlightenment beneath the Bodhi tree, his right hand touching the earth in the **mudra** (symbolic gesture) that calls the earth to witness his authority (Figures **9.28**, **9.29**); the Buddha preaching the *Sermon at Benares*; and the death of the Buddha. In its union of realistic narrative and stylized symbolism, the frieze has much in common with early Christian devotional images (see Figure 9.7).

Between the fourth and sixth centuries, under the sway of the Gupta Empire, India experienced a golden age in the arts as well as in the sciences. Gupta rulers commissioned Sanskrit prose and poetry that ranged from adventure stories and plays to sacred and philosophical works. Gupta mathematicians were the first to use a special sign for the numeric zero and Hindu physicians made significant advances in medicine. (As we shall see in chapter 10, the Arabs transmitted many of these innovations to the West.) In the hands of Gupta sculptors, the image of the Buddha assumed its classic form: a figure seated cross-legged in the position of yoga meditation (Figure **9.30**). The Buddha's oval head, framed by an elaborately ornamented halo, features a mounded protuberance (symbolizing spiritual wisdom), elongated earlobes (a reference to Siddhartha's princely origins), and a third "eye"—a symbol of spiritual vision—between the eyebrows (see Figure 8.5). His masklike face, with downcast eyes and gentle smile, denotes the still state of inner repose. His hands form a *mudra* that indicates the Wheel of the Law, the subject of the Buddha's first sermon (see Figure 9.29). Wheels, symbolizing the Wheel of the Law, are additionally engraved on the palms of his hands and the soles of his feet. The lotus, a favorite Buddhist symbol of enlightenment (and an ancient symbol of procreative life), appears on the seat of the throne and in the decorative motifs on the halo. Finally, in the relief on the base of the throne is the narrative depiction of the Buddha preaching:

Figure 9.26 East *torana* (gate), Great Stupa, Sanchi, India, early Andhra period, mid-first century B.C.E. Sandstone, height of gate 34 ft. Photo: A. F. Kersting, London.

Figure 9.27 (left) *Yakshi* (female fertility spirit) bracket figure, east *torana*, Great Stupa, Sanchi. Sandstone, height approx. 5 ft. Photo: Douglas Dickins, London.

Figure 9.29 (below) *Mudras*.

abhaya mudra
reassurance and
protection

*bhumisparsha
mudra*
calling the earth
to witness

vitarka mudra
intellectual debate

dharmachakra mudra
teaching

dhyana mudra
meditation

Figure 9.28 (below) *Enlightenment*, detail of frieze showing four scenes from the life of Buddha: *Birth, Enlightenment, First Preaching*, and *Nirvana*, from the Gandharan region of Northwest Pakistan, Kushan dynasty, late second–early third century C.E. Dark gray-blue slate, height 26⅜ in., width 114⅛ in., thickness 31³⁄₁₆ in. Courtesy of the Freer Gallery of Art, Smithsonian Institution, Washington, D.C. 49.9.

six disciples flank the Wheel of the Law, while two rampant deer signify the site of the sermon, the Deer Park in Benares (see Reading 2.4). More stylized than their Gandharan predecessors, Gupta figures are typically full-bodied and smoothly modeled with details reduced to decorative linear patterns.

The Gupta period also produced some of the earliest surviving examples of Indian painting. Hundreds of frescoes found on the walls of some thirty rock-cut sanctuaries at Ajanta in Central India show scenes from the lives and incarnations of the Buddha (as told in Mahayana literature), as well as stories from Indian history and legend. In the Ajanta frescoes, musicians, dancers, and lightly clad *bodhisattvas* (Figure 9.31) rival the sensual elegance of the carved goddesses at Sanchi. The Ajanta frescoes are among the best-preserved and most magnificent of Indian paintings. They rank with the frescoes of the catacombs and the mosaic cycles of Early Christian and Byzantine churches, though in their naturalistic treatment of form and in their mythic subject matter (which includes depictions of erotic love), they have no equivalent in the medieval West. They underline the fact that, in Buddhist thought, the divine and the human, the spirit and the body, are considered complementary rather than antagonistic.

Figure 9.30 (above) *Teaching Buddha*, from Sarnath, India, Gupta dynasty, fifth century C.E. Sandstone, height 5 ft. 2 in. Archeological Museum, Sarnath.

Figure 9.31 (left) Palace scene, Cave 17, Ajanta, India. Wall painting. Gupta period, fifth century C.E.

Buddhist Art and Architecture in China

Between the first and third centuries, Buddhist missionaries introduced many of the basic conventions of Indian art and architecture into China. The Chinese adopted the *stupa* as a temple-shrine and place of private worship, transforming its moundlike base and umbrellalike structure into a **pagoda**, or multitiered tower with many roofs. These temple-towers are characterized by sweeping curves and upturned corners similar to those used in ancient watchtowers and multistoried houses (see chapter 7). At the same time, they recreate the image of the spreading pine tree, a beneficent sign in Chinese culture. Favoring timber as the principal building medium, Chinese architects devised complex vaulting systems for the construction of pagodas, of which no early examples have survived.

The earliest Buddhist building in China whose date is known is the twelve-sided brick pagoda on Mount Song in Henan, which served as a shrine for the nearby Buddhist monastery (Figure **9.32**). Constructed in the early sixth century, this pagoda has a hollow interior that may once have held a large statue of the Buddha. Pagodas, whether built in brick or painted wood, became popular throughout Southeast Asia and provided a model for all religious shrines—Daoist and Confucian—as well as for Hindu temples in medieval India.

In addition, the Chinese produced rock-cut sanctuaries modeled on the monastic shrines of India. These contain

Figure 9.32 (right) Pagoda of the Song Yue Temple, Mount Song, Henan, China, 523 C.E.

Figure 9.33 (left) *Large Seated Buddha with Standing Bodhisattva*, Cave 20, Yungang, Shanxi, China, Northern Wei dynasty, ca. 460–470 C.E. Stone, height 44 ft. Werner Forman Archive, London.

Muslim communities in Spain, North Africa, and the Near East cultivated rich traditions in the arts and sciences. Muslim scholars in the cities of Baghdad (in present-day Iraq) and Córdoba (in Andalusia, or Southern Spain) copied Greek manuscripts, creating a rich preserve of classical literature; and Islamic intermediaries carried into the West many of the greatest innovations of Asian culture. These achievements had far-reaching effects on global culture, on the subsequent rise of the European West and, more broadly, on the global humanistic tradition.

The religion of Islam is practiced today by some one billion people, more than two-thirds of whom live outside of Southwest Asia. In the United States, home to over six million Muslims, Islam is the fastest growing religion. These facts suggest that, despite a decline in Islamic culture after 1350, Islam remains one of the most powerful forces in world history.

The Religion of Islam

Muhammad and Islam

Centuries before the time of Christ, nomadic Arabs known as Bedouins lived in the desert peninsula of Arabia east of Egypt. At the mercy of this arid land, they traded along the caravan routes of Southwest Asia. Bedouin Arabs were an animistic, tribal people who worshiped some three hundred different nature deities. Idols of these gods, along with the sacred Black Stone (probably an ancient meteorite), were housed in the **Kaaba**, a sanctuary located in the city of Mecca. Until the sixth century C.E., the Arabs remained polytheistic and disunited, but the birth of the prophet Muhammad in 570 in Mecca changed these circumstances dramatically.

Orphaned at the age of six, Muhammad received little formal education. He traveled with his uncle as a camel driver on caravan journeys that brought him into contact with communities of Jews, Christians, and pagans. At the age of twenty-five he married Khadijah, a wealthy widow fifteen years his senior, and assisted in running her flourishing caravan trade. Periods of solitary meditation in the desert, however, led to a transformation in Muhammad's career: According to Muslim teachings, the Angel Gabriel commanded Muhammad to proclaim his role as the prophet of the one and only Allah (the Arab word for God). Now forty-one years old, Muhammad declared himself the final messenger—human, not divine—in a history of religious revelation that had begun with Abraham and continued through Moses and Jesus. Preaching the revealed word of Allah to his followers—called Muslims ("those who submit")—Muhammad taught that Allah was identical with the god of the Jews and that of the Christians: Fulfilling the long Judeo-Christian biblical tradition of deliverance, Islam ("submission to God's will") completed God's revelation.

Many of Allah's revelations to Muhammad, such as resurrection, the promise of personal immortality, and the concepts of Heaven and Hell, were staples of Christianity, while others, such as an uncompromising monotheism and a set of strict social and ethical commandments, were fundamental to Judaism. Addressed to all people, howev-

Figure 10.1 The *Kaaba*, Mecca, Saudi Arabia. Photo: Mohamed Amin/Robert Harding Picture Library, London.

er, the message of Islam holds simply: "There is no god but Allah [God], and Muhammad is the Messenger of God." Religious practise rests on the "Five Pillars of Faith": (1) declaration of the central belief, that is, the confession of faith, (2) recitation of prayers five times daily, (3) charitable contribution to the welfare of the Islamic community, (4) fasting from dawn until sunset during the sacred month of Ramadan, in which Muhammad received his divine calling, and (5) making the **hajj** or pilgrimage to the city of Mecca, Muhammad's birthplace. Pilgrims who throng to Mecca make the ritual procession that circles the *Kaaba* (Figure **10.1**) seven times (compare Buddhist ritual, as described in chapter 9). The sacred space known as the *Kaaba* is a cubical structure some 48 feet high. Its origins are variously explained. According to Muslim tradition, it was built by Abraham and his son Ishmael as a physical reminder of the links between Islam and Judaism. The shrine is also identified as the sacred spot where, at God's command, the biblical Abraham had prepared to sacrifice his son Isaac. (Both stories reflect the ties that bound the fledgling Muslim faith to biblical Judaism.)

Despite Muhammad's effectiveness as a preacher, the polytheistic Meccans were slow to embrace the new faith. After a series of indecisive battles with the Meccan opposition, the Prophet abandoned his native city, emigrating, in 622, to nearby Medina—a journey known as the **hijra** or *hegira* ("migration"). After converting the population of Medina to Islam, he returned to Mecca with a following of ten thousand men, conquering the city and destroying the idols in the *Kaaba*, with the exception of the Black Stone. Thereafter, Muhammad would assume a position of spiritual and political leadership, and his disciples carried his teachings throughout and beyond Arabia. By the time Muhammad died in 632, the whole Arabian peninsula was united in its commitment to Islam. Since the history of successful missionary activity began with Muhammad's *hijra* in 622, his followers designated that date as the first year of the Muslim calendar.

The Quran

Muhammad himself wrote nothing, but his disciples memorized his teachings and recorded them some ten years after his death. Written in Arabic, the Quran (sometimes transcribed as "Koran"; literally, "recitation") is the Holy Book of Islam (Figure **10.2**). The Muslim guide to spiritual and secular life, the Quran consists of 114 chapters (*suras*) that reveal the nature of God and the inevitability of judgment and resurrection. Muslim Scripture offers guidelines for worship and specific moral and social injunctions for everyday conduct. It condemns drinking wine, eating pork, and all forms of gambling. Islam limits **polygyny** (marriage to several women at the same time) to no more than four wives, provided that a man can support and protect all of them. Although the Quran defends the equality of men and women before God (see Sura 4.3–7), it describes men as being "a degree higher than women" (in that they are the providers) and endorses the pre-Islamic tradition requiring women to veil their bodies from public view (Sura 24:31; see Figure 10.3). Moreover, a husband has unrestricted rights of divorce and can end a marriage by renouncing his wife publicly. Nevertheless, Muhammad's teachings actually raised the status of women by condemning female infanticide, according women property rights, and ensuring their financial support in an age when such protections were not commonly guaranteed.

Muslims consider the Quran the eternal and absolute word of God, and centuries of Muslim leaders have governed according to its precepts. It is sacred poetry, intended to be chanted or recited, not read silently. Committed to memory by devout Muslims, the Quran is considered untranslatable, not only because its contents are deemed holy, but because it is impossible to capture in other languages the musical nuances of the original Arabic. Since the main textbook of the Muslim world is written in Arabic, many non-Arab-speaking Muslims over the centuries have felt it necessary to learn that language. Crucial to Arab culture and Islamic civilization, the Quran is also the primary text for the study of the Arabic language.

Figure 10.2 Kufic calligraphy from the Quran, from Persia, ninth–tenth centuries C.E. Ink and gold leaf on vellum, 8½ × 21 in. The Nelson-Atkins Museum of Art, Kansas City, Missouri. Purchase: Nelson Trust.

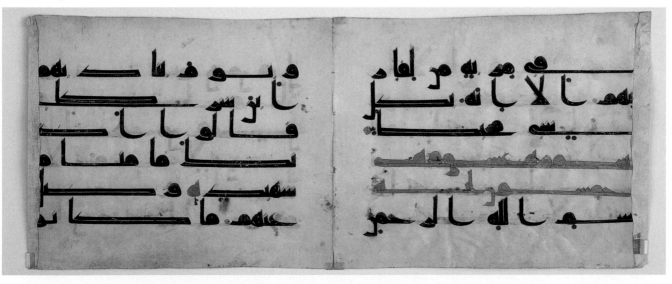

In the name of Allah, most benevolent, ever-merciful.

. . . .

8. O you who believe! Be upright for Allah, bearers of witness with justice, and let not hatred of a people incite you not to act equitably; act equitably, that is nearer to piety, and be careful of (your duty to) Allah; surely Allah is Aware of what you do.

9. Allah has promised to those who believe and do good deeds (that) they shall have forgiveness and a mighty reward.

10. And (as for) those who disbelieve and reject our communications, these are the companions of the flame.[2]

11. O you who believe! remember Allah's favor on you when a people had determined to stretch forth their hands towards you, but He withheld their hands from you, and be careful of (your duty to) Allah; and on Allah let the believers rely.

. . . .

68. Say: O followers of the Book![3] you follow no good till you keep up the [Torah] and the [Gospel] and that which is revealed to you from your Lord; and surely that which has been revealed to you from your Lord shall make many of them increase in inordinacy and unbelief; grieve not therefore for the unbelieving people.

69. Surely those who believe and those who are Jews and the Sebeans[4] and the Christians whoever believes in Allah and the last day and does good—they shall have no fear nor shall they grieve.

70. Certainly We made a covenant with the children of Israel and We sent to them apostles; whenever there came to them an apostle with what that their souls did not desire, some (of them) did they call liars and some they slew.

71. And they thought that there would be no affliction, so they became blind and deaf; then Allah turned to them mercifully, but many of them became blind and deaf; and Allah is well seeing what they do.

72. Certainly they disbelieve who say: Surely Allah, He is the Messiah, son of [Mary];[5] and the Messiah said: O Children of Israel! serve Allah, my Lord and your Lord. Surely whoever associates (others) with Allah, then Allah has forbidden to him the garden,[6] and his abode is the fire; and there shall be no helpers for the unjust.

73. Certainly they disbelieve who say: Surely Allah is the third (person) of the three; and there is no god but the one God, and if they desist not from what they say, a painful chastisement shall befall those among them who disbelieve.

---

[1]Muhammad's followers arranged the 114 chapters of the Quran in order of length, from longest to shortest. The shorter chapters are, however, earlier in date.
[2]That is, Hell.
[3]Jews and Christians.
[4]Semitic merchants from the Saba, a kingdom in southern Arabia.
[5]Muslims believe in Jesus' virgin birth, his miraculous powers, and his ascent to Heaven, but not in his resurrection from the dead nor in his divinity.
[6]Heaven, or Paradise.

74. Will they not then turn to Allah and ask His forgiveness? And Allah is Forgiving, Merciful.

75. The Messiah, son of [Mary] is but an apostle; apostles before him have indeed passed away; and his mother was a truthful woman; they both used to eat food. See how We make the communications clear to them, then behold, how they are turned away.

76. Say: Do you serve besides Allah that which does not control for you any harm, or any profit? And Allah—He is the Hearing, the Knowing.

77. Say: O followers of the Book! be not unduly immoderate in your religion, and do not follow the low desires of people who went astray before and led many astray and went astray from the right path.

. . . .

Chapter 17 The Israelites

In the name of Allah, most benevolent, ever-merciful.

. . . .

9. Surely this Quran guides to that which is most upright and gives good news to the believers who do good that they shall have a great reward.

10. And that (as for) those who do not believe in the hereafter, We have prepared for them a painful chastisement.

11. And man prays for evil as he ought to pray for good, and man is ever hasty.

12. And We have made the night and the day two signs, then We have made the sign of the night to pass away and We have made the sign of the day manifest, so that you may seek grace from your Lord, and that you might know the numbering of years and the reckoning; and We have explained everything with distinctness.

13. And We have made every man's actions to cling to his neck, and We will bring forth to him on the resurrection day a book which he will find wide open:

14. Read your book; your own self is sufficient as a reckoner against you this day.

15. Whoever goes aright, for his own soul does he go aright; and whoever goes astray, to its detriment only does he go astray; nor can the bearer of a burden bear the burden of another, nor do We chastise until We raise an apostle.

16. And when We wish to destroy a town, We send Our commandment to the people of it who lead easy lives, but they transgress therein; thus the word proves true against it, so We destroy it with utter destruction.

17. And how many of the generations did We destroy after [Noah] and your Lord is sufficient as Knowing and Seeing with regard to His servants' faults.

18. Whoever desires this present life, We hasten to him therein what We please for whomsoever We desire, then We assign to him the hell; he shall enter it despised, driven away.

19. And whoever desires the hereafter and strives for it as he ought to strive and he is a believer; (as for) these, their striving shall surely be accepted.

20. All do We aid—these as well as those—out of the bounty of your Lord, and the bounty of your Lord is not confined.

21. See how We have made some of them to excel others, and

certainly the hereafter is much superior in respect of excellence.

22. Do not associate with Allah any other god, lest you sit down despised, neglected.

23. And your Lord has commanded that you shall not serve (any) but Him, and goodness to your parents. If either or both of them reach old age with you, say not to them (so much as) "Ugh" nor chide them, and speak to them a generous word.

24. And make yourself submissively gentle to them with compassion, and say: O my Lord! have compassion on them, as they brought me up (when I was) little.

25. Your Lord knows best what is in your minds; if you are good, then He is surely Forgiving to those who turn (to Him) frequently.

26. And give to the near of kin his due and (to) the needy and the wayfarer, and do not squander wastefully.

. . . .

31. And do not kill your children for fear of poverty; We give them sustenance and yourselves (too); surely to kill them is a great wrong.

32. And go not nigh to fornication; surely it is an indecency and an evil way.

33. And do not kill any one whom Allah has forbidden, except for a just cause, and whoever is slain unjustly, We have indeed given to his heir authority, so let him not exceed the just limits in slaying; surely he is aided.

34. And draw not near to the property of the orphan except in a goodly way till he attains his maturity and fulfill the promise; surely (every) promise shall be questioned about.

35. And give full measure when you measure out, and weigh with a true balance; this is fair and better in the end.

36. And follow not that of which you have not the knowledge; surely the hearing and the sight and the heart, all of these, shall be questioned about that.

37. And do not go about in the land exultingly, for you cannot cut through the earth nor reach the mountains in height.

38. All this—the evil of it—is hateful in the sight of your Lord.

39. This is of what your Lord has revealed to you of wisdom, and do not associate any other god with Allah lest you should be thrown into hell, blamed, cast away.

40. What! has then your Lord preferred to give you sons, and (for Himself) taken daughters from among the angels? Most surely you utter a grievous saying.

. . . .

Chapter 47 Muhammad

In the name of Allah, most benevolent, ever-merciful.

1. (As for) those who disbelieve and turn away from Allah's way, He shall render their works ineffective.

2. And (as for) those who believe and do good, and believe in what has been revealed to Muhammad, and it is the very truth from their Lord, He will remove their evil from them and improve their condition.

3. That is because those who disbelieve follow falsehood, and those who believe follow the truth from their Lord; thus does Allah set forth to men their examples.

4. So when you meet in battle those who disbelieve, then

smite the necks until when you have overcome them, then make (them) prisoners, and afterwards either set them free as a favor or let them ransom (themselves) until the war terminates. That (shall be so); and if Allah had pleased He would certainly have exacted what is due from them, but that He may try some of you by means of others; and (as for) those who are slain in the way of Allah, He will by no means allow their deeds to perish.

5. He will guide them and improve their condition.

6. And cause them to enter the garden which He has made known to them.

7. O you who believe! if you help (the cause of) Allah, He will help you and make firm your feet.

8. And (as for) those who disbelieve, for them is destruction, and He has made their deeds ineffective.

9. That is because they hated what Allah revealed, so He rendered their deeds null.

10. Have they not then journeyed in the land and seen how was the end of those before them: Allah brought down destruction upon them, and the unbelievers shall have the like of it.

11. That is because Allah is the Protector of those who believe, and because the unbelievers shall have no protector for them.

. . . .

Chapter 76 The Man

In the name of Allah, most benevolent, ever-merciful.

1. There surely came over man a period of time when he was a thing not worth mentioning.

2. Surely We have created man from a small life-germ uniting (itself): We mean to try him, so We have made him hearing, seeing.

3. Surely We have shown him the way: he may be thankful or unthankful.

4. Surely We have prepared for the unbelievers chains and shackles and a burning fire.

5. Surely the righteous shall drink of a cup the admixture of which is camphor,[7]

6. A fountain from which the servants of Allah shall drink; they make it to flow a (goodly) flowing forth.

7. They fulfill vows and fear a day the evil of which shall be spreading far and wide.

8. And they give food out of love for Him to the poor and the orphan and the captive:

9. We only feed you for Allah's sake; we desire from you neither reward nor thanks:

10. Surely we fear from our Lord a stern, distressful day.

11. Therefore Allah will guard them from the evil of that day and cause them to meet with ease and happiness;

12. And reward them, because they were patient, with garden and silk [in Paradise],

13. Reclining therein on raised couches, they shall find therein neither (the severe heat of) the sun nor intense cold.

---

[7] A cool and refreshing aromatic.

ards and rubies from India; silk, paper, and porcelain from China; horses and camels from Arabia; topaz and cotton cloth from Egypt. The court of the caliph Harun al-Rashid (ruled 786–809) attracted musicians, dancers, writers, and poets. Harun's sons opened a "house of wisdom" in which scholars prepared Arabic translations of Greek, Persian, Syraic, and Sanskrit manuscripts. In the ninth century, no city in the world could match the breadth of educational instruction or boast a library as large as that of Baghdad. Al-Yaqubi, a late ninth-century visitor to Baghdad, called Iraq "the navel of the earth" and Baghdad "the greatest city, which has no peer in the east or the west of the world in extent, size, prosperity, abundance of water, or health of climate. . . ." He continued:

> To [Baghdad] they come from all countries, far and near, and people from every side have preferred Baghdad to their own homelands. There is no country, the peoples of which have not their own quarter and their own trading and financial arrangements. In it there is gathered that which does not exist in any other city in the world. On its flanks flow two great rivers, the Tigris and the Euphrates, and thus goods and foodstuffs come to it by land and water with the greatest ease, so that every kind of merchandise is completely available, from east and west, from Muslim and non-Muslim lands. Goods are brought from India, Sind [modern Pakistan], China, Tibet, the lands of the Turks, . . . the Ethiopians, and others to such an extent that [products] are more plentiful in Baghdad than in the countries from which they come. They can be procured so readily and so certainly that it is as if all the good things of the world are sent there, all the treasures of the earth assembled there, and all the blessings of creation perfected there. . . . The people excel in knowledge, understanding, letters, manners, insight, discernment, skill in commerce and crafts, cleverness in every argument, proficiency in every calling, and mastery of every craft. There is none more learned than their scholars, better informed than their traditionists,

more cogent than their theologians, more perspicuous than their grammarians, more accurate than their [calligraphers], more skillful than their physicians, more melodious than their singers, more delicate than their craftsmen, more literate than their scribes, more lucid than their logicians, more devoted than their worshipers, more pious than their ascetics, more juridical than their [magistrates], more eloquent than their preachers, more poetic than their poets, and more reckless than their rakes.*

Although this description may reflect the sentiments of an overly enthusiastic tourist, it is accurate to say that, between the eighth and tenth centuries, the cosmopolitan cities of the Muslim world boasted levels of wealth and culture that far exceeded those of Western Christendom. Even after invading Turkish nomads gained control of Baghdad during the eleventh century, the city retained cultural primacy within the civilized world—although Córdoba, with a library of some 400,000 volumes, came to rival Baghdad as a cultural and educational center. The destruction of Baghdad in 1258 at the hands of the Mongols ushered in centuries of slow cultural decline. However, Mongols and Turks, themselves converts to Islam, carried Islamic culture into India and China. In Egypt, an independent Islamic government ruled until the sixteenth century. The Tunisian historian Ibn Khaldun, visiting fourteenth-century Egypt, called Cairo "the mother of the world, the great center of Islam and the mainspring of the sciences and the crafts." Until the mid-fourteenth century, Muslims continued to dominate a system of world trade that stretched from Western Europe to China; thereafter, the glories of medieval Muslim culture waned. The same cannot be said of the religion of Islam: Over the centuries of Islamic expansion, millions of people found Islam responsive to their immediate spiritual needs, and in most of the Asiatic and African regions conquered prior to the late seventh century (see Map 10.1), it is still the dominant faith. To date, Islam has experienced less change and remains closer to its original form than any other world religion.

Islamic Culture

From its beginnings, Islam held the status of a state-sponsored religion; however, the unique feature of Islamic civilization is its diversity, the product of its assimilation of the many different cultures and peoples it encountered. The principal languages of the Islamic world, for instance, are Arabic, Persian, and Turkish, but dozens of other languages, including Berber, Swahili, Kurdish, Tamil, Malay, and Javanese, are spoken by Muslims. Moreover, as Islam expanded, it absorbed many different styles from the arts of non-Arab cultures. "Islamic," then, is a term used to describe the culture of geographically diverse regions—Arab and non-Arab—dominated by Islam.

765	the medical hospital constructed at Baghdad becomes a prototype for those built elsewhere
783	a paper mill (based on a Chinese design) is introduced in Baghdad
820	publication of *Al-jabr wa l mugābalah*, an Arabic adaptation of Hindu numerals to solve equations (called "algebra" in Europe)
ca. 830	Geographers at Baghdad's House of Wisdom estimate the earth's circumference by directly measuring one degree of latitude on the earth's surface
850	the Arabs refine the astrolabe (from Greek prototypes)
950	al-Farabi publishes a treatise, the *Catalogue of the Sciences*, on applied mathematics

*Bernard Lewis, ed. and trans., *Islam from the Prophet Muhammad to the Capture of Constantinople.* New York: Oxford University Press, 1987, 69–71.

Scholarship in the Islamic World

Following Muhammad's dictum to "seek knowledge," Islam was enthusiastically receptive to the intellectual achievements of other cultures and aggressive in its will to understand the workings of the natural world. At a time when few Westerners could read or write Latin and even fewer could decipher Greek, Arab scholars preserved hundreds of ancient Greek manuscripts—the works of Plato, Aristotle, Archimedes, Hippocrates, Galen, Ptolemy, and others—copying and editing them in Arabic translations. An important factor in this burst of literary creativity was the availability of paper, which originated in China as early as the second century (see chapter 14) and came into use in Baghdad during the ninth century. In the copying of classical manuscripts, in the codification of religious teachings (that had heretofore been passed orally), and in the production of new types of literature, such as scientific treatises, cookbooks, poems and tales (see Readings 2.10–12), paper provided a major advance over parchment and papyrus, expensive materials from whose surfaces ink could easily be erased. Between the ninth and twelfth century, Muslims absorbed and preserved much of the medical, botanical, and astrological lore of the Hellenized Mediterranean. This fund of scientific and technological knowledge, along with Arabic translations of Aristotle's works in logic and natural philosophy, and Muslim commentaries on Aristotle, filtered into the urban centers of Europe. There, in the twelfth century, they stimulated a rebirth of learning and contributed to the rise of Western universities (see chapter 12). Muslim philosophers compared the theories of Aristotle and the neoplatonists with the precepts of Islam, seeking a unity of truth that would become the object of inquiry among Italian Renaissance humanists (see chapter 16). Crucial to the advancement of learning was the Muslim transmission of Hindu numbers, which replaced cumbersome Roman numerals with so-called "Arabic numbers" such as those used to paginate this book. Muslims also provided the West with such technological wonders as block printing (after the eighth century) and gunpowder (after the thirteenth century), both of which originated in China (see chapter 14). Muslims thus borrowed and diffused the knowledge of Greek, Chinese, and Indian culture as energetically as they circulated commercial goods.

But the scholars of the Islamic world were not merely copyists; they made original contributions in mathematics, medicine, optics, chemistry, geography, philosophy, and astronomy. In the field of medicine, Islamic physicians wrote treatises on smallpox, measles, and diseases transmitted by animals (such as rabies), on the cauterization of wounds, and on the preparation of medicinal drugs (Figure 10.4). The single most important medieval health handbook, the *Tacuinum Sanitatis*, originated among Arab physicians

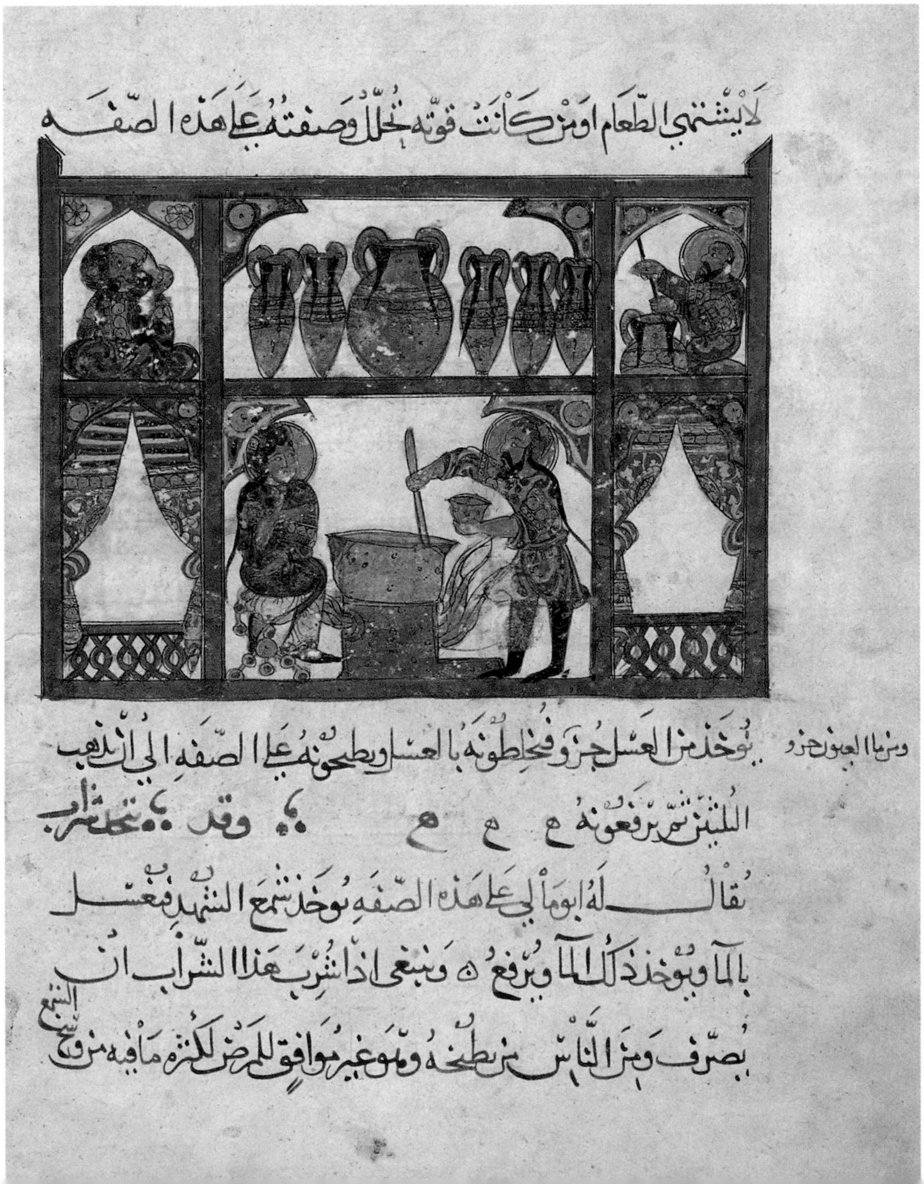

Figure 10.4 *Preparing Medicine from Honey*, from an Arabic manuscript of *Materia Medica* by Dioscorides, thirteenth century. Colors and gilt on paper, 12⅜ × 9 in. The Metropolitan Museum of Art, New York. Cora Timken Burnett Collection of Persian Miniatures and Other Persian Art Objects. Bequest of Cora Timken Burnett, 1956. 57.51.21.

Figure 10.6 Dancing Dervishes from a manuscript of the Diwan by Hafiz. Herat School, Persia, 1490. The Metropolitan Museum of Art, New York. Rogers Fund.

the unity of God: Seeing beyond the dim gropings of the ordinary intellect, the mystic perceives that religions are many, but God is One.

READING 2.11 Rumi's Poems (ca. 1250)

The Man of God

The man of God is drunken while sober.	1
The man of God is full without meat.	
The man of God is perplexed and bewildered.	
The man of God neither sleeps nor eats.	
The man of God is a king clothed in rags.	5
The man of God is a treasure in the streets.	

The man of God is neither of sky nor land.	
The man of God is neither of earth nor sea.	
The man of God is an ocean without end.	
The man of God drops pearls at your feet.	10
The man of God has a hundred moons at night.	
The man of God has a hundred suns' light.	
The man of God's knowledge is complete.	
The man of God doesn't read with his sight.	
The man of God is beyond form and disbelief.	15
The man of God sees good and bad alike.	
The man of God is far beyond non-being.	
The man of God is seen riding high.	
The man of God is hidden, Shamsuddin.	
The man of God you must seek and find.	20

Empty the Glass of Your Desire

Join yourself to friends   1
and know the joy of the soul.
Enter the neighborhood of ruin
with those who drink to the dregs.

Empty the glass of your desire   5
so that you won't be disgraced.
Stop looking for something out there
and begin seeing within.

Open your arms if you want an embrace.
Break the earthen idols and release the radiance.   10
Why get involved with a hag like this world?
You know what it will cost.

And three pitiful meals a day
is all that weapons and violence can earn.
At night when the Beloved comes   15
will you be nodding on opium?

If you close your mouth to food,
you can know a sweeter taste.
Our Host is no tyrant. We gather in a circle.
Sit down with us beyond the wheel of time.   20

Here is the deal: give one life
and receive a hundred.
Stop growling like dogs,
and know the shepherd's care.

You keep complaining about others   25
and all they owe you?
Well, forget about them;
just be in His presence.

When the earth is this wide,
why are you asleep in a prison?   30
Think of nothing but the source of thought.
Feed the soul; let the body fast.

Avoid knotted ideas;
untie yourself in a higher world.
Limit your talk   35
for the sake of timeless communion.

Abandon life and the world,
and find the life of the world.

The One True Light

The lamps are different, but the Light is the same: it
     comes from Beyond.
If thou keep looking at the lamp, thou art lost: for thence   1
     arises the appearance of number and plurality.
Fix thy gaze upon the Light, and thou art delivered from
     the dualism inherent in the finite body.
O thou who art the kernel of Existence, the disagreement
     between Moslem, Zoroastrian and Jew depends on the
     standpoint.

Some Hindus brought an elephant, which they exhibited
     in a dark shed.
As seeing it with the eye was impossible, every one felt it   5

with the palm of his hand.
The hand of one fell on its trunk: he said, "This animal   1
     is like a water-pipe."
Another touched its ear: to him the creature seemed like
     a fan.
Another handled its leg and described the elephant as
     having the shape of a pillar.
Another stroked its back. "Truly," said he, "this elephant
     resembles a throne."   10
Had each of them held a lighted candle, there would
     have been no contradiction in their words.

Islamic Prose Literature

Islam prized poetry over prose, but both forms drew on enduring oral tradition and on the verbal treasures of many regions. Unique to Arabic literature was rhyming prose, which brought a musical quality to everyday speech. One of the most popular forms of prose literary entertainment was a collection of eighth-century animal fables, which instructed as they amused. Another, which narrated the adventures of a rogue or vagabond characters, anticipated by five centuries the picaresque novel in the West (see chapter 24).

The rich diversity of Islamic culture is nowhere better revealed, however, than in the collection of prose tales known as *The Thousand and One Nights*. This literary classic, gradually assembled between the eighth and tenth centuries, brought together in the Arabic tongue various tales from Persian, Arabic, and Indian sources. The framework for the whole derives from an Indian fairy tale: Shahrasad (in English, Scheherazade) marries a king who fears female infidelity so greatly that he kills each new wife on the morning after the wedding night. In order to forestall her own death, Scheherazade entertains the king by telling stories, each of which she carefully brings to a climax just before dawn, so that, in order to learn the ending, the king must allow her to live. Scheherazade—or, more exactly, her storytelling—has a humanizing effect upon the king, who, after a thousand nights, comes to prize his clever wife. *The Thousand and One Nights*, which exists in many versions, actually contains only some 250 tales, many of which have become favorites with readers throughout the world: The adventures of Ali Baba, Aladdin, Sinbad, and other post-medieval stories are filled with fantasy, exotic characters, and spicy romance. The manner in which each tale loops into the next, linking story to story and parts of each story to each other, resembles the regulating principles of design in Islamic art, which include repetition, infinite extension, and the looping together of motifs to form a meandering, overall pattern (Figure **10.7** and **10.8**).

The story of Prince Behram and the Princess Al-Datma, reproduced below, addresses some of the major themes in Islamic literary culture: the power of female beauty, survival through cunning, and the "battle" of the sexes. While the story provides insight into Islamic notions of etiquette, it confirms the subordinate role of women in this, as in Western, society (see Reading 2.15). Nevertheless,

well, modal (each mode bearing association with a specific quality of emotion). Two additional characteristics of Arab music (to this day) are its use of microtones (the intervals that lie between the semitones of the Western twelve-note system) and its preference for improvisation (the performer's original, spur-of-the-moment variations on the melody or rhythm of a given piece). Both of these features, which also occur in modern jazz, work to give Arab music its unique sound. The melodic line of the Arab song weaves and wanders, looping and repeating themes in a kind of aural arabesque; the voice slides and intones in subtle and hypnotic stretches. In its linear ornamentation and in its repetitive rhythmic phrasing, Arab music has much in common with literary and visual forms of Islamic expression. This vocal pattern, resembling Hebrew, Christian, or Buddhist chant, is not unlike the sound of the *muezzin* calling Muslims to prayer.

Instrumental music took second place to the voice everywhere in the Islamic world, except in Persia, where a strong pre-Islamic instrumental tradition flourished. Lyres, flutes, and drums—all light, portable instruments—were used to accompany the songs of Bedouin camel drivers, while bells and tambourines might provide percussion for dancing. By the seventh century, the Arabs developed the lute (in Arabic, *ud*, meaning "wood"), a half-pear-shaped wooden string instrument that was used to accompany vocal performance (Figures **10.15**, **10.16**). The forerunner of the guitar, the lute has a right-angled neck and is played with a small quill. Some time after the eighth cen-

Figure 10.15 (above) Lute with nine strings. Spanish miniature from the *Cantigas de Santa Maria*, 1221–1289. El Escorial de Santa Maria, MS E-Eb-1-2, f.162.

Figure 10.16 (below) Drawing of a lute.

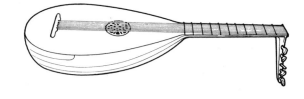

Figure 10.14 Court of the Lions, the Alhambra, Granada, Spain, fourteenth century.

tury, Muslim musicians in Spain began to compose larger orchestral pieces divided into five or more distinct movements, to be performed by string and wind instruments, percussion, and voices. 🎵 It is possible that the Western tradition of orchestral music, along with the development of such instruments as oboes, trumpets, viols, and kettledrums, originated among Arab musicians during the centuries of Muslim rule in Spain. Indeed, the renowned ninth-century musician Ziryab (known for his dark complexion as "the Blackbird") traveled from Baghdad through North Africa to Córdoba to become the founder of the first conservatory of music and patriarch of Arabo-Andalusian musical art. Music composition and theory reached a peak between the ninth and eleventh centuries, when noted Islamic scholars wrote almost two hundred treatises on musical performance and theory. They classified the aesthetic, ethical, and medicinal functions of the modes, recommending specific types of music to relieve specific illnesses. One Arab writer, al-Isfahani (897–967), compiled the *Great Book of Songs*, a twenty-one-volume encyclopedia that remains the most important source of information about Arab music and poetry from its beginnings to the tenth century. The wide range of love songs, many with motifs of complaint and yearning, would have a distinct influence on both the secular and the religious music of the Western Middle Ages and the Renaissance.

🎵 See Music Listening Selections at end of chapter.

SUMMARY

In seventh-century Arabia, Islam emerged as the third of the global monotheistic religions. As the teachings of Muhammad, the Prophet of Allah, came to be recorded in the Quran, Muslims throughout Arabia followed the religious, social, and ethical mandates of a vibrant new faith. Islam rapidly expanded beyond the Arabian homeland to establish the most culturally productive civilization since Roman times. Dominating the Mediterranean and much of Southwest Asia, Muslim traders and travelers formed a global community whose internal cohesiveness was based on a set of common moral and religious values.

Between the eighth and thirteenth centuries, the great centers of Muslim urban life—Baghdad in Iraq, Córdoba in Spain, and Cairo in Egypt—outshone the cities of Western Europe in learning and the arts. Muslims made unique contributions in the realms of poetry and prose, as well as in architecture, the visual arts, and music. The high degree of technical craftsmanship in these forms of expression is matched by a sophisticated taste for complex abstract design. Compositions marked by lyrical repetition and infinite extension are as evident in *The Thousand and One Nights* as in the Great Mosque at Córdoba. Muslim scholars translated into Arabic the valuable corpus of Greek writings, which they transmitted to the West along with the technological and scientific inventions of Asian civilizations. But the scholars of the Islamic world also produced original work in the fields of mathematics, optics, philosophy, geography, and medicine, much of which had profound effects on the course of European culture. As the geographic intermediaries between Asia and Europe, the Muslims created the first truly global culture—a culture united by a single system of belief, but embracing a wide variety of regions, languages, and customs. To this day, Islam, with over one billion adherents, has preserved with little change the teachings of its founder. And, in our own time, Muslim countries and their populations have reassumed positions of worldwide consequence.

SUGGESTIONS FOR READING

Abu-Lughod, Janet L. *Before European Hegemony: The World System A.D. 1250–1350*. New York: Oxford University Press, 1989.

Bloom, Jonathan M., and Sheila S. Blair. *Islamic Arts*. New York: Phaidon, 1997.

Brend, Barbara. *Islamic Art*. Cambridge, Mass.: Harvard University Press, 1980.

Hillerbrand, Robert. *Islamic Art and Architecture*. London: Thames and Hudson, 1999.

Hiskett, Mervyn. *The Course of Islam in Africa*. New York: Columbia University Press, 1994.

Hodgson, Marshall. *The Venture of Islam*. 3 vols. Chicago: University of Chicago Press, 1974.

Lewis, Bernard, ed. *Islam from the Prophet Muhammad to the Capture of Constantinople*. New York: Oxford University Press, 1987.

Martin, Richard. *Islam: A Cultural Perspective*. New York: Prentice-Hall, 1982.

Otto-Dorn, Katharina. *The Art and Architecture of the Islamic World*. Berkeley, Calif. University of California Press, 1991.

Peters, F. E. *Muhammad and the Origins of Islam*. Ithaca, N.Y.: State University of New York, 1994.

Stanton, Charles M. *Higher Learning in Islam: The Classical Period, 700 A.D. to 1300 A.D.* Langham, Md.: Rowman and Littlefield, 1990.

Turner, Howard R. *Science in Medieval Islam: An Illustrated Introduction*. Austin: University of Texas Press, 1998.

MUSIC LISTENING SELECTIONS

CD One Selection 4   Islamic Call to Prayer.
CD One Selection 5   Anonymous, Nouba Raml Al Maya.

GLOSSARY

arabesque a type of ornament featuring plant and flower forms

caliph the official successor to Muhammad and theocratic ruler of an Islamic state

hajj pilgrimage to Mecca, the fifth Pillar of the Faith in Islam

hexafoil having six leaves or arcs

hijra (Arabic, "migration" or "flight") Muhammad's journey from Mecca to Medina in the year 622

illuminated manuscript a handwritten and ornamented book, parts of which (the script, illustrations, or decorative devices) may be embellished with gold or silver paint or with gold foil, hence "illuminated"

imam a Muslim prayer leader

infidel a nonbeliever

jihad (Arabic, "struggle" [to follow God's will]) the struggle to lead a virtuous life and to further the universal mission of Islam through teaching, preaching, and, when necessary, warfare

Kaaba (Arabic, "cube") a religious sanctuary in Mecca; a square temple containing the sacred Black Stone thought to have been delivered to Abraham by the Angel Gabriel

Kufic the earliest form of Arabic script; it originated in the Iraqi town of Kufa

mihrab a special niche in the wall of a mosque that indicates the direction of Mecca

minaret a tall, slender tower usually attached to a mosque and surrounded by a balcony from which the *muezzin* summons Muslims to prayer

minbar a stepped pulpit in a mosque

mosque the Muslim house of worship

muezzin a "crier" who calls the hours of Muslim prayer five times a day

mullah a Muslim trained in Islamic law and doctrine

polygyny the marriage of one man to several women at the same time

sharia the body of Muslim law based on the Quran and the Hadith

stucco fine plaster or cement used to coat or decorate walls

The medieval West

The popular picture of the Middle Ages is colored by knights in shining armor, hooded monks, walled castles, and bloody crusades. There is, indeed, much about the medieval world that provides food for fantasy; but, in reality, the era had a powerful impact on the evolution of Western values, beliefs, and practices. The geographic contours of modern European states and the basic political, religious, and linguistic traditions of Western Europe (to which Americans are deeply indebted) took shape during the Middle Ages. The prototypes of nation-states, cities, and universities emerged at this time, and the Roman Catholic Church reached its peak as a powerful political and spiritual institution. The feudal epic, the courtly romance, and the morality play appeared, along with the vernacular languages used in the West today. Medieval artists and artisans produced works of art and architecture that still dazzle modern beholders.

Three distinctly different cultures combined to produce the Middle Ages: Greco-Roman, Judeo-Christian, and Germanic. As these three strands mingled and blended, a new culture, whose mainstay was Christianity, came to dominate Western Europe. The Greco-Roman and the Judeo-Christian strands have been examined in previous chapters. Our examination, therefore, begins with an appraisal of Germanic culture and the ways in which the tribal invasions of the West affected the identity of the late Roman world. The empire of Charlemagne provides an excellent example of cultural synthesis: Germanic, Classical, and Christian. Though interrupted by Viking invasions, Carolingian culture laid the basis for medieval patterns of life. The feudal and manorial traditions of the Early Middle Ages (ca. 500–1000) established patterns of class and social status that came to shape the economic and political history of the West. In the masterworks of this period—the Song of Roland, the Bayeux Tapestry, Gregorian Chant, and the gloriously illuminated pages of Christian liturgical manuscripts—we see reflected some of the principal features of early medieval culture: the spirit of rugged warfare, the obligations of feudal loyalty, and the rising tide of Christian piety. Between 700 and 1300, the approximate time frame for chapters 11 to 13, the population of medieval Europe rose from 27 million to 73 million people. The High Middle Ages (ca. 1000–1300) saw the onset of the Crusades, the revival of trade, the emergence of towns, and the rise of universities. Medieval Europe's centuries of incubation had given way to a new era, marked by urban growth and global outreach.

Throughout the Middle Ages the Catholic Church assumed a major role in shaping the belief system of medieval Christians. Catholic mystics and preachers articulated the promise of life after death in vivid terms that inspired such great literary works as *Everyman* and Dante's *Divine Comedy*. The great monastic centers, the Romanesque and Gothic churches, the lavishly adorned liturgical objects and manuscripts, and the rise of polyphonic religious music all give evidence of the spiritual yearnings of an age of faith. In the synthesis of all of these forms of expression—architecture, sculpture, painting, stained glass, metalwork, music, poetry, and drama—the Middle Ages provided a unique chapter in the history of the humanistic tradition.

(opposite) *God as Architect of the Universe*, detail, from the Bible Moralisée, thirteenth century. Österreichische Nationalbibliothek, Vienna, MS Cod. 2554, f.1.

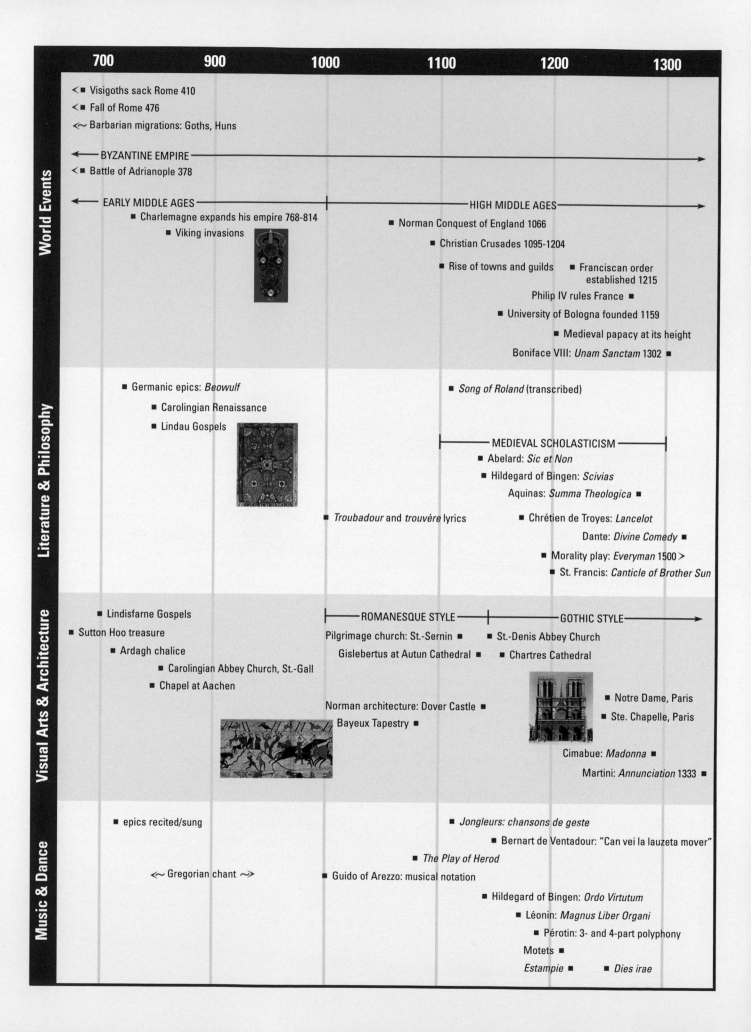

| | 700 | 900 | 1000 | 1100 | 1200 | 1300 |

World Events

<‐ ■ Visigoths sack Rome 410
<‐ ■ Fall of Rome 476
<~ Barbarian migrations: Goths, Huns

←— BYZANTINE EMPIRE —————————————→
<‐ ■ Battle of Adrianople 378

←— EARLY MIDDLE AGES —————| ———————— HIGH MIDDLE AGES —————————→
■ Charlemagne expands his empire 768-814
■ Viking invasions
■ Norman Conquest of England 1066
■ Christian Crusades 1095-1204
■ Rise of towns and guilds   ■ Franciscan order established 1215
Philip IV rules France ■
■ University of Bologna founded 1159
■ Medieval papacy at its height
Boniface VIII: *Unam Sanctam* 1302 ■

Literature & Philosophy

■ Germanic epics: *Beowulf*   ■ *Song of Roland* (transcribed)
■ Carolingian Renaissance
■ Lindau Gospels

————— MEDIEVAL SCHOLASTICISM —————|
■ Abelard: *Sic et Non*
■ Hildegard of Bingen: *Scivias*
Aquinas: *Summa Theologica* ■
■ *Troubadour* and *trouvère* lyrics   ■ Chrétien de Troyes: *Lancelot*
Dante: *Divine Comedy* ■
■ Morality play: *Everyman* 1500 >
■ St. Francis: *Canticle of Brother Sun*

Visual Arts & Architecture

■ Lindisfarne Gospels   —— ROMANESQUE STYLE ——| ——— GOTHIC STYLE ———→
■ Sutton Hoo treasure   Pilgrimage church: St.-Sernin ■   ■ St.-Denis Abbey Church
■ Ardagh chalice   Gislebertus at Autun Cathedral ■   ■ Chartres Cathedral
■ Carolingian Abbey Church, St.-Gall
■ Chapel at Aachen

Norman architecture: Dover Castle ■   ■ Notre Dame, Paris
Bayeux Tapestry ■   ■ Ste. Chapelle, Paris

Cimabue: *Madonna* ■
Martini: *Annunciation* 1333 ■

Music & Dance

■ epics recited/sung   ■ *Jongleurs: chansons de geste*
■ Bernart de Ventadour: "Can vei la lauzeta mover"
■ *The Play of Herod*
<~ Gregorian chant ~>   ■ Guido of Arezzo: musical notation
■ Hildegard of Bingen: *Ordo Virtutum*
■ Léonin: *Magnus Liber Organi*
■ Pérotin: 3- and 4-part polyphony
Motets ■
Estampie ■   ■ *Dies irae*

CHAPTER ELEVEN

Patterns of medieval life

"When they mount chargers, take up their swords and shields,
Not death itself could drive them from the field.
They are good men; their words are fierce and proud."
Song of Roland

In the five centuries following the fall of Rome in 476—a period often called the Dark Ages—Western Europe struggled for order and stability. During this formative era, more aptly termed the Early Middle Ages (ca. 500–1000), three traditions—classical, Christian, and Germanic—became interwoven, ultimately to produce the vigorous new culture of the medieval West. The Germanic tribes that moved upon the West in the first centuries of the Christian era (Map **11.1**) contributed to the decline and decentralization of Roman civilization. Ultimately, however, Germanic tribal people and practices blended with

those of classical Rome and Western Christianity to forge the basic economic, social, and cultural patterns of medieval life. The system of feudalism came to dominate early medieval society, while in the centuries immediately following the Crusades the revival of trade stimulated the rise of cities and the development of an urban culture.

The Germanic Tribes

The Germanic peoples were a tribal folk who followed a migratory existence. Dependent on their flocks and herds,

Map 11.1 The Early Christian World and the Barbarian Invasions, ca. 500 C.E.

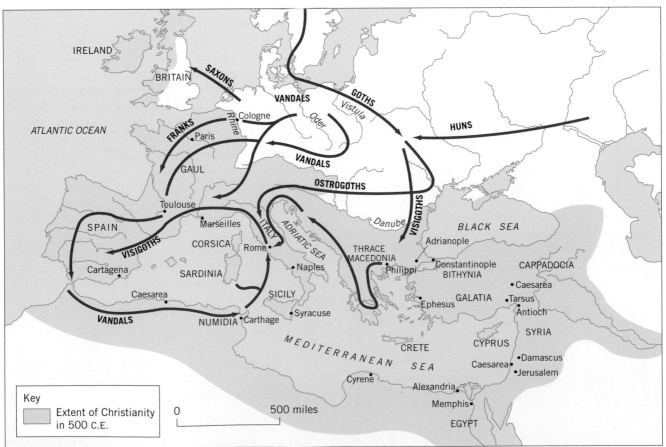

Key
Extent of Christianity in 500 C.E.

0   500 miles

they lived in pre-urban village communities throughout Asia and frequently raided and plundered nearby lands for material gain. They settled no territorial state, nor did they produce any monumental architecture or sculpture. As early as the first century B.C.E., the loose confederacy of Germanic tribes began to threaten Roman territories, but it was not until the fourth century C.E. that these tribes, driven westward by the fierce Central Asian nomads known as Huns, pressed into the Roman Empire. Lacking the hallmarks of civilization—urban settlements, monumental architecture, and the art of writing—the Germanic tribes struck the Romans as inferiors, as outsiders, hence, as "barbarians." In fact, the Germanic peoples were ethnically distinct from the Huns. East Goths (Ostrogoths), West Goths (Visigoths), Franks, Vandals, Burgundians, Angles, and Saxons—to name only a few—belonged to one and the same (Germanic) language family, dialects of which differed from tribe to tribe. The Ostrogoths occupied the steppe region between the Black and Baltic seas, while the Visigoths settled in territories closer to the Danube River (see Map 11.1). As the tribes pressed westward, however, an uneasy alliance was forged: The Romans allowed the barbarians to settle on the borders of the Empire, in exchange for which Germanic warriors afforded Rome protection against other invaders. Antagonisms between Rome and the West Goths led to a military showdown. At the Battle of Adrianople (130 miles northwest of Constantinople) in 378, the Visigoths defeated the "invincible" Roman army, killing the East Roman Emperor Valens and dispersing his army. Almost immediately thereafter, the Visigoths swept across the Roman border, raiding the cities of the declining West, including Rome itself in 410.

The Battle of Adrianople opened the door to a sequence of barbarian invasions. During the fifth century, the Empire fell prey to the assaults of many Germanic tribes, including the Vandals, whose willful, malicious destruction of Rome in 455 produced the English word "vandalize." In 476, a Germanic commander named Odoacer deposed the reigning Roman emperor in the West, an event that is traditionally taken to mark the official end of the Roman Empire. Although the Germanic tribes leveled the final assaults on an already declining empire, they did not utterly destroy Rome's vast resources, nor did they ignore the culture of the late Roman world. The Ostrogoths embraced Christianity and sponsored literary and architectural enterprises modeled on those of Rome and Byzantium, while the Franks and the Burgundians chose to commit their legal traditions to writing, styling their codes of law on Roman models.

568	Germanic tribes introduce stirrups (from China) into Europe
600	a heavy iron plow is used in Northern Europe
770	iron horseshoes are used widely in Western Europe

But Germanic culture differed dramatically from that of Rome: In the agrarian and essentially self-sufficient communities of these nomadic peoples, fighting was a way of life and a highly respected skill. Armed with javelins and shields, Germanic warriors fought fiercely on foot and on horseback. Superb horsemen, the Germanic cavalry would come to borrow from the Mongols spurs and foot stirrups—devices (originating in China) that firmly secured the rider in his saddle and improved his driving force. In addition to introducing to the West superior methods of fighting on horseback, the Germanic tribes imposed their own longstanding traditions on medieval Europe. Every Germanic chieftain retained a band of warriors that followed him into battle, and every warrior anticipated sharing with his chieftain the spoils of victory. At the end of the first century, the Roman historian Tacitus (see chapter 6) wrote an account of the habits and customs of the Germanic peoples. He observes:

> All [men] are bound, to defend their leader . . . and to make even their own actions subservient to his renown. If he dies in the field, he who survives him survives to live in infamy. . . . This is the bond of union, the most sacred obligation. The chief fights for victory; the followers for their chief. . . . The chief must show his liberality, and the follower expects it. He demands, at one time this warlike horse, at another, that victorious lance drenched with the blood of the enemy.*

The bond of **fealty**, or loyalty, between the Germanic warrior and his chieftain and the practice of rewarding the warrior with land or the spoils of battle would become fundamental to the medieval practice of feudalism.

Germanic Law

Germanic law was not legislated by the state, as in Roman tradition, but was, rather, a collection of customs passed orally from generation to generation. Among the Germanic peoples, tribal chiefs were responsible for governing, but general assemblies met to make important decisions: Fully armed, clan warriors demonstrated their assent to propositions "in a military manner," according to Tacitus—by brandishing their javelins. Since warlike behavior was commonplace, tribal law was severe, uncompromising, and directed toward publicly shaming the guilty. Tacitus records that punishment for an adulterous wife was "instant, and inflicted by the husband. He cuts off the hair of his guilty wife, and having assembled her relations, expels her naked from his house, pursuing her with stripes through the village. To public loss of honor no favor is shown. She may possess beauty, youth and riches; but a husband she can never obtain."

As in most ancient societies—Hammurabi's Babylon, for instance—penalties for crimes varied according to the social standing of the guilty party. Among the Germanic tribes, however, a person's guilt or innocence might be

---

* *Tacitus: Historical Works*, translated by Arthur Murphey. London: J. M. Dent, 1907, 320–321.

determined by an ordeal involving fire or water; such trials reflected the faith Germanic peoples placed in the will of nature deities. Some of the names of these gods came to designate days of the week; for instance, the English word "Wednesday" derives from "Woden's day" and "Thursday" from "Thor's day." Similarly, the Germanic dependence on custom had a lasting influence on the development of law, and especially **common law**, in parts of the medieval West.

Germanic Literature

Germanic traditions, including those of personal valor and heroism associated with a warring culture, are reflected in the epic poems of the Early Middle Ages. The three most famous of these, *Beowulf*, *The Song of the Nibelungen*, and the *Song of Roland*, were transmitted orally for hundreds of years before they were written down sometime between the tenth and thirteenth centuries. *Beowulf*, which originated among the Anglo-Saxons around 700, was recorded in Old English, the Germanic language spoken in the British Isles between the fifth and eleventh centuries. *The Song of the Nibelungen*, a product of the Burgundian tribes, was recorded in Old German; and the Frankish *Song of Roland*, in Old French. Celebrating the deeds of warrior-heroes, these three epic poems have much in common with the *Iliad*, the *Mahabharata*, and other orally transmitted adventure poems.

The 3,000-line epic known as *Beowulf* is the first monumental literary composition in a European vernacular language. The tale of a daring Scandinavian prince, *Beowulf* brings to life the heroic world of the Germanic people with whom it originated. In unrhymed Old English verse embellished with numerous two-term metaphors known as **kennings** ("whale-path" for "sea," "ring-giver" for "king"), the poem recounts three major adventures: Beowulf's encounter with the monster Grendel, his destruction of Grendel's hideous and vengeful mother, and (some five decades later) his effort to destroy the fire-breathing dragon which threatens his people. These adventures—the stuff of legend, folk tale, and fantasy—immortalize the mythic origins of the Anglo-Saxons. Composed in the newly Christianized England of the eighth century, the poem was not written down for another two centuries. Only a full reading of *Beowulf* offers an appreciation of its significance as a work of art. However, the passage that follows—from a modern translation by Burton Raffel—offers an idea of the poem's vigorous style and narrative. The excerpt (lines 2510–2601 of the work), which describes Beowulf's assault on the fire-dragon, opens with a "battle-vow" that broadcasts the boastful courage of the epic hero. Those who wish to know the outcome of this gory contest must read further in the poem.

READING 2.13 From *Beowulf*

And Beowulf uttered his final boast: 1
   "I've never known fear; as a youth I fought
In endless battles. I am old, now,
But I will fight again, seek fame still,

If the dragon hiding in his tower dares   5
To face me."
   Then he said farewell to his followers,
Each in his turn, for the last time:
   "I'd use no sword, no weapon, if this beast
Could be killed without it, crushed to death   10
Like Grendel, gripped in my hands and torn
Limb from limb. But his breath will be burning
Hot, poison will pour from his tongue.
I feel no shame, with shield and sword
And armor, against this monster: when he comes to me
I mean to stand, not run from his shooting   15
Flames, stand till fate decides
Which of us wins. My heart is firm,
My hands calm: I need no hot
Words. Wait for me close by, my friends.
We shall see, soon, who will survive   20
This bloody battle, stand when the fighting
Is done. No one else could do
What I mean to, here, no man but me
Could hope to defeat this monster. No one
Could try. And this dragon's treasure, his gold   25
And everything hidden in that tower, will be mine
Or war will sweep me to a bitter death!"
   Then Beowulf rose, still brave, still strong,
And with his shield at his side, and a mail shirt on his breast,
Strode calmly, confidently, toward the tower, under   30
The rocky cliffs: no coward could have walked there!
And then he who'd endured dozens of desperate
Battles, who'd stood boldly while swords and shields
Clashed, the best of kings, saw
Huge stone arches and felt the heat   35
Of the dragon's breath, flooding down
Through the hidden entrance, too hot for anyone
To stand, a streaming current of fire
And smoke that blocked all passage. And the Geats'[1]
Lord and leader, angry, lowered   40
His sword and roared out a battle cry,
A call so loud and clear that it reached through
The hoary rock, hung in the dragon's
Ear. The beast rose, angry,
Knowing a man had come—and then nothing   45
But war could have followed. Its breath came first,
A steaming cloud pouring from the stone,
Then the earth itself shook. Beowulf
Swung his shield into place, held it
In front of him, facing the entrance. The dragon   50
Coiled and uncoiled, its heart urging it
Into battle. Beowulf's ancient sword
Was waiting, unsheathed, his sharp and gleaming
Blade. The beast came closer; both of them
Were ready, each set on slaughter. The Geats'   55
Great prince stood firm, unmoving, prepared
Behind his high shield, waiting in his shining
Armor. The monster came quickly toward him,
Pouring out fire and smoke, hurrying
To its fate. Flames beat at the iron   60

---
[1]The Scandinavian tribe led by Beowulf.

Shield, and for a time it held, protected
Beowulf as he'd planned; then it began to melt,
And for the first time in his life that famous prince
Fought with fate against him, with glory
Denied him. He knew it, but he raised his sword   65
And struck at the dragon's scaly hide.
The ancient blade broke, bit into
The monster's skin, drew blood, but cracked
And failed him before it went deep enough, helped him
Less than he needed. The dragon leaped   70
With pain, thrashed and beat at him, spouting
Murderous flames, spreading them everywhere.
And the Geats' ring-giver did not boast of glorious
Victories in other wars: his weapon
Had failed him, deserted him, now when he needed it   75
Most, that excellent sword. Edgetho's
Famous son stared at death,
Unwilling to leave this world, to exchange it
For a dwelling in some distant place—a journey
Into darkness that all men must make, as death   80
Ends their few brief hours on earth.

    Quickly, the dragon came at him, encouraged
As Beowulf fell back; its breath flared,
And he suffered, wrapped around in swirling
Flames—a king, before, but now   85
A beaten warrior. None of his comrades
Came to him, helped him, his brave and noble
Followers; they ran for their lives, fled
Deep in a wood. And only one of them
Remained, stood there, miserable, remembering,   90
As a good man must, what kinship should mean.

Germanic Art

The artistic production of nomadic peoples consists largely of easily transported objects such as carpets, jewelry, and weapons. Germanic folk often buried the most lavish of these items with their chieftains in boats that were cast out to sea (as described in *Beowulf*). In 1939, archeologists at Sutton Hoo in Eastern England excavated a seventh-century Anglo-Saxon grave that contained weapons, coins, utensils, jewelry, and a small lyre. These treasures were packed, along with the corpse of their chieftain, into an 89-foot-long ship that served as a tomb. Among the remarkable metalwork items found at Sutton Hoo were gold buckles, shoulder clasps, and the lid of a purse designed to hang from the chieftain's waistbelt (Figure 11.1). These objects are adorned with semiprecious stones and **cloisonné**—enamelwork produced by pouring molten colored glass between thin gold partitions (Figure 11.2). The purse lid is ornamented with a series of motifs: interlaced fighting animals, two frontal male figures between pairs of rampant beasts (compare Figure 2.2), and two curved-beaked predators attacking wild birds. These motifs explore the interface between man and beast in what was primarily a hunting society. A 5-pound gold belt buckle is ornamented with a dense pattern of interlaced snakes incised with a black sulfurous substance called **niello** (Figure 11.3). The high quality of so-called "barbarian"

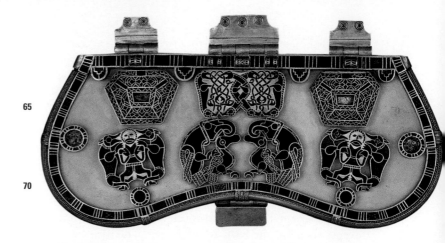

Figure 11.1 (above) Sutton Hoo purse cover, East Anglia, England, ca. 630. Gold with garnets and cloisonné enamel, 8 in. long. British Museum, London.

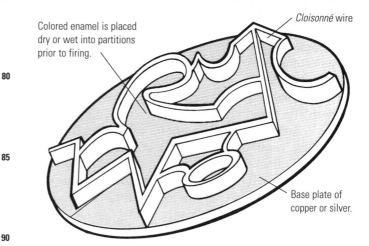

Colored enamel is placed dry or wet into partitions prior to firing.

Cloisonné wire

Base plate of copper or silver.

Base plate is enameled and permanently holds the partitions in place. They may also be soldered to the base metal before the first firing.

Figure 11.2 *Cloisonné* enameling process. From Richard Phipps and Richard Wink, *Introduction to the Gallery.* Copyright © 1987 Wm. C. Brown Publishers, Dubuque, Iowa. All rights reserved. Reprinted by permission.

art, as evidenced at Sutton Hoo and elsewhere, shows that technical sophistication and artistic originality were by no means the monopoly of "civilized" societies. It also demonstrates the continuous diffusion and exchange of styles across Asia and into Europe. The **zoomorphic** (animal-shaped) motifs found on the artifacts at Sutton Hoo, along with many of the metalwork techniques used in their fabrication, are evidence of contact between the Germanic tribes and the nomadic populations of Central Asia, who perpetuated the decorative traditions of ancient Persian, Scythian, and Chinese craftspeople.

As the Germanic tribes poured into Europe, their art and their culture commingled with that of the people with whom they came into contact. A classic example is the fusion of Celtic and Anglo-Saxon styles. The Celts were a non-Germanic, Iron Age folk that had migrated throughout Europe between the fifth and third centuries B.C.E., settling in the British Isles before the time of Christ. A great flowering of Celtic art and literature occurred in Ireland and England following the conversion of the Celts to Christianity in the fifth century C.E. The instrument of this conversion was the fabled Saint Patrick (ca. 385–461), the British monk who is said to have baptized

Figure 11.3 Buckle, from Sutton Hoo, first half of seventh century C.E. Gold and niello, length 5¼in., weight 5 lb. Reproduced by courtesy of the Trustees of the British Museum, London.

Figure 11.4 Bishop Eadfrith (?), "Carpet Page," from the Lindisfarne Gospels, ca. 698–721 C.E. Vellum, 13½ × 9¾ in. British Library, London.

more than 120,000 people and founded three hundred churches in Ireland. In the centuries thereafter, Anglo-Irish monasteries produced a number of extraordinary illuminated manuscripts, the decorative style of which is closely related to the dynamic linear ornamentation of the Sutton Hoo artifacts.

The visual masterpiece of an otherwise bleak period in the West, the seventh-century Lindisfarne Gospels, comes from a monastery located on an island off the east coast of England. In the pages of this remarkable Gospel book, naturalistic representation of the kind associated with classical culture has disappeared entirely. The precisely drawn Lindisfarne "carpet page"—so called for its resemblance to a woven fabric—is dominated by a magnificent **cruciform** (cross-shaped) design (Figure **11.4**), but the entire spatial field writhes with knotted, ribbonlike shapes resembling those on the Sutton Hoo belt buckle (see Figure 11.3). Looking every bit like a metalwork surface or a woven rug, the carpet page combines the illusion of compositional order with a sense of labyrinthine movement. Analysis of the design shows, however, that one's initial impression of perfect symmetry is mistaken, for the composition involves a complex system of mirror images and subtly var-

ied shapes, lines, and colors. The influence of Germanic design in Christian manuscript illumination is a dramatic example of cultural syncretism (the combination of different practices and principles), but it also raises another matter—the similarity between Germanic and Islamic art styles. As did Islamic artists, the Germanic tribes distilled the decorative traditions of Persia, Egypt, and the Mediterranean into a style marked by complex, rhythmically meandering surface designs. Whether the sophisticated abstract vocabularies of these two bodies of art—Germanic and Islamic—are symbolic of the wandering lifestyles of these originally nomadic peoples (as some scholars have suggested), or whether closeness to nature generated a set of unique but similar design principles, may be left to speculation.

The Germanic style influenced not only the illumination of Christian manuscripts, but also the decoration of Christian liturgical objects, such as the **paten** (Eucharistic plate) and the **chalice** (Eucharistic cup). Employed in the celebration of the Mass, these objects usually commanded the finest and most costly materials; and, like the manuscripts that accompanied the sacred rites, they received inordinate care in execution. The Ardagh Chalice, made

his nephew Roland as Charlemagne returned from an expedition against the Muslims in Spain—this *chanson de geste* ("song of heroic deeds") captures the spirit of the Early Middle Ages. Transmitted orally for three centuries, the four-thousand-line poem was not written down until the early 1100s. Generation after generation of *jongleurs* (professional entertainers) wandered from court to court, chanting the story (and possibly embellishing it with episodes of folklore) to the accompaniment of a lyre. Though the music for the poem has not survived, it is likely that it consisted of a single and highly improvised line of melody. The melody was probably syllabic (one note to each syllable) and—like folk song—dependent on simple repetition. As with other works in the oral tradition (the *Epic of Gilgamesh* and the *Iliad*, for instance), the *Song of Roland* is grandiose in its dimensions and profound in its lyric power. Its rugged Old French verse describes a culture that prized the performance of heroic deeds that brought honor to the warrior, his lord, and his religion. The strong bond of loyalty between vassal and chieftain that characterized the Germanic way of life resonates in Roland's declaration of unswerving devotion to his temporal overlord, Charlemagne.

The *Song of Roland* brings to life such aspects of early medieval culture as the practice of naming one's battle gear and weapons (often considered sacred), the dependence on cavalry, the glorification of blood-and-thunder heroism, and the strong sense of comradeship among men-at-arms. Women play almost no part in the epic. The feudal contract did not exclude members of the clergy; hence Archbishop Turpin fights with lance and spear, despite the fact that Church law forbade members of the clergy to shed another man's blood. (Some members of the clergy got around this law by arming themselves with a **mace**—a spike-headed club that could knock one's armored opponent off his horse or do damage short of bloodshed.) Roland's willingness to die for his religious beliefs, fired by the Archbishop's promise of admission into Paradise for those who fall fighting the infidels (in this case, the Muslims), suggests that the militant fervor of Muslims was matched by that of early medieval Christians. Indeed, the *Song of Roland* captures the powerful antagonism between Christians and Muslims that dominated all of medieval history and culminated in the Christian Crusades described later in this chapter.

The descriptive language of the *Song of Roland* is stark, unembellished, and vivid: "He feels his brain gush out," reports the poet in verse 168. Such directness and simplicity lend immediacy to the action. Characters are stereotypical ("Roland's a hero, and Oliver is wise," verse 87), and groups of people are characterized with epic expansiveness: *All* Christians are good and *all* Muslims are bad. The figure of Roland epitomizes the ideals of physical courage, religious devotion, and personal loyalty. Yet, in his refusal to call for assistance from Charlemagne and his troops, who have already retreated across the Pyrenees, he exhibits a foolhardiness—perhaps a "tragic flaw"—that leads him and his warriors to their deaths.

READING 2.14   From the *Song of Roland*

81

Count Oliver has climbed up on a hill;   1
From there he sees the Spanish lands below,
And Saracens[1] assembled in great force.
Their helmets gleam with gold and precious stones,
Their shields are shining, their hauberks[2] burnished gold,   5
Their long sharp spears with battle flags unfurled.
He tries to see how many men there are:
Even battalions are more than he can count.
And in his heart Oliver is dismayed;
Quick as he can, he comes down from the height,   10
And tells the Franks what they will have to fight.

82

Oliver says, "Here come the Saracens—
A greater number no man has ever seen!
The first host carries a hundred thousand shields,
Their helms are laced, their hauberks shining white,   15
From straight wood handles rise ranks of burnished spears.
You'll have a battle like none on earth before!
Frenchmen, my lords, now God give you the strength
To stand your ground, and keep us from defeat."
They say, "God's curse on those who quit the field!   20
We're yours till death—not one of us will yield."   AOI[3]

83

Oliver says, "The pagan might is great—
It seems to me, our Franks are very few!
Roland, my friend, it's time to sound your horn;
King Charles[4] will hear, and bring his army back."   25
Roland replies, "You must think I've gone mad!
In all sweet France I'd forfeit my good name!
No! I will strike great blows with Durendal,[5]
Crimson the blade up to the hilt of gold.
To those foul pagans I promise bitter woe—   30
They all are doomed to die at Roncevaux!"[6]   AOI

84

"Roland, my friend, let the Oliphant[7] sound!
King Charles will hear it, his host will all turn back,
His valiant barons will help us in this fight."
Roland replies, "Almighty God forbid   35
That I bring shame upon my family,
And cause sweet France to fall into disgrace!
I'll strike that horde with my good Durendal;

---

[1]Another name for Muslims.
[2]Long coats of chain mail.
[3]The letters AOI have no known meaning but probably signify a musical appendage or refrain that occurred at the end of each stanza.
[4]Charlemagne.
[5]Roland's sword.
[6]"The gate of Spain," a narrow pass in the Pyrenees where the battle takes place.
[7]A horn made from an elephant's tusk.

My sword is ready, girded here at my side,
And soon you'll see its keen blade dripping blood.   40
The Saracens will curse the evil day
They challenged us, for we will make them pay."   AOI

85

"Roland, my friend I pray you, sound your horn!
King Charlemagne, crossing the mountain pass,
Won't fail, I swear it, to bring back all his Franks."   45
"May God forbid!" Count Roland answers then.
"No man on earth shall have the right to say
That I for pagans sounded the Oliphant!
I will not bring my family to shame.
I'll fight this battle; my Durendal shall strike   50
A thousand blows and seven hundred more;
You'll see bright blood flow from the blade's keen steel.
We have good men; their prowess will prevail,
And not one Spaniard shall live to tell the tale."

86

Oliver says, "Never would you be blamed;   55
I've seen the pagans, the Saracens of Spain.
They fill the valleys, cover the mountain peaks;
On every hill, and every wide-spread plain,
Vast hosts assemble from that alien race;
Our company numbers but very few."   60
Roland replies, "The better, then, we'll fight!
If it please God and His angelic host,
I won't betray the glory of sweet France!
Better to die than learn to live with shame—
Charles loves us more as our keen swords win fame."   65

87

Roland's a hero, and Oliver is wise;
Both are so brave men marvel at their deeds.
When they mount chargers, take up their swords and shields,
Not death itself could drive them from the field.
They are good men; their words are fierce and proud.   70
With wrathful speed the pagans ride to war.
Oliver says, "Roland, you see them now.
They're very close, the king too far away.
You were too proud to sound the Oliphant:
If Charles were with us, we would not come to grief.   75
Look up above us, close to the Gate of Spain:
There stands the guards—who would not pity them!
To fight this battle means not to fight again."
Roland replies, "Don't speak so foolishly!
Cursed be the heart that cowers in the breast!   80
We'll hold our ground; if they will meet us here,
Our foes will find us ready with sword and spear."   AOI

88

When Roland sees the fight will soon begin,
Lions and leopards are not so fierce as he.
Calling the Franks, he says to Oliver: 85
"Noble companion, my friend, don't talk that way!
The Emperor Charles, who left us in command

Of twenty thousand he chose to guard the pass,
Made very sure no coward's in their ranks.
In his lord's service a man must suffer pain,   90
Bitterest cold and burning heat endure;
He must be willing to lose his flesh and blood.
Strike with your lance, and I'll wield Durendal—
The king himself presented it to me—
And if I die, whoever takes my sword   95
Can say its master has nobly served his lord."

89

Archbishop Turpin comes forward then to speak.
He spurs his horse and gallops up a hill,
Summons the Franks, and preaches in these words:
"My noble lords, Charlemagne left us here,   100
And may our deaths do honor to the king!
Now you must help defend our holy Faith!
Before your eyes you see the Saracens.
Confess your sins, ask God to pardon you;
I'll grant you absolution to save your souls.   105
Your deaths would be a holy martyrdom,
And you'll have places in highest Paradise."
The French dismount; they kneel upon the ground.
Then the archbishop, blessing them in God's name,
Told them, for penance, to strike when battle came.   110

. . . .

91

At Roncevaux Count Roland passes by,
Riding his charger, swift-running Veillantif.[8]
He's armed for battle, splendid in shining mail.
As he parades, he brandishes his lance.
Turning the point straight up against the sky,   115
And from the spearhead a banner flies, pure white,
With long gold fringes that beat against his hands.
Fair to behold, he laughs, serene and gay.
Now close behind him comes Oliver, his friend,
With all the Frenchmen cheering their mighty lord.   120
Fiercely his eyes confront the Saracens;
Humbly and gently he gazes at the Franks,
Speaking to them with gallant courtesy:
"Barons, my lords, softly now, keep the pace!
Here come the pagans looking for martyrdom.   125
We'll have such plunder before the day is out,
As no French king has ever won before!"
And at this moment the armies join in war.   AOI

. . . .

161

The pagans flee, furious and enraged,
Trying their best to get away in Spain.   130
Count Roland lacks the means to chase them now,
For he has lost his war-horse Veillantif;
Against his will he has to go on foot.

———

[8]Roland's horse.

Figure 11.18 *Women and Men Reaping*, from the Luttrell Psalter, ca. 1340. Reproduced by permission of the British Library, London, Add. MS 42130, f.172.

800	rigging (gear that controls ships' sails to take advantage of the wind) is invented by the Vikings
900	horse collars come into use in Europe
1050	crossbows are first used in France
ca. 1150	the first windmills appear in Europe

resentations of lower-class life. As illustrations from the Luttrell Psalter indicate, peasant women worked alongside men in raising crops: sowing, reaping, gleaning, threshing, and assisting even in the most backbreaking of farming tasks (Figure 11.18). Medieval women were associated with the professions that involved food-preparation (milking, raising vegetables, brewing, and baking) and the making of cloth (sheep-shearing, carting, spinning, and weaving). The distaff, the pole on which fibers were wound prior to spinning, came to be a symbol of women's work and (universally) of womankind. But lower-class women also shared their husbands' domestic tasks and day to day responsibilities that few noblewomen shared with their upper-class partners.

The Christian Crusades

During the eleventh century, numerous circumstances contributed to a change in the character of medieval life. The Normans effectively pushed the Muslims out of the Mediterranean Sea and, as the Normans and other marauders began to settle down, Europeans enjoyed a greater degree of security. At the same time, rising agricultural productivity and surplus encouraged trade and travel. The Christian Crusades of the eleventh to thirteenth centuries were directly related to these changes. They were both a cause of economic revitalization and a symptom of the increased freedom and new mobility of Western Europeans during the High Middle Ages (ca. 1000–1300).

The Crusades began in an effort to rescue Jerusalem from Muslim Turks who were threatening the Byzantine Empire and denying Christian pilgrims access to the Holy Land. At the request of the Byzantine emperor, the Roman Catholic Church launched a series of military expeditions designed to regain territories dominated by the Turks. The First Crusade, called by Pope Urban II in 1095, began in the spirit of a Holy War but, unlike the Muslim *jihad*, the intention was to recover land, not to convert pagans. Thousands of people—both laymen and clergy—"took up the Cross" and marched overland through Europe to the Byzantine East (Map **11.3**). It soon became apparent, however, that the material benefits of the Crusades outweighed the spiritual ones, especially since the campaigns provided economic and military opportunities for the younger sons of the nobility. While the eldest son of an upper-class family inherited his father's fief under the principle of **primogeniture**, his younger brothers were left to seek their own fortunes. The Crusades stirred the ambitions of these disenfranchised young men. Equally ambitious were the Italian city-states. Eager to expand their commercial activities, they encouraged the Crusaders to become middlemen in trade between Italy and the East. In the course of the Fourth Crusade, Venetian profit seekers persuaded the Crusaders to sack Constantinople and capture trade ports in the Aegean in the interest of Venetian trade. Moral inhibitions failed to restrain the vampires of greed and, in 1204, the Fourth Crusade deteriorated into a contest for personal profit. A disastrous postscript to the Fourth Crusade was the Children's Crusade of 1212, in which thousands of children, aged between ten and fourteen, set out to recapture Jerusalem. Almost all died or were taken into slavery before reaching the Holy Land.

Aside from such economic advantages as those enjoyed by individual Crusaders and the Italian city-states, the gains made by the Crusades were slight. In the first of the four major expeditions, the Crusaders did retake some important cities, including Jerusalem. But by 1291, all recaptured lands were lost again to the Muslims. Indeed, in over two hundred years of fighting, the Christian Crusaders did not secure any territory permanently, nor did they stop the westward advance of the Turks. Constantinople finally fell in 1453 to a later wave of Muslim Turks.

Despite their failure as religious ventures, the Crusades had enormous consequences for the West: The revival of

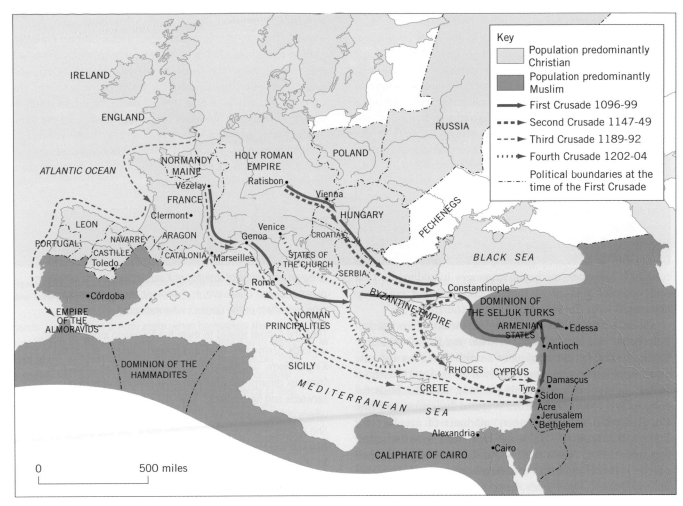

Map 11.3 The Major Crusades, 1096–1204.

trade between East and West enhanced European commercial life, encouraging the rise of towns and bringing great wealth to the cities of Venice, Genoa, and Pisa in Italy. Then, too, in the absence or death of crusading noblemen, feudal lords (including emperors and kings) seized every opportunity to establish greater authority over the lands within their domains, thus consolidating and centralizing political power in the embryonic nation-states of England and France. Finally, renewed contact with Byzantium promoted an atmosphere of commercial and cultural receptivity that had not existed since Roman times. Luxury goods, such as saffron, citrus, silks, and damasks, entered Western Europe, as did sacred relics associated with the lives of Jesus, Mary, and the Christian saints. And, to the delight of the literate, Arabic transla-

tions of Greek manuscripts poured into France, along with all genres of Islamic literature (see chapter 10).

The Medieval Romance and the Code of Courtly Love

The Crusades inspired the writing of chronicles that were an admixture of historical fact, Christian lore, and stirring fiction. As such histories had broad appeal in an age of increasing upper-class literacy, they came to be written in the everyday language of the layperson—the vernacular—rather than in Latin. The Crusades also contributed to the birth of the **medieval romance**, a fictitious tale of love and adventure that became the most popular form of literary entertainment in the West between the years 1200 and 1500. Medieval romances first appeared in twelfth-century France in the form of rhymed verse, but later ones were written in prose. While romances were probably recited before a small, courtly audience rather than read individually, the development of the form coincided with the rise of a European "textual culture," that is, a culture dependent on written language rather than on oral tradition. In this textual culture, vernacular languages gained importance for intimate kinds of literature, while Latin remained the official language of Church and state.

The "spice" of the typical medieval romance was an illicit relationship or forbidden liaison between a man and

ca. 1150	magnetic compasses appear in Europe
1233	the first coal mines are opened in Newcastle, England
1240	European shipbuilders adopt the use of the rudder from the Arabs
1249	Muslims use gunpowder against Christian Crusaders

She laughs to hear my deepest sighs—
then silently I'll leave her sight.
I cast my love of her away. 45
She struck and I accept the blow.
She will not speak and I must stray
in exile. Where, I do not know.

Tristan, I've made an end, I say.
I'm going—where, I do not know. 50
My song is dying, and away
all love and joy I cast, and go.

Peire Cardenal's "Lonely the rich need never be"

Lonely the rich need never be, 1
they have such constant company.

For Wickedness in front we see,
behind, all round, and far and wide.
The giant called Cupidity 5
is always hulking at their side.
Injustice waves the flag, and he
is led along by Pride . . .

If a poor man has snitched a bit of rag,
he goes with downcast head and frightened eye. 10
But when the rich thief fills his greedy bag,
he marches on with head still held as high.
The poor man's hanged, he stole a rotten bridle.
The man who hanged him stole the horse. O fie.
To hang poor thieves the rich thieves still aren't idle. 15
That kind of justice arrow-swift will fly . . .

Figure 11.20 "Herr Konrad von Altretten," *Medieval Lovers*, from the Manesse Codex, Zürich, ca. 1315–1330. Universitätsbibliothek, Heidelberg, Germany, MS Pal. germ. 848, f.84. Rheinisches Köln Bildarchiv, Cologne, Germany.

The rich are charitable? Yes,
as Cain who slew his brother Abel.
They're thieves, no wolves as merciless.
They're liars, like a whoreshop-babel.   20
O stick their ribs, O stick their souls!
No truth comes bubbling from the holes,
but lies. Their greedy hearts, abhorrent,
are rabid as a mountain-torrent . . .

With loving-kindness how they quicken,   25
what hoards of charity they spread.
If all the stones were loaves of bread,
if all the streams with wine should thicken,
the hills turn bacon or boiled chicken,
they'd give no extra crumb. That's flat,   30
   Some people are like that.

The Countess of Dia's "I've been in great anguish"

I've been in great anguish   1
over a noble knight I once had,
and I want everyone to know, for all time,
that I loved him—too much!
Now I see I'm betrayed   5
because I didn't yield my love to him.

For that I've suffered greatly,
both in my bed and when I'm fully clad.

How I'd yearn to have my knight
in my naked arms for one night!   10
He would feel a frenzy of delight
only to have me for his pillow.
I'm more in love with him
than Blancheflor ever was with Floris.[1]
To him I'd give my heart, my love,   15
my mind, my eyes, my life.

Beautiful, gracious, sweet friend,
when shall I hold you in my power?
If I could lie with you for one night,
and give you a kiss of love,   20
you can be sure I would desire greatly
to grant you a husband's place,
as long as you promised
to do everything I wished!

---

[1]The lovers in a popular medieval romance.

The Rise of Medieval Towns

Observing the plight of the poor at the hands of the rich, Peire Cardenal condemns a universal condition; but his poem discloses a new social consciousness associated with economic change. During the High Middle Ages, a class of people "midway" between serfs and landlords—the middle class—was emerging. Many factors, including increased agricultural production and the reopening of trade routes, encouraged the rise of the middle class. During the eleventh century, merchants (often younger sons of noble families) engaged in commercial enterprises that promoted the growth of local markets. Usually established near highways or rivers, outside the walls of the fortified castle (*bourg* in French, *burg* in German, *borough* in English), the trade market became an essential part of manorial life. The permanent market (or *faubourg*) provided the basis for the medieval town—an urban center that attracted farmers and artisans who might buy freedom from their lord or simply run away from the manor. "City air makes a man free" was the cry of those who had discovered the urban alternative to manorial life.

In the newly established towns, the middle class pursued profit from commercial exchange. Merchants and craftspeople in like occupations formed **guilds** for the mutual protection of buyers and sellers. The guilds regulated prices, fixed wages, established standards of quality in the production of goods, and provided training for newcomers in each profession. During the eleventh and twelfth centuries, urban dwellers purchased charters of self-government from lords in whose fiefs their towns were situated. Such charters allowed townspeople (in French, *bourgeois*; in German, *Burghers*) to establish municipal governments and regulate their own economic activities. Such commercial centers as Milan, Florence, and Venice became completely self-governing city-states similar to those of ancient Greece and Rome. The Flemish cities of Bruges and Antwerp exported fine linen and wool to England and to towns along the Baltic Sea. The spirit of urban growth was manifested in the construction of defensive stone walls that protected the citizens, as at Carcassonne in Southwestern France (Figure **11.21**), and in the building of cathedrals and guildhalls that flanked the open marketplace. Although by the twelfth century town dwellers constituted less than fifteen percent of the

Figure 11.21 The walled city of Carcassonne, France, twelfth–thirteenth centuries. Arch. Robert Harding Picture Library, London.

total European population, the middle class continued to expand and ultimately came to dominate Western society.

Middle-class values differed considerably from those of the feudal nobility. Whereas warfare and chivalry preoccupied the nobility, financial prosperity and profit were the principal concerns of the middle class. In European cities, there evolved a lively vernacular literature expressive of middle-class concerns. It included humorous narrative tales (*fabliaux*) and poems (*dits*) describing urban occupations, domestic conflict, and street and tavern life (Figure 11.22). These popular genres, which feature such stereotypes as the miserly husband and the lecherous monk, slyly reflect many of the social tensions and sexual prejudices of the day. A favorite theme of medieval *fabliaux* and *dits* was the antifemale diatribe, a denunciation of women as bitter as Juvenal's (see chapter 6), and one that was rooted in a long tradition of misogyny (the hatred of women). While medieval romances generally cast the female in a positive light, *fabliaux* and *dits* often described all women as sinful and seductive. The hostile attitude toward womankind, intensified perhaps by women's increasing participation in some of the commercial activities traditionally dominated by men, is readily apparent in both urban legislation and in the popular literature of the late

Figure 11.22 *Young Lady Shopping for Belts and Purses,* from the Manesse Codex, Zürich, ca. 1315-1333. Universitätsbibliothek, Heidelberg, Germany, MS Pal. germ. 848, f.64. Rheinisches Köln Bildarchiv, Cologne, Germany.

thirteenth century. The following verse, based on a widely circulated proverb, voices a popular male complaint:

> He who takes a wife trades peace for strife,
> Long weariness, despair, oppress his life,
> A heavy load, a barrel full of chatter,
> Uncorkable, her gossip makes a clatter,
> Now, ever since I took a wife,
> Calamity has marred my life.*

SUMMARY

The progress of the medieval West reflects the commingling of three cultural ingredients: classical, Christian, and Germanic. The westward migrations of the Germanic tribes threatened the stability of the already waning Roman civilization. Nevertheless, these tribes introduced customs and values that came to shape the character of the European Middle Ages. In the first five hundred years of the first millennium, Germanic languages, laws, and forms of artistic expression fused with those of the late Roman and newly Christianized world to fix the patterns of early medieval life. The epic *Beowulf* and the art of Sutton Hoo are two examples of Germanic cultural achievement. By the eighth century, the Empire of the Frankish ruler Charlemagne had become the cultural oasis of the West. Under Charlemagne's influence, much of Europe converted to Christianity, while members of his court worked to encourage education and the arts. In the turbulent century following the fragmentation of the Carolingian Empire, feudalism—the exchange of land for military service— gave noblemen the power to rule locally while providing protection from outside attack. The artistic monuments of the Early Middle Ages—the *Song of Roland*, the Norman castle, and the Bayeux Tapestry—all describe a heroic age that glorified feudal combat, male prowess, and the conquest of land. Manorialism, the economic basis for medieval society, offered the lower classes physical protection in exchange for food production, but it left in its wake little tangible evidence of the lives and values of the majority of the population.

The Christian Crusades—the definitive expression of Christian-Muslim hostility—altered early medieval patterns of economic and cultural life, even as they reflected the new mobility of Europe's High Middle Ages. In the literature of the medieval court, sentiment and sensuousness replaced heroic idealism and chivalric chastity. Romantic love, a medieval invention, dominated both the vernacular romance and *troubadour* poetry. The Crusades also encouraged the rise of towns and trade dominated by a new middle class, whose ambitions were distinctly materialistic and profit oriented. The values of merchants and craftspeople differed from those of the feudal nobility, for whom land provided the basis of wealth and chivalry

*"The Vices of Women," in *Three Medieval Views of Women*, translated by Gloria K. Fiero et al. New Haven: Yale University Press, 1989, 129, 131.

dictated manners and morals. Vernacular tales and poems often satirized inequality between classes and antagonism between sexes. Changing patterns of secular life between the years 750 and 1300 reflect the shift from a feudal society to an urban one distinguished by increasingly complex social interactions between male and female, lord and vassal, farmer and merchant.

SUGGESTIONS FOR READING

Bruce-Mitford, Rupert. *The Sutton Hoo Ship-Burial: A Handbook.* London: British Museum, 1972.

Bury, J. B. *Invasions of Europe by the Barbarians.* New York: Norton, 2000.

Diebold, William J. *Word and Image: An Introduction to Early Medieval Art.* New York: Harpercollins, 2000.

Dodwell, C. R. *The Pictorial Arts of the West 800–1200.* New Haven: Yale University Press, 1992.

Duby, George. *Love and Marriage in the Middle Ages*, translated by Jane Dunnett. Chicago: University of Chicago Press, 1994.

Erickson, Carolly. *Life in a Medieval City.* New York: Harper, 1981.

Gies, Frances, and J. Gies. *Life in a Medieval Village.* New York: Harper, 1991.

Herlihy, David. *Opera Muliera: Women and Work in Medieval Europe.* New York: McGraw-Hill, 1990.

Labarge, Margaret Wade. *A Small Sound of the Trumpet: Women in Medieval Life.* Boston: Beacon Press, 1986.

Lewis, Archibald R. *Knights and Samurai: Feudalism in Northern France and Japan.* London: Temple Smith, 1974.

Maalouf, Amin. *The Crusades Through Arab Eyes.* New York: Schocken, 1984.

Stephenson, Carl. *Medieval Feudalism.* Ithaca, N.Y.: Cornell University Press, 1973.

Trevor-Roper, Hugh. *The Rise of Christian Europe.* New York: Norton, 1989.

MUSIC LISTENING SELECTION

CD One Selection 6 Bernart de Ventadour, "Can vei la lauzeta mover" ("When I behold the lark"), ca. 1150, excerpt.

GLOSSARY

chain mail a flexible medieval armor made of interlinked metal rings

chalice a goblet; in Christian liturgy, the Eucharistic cup

chanson de geste (French, "song of heroic deeds") an epic poem of the Early Middle Ages

chivalry a code of behavior practiced by upper-class men and women of medieval society

cloisonné (French, *cloison*, meaning "fence") an enameling technique produced by pouring molten colored glass between thin metal strips secured to a metal surface; any object ornamented in this manner (see Figure 11.2)

common law the body of unwritten law developed primarily from judicial decisions based on custom and precedent; the basis of the English legal system and that of all states in the United States with the exception of Louisiana

crenellations tooth-shaped battlements surmounting a wall and used for defensive combat

cruciform cross-shaped

fealty loyalty; the fidelity of the warrior to his chieftain

feudalism the system of political organization prevailing in Europe between the ninth and fifteenth centuries and having as its basis the exchange of land for military defense

fief in feudal society, land or property given to a warrior in return for military service

gilt gold-surfaced; covered with gold paint or gold foil

guild an association of merchants or craftspeople organized according to occupation

investiture the procedure by which a feudal lord granted a vassal control over a fief

jongleur a professional entertainer who wandered from court to court in medieval Europe

joust a form of personal combat, usually with lances on horseback, between men-at-arms

keep a square tower, the strongest and most secure part of the medieval castle (see Figure 11.14)

kenning a two-term metaphor used in Old English verse

lord any member of the feudal nobility who invested a vassal with a fief

mace a heavy, spike-headed club used as a weapon in medieval combat

medieval romance a tale of adventure that supplanted the older *chanson de geste* and that deals with knights, kings, and ladies acting under the impulse of love, religious faith, or the desire for adventure

moat a wide trench, usually filled with water, surrounding a fortified place such as a castle (see Figure 11.14)

niello a black sulfurous substance used as a decorative inlay for incised metal surfaces; the art or process of decorating metal in this manner

paten a shallow dish; in Christian liturgy, the Eucharistic plate

primogeniture the principle by which a fief was passed from father to eldest son

renaissance (French, "rebirth") a revival of the learning of former and especially classical culture

serf an unfree peasant

vassal any member of the feudal nobility who vowed to serve a lord in exchange for control of a fief

zoomorphic animal-shaped; having the form of an animal

CHAPTER TWELVE

Christianity and the medieval mind

"All earthly things is but vanity:
Beauty, Strength, and Discretion do man forsake,
Foolish friends and kinsmen, that fair spake,
All fleeth save Good Deeds . . ."
Everyman

For a thousand years after the fall of Rome (ca. 500–1500), the Catholic Church was the primary source of spiritual authority and religious leadership in the European West. Longstanding disagreements over doctrinal, political, and liturgical matters resulted, in 1054, in a permanent breach between the Roman Catholic Church in the West and the Greek Orthodox Church in the East. Both churches, however, shared the view that the terrestrial world mirrored a divine order that was sustained through the ministry of God's representatives on earth. Church doctrine and liturgy gave coherence and meaning to everyday life. More important, the Church offered the sole means by which the medieval Christian might achieve life everlasting.

The Christian Way of Life and Death

The promise of personal immortality was central to Christianity and to the medieval worldview. With the exception of the purest forms of Hinduism and Buddhism, which anticipate the extinction of the Self, most world religions have met the fear of death with an ideology (a body of doctrine supported by myth and symbols) that promises the survival of some aspect of the Self in a life hereafter. The nature of that hereafter usually depends on the moral status of the believer—that is, his or her conduct on earth.

Christianity addressed the question of personal salvation more effectively than any other world religion. Indeed, the Christian immortality ideology* provided a system by which medieval Christians achieved final victory over death. Through the **sacraments**, a set of sacred acts that impart **grace** (the free and unearned favor of God), medieval Christians were assured of the soul's redemption from sin and, ultimately, of eternal life in the world to come. The seven sacraments—the number fixed by the

---

*The phrase is from Ernest Becker, *The Denial of Death*. New York: The Free Press, 1973.

Fourth Lateran Council of 1215—touched every significant phase of human life: At birth, baptism purified the recipient of Original Sin; confirmation admitted the baptized to full church privileges; ordination invested those entering the clergy with priestly authority; matrimony blessed the union of man and woman; penance acknowledged repentance of sins and offered absolution; Eucharist—the central and most important of the sacraments—joined human beings to God by means of the body and blood of Jesus; and finally, just prior to death, extreme unction provided final absolution from sins.

By way of the sacraments, the Church participated in virtually every major aspect of the individual's life, enforcing a set of values that determined the collective spirituality of Christendom. Since only Church officials could administer the sacraments, the clergy held a "monopoly" on personal salvation. Medieval Christians thus looked to representatives of the Mother Church as shepherds guiding the members of their flock on their long and hazardous journey from cradle to grave. Their conduct on earth determined whether their souls went to Heaven, Hell, or Purgatory (the place of purification from sins). But only by way of the clergy might they receive the gifts of grace that made salvation possible.

By the twelfth century, the Christian concepts of sin and divine justice had become ever more complex: Church councils defined Purgatory as an intermediate realm occupied by the soul after death (and before the Last Judgment). In Purgatory punishment was imposed for the unexpiated but repented sins committed in mortal life. While ordinary Christians might suffer punishment in Purgatory, they might also benefit from prayers and good works offered on their behalf. The role of the priesthood in providing such forms of remission from sin would give the medieval Church unassailable power and authority.

The Literature of Mysticism

Most of the religious literature of the Middle Ages was didactic—that is, it served to teach and instruct. Visionary literature, however, functioned in two other ways. It reflected an individual's intuitive and direct knowledge of God (thus constituting a form of autobiography); and it conjured vivid images of the supernatural (thus providing a vocabulary by which the unknowable might actually be known). The leading mystic of the twelfth century, Hildegard of Bingen (1098–1179) was an extraordinary individual. Entering a Benedictine convent at the age of eight, she went on to become its abbess. A scholar of both Latin and her native Germany, she wrote three visionary tracts, treatises on natural science, medicine and the treatment of disease, an allegorical dialogue between the vices and the virtues, and a cycle of seventy-seven songs arranged for devotional performance (see Chapter 13). While some regard Hildegard as the *first* in a long line of female visionaries, she more accurately follows a long line of mystics and seers whose history begins in antiquity (most famously represented by the Delphic priestesses and the Roman sibyls). One of the first great Christian mystics, however, Hildegard produced original works on such topics as the nature of the universe, the meaning of Scripture, and the destiny of the Christian soul. The Church confirmed the divine source of her visions and, along with most of her contemporaries, acknowledged her prophetic powers. In the following selection from *Scivias*, short for *Scito vias domini* (*Know the Ways of the Lord*), her encounter with the "voice from heaven" is followed by two of her most compelling visions. The miniature accompanying one of these visions (Figure **12.1**)—like all of those that illustrate her manuscripts—was supervised by Hildegard herself.

READING 2.17 From Hildegard of Bingen's *Know the Ways of the Lord* (ca. 1146)

1. A Solemn Declaration Concerning the True Vision Flowing from God: *Scivias*. Protestificatio

Lo! In the forty-third year of my temporal course, when I clung **1** to a celestial vision with great fear and tremulous effort, I saw a great splendor. In it came a voice from heaven, saying:

"O frail mortal, both ash of ashes, and rottenness of rottenness, speak and write down what you see and hear. But because you are fearful of speaking, simple at expounding, and unlearned in writing—speak and write, not according to the speech of man or according to the intelligence of human invention, or following the aim of human composition, but according to what you see and hear from the heavens above in **10** the wonders of God! Offer explanations of them, just as one who hears and understands the words of an instructor willingly makes them public, revealing and teaching them according to the sense of the instructor's discourse. You, therefore, O mortal, speak also the things you see and hear. Write them, not according to yourself or to some other person, but according to the will of the Knower, Seer, and Ordainer of all things in the secrets of their mysteries."

And again I heard the voice from heaven saying to me: "Speak these wonders and write the things taught in this **20** manner—and speak!"

Figure 12.1 Hildegard of Bingen, Scivias, ca. 1146. Rheinisches Bildarchiv, MS 13 321, Wiesbaden Codex B, folio 1.

It happened in the year 1141 of the Incarnation of the Son of God, Jesus Christ, when I was forty-two years and seven months old, that a fiery light of the greatest radiance coming from the open heavens flooded through my entire brain. It kindled my whole breast like a flame that does not scorch but warms in the same way the sun warms anything on which it sheds its rays.

Suddenly I understood the meaning of books, that is, the Psalms and the Gospels; and I knew other catholic books of **30** the Old as well as the New Testaments—not the significance of the words of the text, or the division of the syllables, nor did I consider an examination of the cases and tenses.

Indeed, from the age of girlhood, from the time that I was fifteen until the present, I had perceived in myself, just as until this moment, a power of mysterious, secret, and marvelous visions of a miraculous sort. However, I revealed these things to no one, except to a few religious persons who were living under the same vows as I was. But meanwhile, until this time when God in his grace has willed these things to be revealed, **40** I have repressed them in quiet silence.

But I have not perceived these visions in dreams, or asleep, or in a delirium, or with my bodily eyes, or with my external mortal ears, or in secreted places, but I received them awake and looking attentively about me with an unclouded mind, in open places, according to God's will. However this may be, it is difficult for carnal man to fathom. . . .

2. The Iron-Colored Mountain and the Radiant One: *Scivias*. Book I, Vision 1

I saw what seemed to be a huge mountain having the color of iron. On its height was sitting One of such great radiance that it stunned my vision. On both sides of him extended a gentle [50] shadow like a wing of marvelous width and length. And in front of him at the foot of the same mountain stood a figure full of eyes everywhere. Because of those eyes, I was not able to distinguish any human form.

In front of this figure there was another figure, whose age was that of a boy, and he was clothed in a pale tunic and white shoes. I was not able to look at his face, because above his head so much radiance descended from the One sitting on the mountain. From the One sitting on the mountain a great many living sparks cascaded, which flew around those figures [60] with great sweetness. In this same mountain, moreover, there seemed to be a number of little windows, in which men's heads appeared, some pale and some white.

And see! The One sitting on the mountain shouted in an extremely loud, strong voice, saying: "O frail mortal, you who are of the dust of the earth's dust, and ash of ash, cry out and speak of the way into incorruptible salvation! Do this in order that those people may be taught who see the innermost meaning of Scripture, but who do not wish to tell it or preach it because they are lukewarm and dull in preserving God's [70] justice. Unlock for them the mystical barriers. For they, being timid, are hiding themselves in a remote and barren field. You, therefore, pour yourself forth in a fountain of abundance! Flow with mystical learning, so that those who want you to be scorned because of the guilt of Eve may be inundated by the flood of your refreshment!

"For you do not receive this keenness of insight from man, but from that supernal and awesome judge on high. There amidst brilliant light, this radiance will brightly shine forth among the luminous ones. Arise, therefore, and shout and [80] speak! These things are revealed to you through the strongest power of divine aid. For he who potently and benignly rules his creatures imbues with the radiance of heavenly enlightenment all those who fear him and serve him with sweet love in a spirit of humility. And he leads those who persevere in the path of justice to the joys of everlasting vision!"

3. The Fall of Lucifer, the Formation of Hell, and the Fall of Adam and Eve: *Scivias*. Book I, Vision 2

Then I saw what seemed to be a great number of living torches, full of brilliance. Catching a fiery gleam, they received a most radiant splendor from it. And see! A lake appeared here, of great length and depth, with a mouth like a well, [90] breathing forth a stinking fiery smoke. From the mouth of the lake a loathsome fog also arose until it touched a thing like a blood vessel that had a deceptive appearance.

And in a certain region of brightness, the fog blew through the blood vessel to a pure white cloud, which had emerged from the beautiful form of a man, and the cloud contained within itself many, many stars. Then the loathsome fog blew and drove the cloud and the man's form out of the region of brightness.

Once this had happened, the most luminous splendor [100] encircled that region. The elements of the world, which previously had held firmly together in great tranquillity, now, turning into great turmoil, displayed fearful terrors. . . .

Now "that lake of great length and depth" which appeared to you is Hell. In its length are contained vices, and in its deep abyss is damnation, as you see. Also, "it has a mouth like a well, breathing forth a stinking, fiery smoke" means that drowning souls are swallowed in its voracious greed. For although the lake shows them sweetness and delights, it leads them, through perverse deceit, to a perdition of [110] torments. There the heat of the fire breathes forth with an outpouring of the most loathsome smoke, and with a boiling, death-dealing stench. For these abominable torments were prepared for the Devil and his followers, who turned away from the highest good, which they wanted neither to know nor to understand. For this reason they were cast down from every good thing, not because they did not know them but because they were contemptuous of them in their lofty pride. . . .

Sermon Literature

While the writings of Hildegard of Bingen addressed individual, literate Christians, medieval sermons, delivered orally from the pulpit of the church, were directed to the largely illiterate Christian community. Both visionary tracts and sermon literature, however, described grace and salvation in vivid terms. The classic medieval sermon, *On the Misery of the Human Condition*, was written by one of Christendom's most influential popes, Innocent III (d. 1216). This sermon is a compelling description of the natural sinfulness of humankind and a scathing condemnation of the "vile and filthy [human] condition." Such imagery, like that found in Hildegard's visions, proceeded from prevailing views of the human condition: Weighed down by the burden of the flesh, the body is subject to corruption, disease, and carnal desire. As the temple of the soul, the body will be resurrected on Judgment Day, but not before it suffers the trials of mortality. Warning of the "nearness of death," Innocent's sermon functioned as a **memento mori**, a device by which listeners in a predominantly oral culture might "remember death" and thus prepare themselves for its inevitable arrival. Innocent's portrayal of the decay of the human body reflects the medieval disdain for the world of matter, a major theme in most medieval didactic literature. During the Late Middle Ages, especially after the onslaught of the bubonic plague (see chapter 15), the motif of the body as "food for worms"—one of Innocent's most vivid images—became particularly popular in gruesomely forthright tomb sculptures (Figure 12.2).

Innocent's vivid account of the Christian Hell transforms the concept of corruption into an image of eternal

Figure 12.2 Detail of *transi* (effigy of the dead) of François de la Sarra, ca. 1390. La Sarraz, Switzerland. Photo: De Jongh, Lausanne. © Musée de l'Elysée, Lausanne, Switzerland.

punishment for unabsolved sinners—a favorite subject matter for medieval artists (Figure **12.3**). The contrast that Innocent draws between physical death and spiritual life has its visual counterpart in the representations of the Last Judgment depicted in medieval manuscripts and on Romanesque and Gothic church portals (see Figure 13.9).

READING 2.18 From Pope Innocent III's *On the Misery of the Human Condition* (ca. 1200)

Of the Miserable Entrance upon the Human Condition

. . . Man was formed of dust, slime, and ashes: what is even more vile, of the filthiest seed. He was conceived from the itch of the flesh, in the heat of passion and the stench of lust, and worse yet, with the stain of sin. He was born to toil, dread, and trouble; and more wretched still, was born only to die. He commits depraved acts by which he offends God, his neighbor, and himself; shameful acts by which he defiles his name, his person, and his conscience; and vain acts by which he ignores all things important, useful, and necessary. He will become fuel for those fires which are forever hot and burn forever bright; food for the worm which forever nibbles and digests; a mass of rottenness which will forever stink and reek. . . . [10]

On the Nearness of Death

A man's last day is always the first in importance, but his first day is never considered his last. Yet it is fitting to live always on this principle, that one should act as if in the moment of death. For it is written: "Remember that death is not slow."[1] Time passes, death draws near. In the eyes of the dying man a thousand years are as yesterday, which is past. The future is

[1]Ecclesiastes 14:12.

---

forever being born, the present forever dying and what is past is utterly dead. We are forever dying while we are alive; we only cease to die when we cease to live. Therefore it is better to die to life than to live waiting for death, for mortal life is but a living death. . . . [20]

On the Putrefaction of the Dead Body

. . . Man is conceived of blood made rotten by the heat of lust; and in the end worms, like mourners, stand about his corpse. In life he produced lice and tapeworms; in death he will produce worms and flies. In life he produced dung and vomit; in death he produces rottenness and stench. In life he fattened one man; in death he fattens a multitude of worms. What then is more foul than a human corpse? What is more horrible than a dead man? He whose embrace was pure delight in life will be a gruesome sight in death. [30]

Of what advantage, then, are riches, food, and honors? For riches will not free us from death, neither food protect us from the worm nor honors from the stench. That man who but now sat in glory upon a throne is now looked down on in the grave; the dandy who once glittered in his palace lies now naked and vile in his tomb; and he who supped once on delicacies in his hall is now in his sepulcher food for worms. . . .

That Nothing Can Help the Damned

. . . O strict judgment!—not only of actions, but "of every idle word that men shall speak, they shall render an account";[2] payment with the usurer's interest will be exacted to the last penny. "Who hath showed you to flee from the wrath to come?"[3] [40]

"The Son of Man shall send his angels and they shall gather out of his kingdom all scandals, and them that work iniquity, and they will bind them as bundles to be burnt, and shall cast them into the furnace of fire. There shall be weeping and gnashing of teeth,"[4] there shall be groaning and wailing, shrieking and flailing of arms and screaming, screeching, and shouting; there shall be fear and trembling, toil and trouble, holocaust and dreadful stench, and everywhere darkness and anguish; there shall be asperity, cruelty, calamity, poverty, distress, and utter wretchedness; they will feel an oblivion of loneliness and namelessness; there shall be twistings and piercings, bitterness, terror, hunger and thirst, cold and hot, brimstone and fire burning, forever and ever world without end. . . . [50]

The Medieval Morality Play

While medieval churches rang with sermons like those preached by Innocent III, town squares (often immediately adjacent to a cathedral) became open-air theaters for the dramatization of Christian history and legend. To these urban spaces, people flocked to see dramatic performances that might last from sunrise to sunset. The **mystery play** dramatized biblical history from the fall of

[2]Matthew 12:36.
[3]Luke 3:7.
[4]Matthew 13:41–42.

Figure 12.3 *The Mouth of Hell*, from the Psalter of Henry of Blois, Bishop of Winchester, twelfth century. Reproduced by permission of the British Library, London, MS Cotton Nero, C.IV, f.39.

Lucifer to the Last Judgment, while the **miracle play** enacted stories from the Life of Christ, the Virgin, or the saints. The **morality play**, the third type of medieval drama, dealt with the struggle between good and evil and the destiny of the soul in the hereafter. The first medieval morality play, Hildegard of Bingen's *Ordo virtutum* (*Play of the Virtues*) was a twelfth-century allegorical dialogue between vice and virtue. All of these types of plays were performed by members of the local guilds, and mystery plays were usually produced on **pageants** (roofed wagon-stages) that were rolled into the town square. Medieval plays were a popular form of entertainment, as well as a source of religious and moral instruction.

Just as ancient Greek drama originated in religious ritual, so medieval drama had its roots in the performance of Church liturgy. The Catholic Mass, the principal rite of Christian worship, admitted all of the trappings of theater: colorful costumes, symbolic props, solemn processions, dramatic gestures, and ceremonial music. It is likely that the gradual dramatization of Church liturgy (see chapter 13) influenced the genesis of mystery and miracle plays. The morality play, however, had clear precedents in allegorical poetry and sermon literature. Allegory—a literary device we have encountered in Plato's *Republic* (see chapter 4) and in Augustine's *City of God* (see chapter 9)—uses symbolic figures to capture the essence of a person, thing, or idea. The characters in the morality play are personifications of abstract qualities and universal conditions. In the play *Everyman*, for instance, the main character represents *all* Christian souls, Fellowship stands for friends, Goods for worldly possessions, and so forth.

Although *Everyman* has survived only in fifteenth-century Dutch and English editions, plays similar to it originated considerably earlier. The most popular of all medieval morality plays, *Everyman* symbolically recreates the pilgrimage of the Christian soul to its ultimate destiny. The play opens with the Messenger, who expounds on the transitory nature of human life. The subsequent conversation between Death and God, somewhat reminiscent of that between Satan and God in the Book of Job (see chapter 2), shows God to be an angry, petulant figure who regards human beings as "drowned in sin." If left to their own devices, he opines, "they will become much worse than beasts."

As the action unfolds, Everyman realizes that Death has come for him. He soon discovers that his best friends, his kin, his worldly possessions—indeed, all that he so treasured in life—will not accompany him to the grave. Knowledge, Wits, Beauty, and Discretion may point the way to redemption, but they cannot save him. Ultimately, only Good-Deeds will accompany him to confront judgment by "eternal God." *Everyman* is essentially a moral allegory that illustrates the pilgrimage through life to death; but, typical of its time, it is also an exposition on the importance of the Catholic priesthood in helping the medieval Christian achieve salvation. Like Pope Innocent's sermon, *Everyman* teaches that all things contributing to worldly pleasure are ultimately valueless, that life is transient, and that sin can be mitigated solely by salvation earned through grace as dispensed by the Church.

READING 2.19   From *Everyman* (ca. 1500)

Characters

Messenger	Cousin	Strength
God (Adonai)	Goods	Discretion
Death	Good-Deeds	Five-Wits
Everyman	Knowledge	Angel
Fellowship	Confession	Doctor
Kindred	Beauty	

HERE BEGINNETH A TREATISE HOW THE HIGH FATHER OF HEAVEN SENDETH DEATH TO SUMMON EVERY CREATURE TO COME AND GIVE ACCOUNT OF THEIR LIVES IN THIS WORLD AND IS IN MANNER OF A MORAL PLAY.

Messenger: I pray you all give your audience,   1
And hear this matter with reverence,
By figure a moral play—
The Summoning of Everyman called it is,
That of our lives and ending shows
How transitory we be all day.[1]
This matter is wondrous precious,
But the intent of it is more gracious,
And sweet to bear away.
The story saith—Man, in the beginning,   10
Look well, and take good heed to the ending,

----
[1]Always.

Be you never so gay!
Ye think sin in the beginning full sweet,
Which in the end causeth thy soul to weep,
When the body lieth in clay.
Here shall you see how *Fellowship* and *Jollity*,
Both *Strength*, *Pleasure*, and *Beauty*,
Will fade from thee as flower in May.
For ye shall hear, how our heaven king
Calleth *Everyman* to a general reckoning: 20
Give audience, and hear what he doth say.

God: I perceive here in my majesty,
How that all creatures be to me unkind,[2]
Living without dread in worldly prosperity:
Of ghostly[3] sight the people be so blind,
Drowned in sin, they know me not for their God:
In worldly riches is all their mind,
They fear not my right wiseness, the sharp rod:
My law that I shewed, when I for them died,
They forget clean, and shedding of my blood red: 30
I hanged between two, it cannot be denied:
To get them life I suffered to be dead:
I healed their feet, with thorns hurt was my head:
I could do no more than I did truly,
And now I see the people do clean forsake me,
They use the seven deadly sins damnable;
As pride, covetise, wrath, and lechery,
Now in the world be made commendable;
And thus they leave of angels the heavenly company;
Everyman liveth so after his own pleasure, 40
And yet of their life they be nothing sure:
I see the more that I them forbear
The worse they be from year to year;
All that liveth appaireth[4] fast,
Therefore I will in all the haste
Having a reckoning of Everyman's person
For and[5] I leave the people thus alone
In their life and wicked tempests,
Verily they will become much worse than beasts;
For now one would by envy another up eat; 50
Charity they all do clean forget.
I hoped well that Everyman
In my glory should make his mansion,
And thereto I had them all elect;
But now I see, like traitors deject,
They thank me not for the pleasure that I to them meant
Nor yet for their being that I them have lent;
I proffered the people great multitude of mercy,
And few there be that asketh it heartily;
They be so combered with worldly riches, 60
That needs of them I must do justice,
On Everyman living without fear.
Where art thou, Death, thou mighty messenger?

Death: Almighty God, I am here at your will,
Your commandment to fulfil.

God: Go thou to Everyman,
And show him in my name
A pilgrimage he must on him take,
Which he in no wise may escape:
And that he bring with him a sure reckoning 70
Without delay or any tarrying.

Death: Lord, I will in the world go run over all,
And cruelly outsearch both great and small;
Every man will I beset that liveth beastly
Out of God's laws, and dreadeth not folly:
He that loveth riches I will strike with my dart,
His sight to blind, and from heaven to depart,
Except that alms be his good friend,
In hell for to dwell, world without end.
Lo, yonder I see Everyman walking; 80
Full little he thinketh on my coming;
His mind is on fleshly lusts and his treasure,
And great pain it shall cause him to endure
Before the Lord Heaven King.
Everyman, stand still; whither art thou going
Thus gaily? Hast my Maker forgot?

Everyman: Why askst thou?
Wouldest thou wete?[6]

Death: Yea, sir, I will show you;
In great haste I am sent to thee 90
From God out of his majesty.

Everyman: What, sent to me?

Death: Yea, certainly.
Though thou have forget him here,
He thinketh on thee in the heavenly sphere,
As, or we depart, thou shalt know.

Everyman: What desireth God of me?

Death: That shall I show thee;
A reckoning he will needs have
Without any longer respite. 100

Everyman: To give a reckoning longer leisure I crave;
This blind matter troubleth my wit.

Death: On thee thou must take a long journey:
Therefore thy book of count with thee thou bring:
For turn again thou can not by no way.
And look thou be sure of thy reckoning:
For before God thou shalt answer, and show
Thy many bad deeds and good but a few;
How thou hast spent thy life, and in what wise,
Before the chief lord of paradise. 110
Have ado that we were in that way,
For, wete thou well, thou shalt make none attournay.[7]

Everyman: Full unready I am such reckoning to give.
I know thee not: what messenger art thou?

Death: I am Death, that no man dreadeth.
For every man I rest[8] and no man spareth;
For it is God's commandment
That all to me should be obedient.

Everyman: O Death, thou comest when I had thee least
in mind,

---

[2]Ungrateful.
[3]Spiritual.
[4]Decays.
[5]If.

---

[6]Know.
[7]Mediator.
[8]Arrest.

Also of ill deeds, that I have used
In my time, sith[20] life was me lent;   340
And of all virtues that I have refused.
Therefore I pray you go thither with me,
To help to make mine account, for saint charity.

    Cousin: What, to go thither? Is that the matter?
Nay, Everyman, I had liefer[21] fast bread and water
All this five year and more.

    Everyman: Alas, that ever I was bore![22]
For now shall I never be merry
If that you forsake me.

    Kindred: Ah, sir, what, ye be a merry man!   350
Take good heart to you, and make no moan.
But one thing I warn you, by Saint Anne,
As for me, ye shall go alone.

    Everyman: My Cousin, will you not with me go?

    Cousin: No, by our Lady; I have the cramp in my toe.
Trust not to me, for, so God me speed,
I will deceive you in your most need.

    Kindred: It availeth not us to tice.[23]
Ye shall have my maid with all my heart;
She loveth to go to feasts, there to be nice,   360
And to dance, and abroad to start:
I will give her leave to help you in that journey,
If that you and she may agree.

    Everyman: Now show me the very effect of your mind. Will you
go with me, or abide behind?

    Kindred: Abide behind? Yea, that I will and I may! Therefore
farewell until another day.

    Everyman: How should I be merry or glad?
For fair promises to me make,
But when I have most need, they me forsake.   370
I am deceived; that maketh me sad.

    Cousin: Cousin Everyman, farewell now,
For verily I will not go with you;
Also of mine own an unready reckoning
I have to account: therefore I make tarrying.
Now, God keep thee, for now I go.

    Everyman: Ah, Jesus, is all come hereto?
Lo, fair words maketh fools feign;
They promise and nothing will do certain.
My kinsmen promised me faithfully   380
For to abide with me steadfastly,
And now fast away do they flee:
Even so Fellowship promised me.
What friend were best me of to provide?
I lose my time here longer to abide.
Yet in my mind a thing there is:—
All my life I have loved riches;
If that my goods now help me might,
He would make my heart full light.
I will speak to him in this distress.—   390
Where art thou, my Goods and riches?

    Goods: Who calleth me? Everyman? What haste thou
        hast!

I lie here in corners, trussed and piled so high,
And in chests I am locked so fast,
Also sacked in bags, thou mayst see with thine eye,
I cannot stir; in packs low I lie,
What would ye have, lightly me say.[24]

    Everyman: Come hither, Good, in all the haste thou
        may,
For of counsel I must desire thee.

    Goods: Sir, and ye in the world have trouble or adversity.   400
That can I help you to remedy shortly.

    Everyman: It is another disease that grieveth me;
In this world it is not, I tell thee so.
I am sent for another way to go,
To give a straight account general
Before the highest Jupiter of all;
And all my life I have had joy and pleasure in thee.
Therefore I pray thee go with me,
For, peradventure, thou mayst before God Almighty
My reckoning help to clean and purify;   410
For it is said ever among,
That money maketh all right that is wrong.

    Goods: Nay, Everyman, I sing another song.
I follow no man in such voyages;
For and I went with thee
Thou shouldst fare much the worse for me;
For because on me thou did set thy mind,
Thy reckoning I have made blotted and blind
That thine account thou cannot make truly;
And that has thou for the love of me.   420

    Everyman: That would grieve me full sore,
When I should come to that fearful answer.
Up, let us go thither together.

    Goods: Nay, no so, I am too brittle, I may not endure:
I will follow no man one foot, be ye sure.

    Everyman: Alas, I have thee loved, and had great
pleasure
All my life-days on good and treasure.

    Goods: That is to thy damnation without lesing,[25]
For my love is contrary to the love everlasting
But if thou had me loved moderately during,   430
As, to the poor give part of me,
Then shouldst thou not in this dolour[26] be,
Nor in this great sorrow and care.

    Everyman: Lo, now was I deceived or I was ware,
And all I may wyte[27] my spending of time.

    Goods: What, weenest thou that I am thine?

    Everyman: I had wend so.

    Goods: Nay, Everyman, I say no;
As for a while I was lent thee,
A season thou hast had me in prosperity   440
My condition is man's soul to kill;
If I save one, a thousand I do spill;[28]
Weenest thou that I will follow thee?
Nay, from this world, not verily.

---

[20]Since.
[21]Rather.
[22]Born.
[23]It is useless to try to entice us.

[24]Quickly tell me.
[25]Loosing, releasing.
[26]Distress.
[27]Blame.
[28]Ruin.

Everyman: I had wend otherwise.

Goods: Therefore to thy soul Good is a thief;
For when thou art dead, this is my guise
Another to deceive in the same wise
As I have done thee, and all to his soul's reprief.[29]

Everyman: O false Good, cursed thou be!   450
Thou traitor to God, that has deceived me,
And caught me in thy snare.

Goods: Marry,[30] thou brought thyself in care,
Whereof I am glad,
I must needs laugh, I cannot be sad.

Everyman: Ah, Goods, thou has had long my heartly love, I gave
thee that which should be the Lord's above.
But wilt thou not go with me in deed?
I pray thee truth to say.

Goods: No, so God me speed,   460
Therefore farewell, and have good day.

Everyman: O, to whom shall I make moan
For to go with me in that heavy journey?
First Fellowship said he would with me gone;
His words were very pleasant and gay,
But afterward he left me alone.
Then spake I to my kinsmen all in despair,
And also they gave me words fair,
They lacked no fair speaking,
But all forsake me in the ending.   470
Then went I to my Goods that I loved best,
In hope to have comfort, but there had I least:
For my Goods sharply did me tell
That he bringeth many into hell.
Then of myself I was ashamed;
And so I am worthy to be blamed;
Thus may I well myself hate,
Of whom shall I now counsel take?
I think that I shall never speed
Till that I go to my Good-Deed,   480
But alas, she is so weak,
That she can neither go nor speak,
Yet will I venture on her now.—
My Good-Deeds, where be you?

Good-deeds: Here I lie cold on the ground,
Thy sins hath me sore bound,
That I cannot stir.

Everyman: O, Good-Deeds, I stand in fear;
I must you pray of counsel,
For help now should come right well.   490

Good-deeds: Everyman, I have understanding
That ye be summoned account to make
Before Messias, of Jerusalem King;
And you by me[31] that journey what[32] you will I take.

Everyman: Therefore I come to you, my moan to make; I pray
you, that ye will go with me.

Good-deeds: I would full fain,[33] but I cannot stand verily.

Everyman: Why, is there anything on you fall?

Good-deeds: Yea, sir, I may think you of all;
If ye had perfectly cheered me,   500
Your book of account now full ready had be.
Look, the books of your works and deeds eke;[34]
Oh, see how they lie under the feet,
To your soul's heaviness.

Everyman: Our Lord Jesus, help me!
For one letter here I can not see.

Good-deeds: There is a blind reckoning in time of
distress!

Everyman: Good-Deeds, I pray you, help me in this need,
Or else I am for ever damned indeed;
Therefore help me to make reckoning   510
Before the redeemer of all thing,
That king is, and was, and ever shall.

Good-deeds: Everyman, I am sorry of your fall,
And fain would I help you, and I were able.

Everyman: Good-Deeds, your counsel I pray you give me.

Good-deeds: That shall I do verily;
Though that on my feet I may not go,
I have a sister, that shall with you also,
Called Knowledge, which shall with you abide,
To help you to make that dreadful reckoning.   520

*[Knowledge guides Everyman to Confession, Discretion, Strength,
Beauty, and Five-Wits, who direct him to
receive the sacrament of extreme unction.]*

Knowledge: Everyman, hearken what I say;
Go to priesthood, I you advise,
And receive of him in any wise
The holy sacrament and ointment together;
Then shortly see ye turn again hither;
We will all abide you here.

Five-wits: Yea, Everyman, hie[35] you that ye ready were, There is
no emperor, king, duke, ne baron,
That of God hath commission,
As hath the least priest in the world being;   530
For of the blessed sacraments pure and benign,
He beareth the keys and thereof hath the cure
For man's redemption, it is ever sure;
Which God for our soul's medicine
Gave us out of his heart with great pine;[36]
Here in this transitory life, for thee and me
The blessed sacraments seven there be.
Baptism, confirmation, with priesthood good,
And the sacrament of God's precious flesh and blood,
Marriage, the holy extreme unction, and penance;   540
These seven be good to have in remembrance,
Gracious sacraments of high divinity.

Everyman: Fain would I receive that holy body
And meekly to my ghostly father I will go.

Five-wits: Everyman, that is the best that ye can do:
God will you to salvation bring,
For priesthood exceedeth all other thing;
To us Holy Scripture they do teach,
And converteth man from sin heaven to reach;

---

[29]Shame.
[30]The Virgin Mary! (An interjection of surprise or agreement.)
[31]If you do as I advise.
[32]With.
[33]Very willingly.

---

[34]Also.
[35]Hasten.
[36]Suffering.

When we had reached the joint where the great thigh
  merges into the swelling of the haunch,
  my Guide and Master, straining terribly,   **78**

turned his head to where his feet had been
  and began to grip the hair as if he were climbing;
  so that I thought we moved toward Hell again.   **81**

"Hold fast!" my Guide said, and his breath came shrill
  with labor and exhaustion. "There is no way
  but by such stairs to rise above such evil."   **84**

At last he climbed out through an opening
  in the central rock, and he seated me on the rim;
  then joined me with a nimble backward spring.   **87**

I looked up, thinking to see Lucifer
  as I had left him, and I saw instead
  his legs projecting high into the air.   **90**

Now let all those whose dull minds are still vexed
  by failure to understand what point it was
  I had passed through, judge if I was perplexed.   **93**

"Get up. Up on your feet," my Master said.
  "The sun already mounts to middle tierce,
  and a long road and hard climbing lie ahead."   **96**

It was no hall of state we had found there,
  but a natural animal pit hollowed from rock
  with a broken floor and a close and sunless air.   **99**

"Before I tear myself from the Abyss,"
  I said when I had risen, "O my Master,
  explain to me my error in all this: **102**

where is the ice? and Lucifer—how has he
  been turned from top to bottom: and how can the sun
  have gone from night to day so suddenly?"   **105**

And he to me: "You imagine you are still
  on the other side of the center where I grasped
  the shaggy flank of the Great Worm of Evil   **108**

which bores through the world—you *were* while I climbed down,
  but when I turned myself about, you passed
  the point to which all gravities are drawn.   **111**

You are under the other hemisphere where you stand;
  the sky above us is the half opposed
  to that which canopies the great dry land.   **114**

Under the mid-point of that other sky
  the Man who was born sinless and who lived
  beyond all blemish, came to suffer and die.   **117**

You have your feet upon a little sphere
  which forms the other face of the Judecca. [Named
    for Judas Iscariot.]
  There it is evening when it is morning here.   **120**

And this gross Fiend and Image of all Evil
  who made a stairway for us with his hide
  is pinched and prisoned in the ice-pack still.   **123**

On this side he plunged down from heaven's height,
  and the land that spread here once hid in the sea
  and fled North to our hemisphere for fright;   **126**

and it may be that moved by that same fear,
  the one peak that still rises on this side
  fled upward leaving this great cavern here."   **129**

Down there, beginning at the further bound
  of Beelzebub's dim tomb, there is a space
  not known by sight, but only by the sound   **132**

of a little stream descending through the hollow
  it has eroded from the massive stone
  in its endlessly entwining lazy flow.   **135**

My Guide and I crossed over and began
  to mount that little known and lightless road
  to ascend into the shining world again.   **138**

He first, I second, without thought of rest
  we climbed the dark until we reached the point
  where a round opening brought in sight the blest   **141**

and beauteous shining of the Heavenly cars.
And we walked out once more beneath the Stars.

Notes to "Inferno" (Canto 34)

line 1 *On march the banners of the King*: The hymn ("Vexilla regis prodeunt") was written in the sixth century by Venantius Fortunatus, Bishop of Poitiers. The original celebrates the Holy Cross, and is part of the service for Good Friday to be sung at the moment of uncovering the cross.

line 17 *the foul creature*: Satan.

line 38 *three faces*: Numerous interpretations of these three faces exist. What is essential to all explanations is that they be seen as perversions of the qualities of the Trinity.

line 54 *bloody froth and pus*: The gore of the sinners he chews which is mixed with his slaver.

line 62 *Judas*: Note how closely his punishment is patterned on that of the Simoniacs (Canto 19).

line 67 *huge and sinewy arms*: The Cassius who betrayed Caesar was more generally described in terms of Shakespeare's "lean and hungry look." Another Cassius is described by Cicero (*Catiline* III) as huge and sinewy. Dante probably confused the two.

line 68 *the night is coming on*: It is now Saturday evening.

line 82 *his breath came shrill*: Cf. Canto 23, 85, where the fact that Dante breathes indicates to the Hypocrites that he is alive. Virgil's breathing is certainly a contradiction.

line 95 *middle tierce*: In the canonical day tierce is the period from about six to nine a.m. Middle tierce, therefore, is seven-thirty. In going through the center point, they have gone from night to day. They have moved ahead twelve hours.

line 128 *the one peak*: The Mount of Purgatory.

line 129 *this great cavern*: The natural animal pit of line 98. It is also "Beelzebub's dim tomb," line 131.

line 133 *a little stream*: Lethe. In classical mythology, the river of forgetfulness, from which souls drank before being born. In Dante's symbolism it flows down from Purgatory, where it has washed away the memory of sin from the souls who are undergoing purification. That memory it delivers to Hell, which draws all sin to itself.

line 143 *Stars*: As part of his total symbolism Dante ends each of the three divisions of the *Commedia* with this word. Every conclusion of the upward soul is toward the stars, God's shining symbols of hope and virtue. It is just before dawn of Easter Sunday that the Poets emerge—a further symbolism.

From The Vision of God ("Paradiso," Canto 33)

O Light Eternal fixed in Itself alone,
    by Itself alone understood, which from Itself
    loves and glows, self-knowing and self-known;   **126**

that second aureole which shone forth in Thee,
    conceived as a reflection of the first—
    or which appeared so to my scrutiny—   **129**

seemed in Itself of Its own coloration
    to be painted with man's image. I fixed my eyes
    on that alone in rapturous contemplation.   **132**

Like a geometer wholly dedicated
    to squaring the circle, but who cannot find,
    think as he may, the principle indicated—   **135**

so did I study the supernal face.
    I yearned to know just how our image merges
    into that circle, and how it there finds place;   **138**

but mine were not the wings for such a flight.
    Yet, as I wished, the truth I wished for came
    cleaving my mind in a great flash of light.   **141**

Here my powers rest from their high fantasy,
    but already I could feel my being turned—
    instinct and intellect balanced equally   **144**

as in a wheel whose motion nothing jars—
by the Love that moves the Sun and the other stars.

Notes to "Paradiso" (Canto 33)

lines 130-144 *seemed in Itself of Its own coloration . . . instinct and intellect balanced equally*: The central metaphor of the entire Comedy is the image of God and the final triumphant in Godding of the elected soul returning to its Maker. On the mystery of that image, the metaphoric symphony of the *Comedy* comes to rest.

In the second aspect of Triple-unity, in the circle reflected from the first, Dante thinks he sees the image of mankind woven into the very substance and coloration of God. He turns the entire attention of his soul to that mystery, as a geometer might seek to shut out every other thought and dedicate himself to squaring the circle. In *Il Convivio II*, 14, Dante asserted that the circle could not be squared, but that impossibility had not yet been firmly demonstrated in Dante's time and mathematicians still worked at the problem. Note, however, that Dante assumes the impossibility of squaring the circle as a weak mortal example of mortal impossibility. How much more impossible, he implies, to resolve the mystery of God, study as man will.

The mystery remains beyond Dante's mortal power. Yet, there in Heaven, in a moment of grace, God revealed the truth to him in a flash of light—revealed it, that is, to the God-enlarged power of Dante's emparadised soul. On Dante's return to the mortal life, the details of that revelation vanished from his mind but the force of the revelation survives in its power on Dante's feelings.

So ends the vision of the *Comedy* and yet the vision endures, for ever since that revelation, Dante tells us, he feels his soul turning ever as one with the perfect motion of God's love.

The Medieval Church

During the High Middle Ages, the Catholic Church exercised great power and authority not only as a religious force, but also as a political institution. The papacy took strong measures to ensure the independence of the Church from secular interference, especially that of the emerging European states. In 1022, for instance, the Church formed the College of Cardinals as the sole body responsible for the election of popes. Medieval pontiffs functioned much like secular monarchs, governing a huge and complex bureaucracy that incorporated financial, judicial, and disciplinary branches. The Curia, the papal council and highest Church court, headed a vast network of ecclesiastical courts, while the Camera (the papal treasury) handled financial matters. The medieval Church was enormously wealthy. Over the centuries, Christians had donated and bequeathed to Christendom so many thousands of acres of land that, by the end of the twelfth century, the Catholic Church was the largest single landholder in Western Europe.

Among lay Christians of every rank the Church commanded religious obedience. It enforced religious conformity by means of such spiritual penalties as **excommunication** (exclusion from the sacraments) and **interdict**, the excommunication of an entire city or state—used to dissuade secular rulers from opposing papal policy. In spite of these spiritual weapons, **heresy** (the denial of the revealed truths of the Christian faith) spread rapidly within the increasingly cosmopolitan centers of twelfth-century Europe. Such anticlerical groups as the Waldensians, followers of the French thirteenth-century reformer Peter Waldo, denounced the growing worldliness of the Church. Waldo proposed that lay Christians administer the sacraments and that the Bible—sole source of religious authority—should be translated into the vernacular.

Condemning such views as threats to civil and religious order, the Church launched antiheretical crusades that were almost as violent as those advanced against the Muslims. Further, in 1233, the pope established the Inquisition, a special court designed to stamp out heresy. The Inquisition brought to trial individuals whom local townspeople denounced as heretics. The accused were deprived of legal counsel and were usually tried in secret. Inquisitors might use physical torture to obtain confession, for the Church considered injury to the body preferable to the eternal damnation of the soul. If the Inquisition failed to restore accused heretics to the faith, it might impose such penalties as exile or excommunication, or it might turn over the defendants to the state to be hanged or burned at the stake—the preferred punishment for female heretics. With the same energy that the Church persecuted heretics, it acted as a civilizing agent. It preserved order by enforcing periods in which warfare was prohibited. It assumed moral and financial responsibility for the poor, the sick, and the homeless; and it provided for the organization of hospitals, refuges, orphanages, and other charitable institutions.

The power and prestige of the Church were enhanced by the outstanding talents of some popes as diplomats, canon lawyers, and administrators. Under the leadership of the lawyer/pope Innocent III, the papacy emerged as the most powerful political institution in Western Europe. Pope Innocent enlarged the body of canon law and refined

without disturbing the monks at the main altar (Figure **13.4**). In the construction of these new, all-stone structures, the Normans led the way. The technical superiority of Norman stonemasons, apparent in their castles (see Figure 11.14), is reflected in the abbey churches at Caen and Jumièges in Northwestern France. At the abbey of Jumièges, consecrated in 1067 in the presence of William the Conqueror, little remains other than the **westwork** (west facade), with its 141-foot-high twin towers (Figure **13.5**). This austere entrance portal, with its **tripartite** (three-part) division and three round arches, captures the geometric simplicity and rugged severity typical of the Romanesque style in France and England. It also anticipates some of the central features of medieval church architecture: Massive towers pointed heavenward and made the church visible from great distances; stone portals separated the secular from the divine realm (see chapter 9) and dramatized the entrance door as the gateway to paradise.

The church of Saint-Sernin at Toulouse, on the southernmost pilgrimage route to Compostela, is one of the largest of the French pilgrimage churches (Figure **13.6**). Constructed of magnificent pink granite, Saint-Sernin's spacious nave is covered by a barrel vault divided by ornamental transverse arches (Figure **13.7**). Thick stone walls and heavy piers carry the weight of the vault and provide lateral support (see Figure 13.19). Since window openings might have weakened the walls that buttressed the barrel vault, the architects of Saint-Sernin eliminated the clerestory. Beneath the vaults over the double side-aisles, a gallery that served weary pilgrims as a place of overnight refuge provided additional lateral buttressing.

The formal design of Saint-Sernin follows rational and harmonious principles: The square represented by the crossing of the nave and transept is the module for the organization of the building and its parts (see Figure 13.4). Each nave **bay** (vaulted compartment) equals one-half the module, while each side-aisle bay equals one-fourth of the

Figure 13.5 West facade of the Abbey of Jumièges, on the lower Seine near Rouen, France, 1037–1067. Height of towers 141 ft. Photo: Serge Chirol, Paris.

module. Clarity of design is also visible in the ways in which the exterior reflects the geometry of the interior: At the east end of the building, for instance, five reliquary chapels protrude uniformly from the ambulatory, while at the crossing of the nave and transept, a tower (enlarged in the thirteenth century) rises as both a belfry and a beacon to approaching pilgrims (see Figure 13.5). Massive and stately in its exterior, dignified and somber in its interior,

Figure 13.6 (below) Saint-Sernin, Toulouse, France, ca. 1080–1120 (tower enlarged in the thirteenth century). Photo: Yan, Toulouse.

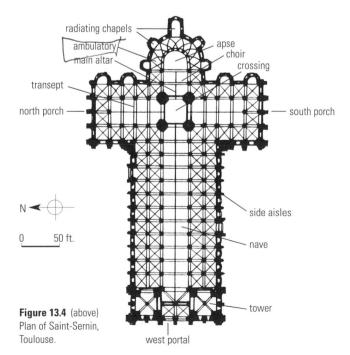

radiating chapels
ambulatory
main altar
apse
choir
crossing
transept
north porch
south porch
N
0   50 ft.
side aisles
nave
tower
west portal

Figure 13.4 (above) Plan of Saint-Sernin, Toulouse.

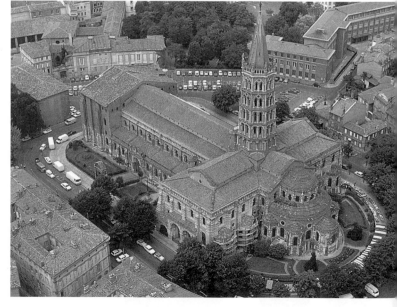

Saint-Sernin conveys the effect of a monumental spiritual fortress.

Romanesque architects experimented with a wide assortment of regional variation in stone vaulting techniques. At the pilgrimage church of Sainte Madeleine (Mary Magdalene) at Vézelay in France—the site from which the Second Crusade was launched—the nave was covered with groin vaults separated by pronounced transverse arches. The concentration of weight along the arches, along with lighter masonry, allowed the architect to enlarge the width of the nave to 90 feet and to include a clerestory that admitted light into the dark interior (Figure 13.8). The alternating light and dark stone **voussoirs** (wedges) in the arches of this dramatic interior indicate the influence of Muslim architecture (see Figure 10.10) on the development of the Romanesque church.

Figure 13.7 Nave and choir of Saint-Sernin, Toulouse. Pink granite, length of nave 377 ft. 4 in. Photo: Serge Chirol, Paris.

Figure 13.8 Nave of Sainte Madeleine, Vézelay, France, ca. 1104–1132. Width 90 ft. © Paul M. R. Maeyaert, Belgium.

Figure 13.13 Jeremiah the Prophet, early twelfth century. Trumeau of south portal, Saint Pierre, Moissac, France. Giraudon, Paris.

Figure 13.14 *The Flight to Egypt*, eleventh century. Capital, Autun Cathedral, France.

The Gothic Cathedral

Romanesque architects drew on Greco-Roman principles and building techniques. Gothic architects, on the other hand, represented a clear break with the classical past. Whereas classical temples seemed to hug the earth, Gothic cathedrals soared heavenward; whereas classical structures enforced a static relationship between building parts, Gothic structures engaged a dynamic system of thrusts and counterthrusts; and whereas classical architects rationalized form, Gothic architects infused form with symbolism. Seventeenth-century neoclassicists coined the term "Gothic" to condemn a style they judged to be a "rude and barbarous" alternative to the classical style. But modern critics have recognized the *Gothic style* as the sophisticated and majestic expression of an age of faith.

The Gothic style was born in Northern France and spread quickly throughout medieval Europe. In France alone, 80 Gothic cathedrals and nearly 500 cathedral-class churches were constructed between 1170 and 1270. Like all Christian churches, the Gothic cathedral was the sanctuary in which priests conducted Masses for all occasions. But, reflecting a shift of intellectual life from the monastery to the town, the Gothic cathedral was also the administrative seat or throne (*cathedra*) of a bishop, the site of ecclesiastical authority, and an educational center—a fount of theological doctrine and divine precept. The Gothic cathedral was a monumental shrine that honored one or more saints, including and especially the Virgin Mary—the principal intercessor between God and the Christian believer. Indeed, most of the prominent churches of the Middle Ages were dedicated

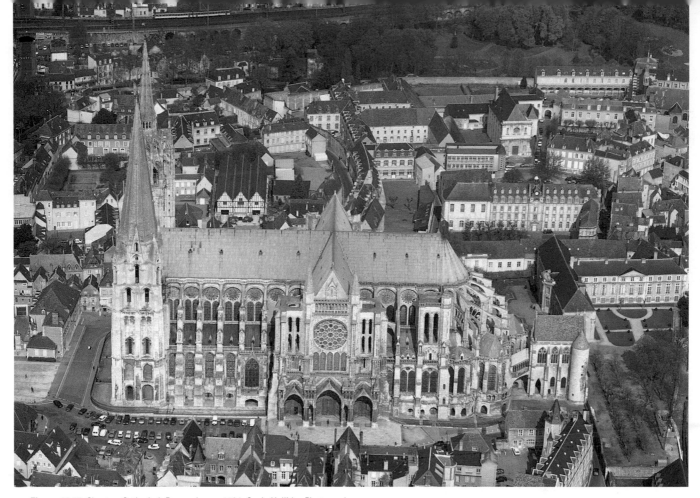

Figure 13.15 Chartres Cathedral, France, begun 1194. Sonia Halliday Photographs.

to Notre Dame ("Our Lady"). On a symbolic level, the church was both the Heavenly Jerusalem, the City of God, and a model of the Virgin as Womb of Christ and Queen of Heaven. In the cathedral, the various types of religious expression converged: Sculpture appeared in its portals, capitals, and choir screens; stained glass diffused divine light through its windows; painted altarpieces embellished its chapels; religious drama was enacted both within its walls and outside its portals; liturgical music filled its choirs.

Finally, the Gothic cathedral, often large enough to hold the entire population of a town, was the municipal center. If the Romanesque church constituted a rural retreat for monastics and pilgrims, the Gothic cathedral served as the focal point for an urban community. Physically dominating the town, its spires soaring above the houses and shops below (Figure **13.15**), the cathedral attracted civic events, public festivals, and even local business. The construction of a Gothic cathedral was a town effort, supported by the funds and labors of local citizens and guild members, including stonemasons (Figure **13.16**), carpenters, metalworkers, and glaziers.

The definitive features of the Gothic style were first assembled in a monastic church just outside the gates of Paris: the abbey church of Saint-Denis—the church that held the relics of the patron saint of France and, for centuries, the burial place of French royalty. Between 1122 and 1144, Abbot Suger (1085–1151), a personal friend

Figure 13.16 *Thirteenth-Century Masons*, French miniature from an Old Testament building scene, ca. 1240. 15⅓ × 11⅞ in. © The J. Pierpont Morgan Library, New York, 1991, MS 638 f.3. Art Resource, NY. Stones, shaped by the two men (bottom right), are lifted by a hoisting engine powered by the treadwheel on the left. Another man is carrying mortar up the ladder on his back.

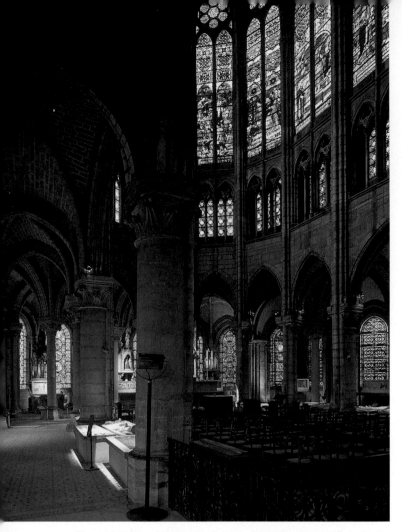

and adviser of the French kings Louis VI and VII, enlarged and remodeled the old Carolingian church of Saint-Denis. Suger's designs for the east end of the church called for a combination of three architectural innovations that had been employed only occasionally or experimentally: the pointed arch, the rib vault, and stained glass windows. The result was a spacious choir and ambulatory, free of heavy stone supports and flooded with light (Figure **13.17**).

While Gothic cathedrals followed Saint-Denis in adopting a new look, their floor plan—the Latin cross—

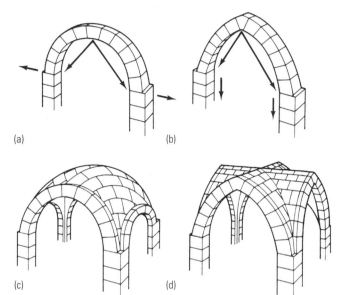

(a)   (b)

(c)   (d)

Figure 13.17 (above) Choir and ambulatory of the Abbey Church of Saint-Denis, France, 1140-1144. © Paul M. R. Maeyaert, Belgium.

Figure 13.19 (above) Round and pointed arches and vaults. The round arch (a) spreads the load laterally, while the pointed arch (b) thrusts its load more directly toward the ground. The pointed arch can rise to any height while the height of the semicircular arch is governed by the space it spans. Round arches create a dome-shaped vault (c). The Gothic rib-vault (d) permits a lighter and more flexible building system with larger wall-openings that may accommodate windows.

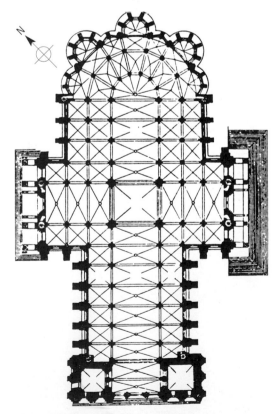

Figure 13.18 Floor plan of Chartres Cathedral.

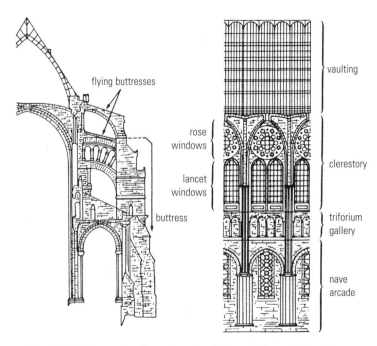

flying buttresses

vaulting

rose windows

lancet windows

buttress

clerestory

triforium gallery

nave arcade

Figure 13.20 Diagram of vaulting and section of nave wall, Chartres Cathedral.

remained basically the same as that of the Romanesque church; only the transept might be moved further west to create a larger choir area (Figure **13.18**). The ingenious combination of rib vault and pointed arch, however, had a major impact on the size and elevation of Gothic structures. Stone ribs replaced the heavy stone masonry of Romanesque vaults, and pointed arches raised these vaults to new heights. Whereas the rounded vaults of the Romanesque church demanded extensive lateral buttressing, the steeply pointed arches of the Gothic period, which directed weight downward, required only the combination of slender vertical piers and thin lateral ("flying") buttresses (Figures **13.19**, **13.20**). In place of masonry,

broad areas of glass filled the interstices of this "cage" of stone. The nave wall consisted of an arcade of pier bundles that swept from floor to ceiling, an ornamental **triforium** gallery (the arcaded passage between the nave arcade and the clerestory), and a large clerestory consisting of **rose** (from the French *roue*, "wheel") and **lancet** (vertically pointed) windows (see Figure 13.20). Above the clerestory hung elegant canopies of **quadripartite** (four-part; Figure **13.21**) or **sexpartite** (six-part) rib vaults. Lighter and more airy than Romanesque churches, Gothic interiors seem to expand and unfold in vertical space. The pointed arch, the rib vault, and stained glass windows, along with the flying buttress (first used at the cathedral of

Figure 13.21 Nave facing east, Chartres Cathedral. Height of nave 122 ft. © Paul M. R. Maeyaert, Belgium.

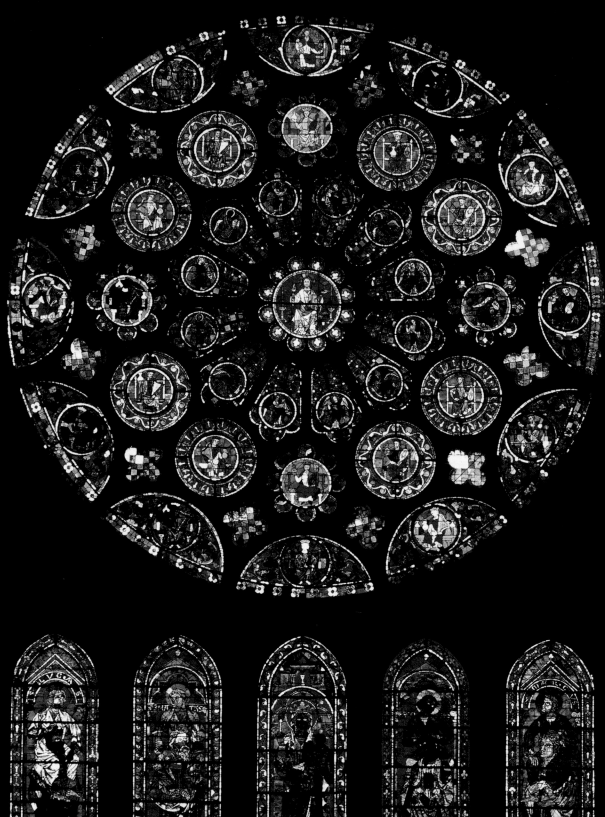

man to exploit the aesthetic potential of stained glass, produced blue glass by grinding up sapphires—a story that, although untrue, reflects the popular equation of precious gems with sacred glass.

Suger exalted stained glass as a medium that filtered divine truth. To the medieval mind, light was a symbol of Jesus, who had proclaimed to his apostles, "I am the light of the world" (John 8.12). Drawing on this mystical bond between Jesus and light, Suger identified the *lux nova* ("new light") of the Gothic church as the symbolic equivalent of God and the windows as mediators of God's love. But for Suger, light—especially as it passed through the stained glass windows of the church—also signified the sublime knowledge that accompanied the progressive purification of the ascending human spirit (compare Canto 33 of Dante's "Paradiso," Reading 2.20). Suger's mystical interpretation of light, inspired by his reading of neoplatonic treatises (see chapter 8), sustained his belief that contemplation of the "many-colored gems" of church glass could transport the Christian from "the slime of this earth" to "the purity of heaven." On the wall of the ambulatory at Saint-Denis, Abbot Suger had these words inscribed: "That which is united in splendor, radiates in splendor/And the magnificent work inundated with the new light shines."

The light symbolism that Suger embraced was as distinctive to medieval sermons and treatises as it was to the everyday liturgy of the church. It permeates the writings of Hildegard of Bingen (see Reading 2.17), who referred to God as "the Living Light," and it is the principal theme in Saint Ambrose's sixth-century song of praise, the "Ancient Morning Hymn" (see Reading 2.6).

The Windows at Chartres

The late twelfth and early thirteenth centuries were, without doubt, the golden age of stained glass. At Chartres, the 175 surviving glass panels with representations of more than four thousand figures comprise a cosmic narrative of humankind's religious and secular history. Chartres' windows, which were removed for safekeeping during World War II and thereafter returned to their original positions, follow a carefully organized theological program designed, as Abbot Suger explained, "to show simple folk . . . what they ought to believe." Like most Gothic cathedrals, Chartres was dedicated to the Virgin Mary. Chartres housed the sacred tunic Mary was said to have worn when she gave birth to Jesus; and since that tunic had survived the late twelfth-century fire that destroyed most of the old church—a miracle that was taken to indicate the Virgin's desire to see the cathedral rebuilt—her image dominated the iconographic program. In one of Chartres' oldest windows, whose vibrant combination of red and blue glass inspired the title *Notre Dame de la Belle Verrière* ("Our Lady of the Beautiful Glass"), the Virgin appears in her dual role as Mother of God and Queen of Heaven (Figure 13.32). Holding the Christ child on her lap and immedi-

ately adjacent to her womb, she also symbolizes the Seat of Wisdom. In the lancet windows below the rose of the south transept wall (Figure 13.33), Mary and the Christ child are flanked by four Old Testament prophets who carry on their shoulders the four evangelists, a symbolic rendering of the Christian belief that the Old Dispensation upheld the New (compare Figure 13.13). Often, the colors chosen for parts of the design carry symbolic value. For instance, in scenes of the Passion from the west-central lancet window, the cross carried by Jesus is green—the color of vegetation—to symbolize rebirth and regeneration.

Many of Chartres' windows were donated by members of the nobility, who are frequently shown kneeling in prayer below the images of the saints (see Figure 13.33)—the activities of bakers, butchers, stonemasons, and other workers often appear among the windows commemorating the patron saints of each guild (see Figure 11.17).

Sainte Chapelle: Medieval "Jewelbox"

The art of stained glass reached its highest point in Sainte Chapelle, the small palace chapel commissioned for the Ile de France by King Louis IX ("Saint Louis") (Figure 13.34). Executed between 1245 and 1248, the chapel was

Figure 13.34 Sainte Chapelle, Paris, from the southwest, 1245–1248. Photo: A. F. Kersting, London.

Figure 13.33 (opposite) South rose and lancets, Chartres Cathedral, thirteenth century. Photo: © Sonia Halliday, Western Turville, UK.

Figure 13.35 Upper chapel of Sainte Chapelle, Paris. Height of lancet windows 49 ft. Sonia Halliday Photographs.

designed to hold the Crown of Thorns, a prized relic that Christian Crusaders claimed to have recovered along with other symbols of Christ's Passion. The lower level of the chapel is richly painted with frescoes that imitate the canopy of Heaven, while the upper level consists almost entirely of 49-foot-high lancet windows dominated by ruby red and purplish blue glass (Figure **13.35**). More than a thousand individual stories are depicted within the stained glass windows that make up two-thirds of the upper chapel walls. In its vast iconographic program and its dazzling, ethereal effect, this medieval "jewelbox" is the crowning example of French Gothic art.

Medieval Painting

Medieval painting shared the graphic character of Romanesque sculpture. Responsive to the combined influence of Germanic, Islamic, and Byzantine art, medieval artists developed a taste for decorative abstraction through line. In fresco, manuscript illumination, and panel painting, line worked to flatten form, eliminate space, and enhance the symbolic nature of the image. Line also helped to emphasize gesture, an important symbolic device. In an age dominated by sermons, liturgical chant, and other oral genres, a single, symbolic gesture was truly "worth a thousand words."

Graceful draftsmanship characterizes the illustrations in the thirteenth-century Psalter of Saint Swithin (Figure **13.36**). Like the figures at Moissac and Autun, those

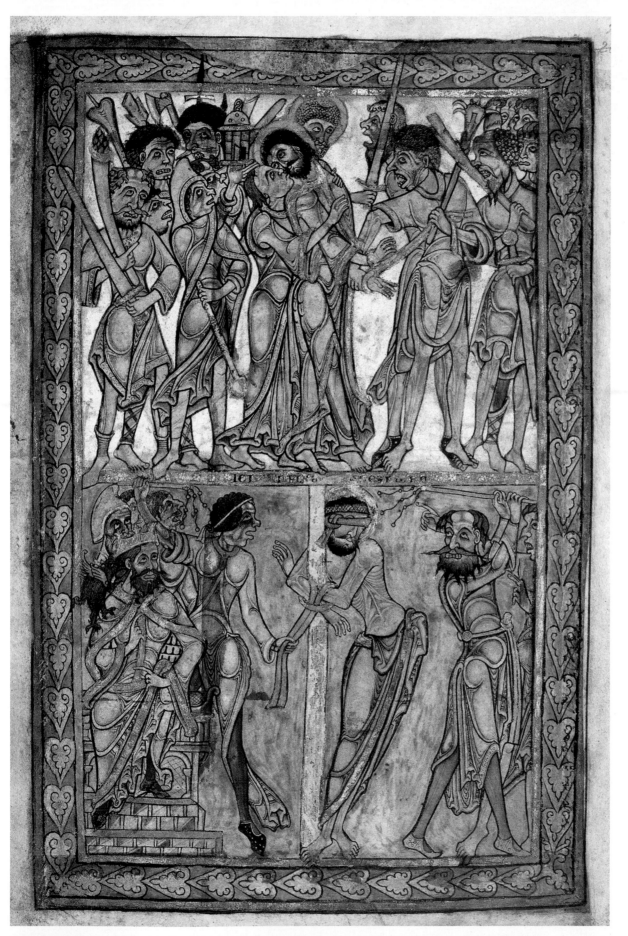

Figure 13.36 Capture of Christ and the Flagellation, from the *Psalter of Saint Swithin*, ca. 1250. Reproduced by permission of the British Library, London.

Figure 13.37 Crucifixion and Deposition of Christ with the Church and the Synogogue, from the *Psalter of Blanche of Castile*, ca. 1235. Bibliothèque de l'Arsenal, Paris, MS 1186, f.24.

parchment (or, if derived from calves, vellum) that made up the book itself. Gold was used lavishly to "illuminate" the images, while rich colors, such as the blue used in Figure 13.37, might come from places as far away as Afghanistan, hence the name "ultramarine" ("beyond the sea") to designate that color.

Some of the finest examples of medieval painting appear on thirteenth-century altarpieces. The typical Gothic altarpiece consisted of a wooden panel or panels covered with **gesso** (a chalky white plaster), on which images were painted in **tempera** (a powdered pigment that produces dry, flat surface colors), and embellished with gold leaf. Installed on or behind the church altar, the altarpiece usually displayed scenes from the Life of Jesus, the Virgin Mary, or a favorite saint or martyr. A late thirteenth-century altarpiece by the Florentine painter Cimabue (1240–1302) shows the Virgin and Child elevated on a monumental seat that is both a throne and a tower (Figure **13.38**). Angels throng around the throne, while, beneath the

Figure 13.38 CIMABUE, *Madonna Enthroned*, ca. 1280–1290. Tempera on wood, 12 ft. 7½ in. × 7 ft. 4 in. Uffizi Gallery, Florence. © Studio Fotografico Quattrone, Florence.

depicted in the Capture and Flagellation of Christ are tall, thin, and lively, their gestures and facial expressions exaggerated to emphasize the contrasting states of arrogance and humility. The artist who painted the Crucifixion and Deposition of Christ for the Psalter of Blanche of Castile (the mother of Saint Louis) imitates the geometric compositions and strong, simple colors of stained glass windows (Figure **13.37**). To the right and left of Jesus are depicted the Church (representing the New Dispensation) and the Synagogue (representing the Old Dispensation). Book illuminators often used pattern books filled with stock representations of standard historical and religious subjects, a practice that encouraged stylistic conservatism. Nevertheless, in the execution of thousands of miniatures and marginal illustrations for secular and religious manuscripts, the imagination of medieval artists seems unbounded. The preparation of medieval manuscripts was a time-consuming and expensive enterprise, usually shared by many different workers. The production of a bible might require the slaughter of some two hundred sheep or calves, whose hides were then scraped, bleached, and carefully processed before becoming the folded sheets of

Figure 13.39 SIMONE MARTINI, *Annunciation*, 1333. (Saints in side panels by **LIPPO MEMMI**.) Tempera on wood, 8 ft. 8 in. × 10 ft. Uffizi Gallery, Florence. Scala/Art Resource, New York.

Virgin's feet, four Hebrew prophets display scrolls predicting the coming of Jesus. To symbolize their lesser importance, angels and prophets are pictured considerably smaller than the enthroned Mary. Such hierarchic grading, which was typical of medieval art, also characterized Egyptian and Byzantine compositional design.

Cimabue's lavishly gilded devotional image has a schematic elegance: Line elicits the sharp, metallic folds of the Virgin's dark blue mantle, the crisp wings of the angels, the chiseled features of the Christ child, and the decorative surface of the throne. The figure of the Virgin combines the hypnotic grandeur of Byzantine icons (by which many Italian artists were influenced) and the weightless, hieratic clarity of Gislebertus' Christ in Majesty at Autun (see Figure 13.9). Although Cimabue's Virgin is more humanized than either of these, she is every bit as regal an object of veneration.

Medieval artists often imitated the ornamental vocabulary of Gothic architecture and the bright colors of stained glass windows. The Sienese painter Simone Martini (1284–1344) made brilliant use of Gothic architectural motifs in his Annunciation altarpiece of 1333 (Figure **13.39**). The frame of the altarpiece consists of elegant Gothic spires and heavily gilded **ogee** arches (pointed arches with S-shaped curves near the apex) sprouting finials and crockets. Set on a gold leaf ground, the petulant Virgin, the Angel Annunciate, and the vase of lilies (symbolizing Mary's purity) seem suspended in time and space. Martini's composition depends on a refined play of lines: The graceful curves of the Angel Gabriel's wings are echoed in his fluttering vestments, in the contours of the Virgin's body as she shrinks from the angel's greeting, and in the folds of her mantle, the pigment for which was ground from semiprecious lapis lazuli.

Medieval Music

Early Medieval Music and Liturgical Drama

The major musical developments of the Early Middle Ages, like those in architecture, came out of the monasteries. In Charlemagne's time, monastic reforms in Church liturgy and in sacred music accompanied the renaissance in the visual arts. Early Church music took the form of unaccompanied monophonic chant (see chapter 9), a solemn sound that inspired one medieval monk to write in the margin of his songbook, "The tedious plainsong grates my tender ears." Perhaps to remedy such complaints, the monks at Saint-Gall enlarged the range of expression of the classical Gregorian chant by adding **antiphons**, or verses sung as responses to the religious text. Carolingian monks also embellished plainsong with the **trope**, an addition of music or words to the established liturgical chant. Thus, "Lord, have mercy upon us" became "Lord, omnipotent Father, God, Creator of all, have mercy upon us." A special kind of trope, called a **sequence**, added words to the long, melismatic passages—such as the alleluias and amens—that occurred at the end of each part of the Mass.

By the tenth century, singers began to divide among themselves the parts of the liturgy for Christmas and Easter, now embellished by tropes and sequences. As more and more dramatic incidents were added to the texts for these Masses, full-fledged music-drama emerged. Eventually, liturgical plays broke away from the liturgy and were performed in the intervals between the parts of the Mass. Such was the case with the eleventh-century *Play of Herod*, whose dramatic "action" brought to life the legend of the three Magi 🎵 and the massacre of the innocents by King Herod of Judea—incidents surrounding the Gospel story of the birth of Christ appropriate to the Christmas season. By the twelfth century, spoken dialogue and possibly musical instruments were introduced. At the monastery of the German abbess, Hildegard of Bingen, Benedictine nuns may have performed her *Ordo virtutum* (see chapter 12). In this music drama, the earliest known morality play in Western history, the Virtues contest with the Devil for the Soul of the Christian. The Devil's lines are spoken, not sung, consistent with Hildegard's belief that satanic evil was excluded from knowing music's harmony and order. Hildegard's most important musical compositions, however, were liturgical. Her monophonic hymns and antiphons in honor of the saints, performed as part of the Divine Office, are exercises in musical meditation. Some offer praise for womankind and for the virgin saints, while others such as the chant *O Successores* 🎵 celebrate the holy confessors—Christ's "successors," who hear confession and give absolution.

Medieval Musical Notation

Musical notation was invented in the monasteries. As with Romanesque architecture, so with medieval musical theory and practice, Benedictine monks at Cluny and elsewhere were especially influential. During the eleventh century, they devised the first efficient Western system of musical notation, thus facilitating the performance and transmission of liturgical music. They arranged the tones of the commonly used scale in progression from A through G and developed a formal system of notating pitch. The Italian Benedictine Guido of Arezzo (ca. 990–ca. 1050) introduced a staff of colored lines (yellow for C, red for F, etc.) on which he registered neumes—marks traditionally written above the words to indicate tonal ascent or descent (see chapter 9). Guido's system established a precise means of indicating shifts in pitch. Instead of relying on memory alone, singers could consult songbooks inscribed with both words and music. Such advances encouraged the kinds of compositional complexity represented by medieval polyphony.

Medieval Polyphony

Although our knowledge of early medieval music is sparse, there is reason to believe that, even before the year 1000, choristers were experimenting with multiple lines of music as an alternative to the monophonic style of Gregorian chant. **Polyphony** (music consisting of two or more lines of melody) was a Western invention; it did not make its appearance in Asia until modern times. The earliest polyphonic compositions consisted of Gregorian melodies sung in two parts simultaneously, with both voices moving note-for-note in parallel motion (parallel **organum**), 🎵 or with a second voice moving in contrary motion (free organum), 🎵 perhaps also adding many notes to the individual syllables of the text (melismatic organum). 🎵 Consistent with rules of harmony derived from antiquity, and with the different ranges of men's voices, the second musical part was usually pitched a fourth or a fifth above or below the first, creating a pure, hollow sound.

Throughout the High Middle Ages, Northern France—and the city of Paris in particular—was the center of the art of polyphonic composition. From the same area that produced the Gothic cathedral came a new musical style that featured several lines of melody arranged in counterpoised rhythms. The foremost Parisian composer toward the end of the twelfth century was Pérotin. A member of the Notre Dame School, Pérotin enhanced the splendor of the Christian Mass by writing three- and four-part polyphonic compositions based on Gregorian chant. Pérotin's music usually consisted of a principal voice or "tenor" (from the Latin *tenere*, meaning "to hold") that sang the "fixed song" (Latin, *cantus firmus*) and one or more voices that moved in shorter-phrased and usually faster tempos. 🎵 The combination of two or three related but independent voices, a musical technique called **counterpoint**, enlivened late twelfth- and thirteenth-century music. Indeed, the process of vertical superimposition of voice on voice enhanced sonority and augmented the melodic complexity of medieval music much in the way that the counterbalanced parts of the Gothic structure enriched its visual texture.

🎵 See Music Listening Selections at end of chapter.

🎵 See Music Listening Selections at end of chapter.

As medieval polyphony encouraged the addition of voices and voice parts, the choir areas of Gothic cathedrals were enlarged to accommodate more singers. Performed within the acoustically resonant bodies of such cathedrals as Notre Dame in Paris, the polyphonic Mass produced an aural effect as resplendent as the multicolored glass that shimmered throughout the interior. Like the cathedral itself, the polyphonic Mass was a masterful synthesis of carefully arranged parts—a synthesis achieved in *time* rather than in *space*.

The "Dies Irae"

One of the best examples of the medieval synthesis, particularly as it served the Christian immortality ideology, is the "Dies irae" ("Day of Wrath"). The fifty-seven-line hymn, which originated among the Franciscans during the thirteenth century, was added to the Roman Catholic **requiem** (the Mass for the Dead) and quickly became a standard part of the Christian funeral service. Invoking a powerful vision of the end of time, the "Dies irae" is the musical counterpart of the sermons and Last Judgment portals (see Figure 13.9) that issued forth solemn warnings of final doom. The hymn opens with the words:

> Day of Wrath! O day of mourning!
> See fulfilled the prophets' warning,
> Heaven and earth in ashes burning!

But, as with most examples of apocalyptic art, including Dante's *Commedia*, the hymn holds out hope for absolution and deliverance:

> With Thy favored sheep, oh, place me!
> Nor among the goats abase me,
> But to Thy right hand upraise me.
>
> While the Wicked are confounded,
> Doomed to flames of woe unbounded,
> Call me, with Thy saints surrounded.

Like so many other forms of medieval expression, the "Dies irae" brings into vivid contrast the destinies of sinners and saints. In later centuries, it inspired the powerful requiem settings of Mozart, Berlioz, and Verdi, and its music became a familiar symbol of apocalyptic death and damnation.

The Motet

The thirteenth century also witnessed the invention of a new religious musical genre, the **motet**—a short, polyphonic choral composition based on a sacred text. Performed both inside and outside the church, it was the most popular kind of medieval religious song. Like the trope, the motet (from the French word *mot*, meaning "word") developed from the practice of adding words to the melismatic parts of a melody. Medieval motets usually juxtaposed two or more uncomplicated themes, each with its own lyrics and metrical pattern, in a manner that was

lilting and lively. ♪ Motets designed to be sung outside the church often borrowed secular tunes with vernacular words. A three-part motet might combine a love song in the vernacular, a well-known hymn of praise to the Virgin, and a Latin liturgical text in the *cantus firmus*. Thirteenth-century motets were thus polytextual as well as polyphonic and polyrhythmic. A stock of melodies (like the stock of images in medieval pattern books) was available to musicians for use in secular and sacred songs, and the same one might serve both types of song. Subtle forms of symbolism occurred in many medieval motets, as for instance where a popular song celebrating spring might be used to refer to the Resurrection of Jesus, the awakening of romantic love, or both.

Instrumental Music of the Middle Ages

Medieval music relied upon the human voice. Musical instruments first appeared in religious music not for the purpose of accompanying songs, as with troubadour poems and folk epics, but to substitute for the human voice in polyphonic compositions. Medieval music depended on **timbre** (tone color) rather than volume for its effect, and

Figure 13.40 Music and Her Attendants, from **BOETHIUS**, *De Arithmetica*, fourteenth century. Scala/Art Resource, New York. Holding a portable pipe organ, the elegant lady who symbolizes the civilized art of courtly music is surrounded by an ensemble of female court musicians. In the circle at the top, King David plays a psaltery, the instrument named after the Psalms (Psaltery) of David. Clockwise from right: lute, clappers, trumpets, nakers (kettledrums), bagpipe, shawm, tambourine, rebec (viol).

most medieval instruments produced sounds that were gentle and thin by comparison with their modern (not to mention electronically amplified) counterparts. Medieval string instruments included the harp, the psaltery, and the lute (all three are plucked), and bowed fiddles such as the vielle and the rebec (Figure 13.40). Wind instruments included portable pipe organs, recorders, and bagpipes. Percussion was produced by chimes, cymbals, bells, tambourines, and drums. Instrumental music performed without voices accompanied medieval dancing. Percussion instruments established the basic rhythms for a wide variety of high-spirited dances, including the estampie, ♪ a popular round dance consisting of short, repeated phrases.

SUMMARY

Medieval churches and cathedrals were the monumental expressions of an age of faith. In Carolingian times, the abbey church became the focal point of monastic life as well as the repository of sacred relics that drew pilgrims from neighboring areas. After the year 1000, Romanesque pilgrimage churches were constructed in great numbers throughout Western Europe. They feature all-stone masonry with round arches and thick barrel and groin vaults. The sculptures on their stone portals and capitals illustrate the Christian themes of redemption and salvation.

While the Romanesque church was essentially a rural phenomenon, the Gothic cathedral was the focus and glory of the medieval town. First developed in the region of Paris, the cathedral was an ingenious synthesis of three structural elements—rib vaults, pointed arches, and flying buttresses—the combination of which permitted the extensive use of stained glass. Raised to breathtaking heights, the Gothic cathedral was, in the words recited at the Mass for the consecration of a Catholic church, "the Court of God and the Gate of Heaven." The sculptural facade, a "bible in stone," presented a panorama of Old and New Testament history, medieval lore, and everyday life. Medieval sculpture and painting styles were generally abstract, symbolic, and characterized by expressive linearity, the use of bright colors, and a decorative treatment of form. Gradually, however, medieval art moved in the direction of greater realism and descriptive detail.

As in the visual arts, the music of the Middle Ages was closely related to religious ritual. In Carolingian times, tropes and sequences came to embellish Christian chant, a process that led to the birth of liturgical drama. In the eleventh century, Benedictine monks devised a system of musical notation that facilitated performance and made possible the accurate transmission of music from generation to generation. At about the same time, polyphony—

a uniquely Western form of musical expression—emerged. In polyphonic compositions, up to three further melodic lines provided counterpoint to the fixed melody. Polyphonic religious compositions known as motets often borrowed vernacular texts and secular melodies.

Like the Gothic cathedral, the polyphonic motet may be said to illustrate the medieval practice of juxtaposing and reconciling opposing elements. Collectively, all of the arts worked to form a coherent whole—a synthesis that projected the medieval view of nature as the expression of a preordained, divine order.

SUGGESTIONS FOR READING

Boney, Jean. *French Gothic Architecture of the Twelfth and Thirteenth Centuries*. Berkeley, Calif.: University of California Press, 1983.

Calkins, Robert. *Monuments of Medieval Art*. Ithaca, N.Y.: Cornell University Press, 1989.

Dodwell, C. R. *The Pictorial Arts of the West 800–1200*. New Haven: Yale University Press, 1993.

Gies, Francis and Joseph. *Cathedral, Forge, and Waterwheel: Technology and Invention in the Middle Ages*. New York: Harperperennial, 1995.

Gimpel, Jean. *The Cathedral Builders*, translated by D. King. Ithaca, N.Y.: Cornell University Press, 1980.

Macauley, David. *Cathedral: The Story of its Construction*. Boston: Houghton Mifflin, 1973.

Martindale, Andrew. *Gothic Art from the Twelfth to the Fifteenth Century*. London: Thames and Hudson, 1985.

Seay, Albert. *Music in the Medieval World*. 2nd ed. Englewood Cliffs, N.J.: Prentice-Hall, 1991.

Simson, Otto von. *The Gothic Cathedral*. Expanded edition. Princeton, N.J.: Princeton University Press, 1988.

Stokstad, Marilyn. *Medieval Art*. New York: Harper, 1986.

Yudkin, Jeremy. *Music in the Middle Ages*. Upper Saddle River, N.J.: Prentice-Hall, 1989.

MUSIC LISTENING SELECTIONS

CD One Selection 7 Medieval liturgical drama, *The Play of Herod*, Scene 2, "The Three Magi."

CD One Selection 8 Hildegard of Bingen, *O Successores* (Your Successors), ca. 1150.

CD One Selection 9 Three examples of early medieval polyphony: parallel organum, "Rex caeli, Domine"; free organum, trope, "Agnus Dei"; melismatic organum, "Benedicamus Domino"; ca. 900–1150; excerpts.

CD One Selection 10 Pérotin, Three-part organum, "Alleluya" (Nativitas), twelfth century.

CD One Selection 11 Anonymous, Motet, "En non Diu! Quant voi; Eius in Oriente," thirteenth century, excerpt.

CD One Selection 12 French dance, "Estampie," thirteenth century.

♪ See Music Listening Selections at end of chapter.

GLOSSARY

antiphon a verse sung in response to the text; see also "antiphonal" in Glossary, chapter 9

archivolt a molded or decorated band around an arch or forming an archlike frame for an opening

bay a regularly repeated spatial unit of a building; in medieval architecture, a vaulted compartment

counterpoint a musical technique that involves two or more independent melodies; the term is often used interchangeably with "polyphony"

crocket a stylized leaf used as a terminal ornament

finial an ornament, usually pointed and foliated, that tops a spire or pinnacle

gargoyle a waterspout usually carved in the form of a grotesque figure

gesso a chalky white plaster used to prepare the surface of a panel for painting

historiated capital the uppermost member of a column, ornamented with figural scenes

lancet a narrow window topped with a pointed arch

lintel a horizontal beam or stone that spans an opening (see Figure 13.10)

motet a short, polyphonic religious composition based on a sacred text

mullion the slender, vertical pier dividing the parts of a window, door, or screen

ogee a pointed arch with an S-shaped curve on each side

organum the general name for the oldest form of polyphony: In *parallel organum*, the two voices move exactly parallel to one another; in *free organum* the second voice moves in contrary motion; *melismatic organum* involves the use of multiple notes for the individual syllables of the text

polyphony (Greek, "many voices") a musical texture

consisting of two or more lines of melody that are of equal importance

psaltery a stringed instrument consisting of a flat soundboard and strings that are plucked

quadripartite consisting of or divided into four parts

refectory the dining hall of a monastery

reliquary a container for a sacred relic or relics

requiem a Mass for the Dead; a solemn chant to honor the dead

rose (from the French *roue*, "wheel") a large circular window with stained glass and stone tracery

sequence a special kind of trope consisting of words added to the melismatic passages of Gregorian chant

sexpartite consisting of or divided into six parts

tempera a powdered pigment that produces dry, flat colors

timbre tone color; the distinctive tone or quality of sound made by a voice or a musical instrument

triforium in a medieval church, the shallow arcaded passageway above the nave and below the clerestory (see Figure 13.20)

tripartite consisting of or divided into three parts

trope an addition of words, music, or both to Gregorian chant

trumeau the pillar that supports the superstructure of a portal (see Figure 13.10)

tympanum the semicircular space enclosed by the lintel over a doorway and the arch above it (see Figure 13.10)

voussoir (French, "wedge") a wedge-shaped block or unit in an arch or vault

westwork (from the German, *Westwerk*) the elaborate west end of a Carolingian or Romanesque church

PART THREE

The world beyond the West

Western students often overlook the fact that Europe—home of the culture that is most familiar to them—occupies only a tiny area at the far western end of the vast continental landmass of Asia. At the eastern end of that landmass lie two geographic and cultural giants, India and China, and the small but mighty Japan (see Maps 14.1 and 14.2). During the European Middle Ages, East and West had little contact with each other, apart from periodic exchanges of goods and technology facilitated by Muslim intermediaries. Although neither India nor China nor Japan had a direct impact on the West, their indirect influence was considerable, especially in the areas of science and technology.

Between 500 and 1300 C.E., India produced some of the finest Sanskrit literature ever written. Hindu temple architecture and sculpture reached new levels of imagination and complexity, and Indian music flourished. In China, during roughly the same period, the Tang and Song dynasties fostered a golden age in poetry and painting. The Chinese surpassed the rest of the world in technological invention and led global production in fine pottery and textiles. Even at the peak of productivity in medieval Europe, and especially between the years 1250 and 1350, China's technical sophistication, naval power, and cultural fertility exceeded that of any country in the West. Medieval Japan originated the world's oldest prose fiction and cultivated a style governed by beauty of effect in art and life. Deeply infused with the values of Buddhism, Hinduism, Daoism, and the precepts of Confucius, the artistic record of India, China, and Japan reflects a holistic view of nature that has worked broadly to universalize the human experience. A brief examination of these achievements puts our study of the humanistic tradition in a global perspective and provides a basis for the appreciation of three of Asia's most notable cultures.

(opposite) Chang Tse-tuan, detail from *Life Along the River on the Eve of The Ch'ing Ming Festival*, late eleventh to early twelfth century. Handscroll, ink on silk. Collection of the Palace Museum, Beijing.

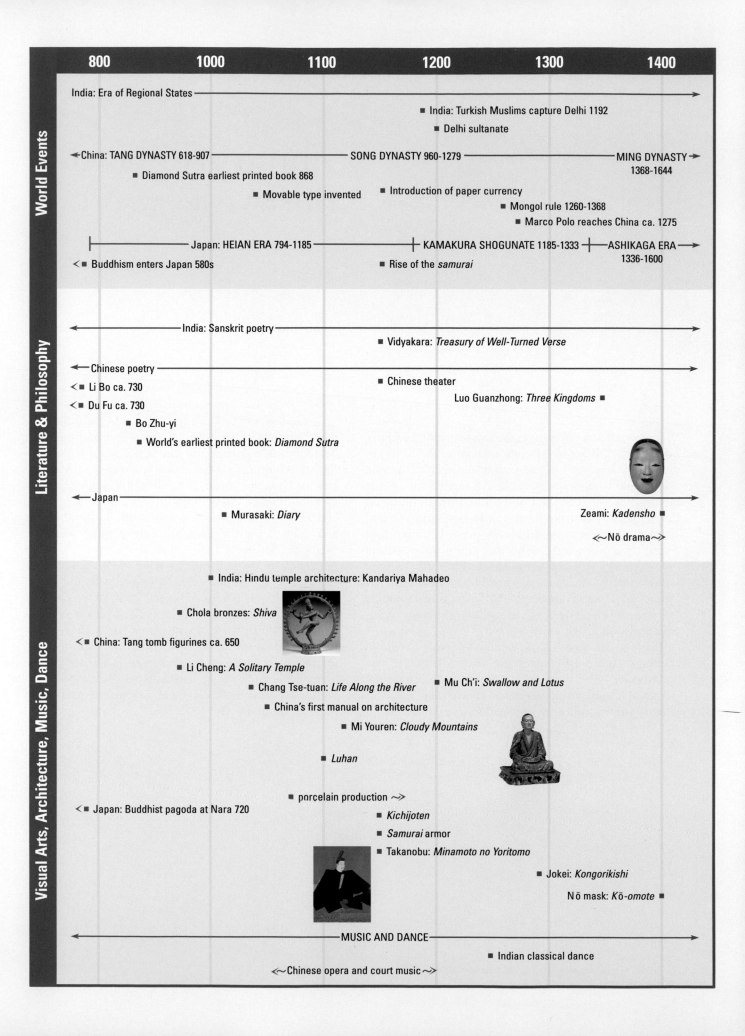

	800	1000	1100	1200	1300	1400

World Events

India: Era of Regional States →

■ India: Turkish Muslims capture Delhi 1192
■ Delhi sultanate

←China: TANG DYNASTY 618-907——————SONG DYNASTY 960-1279——————MING DYNASTY →
1368-1644

■ Diamond Sutra earliest printed book 868
■ Movable type invented
■ Introduction of paper currency
■ Mongol rule 1260-1368
■ Marco Polo reaches China ca. 1275

Japan: HEIAN ERA 794-1185——————KAMAKURA SHOGUNATE 1185-1333——ASHIKAGA ERA →
1336-1600

< ■ Buddhism enters Japan 580s
■ Rise of the *samurai*

Literature & Philosophy

←——————India: Sanskrit poetry——————→
■ Vidyakara: *Treasury of Well-Turned Verse*

←Chinese poetry
< ■ Li Bo ca. 730
■ Chinese theater
< ■ Du Fu ca. 730
Luo Guanzhong: *Three Kingdoms* ■
■ Bo Zhu-yi
■ World's earliest printed book: *Diamond Sutra*

←Japan
■ Murasaki: *Diary*
Zeami: *Kadensho* ■
<~Nō drama~>

Visual Arts, Architecture, Music, Dance

■ India: Hindu temple architecture: Kandariya Mahadeo
■ Chola bronzes: *Shiva*
< ■ China: Tang tomb figurines ca. 650
■ Li Cheng: *A Solitary Temple*
■ Chang Tse-tuan: *Life Along the River*
■ Mu Ch'i: *Swallow and Lotus*
■ China's first manual on architecture
■ Mi Youren: *Cloudy Mountains*
■ *Luhan*
■ porcelain production ~>
< ■ Japan: Buddhist pagoda at Nara 720
■ *Kichijoten*
■ *Samurai* armor
■ Takanobu: *Minamoto no Yoritomo*
■ Jokei: *Kongorikishi*
Nō mask: *Kō-omote* ■

←——————MUSIC AND DANCE——————→
■ Indian classical dance
<~Chinese opera and court music~>

CHAPTER FOURTEEN

Asian civilizations: the artistic record

"Heaven is my father and earth is my mother, and even such a small creature as I finds an intimate place in their midst."
Zhang Zai

The Medieval Period in India

Although the term "medieval" does not apply to the history of India in the Western sense of an interlude between classical and early modern times, scholars have used that term to designate the era between the end of the Gupta dynasty (ca. 500) and the Mongol conquest of India in the fourteenth century—a thousand-year period that roughly approximates the Western Middle Ages. The dissolution of the Gupta Empire at the hands of Central Asian Huns, an event that paralleled the fall of Rome in the West and the collapse of the Han Empire in China, destroyed the remains of South Asia's greatest culture. Following this event, amidst widespread political turmoil and anarchy, India became a conglomeration of fragmented, rival local kingdoms dominated by a warrior caste (not unlike the feudal aristocracy of medieval Europe). Ruling hereditary chiefs or *rajputs* ("sons of kings") followed a code of chivalry that set them apart from the lower classes. The caste system (see chapter 3), which had been practiced in India for many centuries, worked to enforce the distance between rulers and the ruled. And as groups were subdivided according to occupation and social status, caste distinctions became more rigid and increasingly fragmented. Extended families of the same caste were ruled by the eldest male, who might take a number of wives. Children were betrothed early in life and women's duties—to tend the household and raise children (preferably sons)—were carefully prescribed. In a society where males were masters, a favorite Hindu proverb ran, "A woman is never fit for independence." The devotion of the upper-caste Hindu woman to her husband was dramatically expressed in *sati*, a custom by which the wife threw herself on her mate's funeral pyre.

Early in the eighth century, Arab Muslims entered India and began to convert members of the native population to Islam. Muslim authority took hold in Northern India, and Muslims rose to power as members of the ruling caste. During the tenth century, the invasions of Turkish

Muslims brought further chaos to India, resulting in the capture of Delhi (Map **14.1**) in 1192 and the destruction of the Buddhist University of Nalanda in the following year. Muslim armies destroyed vast numbers of Hindu and Buddhist religious statues, which they regarded as idols, and Islam supplanted Hinduism and Buddhism in the Indus valley (modern Pakistan) and in Bengal (modern

Map 14.1 India in the Eleventh Century.

Bangladesh). Elsewhere, however, the native traditions of India and Hinduism itself prevailed. Indeed, most of India—especially the extreme south, which held out against the Muslims until the fourteenth century—remained profoundly devoted to the Hindu faith. Today, approximately eighty-five percent of India's population is Hindu. Buddhism, on the other hand, had virtually disappeared from India by the twelfth century.

Hinduism in Medieval India

In the medieval period, the philosophic aspects of Hinduism (as defined in the principal religious writings, the *Upanishads* and the *Bhagavad-Gita*; see chapter 3) were overshadowed by growing devotion to the gods and goddesses of Hindu mythology. These personal deities, rooted in India's most ancient texts—the *Vedas*—are personifications of the powerful, life-giving forces of nature. Although the worship of these gods suggests that Hindus are polytheistic, it is more accurate to say that Hinduism, fundamentally pantheistic, perceives all of nature—divine, human, and animal—as one. At the very core of Indian civilization, Hinduism confirms the oneness of nature. It teaches that all individual aspects of being belong to the same divine substance: the impersonal, all-pervading Absolute Spirit known as Brahman. Hindus view regional deities and the gods of ancient India as **avatars** (Sanskrit, "incarnations") of Brahman, much in the way that Christians regard Jesus as the incarnate form of God. Indeed, since Hindus believe that the avatars of Brahman may assume different names and forms (even those of animals), they freely honor the Buddha and Jesus as human guises of the Divine Reality. Having no single founder, no spokesman, and no priesthood comparable with that of medieval Christianity, nor any uniform set of sacred practices, Hinduism encourages its devotees to seek union with Brahman in their own fashion, whether through meditation or by worshiping the many gods and spirits of Hindu myth and legend. The plural character of Hinduism contrasts sharply with Judaism, Christianity, and Islam, all of which hold divinity as a singular concept. The many gods of the Hindus—like the facets of a diamond—exist only, however, as individual aspects (or manifestations) of the Whole.

In medieval India, three principal gods dominated the Hindu pantheon: Brahma, Vishnu, and Shiva. Hindus associated this "trinity" with the three main expressions of Brahmanic power: creation, preservation, and destruction. They honored Brahma—his name is the masculine form of Brahman—as the creator of the world. They prized Vishnu (identified with the sun in ancient Vedic hymns) as the preserver god. Hindu mythology recounts Vishnu's appearance on earth in nine different incarnations, including that of Krishna, the hero-god of the Mahabharata (see chapter 3). Icons of Vishnu often resemble those of the Buddha, who is accepted by Hindus as an avatar of Vishnu (Figure **14.1**). Such ritual icons, cast in bronze by the lost-wax method (see Introduction), are among the finest free-standing figural sculptures executed since golden-age Greece. Produced in large numbers in tenth-century Tamil

Figure 14.1 *Standing Vishnu*, from Southern India, Chola dynasty, tenth century C.E. Bronze, with greenish-blue patination, height 33¾ in. The Metropolitan Museum of Art, New York, Purchase 1962. Gift of Mr. and Mrs. John D. Rockefeller.

Nadu in South India, bronze effigies of the god were often bedecked with flowers and carried in public processions. (Note the rings at the four corners of the base of the *Standing Vishnu*, which once held poles for transporting the statue.)

The third god of the trinity, Shiva, is the Hindu lord of regeneration. A god of destruction and creation, of disease and death, and of sexuality and rebirth, Shiva embodies the dynamic rhythms of the universe. While often shown in a dual male and female aspect, Shiva is most commonly portrayed as Lord of the Dance, an image that evokes the Hindu notion of time. Unlike the Western view of time, which is linear and progressive, the Hindu perception of time is cyclical; it moves like an ever-turning cosmic wheel. Hindus believe that the worship of the gods, their avatars, and their female consorts is an expression of intense personal devotion by which one gains the blessing of the divine. Hindus perceive the god to be present in its representation; hence the act of worship puts one in direct

Figure 14.2 *Shiva Nataraja, Lord of the Dance,* from Southern India, Chola period, eleventh century. Copper, height 43⅞ in. The Cleveland Museum of Art. Purchase from the J. H. Wade Fund, 30.331.

physical and visual contact with the god: "Beholding the image is an act of worship."*

The four-armed figure of Shiva as Lord of the Dance is one of medieval India's most famous Hindu icons (Figure **14.2**)—so popular, in fact, that Tamil sculptors cast multiple versions of the image. Framed in a celestial circle of fire, Shiva seems to gyrate, thus symbolizing cosmic creation and destruction, the living cycle of birth and death. His serpentine body bends at the neck, waist, and knees in accordance with specific and prescribed dance movements (Figure **14.3**). Every part of the statue has symbolic meaning: In one right hand Shiva carries a small drum, the symbol of creation; a second right hand (the arm wreathed by a snake, ancient symbol of regeneration) forms the *mudra* meaning protection (see chapter 9); one left hand holds a flame, the symbol of destruction; the second left hand points toward the feet, the left one "released" from worldliness, the right one crushing a dwarf that symbolizes ignorance. Utterly peaceful in countenance, Shiva displays the five activities of the godhead: creation, protection, destruction, release from destiny, and enlightenment. By these activities, the god dances the universe in and out of existence.

Indian Religious Literature

Medieval Indian literature drew heavily on the mythology and legends of early Hinduism as found in the Vedic hymns and in India's two great epics, the *Mahabharata* and the *Ramayana* (see chapter 2). This body of classic Indian literature was recorded in Sanskrit, the language of India's educated classes. Serving much the same purpose that Latin served in the medieval West, Sanskrit functioned for centuries as a cohesive force amidst India's diverse groups of regional vernacular dialects.

Among the most popular forms of Hindu literature in the medieval period were the Puranas (Sanskrit, "old stories"), a collection of eighteen religious books that preserved the myths and legends of the Hindu gods. Transmitted orally for centuries, they were not written down until well after 500 C.E. Many of the tales in the *Puranas* illustrate the special powers of Vishnu and Shiva or their avatars. In the *Vishnu Purana*, for instance, Krishna is pictured as a lover who courts his devotees with sensual abandon, seducing them to become one with the divinity. In contrast to medieval Christianity's somber condemnation of the sensual life, Hinduism regards the physical union of male and female as symbolic of the eternal mingling of flesh and spirit, a sublime metaphor for the fusion of the Self (Atman) and the Absolute Spirit (Brahman) that culminates in *nirvana*. The *Upanishads* make clear the analogy:

> In the embrace of his beloved a man forgets the
> whole world—everything both within and without.
> In the same manner, he who embraces the Self
> knows neither within nor without.

The Hindu view of human sexuality as a metaphor for spiritual knowledge recalls the rituals of pre-Christian fertility cults, which exalted the life-affirming and regenerative aspects of erotic love. In the following passage from the *Vishnu Purana*, Krishna's cajoling and sensuous courtship, culminating in the circle of the dance, symbolizes the god's love for the human soul and the soul's unswerving attraction to the One.

---

*Diana L. Eck, *Dars'an: Seeing the Divine Image in India.* Chambersburg, Pa.: Anima Books, 1981, 3.

Figure 14.8 Ravi Shankar playing the sitar (right); others with tabla (hand drums) and tamboura (plucked string instrument). Photo: © Silverstone/Magnum Photos, Inc.

ditional dances requires a combination of complex body positions, of which there are more than one hundred. The close relationship among the arts of medieval India provides something of a parallel with the achievement of the medieval synthesis in the West. On the other hand, the sensual character of the arts of India distinguishes them sharply from the arts of Christian Europe.

The Medieval Period in China

Nowhere else in the world has a single cultural tradition dominated so consistently over so long a period as in China. When European merchants visited China in the thirteenth century, the Chinese had already enjoyed 1,700 years of civilization. China's agrarian landmass, rich in vast mineral, vegetable, and animal resources, readily supported a large and self-sufficient population, the majority of which constituted a massive land-bound peasantry. Despite internal shifts of power and repeated barbarian attacks, China experienced a single form of government— imperial monarchy—and a large degree of political order until the invasion of the Mongols in the thirteenth century. But even after the establishment of Mongol rule under Kubilai Khan (1215–1294), the governmental bureaucracy on which China had long depended remained intact, and Chinese culture continued to flourish. The wealth and splendor of early fourteenth-century China inspired the awe and admiration of Western visitors, such as the famous Venetian merchant-adventurer Marco Polo (1254–1324). Indeed, in the two centuries prior to Europe's rise to economic dominion (but especially between 1250 and 1350), China was "the most extensive, populous, and technologically advanced region of the medieval world."*

China in the Tang Era

Tang China (618–907 C.E.) was a unified, centralized state that had no equal in Asia or the West. In contrast with

---

*Janet L. Abu-Lughod, *Before European Hegemony: The World System* A.D. 1250–1350. New York: Oxford University Press, 1989, 316.

India, class distinctions in China were flexible and allowed a fair degree of social mobility: Even commoners could rise to become members of the ruling elite. Nevertheless, as in all Asian and European civilizations of premodern times, the great masses of Chinese peasants had no voice in political matters.

Despite the success of Buddhism in China (see chapters 8 and 9), Confucianism remained China's foremost moral philosophy. Confucian teachings encouraged social harmony and respect for the ruling monarch, whom the Chinese called the "Son of Heaven." The Confucian equation of virtue and authority, which linked the destiny of the community with the ruler's obedience to moral law (see chapter 3), and Confucian respect for the universal order (expressed in the creative interaction of yin and yang) were humanizing forces in Chinese culture. Confucianism was generally tolerant of all religious creeds, though it disapproved of the Buddhist commitment to celibacy, which contravened the Confucian esteem for family. The growth of Buddhist sects and the popularity of a religion that attracted large numbers of talented men to the cloister encouraged eighth-century emperors to restrict the number of Buddhist monasteries and to limit the ordination of new monks and nuns. Nevertheless, the monkish image of the Buddhist *luhan* ("worthy one"), humbly attired and transfixed in a state of deep meditation (Figure **14.9**), became a popular model of self-control and selflessness—an ideal type not unlike that of the Christian saint. In contrast to medieval Europe, however, where

700	the Chinese perfect the making of porcelain, which reaches Europe as "china"
725	the Chinese build a water clock with a regulating device anticipating mechanical clocks
748	the first printed newspaper appears in Beijing
868	the *Diamond Sutra*, the first known printed book, is produced in China

transcendental Christianity guided the soul's journey to the hereafter, China held firmly to a secular ethic that emphasized proper conduct (*li*) and the sanctity of human life on earth. These Confucian tenets—renewed in the neo-Confucian movement of the eleventh century—challenged neither the popular worship of a large number of Chinese nature deities nor ancient rites that honored the souls of the dead. Likewise, Confucian ideals of order, harmony, and filial duty were easily reconciled with holistic Daoism (see chapter 7). Tolerant of all religions, the Chinese never engaged in religious wars or massive crusades of the kind that disrupted both Christian and Islamic civilizations.

Under the rule of the Tang emperors, China experienced a flowering of culture that was unmatched anywhere in the world. Often called the greatest dynasty in Chinese history, the Tang brought unity and wealth to a vast Chinese empire (Map **14.2**). Tang emperors perpetuated the economic policies of their immediate predecessors, but they employed their vast powers to achieve a remarkable series of reforms. They completed the Grand Canal connecting the lower valley of the Yellow River to the eastern banks of the Yangzi, a project that facilitated shipping and promoted internal cohesion and wealth. They initiated a full census of the population (some four centuries before a similar survey was undertaken in Norman England), which was repeated every three years. They also humanized the penal code and tried to guarantee farmlands to the peasants. They stimulated agricultural production, encouraged the flourishing silk trade,

Figure 14.9 *Luhan*, China, tenth to thirteenth centuries. Pottery with three-color glaze, height 46½ in. Nelson-Atkins Museum of Art, Kansas City.

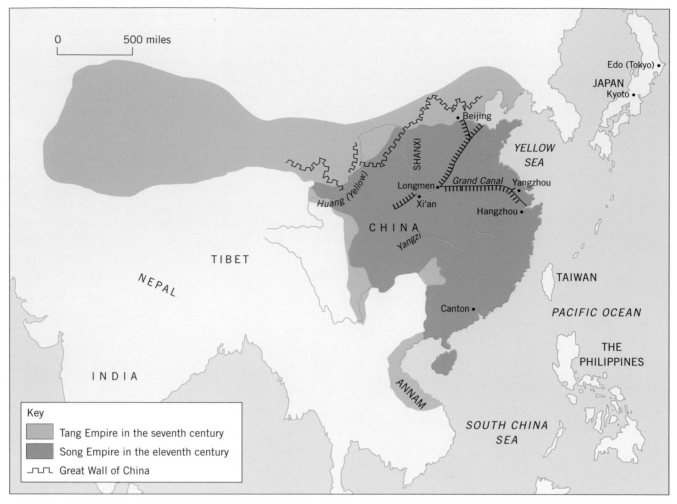

Map 14.2 East Asia.

launched a tax reform that based assessments on units of land rather than agricultural output, and they commuted payments from goods to coins.

The Tang Empire dwarfed the Carolingian Empire in the West not only by its geographic size and population but also by its intellectual and educational accomplishments. Tang bureaucrats, steeped in Confucian traditions and rigorously trained in the literary classics, were members of an intellectual elite that rose to service on the basis of merit. Beginning in the seventh century (but rooted in a long tradition of leadership based on education and ability), every government official was subject to a rigorous civil service examination. A young man gained a political position by passing three levels of examinations (district, provincial, and national) that tested his familiarity with the Chinese classics as well as his grasp of contemporary political issues. For lower-ranking positions, candidates took exams in law, mathematics, and calligraphy. As in the Islamic world and the Christian West, higher education in China required close familiarity with the basic religious and philosophical texts. But because Chinese characters changed very little over the centuries, students could read 1,500-year-old texts as easily as they could read contemporary ones. Chinese classics were thus accessible to Chinese scholars in a way that the Greco-Roman classics

were not accessible to Western scholars. Training for the arduous civil service examinations required a great degree of memorization and a thorough knowledge of the Chinese literary tradition, but originality was also important: Candidates had to prove accomplishment in the writing of prose and poetry, as well as in the analysis of administrative policy. Strict standards applied to grading, and candidates who failed the exams (only one to ten percent passed the first level) could take them over and over, even into their middle and old age.

During the seventh century, the imperial college in the capital city of Chang'an (present-day Xi'an) prepared some three thousand men for the civil service examinations. (As in the West, women were excluded from education in colleges and universities.) Such scholar officials constituted China's highest social class. And while the vast population of Chinese peasants lived in relative ignorance and poverty, the aristocratic bureaucracy of the Tang generally enjoyed lives of wealth and position. Nowhere else in the world (except perhaps Baghdad) was such prestige attached to scholarship and intellectual achievement. Despite instances in which family connections influenced political position, the imperial examination system remained the main route to official status in China well into the twentieth century.

A less enlightened Chinese practice survived into the modern period: the binding of women's feet. From earliest times, Chinese women participated in agricultural activities as well as in the manufacture of silk (Figure **14.10**); many were trained in dance and musical performance (Figure **14.11**). In the early 900s, however, as women seem to have assumed a more ornamental role in Chinese society, footbinding became common among the upper classes. To indicate that their female offspring were exempt from common labor, prosperous urban families bound the feet of their infant daughters—a practice that broke the arch and dwarfed the foot to half its normal growth. Footbinding, a cruel means of signifying social status, persisted into the early twentieth century.

Figure 14.10 Attributed to the Song emperor **HUIZONG** (reigned 1101–1125), but probably by court academician, after a lost painting by Zhang Xuan (fl. 713–741 C.E.), *Women Combing Silk*, detail of *Court Ladies Preparing Newly Woven Silk*, Northern Song dynasty, early twelfth century. Ink, color, and gold on silk handscroll, height 14½ in., length 57¼ in. Courtesy, Museum of Fine Arts, Boston. Chinese and Japanese Special Fund.

Figure 14.11 Attributed to **ZHOU WENJU**, detail of a girls' ensemble performing court banquet music during the reign of Emperor Xuanzong, with (upper group, left to right) lute, angular harp, long zither, stone-chime, mouth organ, hourglass drum, transverse flute, and clapper, Song dynasty. Ink and color on silk handscroll, 16⅜ in. × 71⅞ in. The Art Institute of Chicago. Kate S. Buckingham Purchase Fund, 1950. Photograph © 1998 The Art Institute of Chicago. All rights reserved.

China in the Song Era

After a brief period of political turmoil resulting from the attacks of nomadic tribes, the Song dynasty (960–1279) restored stability to China. The three centuries of Song rule corresponded roughly to the golden age of Muslim learning, the waning of the Abbasid Empire and the era of Norman domination in Europe (see chapters 10, 11). The Song Era was a period of population growth, agricultural productivity, and vigorous commercial trade centering on the exportation of tea, silk, and porcelain. China's new economic prosperity caused a population shift from the countryside to the city, where social mobility was on the rise. The port city of Hangzhou (see Map 14.2), with a population of almost two million people, boasted a variety of restaurants, teahouses, temples, gardens, and shops, including bookstores and pet shops (Figure **14.12**). Chinese cities were larger and more populous than those in the West and city dwellers enjoyed conditions of safety that are enviable even today—in Hangzhou, the streets were patrolled at night, and bridges and canals were guarded and fitted with balustrades to prevent drunken revelers from falling into the water.

Although the Song Era was a time of peace, a ready army was a necessity. However, mercenaries came to replace peasant-soldiers in the ranks. Whereas medieval Islam and the feudal West prized heroism and the art of war, the Chinese despised military life. A Chinese proverb claimed that good steel should not be made into common nails, nor good men into soldiers. Chinese poets frequently lamented the disruption of family life as soldiers left home to defend remote regions of the Empire. In combat, the Chinese generally preferred starving out their enemies to confronting them in battle. The peaceful nature of the Chinese impressed its first Western visitors: Arriving in China a half century after the end of the Song Era, Marco Polo observed with some astonishment that no one carried arms. Indeed, from the twelfth to the early twentieth century China espoused the Confucian idea that everything partakes of a single Nature—a notion of cosmic harmony best expressed in the writings of the Neo-Confucian philosopher Zhang Zai (1020–1077):

> Heaven is my father and earth is my mother, and even such a small creature as I finds an intimate place in their midst. Therefore that which extends throughout the universe I regard as my body and that which directs the universe I consider as my nature. All people are my brothers and sisters, and all things are my companions.*

Technology in the Tang and Song Eras

Chinese civilization is exceptional in the extraordinary number of its technological inventions, many of which came into use elsewhere in the world only long after their utilization in China. A case in point is printing, which originated in ninth-century China but was not perfected in the West until the fifteenth century. The earliest printed document, the *Diamond Sutra*, dated 868, is a Buddhist text produced from large woodcut blocks (Figure **14.13**). In the mid-eleventh century, the Chinese invented movable type and, by the end of the century, the entire body of Buddhist and Confucian classics, including the commentaries, were available in printed editions. One such classic (a required text for civil service candidates) was *The Book of Songs*, a venerable collection of over three hundred

1000	the magnetic needle compass is developed in China
1009	the Chinese first use coal as fuel
ca. 1040	three varieties of gunpowder are described by Zeng Kongliang
1041	movable type is utilized in China

*William H. McNeill and J. W. Sedlar, eds. *China, India, and Japan: The Middle Period*. New York: Oxford University Press, 1971, 78.

Figure 14.12 CHANG TSE-TUAN, detail from *Life Along the River on the Eve of the Ch'ing Ming Festival*, late eleventh to early twelfth century. Handscroll, ink on silk. Collection of the Palace Museum, Beijing.

Figure 14.13 The *Diamond Sutra*, the world's earliest printed book, dated 868 C.E. 72 × 30 in. Reproduced by courtesy of the British Library, London. Department of Oriental Manuscripts and Books.

poems dating from the first millennium B.C.E. By the twelfth century, the Chinese were also printing paper money—a practice that inevitably gave rise to the "profession" of counterfeiting. Although in China movable type did not inspire a revolution in the communication of ideas (as it would in Renaissance Europe), it encouraged literacy, fostered scholarship, and facilitated the preservation of the Chinese classics.

Chinese technology often involved the intelligent application of natural principles to produce labor-saving devices. Examples include the water mill (devised to grind tea leaves and to provide power to run machinery), the wheelbarrow (used in China from at least the third century but not found in Europe until more than ten centuries later), and the stern-post rudder and magnetic compass (Song inventions that facilitated maritime trade). The latter two devices had revolutionary consequences for Western Europeans, who used them to inaugurate an age of exploration and discovery (see chapter 19). Gunpowder, invented by the Chinese as early as the seventh century and used in firework displays, was employed (in the form of fire-arrow incendiary devices) for military purposes in the mid-tenth century, but arrived in the West only in the fourteenth century. Other contrivances, such as the abacus and the hydromechanical clock, and such processes as iron-casting (used for armaments, for suspension bridges, and for the construction of some Tang and Song pagodas)

were unknown in the West for centuries or were invented independently of Chinese prototypes. Not until the eighteenth century, for instance, did Western Europeans master the technique of steel-casting, which had been in use in China since the sixth century C.E.; and the seismograph (invented in China around 100 B.C.E.) remained unknown to Europe until modern times.

Some of China's most important technological contributions, such as the foot stirrup (in use well before the fifth century) and gunpowder, improved China's ability to withstand the attacks of Huns, Turks, and other tribal peoples who repeatedly attacked China's northern frontiers. In the West, however, the foot stirrup and gunpowder had revolutionary results: The former ushered in the military aspect of medieval feudalism; and the latter ultimately undermined siege warfare and inaugurated modern forms of combat. While thirteenth-century China was far ahead of the medieval West in science and technology, its wealth in manpower—a population of some hundred million people—may have made a technology of industrial power (like that pursued in the early modern West) unnecessary.

In addition to their ingenuity in engineering and metallurgy, the Chinese advanced the practice of medicine. From the eleventh century on, they used vaccination to prevent diseases, thus establishing the science of immunology. Their understanding of human anatomy and

My mad singing startles the valleys and hills:
The apes and birds all come to peep.
Fearing to become a laughing-stock to the world,
I choose a place that is unfrequented by men.

Chinese Landscape Painting

During the Tang Era, figural subjects dominated Chinese art (see Figure 14.10), but by the tenth century, landscape painting became the favorite genre. The Chinese, and especially the literati of Song China, referred to landscape paintings as wordless poems and poems as formless paintings; such metaphors reflect the intimate relationship between painting and poetry in Chinese art. In subjects dealing with the natural landscape, both Chinese paintings and Chinese poems seek to evoke a mood rather than provide a literal, objective description of reality. Chinese landscapes work to convey a spirit of harmony between heaven and earth. This cosmic approach to nature, fundamental to both Daoism and Buddhism, asks the beholder to contemplate, rather than simply to view the painted image. The contemplative landscape may require the beholder to integrate multiple viewpoints, and to shift between foreground, middleground, and background in ways that resemble the mental shifts employed in reading lines of poetry.

Chinese paintings generally assume one of three basic formats: the handscroll, the hanging scroll, or the album leaf (often used as a fan). Between one and forty feet long, the handscroll is viewed continuously from right to left (Figure **14.14**). Like a poem, the visual "action" unfolds in time—an object of lingering contemplation and delight. The hanging scroll, on the other hand, is vertical in format and is meant to be read from the bottom up—from earth to heaven, so to speak (see Figure 14.15). The album leaf usually belongs to a book that combines poems and paintings in a sequence. Both leaves and scrolls are made of silk or paper and ornamented with ink or thin washes of paint applied in monochrome or in muted colors. An interesting Chinese practice is the addition of the seals or signatures of collectors who have owned the work of art. These appear along with occasional marginal comments or brief poems inspired by the visual image. The poem may also serve as an extension of the content of the work of art. The Chinese painting, then, is a repository of the personal expressions of both artist and art lover.

By comparison with medieval and Renaissance art in the West, much of which is religious in subject matter, Chinese painting draws heavily on the visual world and the everyday activities of men, women, and children. Whereas Western artists exalt the heroic deeds and historical achievements of individuals, Chinese artists rarely glorify human accomplishments. Indeed, in Chinese paintings, the landscape often dwarfs the figures so that human occupations seem mundane and incidental within the vast sweep of nature.

A Solitary Temple Amid Clearing Peaks, attributed to Li Cheng (active 940–967), is meditative in mood and subtle in composition (Figure **14.15**). There is no single viewpoint from which to observe the mountains, trees, waters, and human habitations. Rather, we perceive the whole from what one eleventh-century Chinese art critic called the "angle of totality." We look down upon some elements, such as the rooftops, and up to others, such as the mountains. The lofty mountains and gentle waterfall seem protective of the infinitely smaller images of houses and people. Misty areas act as transition points between foreground, middleground, and background, but each plane—even the background—is delineated with identical precision. The visual voyage through discontinuous space engages our recognition of the subtle relationships between all parts of the painting, putting us in touch with the physical and spiritual energies of nature. Mountains, Chinese symbols of immortality, were regarded as living organisms that emanated the life force (*qi*) in the form of cloud vapor. As with Chinese poetry, in which a few well-

Figure 14.14 MI YOUREN, *Cloudy Mountains*, 1130. Ink, white lead, and slight touches of color on silk handscroll, 13 ft. 6 in. × 6 ft. 3 in. The Cleveland Museum of Art. Purchase from the J. H. Wade Fund.

Figure 14.15 (above) Attributed to **LI CHENG**, *A Solitary Temple Amid Clearing Peaks*, Northern Song dynasty, ca. 950 C.E. Ink and slight color on silk hanging scroll, 44 × 22 in. The Nelson-Atkins Museum of Art, Kansas City, Missouri. Purchase: Nelson Trust. 47–71.

right (added by the artist's patron) extends the "message" of the image as fragile, elegant, fleeting:

> Meeting the wind, they offer their artful charm;
> Moist with dew, they boast their pink beauty.*

The earliest treatises on Chinese painting appeared in the Song Era. They describe the artist's practice of integrating complementary pictorial elements: dark and light shapes, bold and muted strokes, dense and sparse textures, large and small forms, and positive and negative shapes, each pair interacting in imitation of the *yin/yang* principle that underlies cosmic wholeness. Specific brushstrokes, each bearing an individual name, are prescribed for depicting

*Maxwell Hearn, *Splendors of Imperial China: Treasures from the National Palace Museum, Taipei.* New York: The Metropolitan Museum of Art, 1996, 33.

Figure 14.16 (below) **MU QI**, *Swallow and Lotus*, Song dynasty. Hanging scroll, ink on silk, 36⅛ × 18½ in. The Cleveland Museum of Art. Purchase from the J. H Wade Fund.

chosen words may convey a distinct mood, Chinese painting displays a remarkable economy of line and color—that is, a memorable image is achieved by means of a limited number of brushstrokes and tones. Li Cheng fulfilled the primary aim of the Chinese landscape painter (as defined by Song critics): to capture the whole universe within a few inches of space.

More intimate in detail but equally subtle in its organization of positive and negative space, *Swallow and Lotus* by Mu Qi reflects the Song taste for decorative works featuring floral and bird motifs (Figure **14.16**). Refined nature studies like this one, executed in ink and color on silk, dwell on a single element in nature (the "broken branch") rather than the expansive landscape. The couplet at the

SUMMARY

Between roughly 500 and 1300, India, China, and Japan produced arts and ideas that, although markedly different from those of the European West, contributed richly to the corpus of the humanistic tradition. Asian art of this period reveals a profound respect for the interdependence of natural and divine forces, of body and mind, and of matter and spirit. The sacred literature of Hinduism, as well as the rich fund of Sanskrit secular poetry, manifests a distinctly sensual approach to nature. In literature, architecture, and sculpture, the Hindu gods are identified with the creative, cyclical, and regenerative forces of the Absolute Spirit. The Hindu notion that nature and humankind belong to one and the same unifying, organic order differs sharply from the medieval Christian view that humankind was distinct and separate from both lower (animal) and higher (divine) forms of reality. In Indian visual art, as in Indian music and dance, the holistic view is expressed as a celebration of cyclical and natural universal rhythms.

The arts of China blossomed under the centralized leadership of the Tang and Song dynasties. Chinese religious philosophy—a synthesis of Buddhist, Confucian, and Daoist precepts—emphasized natural harmony and the unity of all living things. These concepts found sublime expression in Chinese poetry and landscape painting—two of China's greatest contributions to world culture. The Chinese imperial examination system produced an elite class of scholar-officials, while China's high regard for scholarship also generated a class of scholar-poets known as literati. China manufactured high-quality luxury goods and exported these to the rest of the world. Until at least the fourteenth century, China's technological and commercial achievements (such as the invention of printing, the magnetic compass, gunpowder, and the manufacture of magnificent porcelains and silks) far outstripped those of the West.

Japan's artistic record bears the stamp of Chinese culture. In the Heian period, however, a literary form unique to medieval Japan—the psychological novel—made its way into world literature. The samurai culture of the Kamakura shogunate and a rich heritage of Mahayana Buddhism played distinctive roles in the arts: The former commissioned magnificent weapons, armor, and palace portraiture, while the latter supported a flourishing industry in shrine architecture and sculpture. The medieval Japanese preference for refined form and beauty of effect is illustrated in the visual arts, in literature, and perhaps most distinctively in Nō theater, the classic drama of Japan.

Deeply committed to the concept of natural harmony, the civilizations of India, China, and Japan produced an extraordinary fund of arts and ideas. As modern forms of communication have worked to bring all parts of the world closer together, the Asian contributions to the humanistic tradition have gained greater recognition, better understanding, and deeper appreciation among Westerners.

SUGGESTIONS FOR READING

Bhavnani, Enakshi. *The Dance in India*, 2nd ed. Bombay: Taraporevala, 1970.

Cahill, James. *The Painter's Practice: How Artists Lived and Worked in Traditional China*. New York: Columbia University Press, 1994.

Clunas, Craig. *Art in China*. New York: Oxford University Press, 1997.

Coomaraswamy, Ananda. *The Dance of Shiva*. Reprint edition. New York: South Asian Books, 1997.

Ellgood, Heather. *Hinduism and the Religious Arts*. London: Cassell, 1999.

Fisher, Robert E. *Buddhist Art and Architecture*. London: Thames and Hudson, 1993.

Massey, Reginald. *The Music of India*. New York: South Asian Books, 1998.

Morris, Ivan. *The World of the Shining Prince: Court Life in Ancient Japan*. New York: Kodansha International, 1994.

Murck, Alfreda, and Wen Fong. *Words and Images: Chinese Poetry, Calligraphy, and Painting*. Princeton, N.J.: Princeton University Press, 1991.

Rawson, Jessica, ed. *The British Museum Book of Chinese Art*. New York: Thames and Hudson, 1992.

Schirokauer, Conrad. *A Brief History of Chinese and Japanese Civilizations*. San Diego: Harcourt, 1991.

Yoshikawa, Itsuji. *Major Themes in Japanese Art*. New York: Weatherhill/Heibonsha, 1976.

MUSIC LISTENING SELECTIONS

CD One Selection 13 Indian music, *Thumri*, played on the sitar by Ravi Shankar.

CD One Selection 14 Chinese music: Cantonese music drama for male solo, zither, and other instruments, "Ngoh wai heng kong" ("I'm Mad About You").

GLOSSARY

alliteration a literary device involving the repetition of initial sounds in successive or closely associated words or syllables

assonance a literary device involving a similarity in sound between vowels followed by different consonants

avatar (Sanskrit, "incarnation") the incarnation of a Hindu deity

luhan (or luohan) (Chinese, "worthy one") a term for enlightened being, portrayed as a sage or mystic

mithuna the Hindu representation of a male and a female locked in passionate embrace

novel an extended fictional prose narrative

opera a drama set to music and making use of vocal pieces with orchestral accompaniment

porcelain a hard, translucent ceramic ware made from clay fired at high heat

raga a mode or melodic form in Hindu music; a specific combination of notes associated with a particular mood or atmosphere

sitar a long-necked stringed instrument popular in Indian music

tala a set rhythmic formula in Hindu music

Yolande de Soissons kneeling before a statue of the Virgin and Child. Psalter and Book of Hours, Northern France, ca. 1290. The Pierpont Morgan Library NY. Art Resource, NY.

PART ONE

The age of the Renaissance

The three hundred years between 1300 and 1600 brought Western Europe out of the Middle Ages and onto the threshold of modernity. In economic life, manorialism succumbed to entrepreneurial capitalism. In political life, the medieval order gave way to centralized forms of government and the advent of national states. Ascendant individualism, secularism, and rationalism challenged devotional sentiment and religious fervor. The printing press made liberal education available to an increasingly literate population, while the science of navigation and advancing technology encouraged European expansion and cross-cultural contacts. By 1600, Europe would assume a dominant presence in parts of the world whose geography had only recently been mapped with any accuracy.

The Renaissance, or "rebirth" of classicism, was the cultural hinge between medieval and modern times. Originating in fourteenth-century Italy, and spreading northward during the fifteenth and sixteenth centuries, this dynamic movement shaped some of the West's most fundamental political, economic, and cultural values—values associated with the rise of nation-states, the formation of the middle class, and the advancement of classically based education and classically inspired art.

The fourteenth century was a period of transition marked by the struggle for survival against the devastating bubonic plague, the trials of a long and debilitating war between England and France, and the dramatic decline of the Roman Catholic Church. These events radically altered all aspects of Western European life and cultural expression. In the arts of this era there are distinct signs of a revived self-consciousness, increasing fidelity to nature, and a growing preoccupation with gender and class. But it was in Italy that the definitive aspect of the Renaissance—classical humanism—unfolded. Classical humanism—the movement to recover, study, and disseminate ancient Greek and Latin texts—stimulated a sense of individualism, a boundless vitality, and an optimistic view of the human potential for fulfillment on earth. The writings of Petrarch, Alberti, Pico, Castiglione, and Machiavelli are evidence of the Renaissance effort to apply classical precepts to matters of education, diplomacy, politics, and social life.

Renaissance artists looked to classical Greece and Rome as sources of aesthetic authority, but competed with their classical predecessors in the search for more scientific methods of describing the visual world. To portraiture and landscape painting, they brought keen objectivity; to monumental sculpture a sense of heroic individualism, and to architecture a new unity of design. The development of vernacular song forms, the rise of instrumental music, and the beginnings of choreography all mark the growing secularism of an age of rebirth.

(opposite) **LUCCA DELLA ROBBIA**, *Drummers* (detail of the *Cantoria*). Museo dell'Opera del Duomo, Florence. Scala, Florence.

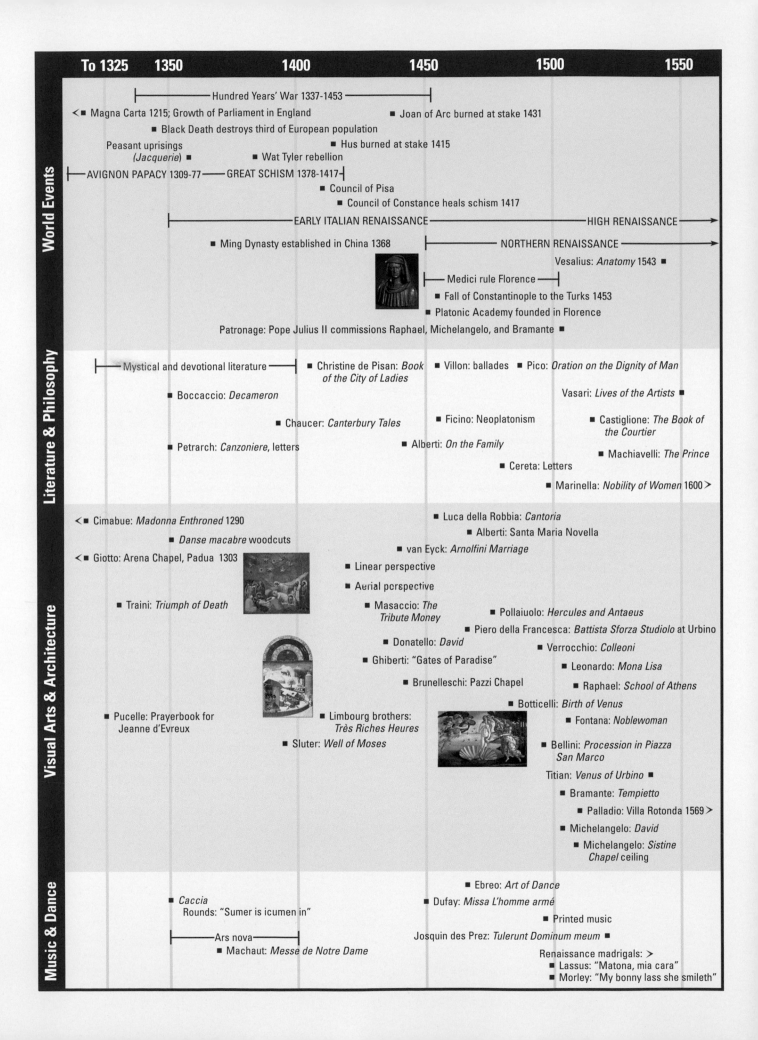

	To 1325	**1350**	**1400**	**1450**	**1500**	**1550**

World Events

Hundred Years' War 1337-1453

< ■ Magna Carta 1215; Growth of Parliament in England   ■ Joan of Arc burned at stake 1431

■ Black Death destroys third of European population

Peasant uprisings   ■ Hus burned at stake 1415
(Jacquerie) ■   ■ Wat Tyler rebellion

├ ■ AVIGNON PAPACY 1309-77 ──── GREAT SCHISM 1378-1417 ┤

■ Council of Pisa

■ Council of Constance heals schism 1417

── EARLY ITALIAN RENAISSANCE ──────────── HIGH RENAISSANCE ──→

■ Ming Dynasty established in China 1368   ── NORTHERN RENAISSANCE ──→

Vesalius: *Anatomy* 1543 ■

├ ■ Medici rule Florence ──┤

■ Fall of Constantinople to the Turks 1453

■ Platonic Academy founded in Florence

Patronage: Pope Julius II commissions Raphael, Michelangelo, and Bramante ■

Literature & Philosophy

├ ── Mystical and devotional literature ──┤ ■ Christine de Pisan: *Book of the City of Ladies*   ■ Villon: ballades   ■ Pico: *Oration on the Dignity of Man*

Vasari: *Lives of the Artists* ■

■ Boccaccio: *Decameron*

■ Chaucer: *Canterbury Tales*   ■ Ficino: Neoplatonism   ■ Castiglione: *The Book of the Courtier*

■ Petrarch: *Canzoniere*, letters   ■ Alberti: *On the Family*   ■ Machiavelli: *The Prince*

■ Cereta: Letters

■ Marinella: *Nobility of Women* 1600 >

Visual Arts & Architecture

< ■ Cimabue: *Madonna Enthroned* 1290   ■ Luca della Robbia: *Cantoria*

■ *Danse macabre* woodcuts   ■ Alberti: Santa Maria Novella

< ■ Giotto: Arena Chapel, Padua 1303   ■ van Eyck: *Arnolfini Marriage*

■ Linear perspective

■ Aerial perspective

■ Traini: *Triumph of Death*   ■ Masaccio: *The Tribute Money*   ■ Pollaiuolo: *Hercules and Antaeus*

■ Piero della Francesca: *Battista Sforza Studiolo* at Urbino

■ Donatello: *David*   ■ Verrocchio: *Colleoni*

■ Ghiberti: "Gates of Paradise"   ■ Leonardo: *Mona Lisa*

■ Brunelleschi: Pazzi Chapel   ■ Raphael: *School of Athens*

■ Botticelli: *Birth of Venus*

■ Pucelle: Prayerbook for Jeanne d'Evreux   ■ Fontana: *Noblewoman*

■ Limbourg brothers: *Très Riches Heures*   ■ Bellini: *Procession in Piazza San Marco*

■ Sluter: *Well of Moses*

Titian: *Venus of Urbino* ■

■ Bramante: *Tempietto*

■ Palladio: Villa Rotonda 1569 >

■ Michelangelo: *David*

■ Michelangelo: *Sistine Chapel* ceiling

Music & Dance

■ Ebreo: *Art of Dance*

■ *Caccia*   ■ Dufay: *Missa L'homme armé*
Rounds: "Sumer is icumen in"

■ Printed music

├ ── Ars nova ──┤   Josquin des Prez: *Tulerunt Dominum meum* ■

■ Machaut: *Messe de Notre Dame*

Renaissance madrigals: >
■ Lassus: "Matona, mia cara"
■ Morley: "My bonny lass she smileth"

Adversity and challenge: the fourteenth-century transition

"So many bodies were brought to the churches every day that the consecrated ground did not suffice to hold them . . ."
Boccaccio

Traditions normally undergo modification only over long periods of time. However, natural disasters, epidemic disease, and protracted warfare generally accelerate cultural change. The fourteenth century provides a case in point, for during that dramatic time all of these catalytic phenomena occurred in Western Europe, causing widespread havoc and wrenching medieval customs and practices out of their steady, dependable rhythms. As a result, the period between roughly 1300 and 1400 became a time of transition between medieval and early modern history. During this age, many medieval traditions were revised or discarded and new cultural patterns contributed to the formation of a modern world system dominated by the rise of the West.

The Black Death

The most devastating natural catastrophe of the early modern era was the bubonic plague, which struck Europe in 1347 and destroyed one third to one half of its population within less than a century. Originating in Asia and spread by the Mongol tribes that dominated that vast area, the disease devastated China and the Middle East, interrupting long-distance trade and cross-cultural encounters that had flourished for two centuries. The plague was carried into Europe by flea-bearing black rats infesting the commercial vessels that brought goods to Mediterranean ports. Within two years of its arrival it ravaged much of the Western world. In its early stages, it was transmitted by the bite of either the infected flea or the host rat; in its more severe stages, it was passed on by those infected with the disease. The symptoms of the malady were terrifying: Buboes (or abscesses) that began in the lymph glands of the groin or armpits of the afflicted slowly filled with pus, turning the body a deathly black, hence the popular label "the Black Death." Once the boils and accompanying fever

appeared, death usually followed within two to three days. Traditional treatments, such as the bleeding of victims and fumigation with vapors of vinegar, proved useless. No connection was perceived between the ubiquitous rats and the plague itself, and in the absence of a clinical understanding of bacterial infection, the medical profession of the day was helpless. (Indeed, the bacillus of the bubonic plague was not isolated until 1894.)

The plague hit hardest in the towns, where a concentration of population and the lack of sanitation made the disease all the more difficult to contain. Four waves of bubonic plague spread throughout Europe between 1347 and 1375, infecting some European cities several times and nearly wiping out their entire populations (Figure **15.1**). The virulence of the plague and the mood of mounting despair horrified the Florentine writer Giovanni Boccaccio (1313–1375). In his preface to the *Decameron*, a collection of tales told by ten young people who abandoned plague-ridden Florence for the safety of a country estate, Boccaccio described the physical conditions of the pestilence, as well as its psychological consequences. He recorded with somber precision how widespread death had forced Florentine citizens to abandon the traditional forms of grieving and the rituals associated with death and burial. The stirring vernacular prose captured the mood of dread that prevailed in Florence, as people fled their cities, homes, and even their families.

READING 3.1   From Boccaccio's Introduction to the *Decameron* (1351)

. . . In the year of Our Lord 1348 the deadly plague broke   **1**
out in the great city of Florence, most beautiful of Italian
cities. Whether through the operation of the heavenly
bodies or because of our own iniquities which the just
wrath of God sought to correct, the plague had arisen in
the East some years before, causing the death of
countless human beings. It spread without stop from one

Figure 15.1 *The Black Death*, miniature from a rhymed Latin chronicle of the events of 1349–1352 by Egidius, abbot of Saint Martin's, Tournai, France, ca. 1355. Manuscript illumination. Bibliothèque Royale, Brussels, MS13076–77, f.24v.

place to another, until, unfortunately, it swept over the West. Neither knowledge nor human foresight availed against it, though the city was cleansed of much filth by chosen officers in charge and sick persons were forbidden to enter it, while advice was broadcast for the preservation of health. Nor did humble supplications serve. Not once but many times they were ordained in the form of processions and other ways for the propitiation of God by the faithful, but, in spite of everything, toward the spring of the year the plague began to show its ravages in a way short of miraculous.

It did not manifest itself as in the East, where if a man bled at the nose he had certain warning of inevitable death. At the onset of the disease both men and women were afflicted by a sort of swelling in the groin or under the armpits which sometimes attained the size of a common apple or egg. Some of these swellings were larger and some smaller, and all were commonly called boils. From these two starting points the boils began in a little while to spread and appear generally all over the body. Afterwards, the manifestation of the disease changed into black or livid spots on the arms, thighs and the whole person. In many these blotches were large and far apart, in others small and closely clustered. Like the boils, which had been and continued to be a certain indication of coming death, these blotches had the same meaning for everyone on whom they appeared.

Neither the advice of physicians nor the virtue of any medicine seemed to help or avail in the cure of these diseases. Indeed, whether the nature of the malady did not suffer it, or whether the ignorance of the physicians could not determine the source and therefore could take no preventive measures against it, the fact was that not only did few recover, but on the contrary almost everyone died within three days of the appearance of the signs—some sooner, some later, and the majority without fever or other ill. Moreover, besides the qualified medical men, a vast number of quacks, both men and women, who had never studied medicine, joined the ranks and practiced cures. The virulence of the plague was all the greater in that it was communicated by the sick to the well by contact, not unlike fire when dry or fatty things are brought near it. But the evil was still worse. Not only did conversation and familiarity with the diseased spread the malady and even cause death, but the mere touch of the clothes or any other object the sick had touched or used, seemed to spread the pestilence. . . .

Because of such happenings and many others of a like sort, various fears and superstitions arose among the survivors, almost all of which tended toward one end—to flee from the sick and whatever had belonged to them. In this way each man thought to be safeguarding his own health. Some among them were of the opinion that by living temperately and guarding against excess of all kinds, they could do much toward avoiding the danger; and forming a band they lived away from the rest of the world. Gathering in those houses where no one had been ill and living was more comfortable, they shut themselves in. They ate moderately of the best that could be had and drank excellent wines, avoiding all luxuriousness. With music and whatever other delights they could have, they lived together in this fashion, allowing no one to speak to them and avoiding news either of death or sickness from the outer world.

Others, arriving at a contrary conclusion, held that plenty of drinking and enjoyment, singing and free living and the gratification of the appetite in every possible way, letting the devil take the hindmost, was the best preventative of such a malady; and as far as they could, they suited the action to the word. Day and night they went from one tavern to another drinking and carousing unrestrainedly. At the least inkling of something that suited them, they ran wild in other people's houses, and there was no one to prevent them, for everyone had abandoned all responsibility for his belongings as well as for himself, considering his days numbered. Consequently most of the houses had become common property and strangers would make use of them at will whenever they came upon them even as the rightful owners might have done. Following this uncharitable way of thinking, they did their best to run away from the infected.

Meanwhile, in the midst of the affliction and misery that had befallen the city, even the reverend authority of divine and human law had almost crumbled and fallen into decay, for its ministers and executors, like other men, had either died or sickened, or had been left so entirely without assistants that they were unable to attend to their duties. As a result everyone had leave to do as he saw fit.

[Others, in an effort to escape the plague, abandoned the city, their houses, their possessions, and their relatives.] The calamity had instilled such horror into the hearts of men and women that brother abandoned brother, uncles, sisters and wives left their dear ones to perish, and, what is more serious and almost incredible, parents avoided visiting or nursing their very children, as though these were not their own flesh. . . . So great was the multitude of those who died in the city night and day, what with lack of proper care and the virulence of the plague, that it was terrible to hear of, and worse still to see. Out of sheer necessity, therefore, quite different customs arose among the survivors from the original laws of the townspeople.

It used to be common, as it is still, for women, friends and neighbors of a dead man, to gather in his house and mourn there with his people, while his men friends and many other citizens collected with his nearest of kin outside the door. Then came the clergy, according to the standing of the departed, and with funereal pomp of tapers and singing he was carried on the shoulders of his peers to the church he had elected before death. Now, as the plague gained in violence, these customs were either modified or laid aside altogether, and new ones were instituted in their place, so that, far from dying among a crowd of women mourners, many passed away without the benefit of a single witness. Indeed, few were those who received the piteous wails and bitter tears of friends and relatives, for often, instead of mourning, laughter, jest and carousal accompanied the dead—usages which even naturally compassionate women had learned to perfection for their health's sake. It was a rare occurrence for a corpse to be followed to church by more than ten or twelve mourners—not the usual respectable citizens, but a class of vulgar grave-diggers who called themselves "sextons" and did these services for a price. They crept under the bier and shouldered it, and then with hasty steps rushed it, not to the church the deceased had designated before death, but oftener than not to the nearest one. . . .

More wretched still were the circumstances of the common people and, for a great part, of the middle class, for, confined to their homes either by hope of safety or by poverty, and restricted to their own sections, they fell sick daily by thousands. There, devoid of help or care, they died almost without redemption. A great many breathed their last in the public streets, day and night; a large number perished in their homes, and it was only by the stench of their decaying bodies that they proclaimed their death to their neighbors. Everywhere the city was teeming with corpses. A general course was now adopted by the people, more out of fear of contagion than of any charity they felt toward the dead. Alone, or with the assistance of whatever bearers they could muster, they would drag the corpses out of their homes and pile them in front of the doors, where often, of a morning, countless bodies might be seen. Biers were sent for. When none was to be had, the dead were laid upon ordinary boards, two or three at once. It was not infrequent to see a single bier carrying husband and wife, two or three brothers, father and son, and others besides. . . .

So many bodies were brought to the churches every day that the consecrated ground did not suffice to hold them, particularly according to the ancient custom of giving each corpse its individual place. Huge trenches were dug in the crowded churchyards and the new dead were piled in them, layer upon layer, like merchandise in the hold of a ship. A little earth covered the corpses of each row, and the procedure continued until the trench was filled to the top. . . .

The Effects of the Black Death

Those who survived the plague tried to fathom its meaning and purpose. Some viewed it as the manifestation of God's displeasure with the growing worldliness of contemporary society, while others saw it as a divine warning to all Christians, but especially to the clergy, whose profligacy and moral laxity were commonly acknowledged facts. Those who perceived the plague as God's scourge urged a return to religious orthodoxy, and some devised fanatic kinds of atonement. Groups of flagellants, for instance, wandered the countryside lashing their bodies with whips in frenzies of self-mortification. At the other extreme, there were many who resolved to "eat, drink, and be

Figure 15.4 *The End of the Siege of Ribodane: English Soldiers Take a French Town*, late fifteenth century. Manuscript illumination. Note longbow and light cannon. By permission of the British Library, London, MS Roy.14.E.IV, f.281v.

bow. Because the thin arrows of the longbow easily pierced the finest French chain mail, plate mail soon came to replace chain mail. However, within the next few centuries, even plate mail became obsolete, since it proved useless against artillery that employed gunpowder.

Introduced into Europe by the Muslims, who borrowed it from the Chinese, gunpowder was first used in Western combat during the Hundred Years' War. In the first battle of the war, however, the incendiary substance proved too potent for the poorly cast English cannons, which issued little more than terrifying noise. Still, gunpowder, which could lay waste a city, constituted an extraordinary advance in military technology, one that ultimately outmoded hand-to-hand combat and rendered obsolete the medieval code of chivalry. Froissart's account of the Hundred Years' War—which reads like a Crusade chronicle—glorifies the performance of chivalric deeds, even though many of the methods of combat Froissart describes

clearly anticipate a new era. For instance, because the English were greatly outnumbered by the French, they resorted to ambush, thus violating medieval rules of war. It can be said, then, that the Hundred Years' War inaugurated the impersonal style of combat that has come to dominate modern warfare.

Although throughout the Hundred Years' War the English repeatedly devastated the French armies, the financial and physical burdens of garrisoning French lands ultimately proved too great for the English, who, facing a revitalized army under the charismatic leadership of Joan of Arc, finally withdrew from France in 1429. Of peasant background, the seventeen-year-old Joan begged the French king to allow her to obey the voices of the Christian saints who had directed her to expel the English (Figure **15.5**). Donning armor and riding a white horse, she led the French into battle. Her success, which forced the English to withdraw from Orléans, initiated her

Figure 15.5 Joan of Arc, from **ANTOINE DUFOUR'S** *Lives of Famous Women*, French MS, 1504, Musée Dobrée, Nantes, MS 17, f. 176. Photo: Giraudon, Paris.

martyrdom; in 1431, she was condemned as a heretic and burned at the stake.

The Hundred Years' War dealt a major blow to feudalism. By the mid-fifteenth century, the French nobility was badly depleted, and those knights who survived the war found themselves "outdated." In France, feudal allegiances were soon superseded by systems of national conscription, and in the decades following the English withdrawal, both countries were ready to move in separate directions, politically and culturally.

The Decline of the Church

The growth of the European nation-states contributed to the weakening of the Christian commonwealth, especially where Church and state competed for influence and authority. The two events that proved most damaging to

Figure 15.7 GIOTTO, *Madonna Enthroned*, ca. 1310. Tempera on panel, 10 ft. 8 in. × 6 ft. 8 in. Uffizi Gallery, Florence. Scala/Art Resource, New York.

Figure 15.8 GIOTTO,
Lamentation, 1305–1306. Fresco,
7 ft. 7 in. × 7 ft. 9 in. Arena
Chapel, Padua.

While they are not individualized to the point of portraiture, neither are they stereotypes. Giotto's style advanced the trend toward realism already evident in late Gothic sculpture (see chapter 13). At the same time, it gave substance to the spirit of lay piety and individualism that marked the fourteenth century.

Devotional Realism and Portraiture

In religious art, realism enhanced the devotional mood of the age. Traditional scenes of the lives of Christ and the Virgin became at once more pictorial and detailed, a reflection of the new concern with Christ's human nature and his suffering. Images of the Crucifixion and the Pietà (the Virgin holding the dead Jesus), which had been a popular object of veneration since the tenth century, were now depicted with a new expressive intensity. One anonymous German artist of the mid-fourteenth century rendered the Pietà (the word means both "pity" and "piety") as a traumatic moment between a despairing Mother and her Son, whose broken torso and elongated arms are as rigid as the wood from which they were carved (Figure **15.10**). The sculpture captures the torment of Christ's martyrdom with a fierce energy more frequently found in African wood sculpture (see Figures 18.9, 18.10) than in traditional European art.

The most notable personality in the domain of fourteenth-century monumental sculpture was the Dutch artist Claus Sluter (ca. 1350–1406). Sluter's *Well of Moses*,

executed between 1395 and 1406 for the Carthusian monastery at Champmol just outside of Dijon, France, was originally part of a 25-foot-tall stone fountain designed to celebrate the sacraments of Eucharist and Baptism. The Crucifixion group that made up the superstructure is lost, but the pedestal of the fountain with its six Old Testament prophets—Moses, David, Jeremiah, Zachariah, Daniel, and Isaiah—survives in its entirety (Figure **15.11**). However, time has robbed the piece of the brightly colored paint and metal accessories (the scholarly Jeremiah bore a pair of copper spectacles) that once gave it a startlingly lifelike presence. Carrying scrolls engraved with their messianic texts, the life-sized prophets are swathed in deeply cut, voluminous draperies. Facial features are individualized so as to render each prophet with a distinctive personality. As in Giotto's *Lamentation*, mourning angels (at the corners of the pedestal above the heads of the prophets) cover their faces or wring their hands in gestures of anguish and despair. So intensely theatrical is the realism of the Champmol ensemble that scholars suspect Sluter might have been inspired by contemporary mystery plays, where Old Testament characters regularly took the stage between the acts to "prophesy" New Testament events.

Devotional realism is equally apparent in illuminated manuscripts, and especially in the popular prayerbook known as the Book of Hours. This guide to private prayer featured traditional recitations for the canonical hours

Figure 15.11 CLAUS SLUTER, figure of Moses on the *Well of Moses*, Carthusian Monastery of Champmol, Dijon, France, 1395–1406. Painted stone, height approx. 6 ft. Photo: Erich Lessing/Art Resource. NY.

of Our Lady). Departing from the medieval tradition of treating the Mass as five separate compositions (based on Gregorian chant), he unified the parts into a single musical composition. He is the first known composer to have provided this type of unified setting for the textually fixed portions of the Mass. Machaut's effort at coherence of design is clear evidence that composers had begun to rank musical effect as equal to liturgical function. He also added to the Mass a sixth movement, the "Ite missa est." ♪ Machaut's new treatment of the Catholic liturgy set a precedent for such composers as the sixteenth-century Palestrina and the baroque master Johann Sebastian Bach (see chapter 22). Machaut's sacred compositions represent only a small part of his total musical output. Indeed, his secular music parallels the rise of vernacular art in his time. Typical of this trend are his 142 polyphonic **ballades** (secular songs), which look back to the music of the *trouvères*. They introduce new warmth and lyricism, as well as vivid poetic imagery—features that parallel the humanizing currents in fourteenth-century art

and literature. "One who does not compose according to feelings," wrote Machaut, "falsifies his work and his song."

Although fourteenth-century polyphony involved both voices and instruments, manuscripts of the period did not usually specify whether a given part of a piece was instrumental or vocal. Custom probably dictated the performance style, not only for vocal and instrumental ensembles, but for dance as well. Outside France, polyphonic music flourished. The blind Italian composer Francesco Landini (ca. 1325–1397) produced graceful instrumental compositions and eloquent two- and three-part songs. Landini's 150 works constitute more than one third of the surviving music of the fourteenth century—evidence of his enormous popularity. Italian composers anticipated Renaissance style (see chapter 17) with florid polyphonic compositions that featured a close relationship between musical parts. The *caccia* (Italian for "chase"), for instance, which dealt with such everyday subjects as hunting, was set to lively music in which one voice part "chased" another. Another popular fourteenth-century polyphonic composition, the **round**, featured successive voices that repeated a single melody (as in "Row, Row,

_____

♪ See Music Listening Selections at end of chapter.

Figure 15.12 JEAN PUCELLE, *Betrayal* and *Annunciation* from the *Book of Hours of Jeanne d'Evreux, Queen of France*, 1325–1328. Miniature on vellum, each folio 3½ × 2⁷⁄₁₆ in. The Metropolitan Museum of Art, New York. The Cloisters Collection, 1954 (54.1.2. ff.15v and 16r).

While Ficino was engaged in popularizing Plato, one of his most learned contemporaries, Giovanni Pico della Mirandola (1463–1494), undertook the translation of various ancient literary works in Hebrew, Arabic, Latin, and Greek. Humanist, poet, and theologian, Pico sought not only to bring to light the entire history of human thought, but to prove that all intellectual expression shared the same divine purpose and design. This effort to discover a "unity of truth" in all philosophic thought—similar to but more comprehensive than the medieval quest for synthesis and so dramatically different from our own modern pluralistic outlook—dominated the arts and ideas of the High Renaissance (see chapter 17).

Pico's program to recover the past and his reverence for the power of human knowledge continued a tradition that looked back to Petrarch; at the same time, his monumental efforts typified the activist spirit of Renaissance *individualism*—the affirmation of the unique, self-fashioning potential of the human being. In Rome, at the age of twenty-four, Pico boldly challenged the Church to debate some 900 theological propositions that challenged the institutional Church in a variety of theological and philosophical matters. The young scholar did not get the opportunity to debate his theses; indeed, he was persecuted for heresy and forced to flee Italy. As an introduction to the disputation, Pico had prepared the Latin introduction that has come to be called the *Oration on the Dignity of Man*. In this "manifesto of humanism," Pico drew on a wide range of literary sources to build an argument for free will and the perfectibility of the individual. Describing the individual's position as only "a little lower than the angels," he stressed man's capacity to determine his own destiny on the hierarchical "chain of being" that linked the divine and brute realms. The Renaissance view that the self-made individual occupies the center of a rational universe is nowhere better described than in the following excerpt.

READING 3.7 From Pico's *Oration on the Dignity of Man* (1486)

Most esteemed Fathers,[1] I have read in the ancient writings 1
of the Arabians that Abdala the Saracen[2] on being asked
what, on this stage, so to say, of the world, seemed to him
most evocative of wonder, replied that there was nothing to
be seen more marvelous than man. And that celebrated
exclamation of Hermes Trismegistus,[3] "What a great miracle
is man, Asclepius"[4] confirms this opinion.

And still, as I reflected upon the basis assigned for these
estimations, I was not fully persuaded by the diverse

reasons advanced by a variety of persons for the 10
preeminence of human nature; for example: that man is the
intermediary between creatures, that he is the familiar
of the gods above him as he is lord of the beings beneath
him; that, by the acuteness of his senses, the inquiry of his
reason and the light of his intelligence, he is the interpreter
of nature, set midway beween the timeless unchanging and
the flux of time; the living union (as the Persians say), the
very marriage hymn of the world, and, by David's testimony[5]
but little lower than the angels. These reasons are all,
without question, of great weight; nevertheless, they do 20
not touch the principal reasons, those, that is to say, which
justify man's unique right to such unbounded admiration.
Why, I asked, should we not admire the angels themselves
and the beatific choirs more?

At long last, however, I feel that I have come to some
understanding of why man is the most fortunate of living
things and, consequently, deserving of all admiration; of
what may be the condition in the hierarchy of beings
assigned to him, which draws upon him the envy, not of
the brutes alone, but of the astral beings and of the very 30
intelligences which dwell beyond the confines of the
world. A thing surpassing belief and smiting the soul with
wonder. Still, how could it be otherwise? For it is on this
ground that man is, with complete justice, considered and
called a great miracle and a being worthy of all admiration.

Hear then, oh Fathers, precisely what this condition of
man is; and in the name of your humanity, grant me your
benign audition as I pursue this theme.

God the Father, the Mightiest Architect, had already
raised, according to the precepts of His hidden wisdom, 40
this world we see, the cosmic dwelling of divinity, a temple
most august. He had already adorned the supercelestial
region with Intelligences, infused the heavenly globes with
the life of immortal souls and set the fermenting dung-
heap of the inferior world teeming with every form of
animal life. But when this work was done, the Divine
Artificer still longed for some creature which might
comprehend the meaning of so vast an achievement, which
might be moved with love at its beauty and smitten with
awe at its grandeur. When, consequently, all else had been 50
completed, . . . in the very last place, He bethought Himself
of bringing forth man. Truth was, however, that there
remained no archetype according to which He might
fashion a new offspring, nor in His treasure-houses the
wherewithal to endow a new son with a fitting
inheritance, nor any place, among the seats of the
universe, where this new creature might dispose himself to
contemplate the world. All space was already filled; all
things had been distributed in the highest, the middle and
the lowest orders. Still, it was not in the nature of the 60
power of the Father to fail in this last creative élan; nor
was it in the nature of that supreme Wisdom to hesitate
through lack of counsel in so crucial a matter; nor, finally,
in the nature of His beneficent love to compel the creature
destined to praise the divine generosity in all other things
to find it wanting in himself.

[1]The assembly of clergymen to whom the oration was to be addressed.
[2]The Arabic philosopher and translator Abd-Allah Ibn al Muqaffa (718–775).
[3]The Greek name (Hermes Thrice-Great) for the Greek god Thoth, the presumed author of a body of occult philosophy that mingled neoplatonism, alchemy, and mystical interpretations of the Scriptures.
[4]The Greek god of healing and medicine.
[5]In Psalms 8.6.

At last, the Supreme Maker decreed that this creature, to whom He could give nothing wholly his own, should have a share in the particular endowment of every other creature. Taking man, therefore, this creature of indeterminate image, He set him in the middle of the world and thus spoke to him: 70

"We have given you, Oh Adam, no visage proper to yourself, nor any endowment properly your own, in order that whatever place, whatever form, whatever gifts you may, with premeditation, select, these same you may have and possess through your own judgment and decision. The nature of all other creatures is defined and restricted within laws which We have laid down; you, by contrast, impeded by no such restrictions, may, by your own free will, to whose custody We have assigned you, trace for yourself the lineaments of your 80 own nature. I have placed you at the very center of the world, so that from that vantage point you may with greater ease glance round about you on all that the world contains. We have made you a creature neither of heaven nor of earth, neither mortal nor immortal, in order that you may, as the free and proud shaper of your own being, fashion yourself in the form you may prefer. It will be in your power to descend to the lower, brutish forms of life; [or] you will be able, through your own decision, to rise again to the superior orders whose life is divine." 90

Oh unsurpassed generosity of God the Father, Oh wondrous and unsurpassable felicity of man, to whom it is granted to have what he chooses, to be what he wills to be! The brutes, from the moment of their birth, bring with them, as Lucilius[6] says, "from their mother's womb" all that they will ever possess. The highest spiritual beings were, from the very moment of creation, or soon thereafter, fixed in the mode of being which would be theirs through measureless eternities. But upon man, at the moment of his creation, God bestowed seeds pregnant with all possibilities, the germs of every 100 form of life. Whichever of these a man shall cultivate, the same will mature and bear fruit in him. If vegetative, he will beome a plant; if sensual, he will become brutish; if rational, he will reveal himself a heavenly being; if intellectual, he will be an angel and the son of God. And if, dissatisfied with the lot of all creatures, he should recollect himself into the center of his own unity, he will there, become one spirit with God, in the solitary darkness of the Father, Who is set above all things, himself transcend all creatures.

Who then will not look with awe upon this our chameleon, 110 or who, at least, will look with greater admiration on any other being? This creature, man, whom Asclepius the Athenian, by reason of this very mutability, this nature capable of transforming itself, quite rightly said was symbolized in the mysteries by the figure of Proteus. This is the source of those metamorphoses, or transformations, so celebrated among the Hebrews and among the Pythagoreans;[7] . . . . while the Pythagoreans transform men guilty of crimes into brutes or even, if we are to believe Empedocles,[8] into

plants; and Mohamet,[9] imitating them, was known 120 frequently to say that the man who deserts the divine law becomes a brute. And he was right; for it is not the bark that makes the tree, but its insensitive and unresponsive nature; nor the hide which makes the beast of burden, but its brute and sensual soul; nor the orbicular form which makes the heavens, but their harmonious order. Finally, it is not freedom from a body, but its spiritual intelligence, which makes the angel. If you see a man dedicated to his stomach, crawling on the ground, you see a plant and not a man; or if you see a man bedazzled by the empty forms of the imagination, as 130 by the wiles of Calypso,[10] and through their alluring solicitations made a slave to his own senses, you see a brute and not a man. If, however, you see a philosopher, judging and distinguishing all things according to the rule of reason, him shall you hold in veneration, for he is a creature of heaven and not of earth; if, finally, a pure contemplator, unmindful of the body, wholly withdrawn into the inner chambers of the mind, here indeed is neither a creature of earth nor a heavenly creature, but some higher divinity, clothed with human flesh.

. . . .

Alberti and Renaissance *Virtù*

Although Pico's *Oration* was not circulated until after his death, its assertion of free will and its acclamation of the unlimited potential of the individual came to symbolize the collective ideals of the Renaissance humanists. In words hauntingly reminiscent of Sophocles (compare the choral eulogy for humankind in *Antigone*; see chapter 4), Pico gave voice to the optimistic view of the individual as free and perfectible. This view—basic to so much Renaissance literature—was central to the life and thought of the Florentine humanist Leon Battista Alberti (1404–1474) (Figure **16.7**). A mathematician, architect, engineer, musician, and playwright, Alberti's most original literary contribution (and that for which he was best known in his own time) was his treatise *On the Family*. Published in 1443, *On the Family* is the first sociological inquiry into the structure, function, and responsibilities of the family. It is also a moralizing treatise that defends the importance of a classical education and hard work as prerequisites for worldly success. In Alberti's view, skill, talent, fortitude, ingenuity, and the ability to determine one's destiny—qualities summed up in the single Italian word *virtù*—are essential to human enterprise. *Virtù*, Alberti observes, is not inherited; rather, it must be cultivated. Not to be confused with the English word "virtue," *virtù* describes the self-confident vitality of the self-made Renaissance individual.

In *On the Family*, Alberti warns that idleness is the enemy of human achievement, while the performance of "manly tasks" and the pursuit of "fine studies" are sure means to worldly fame and material fortune. Pointing to

---

[6]A Roman writer of satires (180–102 B.C.E.).
[7]Followers of the Greek philosopher and mathematician Pythagoras (fl. 530 B.C.E.); see chapter 5.
[8]A Greek philosopher and poet (495–435 B.C.E.).

---

[9]The prophet Muhammad (570–632); see chapter 10.
[10]In Greek mythology, a sea nymph who lured Odysseus to remain with her for seven years.

the success of his own family, he defends the acquisition of wealth as the reward of free-spirited *virtù*. The buoyant optimism so characteristic of the age of the Renaissance is epitomized in Alberti's statement that "man can do anything he wants." Alberti himself—architect, mathematician, and scholar—was living proof of that viewpoint.

READING 3.8 From Alberti's *On the Family*

(1443)

... Let Fathers ... see to it that their sons pursue the study of letters assiduously and let them teach them to understand and write correctly. Let them not think they have taught them if they do not see that their sons have learned to read and write perfectly, for in this it is almost the same to know badly as not to know at all. Then let the children learn arithmetic and gain a sufficient knowledge of geometry, for these are enjoyable sciences suitable to young minds and of great use to all regardless of age or social status. Then let them turn once more to the poets, orators, and philosophers. Above all, one must try to have good teachers from whom the children may learn excellent customs as well as letters. I should want my sons to become accustomed to good authors. I should want them to learn grammar from Priscian and Servius and to become familiar, not with collections of sayings and extracts, but with the works of Cicero, Livy, and Sallust above all, so that they might learn the perfection and splendid eloquence of the elegant Latin tongue from the very beginning. They say that the same thing happens to the mind as to a bottle: if first one puts bad wine in it, its taste will never disappear. One must, therefore, avoid all crude and inelegant writers and study those who are polished and elegant, keeping their works at hand, reading them continuously, reciting them often, and memorizing them. ...

Think for a moment: can you find a man—or even imagine one—who fears infamy, though he may have no strong desire for glory, and yet does not hate idleness and sloth? Who can ever think it possible to achieve honors and dignity without the loving study of excellent arts, without assiduous work, without striving in difficult manly tasks. If one wishes to gain praise and fame, he must abhor idleness and laziness and oppose them as deadly foes. There is nothing that gives rise to dishonor and infamy as much as idleness. Idleness has always been the breeding-place of vice. ...

Therefore, idleness which is the cause of so many evils must be hated by all good men. Even if idleness were not a deadly enemy of good customs and the cause of every vice, as everyone knows it is, what man, though inept, could wish to spend his life without using his mind, his limbs, his every faculty? Does an idle man differ from a tree trunk, a statue, or a putrid corpse? As for me, one who does not care for honor or fear shame and does not act with prudence and intelligence does not live well. But one who lies buried in idleness and sloth and completely neglects good deeds and fine studies is

Figure 16.7 LEON BATTISTA ALBERTI, *Self-Portrait*, ca. 1435. Bronze, 7²⁹⁄₃₂ × 5¹¹⁄₃₂ in. © 2000 Board of Trustees, National Gallery of Art, Washington, D.C. Samuel H. Kress Collection.

altogether dead. One who does not give himself body and soul to the quest for praise and virtue is to be deemed unworthy of life. ...

... [Man] comes into this world in order to enjoy all things, be virtuous, and make himself happy. For he who may be called happy will be useful to other men, and he who is now useful to others cannot but please God. He who uses things improperly harms other men and incurs God's displeasure, and he who displeases God is a fool if he thinks he is happy. We may, therefore, state that man is created by Nature to use, and reap the benefits of, all things, and that he is born to be happy. ...

... I believe it will not be excessively difficult for a man to acquire the highest honors and glory, if he perseveres in his studies as much as is necessary, toiling, sweating, and striving to surpass all others by far. It is said that man can do anything he wants. If you will strive with all your strength and skill, as I have said, I have no doubt you will reach the highest degree of perfection and fame in any profession. ...

... To those of noble and liberal spirit, no occupations seem less brilliant than those whose purpose is to make money. If you think a moment and try to remember which are the occupations for making money, you will see that they consist of buying and selling, lending and collecting. I believe that these occupations whose purpose is gain may seem vile and worthless to you, for you are of noble and lofty spirit. In fact, selling is a mercenary trade; you serve the buyer's needs, pay yourself for your work, and make a profit by charging others more than you yourself have paid. You are not selling goods, therefore, but your labors; you are 80 reimbursed for the cost of your goods, and for your labor you receive a profit. Lending would be a laudable generosity if you did not seek interest, but then it would not be a profitable business. Some say that these occupations, which we shall call pecuniary, always entail dishonesty and numerous lies and often entail dishonest agreements and fraudulent contracts. They say, therefore, that those of liberal spirit must completely avoid them as dishonest and mercenary. But I believe that those who judge all pecuniary occupations in this 90 manner are wrong. Granted that acquiring wealth is not a glorious enterprise to be likened to the most noble professions. We must not, however, scorn a man who is not naturally endowed for noble deeds if he turns to these other occupations in which he knows he is not inept and which, everyone admits, are of great use to the family and to the state. Riches are useful for gaining friends and praise, for with them we can help those in need. With wealth we can gain fame and prestige if we use it munificently for great and noble projects. . . . 100

Castiglione and "l'uomo universale"

By far the most provocative analysis of Renaissance individualism is that found in *The Book of the Courtier*, a treatise written between 1513 and 1518 by the Italian diplomat and man of letters Baldassare Castiglione (1478–1529) (Figure **16.8**). Castiglione's *Courtier* was inspired by a series of conversations that had taken place among a group of sixteenth-century aristocrats at the court of Urbino, a mecca for humanist studies located in central Italy. The subject of these conversations, which Castiglione probably recorded from memory, concerns the qualifications of the ideal Renaissance man and woman. Debating this subject at length, the members of the court arrive at a consensus that afforded the image of *l'uomo universale*, the well-rounded person. Castiglione reports that the ideal man should master all the skills of the medieval warrior and display the physical proficiency of a champion athlete. But, additionally, he must possess the refinements of a humanistic education. He must know Latin and Greek (as well as his own native language), be familiar with the classics, speak and write well, and be able to compose verse, draw, and play a musical instrument. Moreover, all that the Renaissance gentleman does, he should do with an air of nonchalance and grace, a quality summed up in the Italian word *sprezzatura*. This unique combination of breeding and education would produce a cultured individual to serve a very special end: the perfection of the state. For, as Book Four of *The Courtier* explains, the primary duty of *l'uomo universale* is to influence the ruler to govern wisely.

Although, according to Castiglione, the goal of the ideal gentleman was to cultivate his full potential as a human being, such was not the case with the Renaissance gentlewoman. The Renaissance woman should have a knowledge of letters, music, and art—that is, like the gentleman, she should be privileged with a humanistic education—but in no way should she violate that "soft and delicate tenderness that is her defining quality." Castiglione's peers agreed that "in her ways, manners, words, gestures, and bearing, a woman ought to be very unlike a man." Just as the success of the courtier depends on his ability to influence those who ruled, the success of the lady rests with her skills in entertaining the male members of the court.

Castiglione's handbook of Renaissance etiquette was based on the views of a narrow, aristocratic segment of society. But despite its selective viewpoint, it was immensely popular: It was translated into five languages and went through fifty-seven editions before the year 1600. Historically, *The Book of the Courtier* is an index to cultural changes that were taking place between medieval and early modern times. It departs from exclusively feudal and Christian educational ideals and formulates a program for the cultivation of both mind *and* body that has become fundamental to modern Western education. Representative also of the shift from medieval to

Figure 16.8 RAPHAEL, *Portrait of Baldassare Castiglione*, ca. 1515. Oil on canvas, approx. 30¼ × 26½ in. Louvre, Paris. © R.M.N.

CHAPTER SEVENTEEN

Renaissance artists: disciples of nature, masters of invention

"The eye, which is called the window of the soul, is the chief means whereby the understanding may most fully and abundantly appreciate the infinite works of nature."
Leonardo

The Renaissance produced a flowering in the visual arts rarely matched in the annals of world culture. Artists embraced the natural world with an enthusiasm that was equalled only by their ambition to master the lessons of classical antiquity. The result was a unique and sophisticated body of art that set the standards for most of the painting, sculpture, and architecture produced in the West until the late nineteenth century.

During the Early Renaissance, the period from roughly 1400 to 1490, Florentine artists worked side by side with literary humanists to revive the classical heritage. These artist-scientists combined their interest in Greco-Roman art with an impassioned desire to understand the natural world and imitate its visual appearance. As disciples of nature, they studied its operations and functions; as masters of invention, they devised techniques by which to represent the visible world more realistically. In the years of the High Renaissance—approximately 1490 to 1530—the spirit of individualism reached heroic proportions, as artists such as Leonardo da Vinci, Raphael, and Michelangelo integrated the new techniques of naturalistic representation with the much respected principles of classical art.

While the subject matter of Renaissance art was still largely religious, the style was more lifelike than ever. Indeed, in contrast with the generally abstract and symbolic art of the Middle Ages, Renaissance art was concrete and realistic. Most medieval art served liturgical or devotional ends; increasingly, however, wealthy patrons commissioned paintings and sculptures to embellish their homes and palaces or to commemorate secular and civic achievements. Portrait painting, a genre that glorified the individual, became popular during the Renaissance, along with other genres that described the physical and social aspects of urban life. These artistic developments reflect the needs of a culture driven by material prosperity, civic pride, and personal pleasure.

Renaissance Art and Patronage

In the commercial cities of Italy and the Netherlands, painting, sculpture, and architecture were the tangible expressions of increased affluence. In addition to the traditional medieval source of patronage—the Catholic Church—merchant princes and petty despots vied with growing numbers of middle-class patrons and urban-centered guilds whose lavish commissions brought prestige to their businesses and families. Those who supported the arts did so at least in part with an eye toward leaving their mark upon society or immortalizing themselves for posterity. Thus art became the evidence of material well-being as well as the visible extension of the ego in an age of individualism.

Active patronage enhanced the social and financial status of Renaissance artists. Such artists were first and foremost craftspeople, apprenticed to studios in which they might achieve mastery over a wide variety of techniques, including the grinding of paints, the making of brushes, and the skillful copying of images. While trained to observe firmly established artistic convention, the more innovative amongst them moved to create a new visual language. Indeed, for the first time in Western history, artists came to wield influence as humanists, scientists, and poets: A new phenomenon of the artist as hero and genius was born. The image of the artist as hero was promoted by the self-publicizing efforts of these artists, as well as by the adulation of their peers. The Italian painter, architect, and critic Giorgio Vasari (1511–1574) immortalized hundreds of Renaissance artists in his monumental biography *The Lives of the Most Excellent Painters, Architects, and Sculptors*, published in 1550. Vasari drew to legendary proportions the achievements of notable Renaissance figures, many of whom he knew personally. Consider, for instance, this terse characterization of Leonardo da Vinci (an artist whose work is featured in this chapter):

. . . He might have been a scientist if he had not been so versatile. But the instability of his character caused him to take up and abandon many things. In arithmetic, for example, he made such rapid progress during the short time he studied it that he often confounded his teacher by his questions. He also began the study of music and resolved to learn to play the lute, and as he was by nature of exalted imagination, and full of the most graceful vivacity, he sang and accompanied himself most divinely, improvising at once both verses and music. He studied not one branch of art only, but all. Admirably intelligent, and an excellent geometrician besides, Leonardo not only worked in sculpture . . . but, as an architect, designed ground plans and entire buildings; and, as an engineer, was the one who first suggested making a canal from Florence to Pisa by altering the river Arno. Leonardo also designed mills and water-driven machines. But, as he had resolved to make painting his profession, he spent most of his time drawing from life. . . .

The Early Renaissance

The Revival of the Classical Nude

Like the classical humanists, artists of the Renaissance were the self-conscious beneficiaries of ancient Greek and Roman culture. One of the most creative forces in Florentine sculpture, Donato Bardi, known as Donatello (1386–1466), traveled to Rome to study antique statuary. The works he observed there inspired his extraordinary likeness of the biblical hero David (Figure **17.1**). Completed in 1432, Donatello's bronze was the first free-standing, life-sized nude sculpture since antiquity. While not an imitation of any single Greek or Roman statue, the piece reveals an indebtedness to classical models in its correct anatomical proportions and gentle **contrapposto** stance (compare the *Kritios Boy* and *Doryphorus* in chapter 5). However, the sensuousness of the youthful figure—especially apparent in the surface modeling—surpasses that of any antique statue. Indeed, in this tribute to male beauty, Donatello rejected the medieval view of the human body as the wellspring of sin and anticipated the modern Western exaltation of the body as the seat of pleasure.

Donatello's colleague Lucca della Robbia (1400–1482) would become famous for his enameled terra-cotta religious figures; but in his first documented commission—the *Cantoria* (Singing Gallery) for the Cathedral of Florence—he exhibited his talents as a sculptor of marble and as a student of antiquity (Figure **17.2**). Greco-Roman techniques of high and low relief are revived in the ten panels representing choristers, musicians, and dancers—the latter resembling the *putti* (plump, nude boys), often used to depict Cupid in ancient art. In a spirited display of physical movement, Lucca brought to life Psalm 150, which enjoins one to praise God with "trumpet sound," "lute and harp," "strings and pipe," and "loud clashing cymbals." Just as Donatello conceived the biblical David

Figure 17.1 DONATELLO, *David*, completed 1432. Bronze, height 5 ft. 2 in. Museo Nazionale del Bargello, Florence. © Studio Fotografico Quattrone, Florence.

Figure 17.2 LUCCA DELLA ROBBIA, *Drummers* (detail of the *Cantoria*). Marble, 42⅛ × 40¹⁹⁄₂₀ in. Museo dell'Opera del Duomo, Florence. Scala, Florence.

in the language of classical antiquity, so Lucca invested the music of Scripture with a lifelike, classicized vigor.

The Renaissance revival of the classical nude was accompanied by a quest to understand the mechanics of the human body. Antonio Pollaiuolo (ca. 1431–1498) was among the first artists to dissect human cadavers in order to study anatomy. The results of his investigations are documented in a bronze sculpture depicting the combat between Hercules and Antaeus, a story drawn from Greco-Roman legend (Figure **17.3**). This small but powerful sculpture in the round is one of many examples of the

Renaissance use of classical mythology to glorify human action, rather than as an exemplum of Christian morality. The wrestling match between the two legendary strongmen of antiquity, Hercules (the most popular of all Greek heroes) and Antaeus (the son of Mother Earth), provided Pollaiuolo with the chance to display his remarkable understanding of the human physique, especially as it responds to stress. Pollaiuolo concentrates on the moment when Hercules lifts Antaeus off the ground, thus divesting him of his maternal source of strength and crushing him in a "body lock." The human capacity for tension and

metho
all o
Brune
dome
inable

Br
Rena
and p
tle cl
(Figu
the i
barre
struct
it is
medi
repet
visua
acces
and g
gular
the "
white
that
Whe
enwa
on ea

B
niou
the
Albe
pain
for R
ings
Arch
Albe
from
metr
for a
becc
posit

I
Rucc
for v
story
chap
appe
well
lowe
Albe
enga
the
west
17.

Figure 17.3 ANTONIO POLLAIUOLO, *Hercules and Antaeus*, ca. 1475. Bronze, height 18 in. with base. Museo Nazionale del Bargello, Florence. Scala, Florence.

energy is nowhere better captured than in the straining muscles and tendons of the two athletes in combat.

The classically inspired nude fascinated Renaissance painters as well as sculptors. In the *Birth of Venus* (Figure **17.4**) by Sandro Botticelli (1445–1510), the central image (Figure **17.5**) is an idealized portrayal of womankind based on an antique model, possibly a statue in the Medici collection (Figure **17.6**). Born of sea foam (according to the Greek poet Hesiod), Venus floats on a pearlescent scallop shell to the shore of the island of Cythera. To her right are two wind gods locked in sensuous embrace, while to her left is the welcoming figure of Pomona, the ancient Roman goddess of fruit trees and fecundity. Many elements in the painting—water, wind, flowers, trees— suggest procreation and fertility, powers associated with Venus as goddess of earthly love. But Botticelli, inspired by a contemporary neoplatonic poem honoring Aphrodite/ Venus as goddess of divine love, renders Venus also as an object of ethereal beauty and spiritual love. His painting pictorializes ideas set forth at the Platonic Academy of Florence (see chapter 16), particularly the neoplatonic notion that objects of physical beauty move the soul to desire union with God, divine fount of all beauty and truth. Botticelli's wistful goddess assumes the double role accorded her by the neoplatonists: goddess of earthly love and goddess of divine (or Platonic) love.

Botticelli executed the *Birth of Venus* in tempera on a large canvas. He rendered the figures with a minimum of shading, so that they seem weightless, suspended in space.

Figure 17.4 SANDRO BOTTICELLI, *Birth of Venus*, after 1482. Tempera on canvas, 5 ft. 9 in. × 9 ft. ½ in. Uffizi Gallery, Florence. Scala/Art Resource, New York.

Figure 17.13 JAN VAN EYCK, *Marriage of Giovanni Anolfini and His Bride*, 1434. Tempera and oil on panel, 32¼ × 23½ in. National Gallery, London.

suggest a sacred union: the burning candle (traditionally carried to the marriage ceremony by the bride) symbolizes the divine presence of Christ, the dog represents fidelity, the ripening fruit that lies near and on the window sill alludes to the union of the first Couple in the Garden of Eden, and the carved image of Saint Margaret (on the chairback near the bed), patron of women in childbirth, signifies aspirations for a fruitful alliance. Whoever the figures actually are, their gestures, the setting, and the objects that surround them constitute a symbolic text that suggests some type of betrothal. Ultimately, however, the power of the painting lies not with the identity of the sitters, but with Jan van Eyck's consummate mastery of minute, realistic details—from the ruffles on the female's headcovering to the whiskers of the monkey-faced dog. The immediacy of the material world is enhanced by the technique of oil painting, which Jan brought to perfection. By applying thin, translucent glazes of pigments bound with linseed oil, he achieved the impression of dense, atmospheric space and simulated the naturalistic effect of light reflecting off the surfaces of objects.

To the Renaissance affection for realistic self-representation, Jan introduced the phenomenon of the psychological portrait—the portrait that probed the temperament, character, or unique personality of the subject. In his brilliant self-image (Figure **17.14**), whose level gaze and compressed lips suggest the personality of a shrewd realist, facial features are finely (almost photographically)

Figure 17.14 JAN VAN EYCK, *Man in a Turban* (*Self-Portrait?*), 1433. Tempera and oil on panel, 13⅛ × 10⅛ in. National Gallery, London.

detailed. Complex folds of crimson fabric make up the turban that crowns his head. Jan deliberately abandoned the profile portrait (see Figure 15.15) in favor of a three-quarter view that gave the figure a more aggressive spatial presence.

While Early Renaissance artists usually represented their sitters in domestic interiors, High Renaissance masters preferred to situate them in *plein-air* (outdoor) settings, as if to suggest human consonance with nature. Leonardo da Vinci's *Mona Lisa* (Figure **17.15**), the world's best-known portrait, brings figure and landscape into exquisite harmony: The pyramidal shape of the sitter (probably the wife of the Florentine banker Francesco del Giocondo) is echoed in the rugged mountains; the folds of her tunic are repeated in the curves of distant roads and rivers. Soft golden tones highlight the figure which, like the landscape, is modeled in soft, smoky (in Italian, *sfumato*) gradations of light and shade. The setting, a rocky and ethereal wilderness, is as elusive as the sitter, whose eyes and mouth are delicately blurred to produce a facial expression that is almost impossible to decipher—a smile both melancholic and mocking. While the shaved eyebrows and plucked hairline are hallmarks of fifteenth-century female fashion, the figure resists classification by age and (in the opinion of some) by gender. Praised by Renaissance copyists for its "lifelikeness," the *Mona Lisa* has remained an object of fascination and mystery for generations of beholders.

Renaissance portraits often took the form of life-sized sculptures in the round, some of which were brightly painted to achieve naturalistic effects. Such is also the case with the polychrome terra-cotta likeness of Lorenzo de' Medici (see Figure 16.2), executed by the Florentine sculptor Andrea del Verrocchio (1435–1488), which reveals a spirited naturalism reminiscent of Roman portraiture (see chapter 6). Verrocchio was the Medici court sculptor and the close companion of Lorenzo, whose luxurious lifestyle and opulent tastes won him the title "Il Magnifico" ("the Magnificent"). Verrocchio immortalized the physical appearance of the Florentine ruler, who was also a humanist, poet, and musician. At the same time, he captured the willful vitality of the man whose *virtù* made him a legend in his time.

Renaissance sculptors revived still another antique genre: the equestrian statue. Verrocchio's monumental bronze statue of the *condottiere* Bartolommeo Colleoni (Figure **17.16**), commissioned to commemorate the mercenary soldier's military victories on behalf of the city of Venice, recalls the Roman statue of Marcus Aurelius on horseback (see Figure 6.23) as well as the considerably smaller equestrian statue of Charlemagne (see chapter 11). However, compared with these works, Verrocchio's masterpiece displays an unprecedented degree of scientific naturalism and a close attention to anatomical detail—note the bulging muscles of Colleoni's mount. Verrocchio moreover makes his towering mercenary twist dramatically in his saddle and scowl fiercely. Such expressions of *terribilità*, or awe-inspiring power, typify the aggressive spirit that fueled the Renaissance.

Figure 17.23 (right) **LORENZO GHIBERTI**, *Meeting of Solomon and Sheba* (single panel of the "Gates of Paradise," Figure 17.22). Gilt-bronze relief, 31¼ × 31¼ in. Alinari/Art Resource, New York.

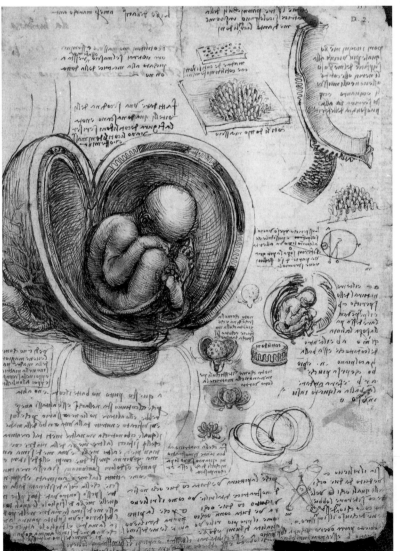

Figure 17.24 (left) **LEONARDO DA VINCI**, *Embryo in the Womb*, ca. 1510. Pen and brown ink, 11¾ × 8½ in. The Royal Collection, Windsor Castle, Royal Library. © 1998 Her Majesty Queen Elizabeth II.

nature includes anatomical drawings whose accuracy remained unsurpassed until 1543, when the Flemish physician Andreas Vesalius published the first medical illustrations of the human anatomy. Some of Leonardo's studies explore ideas (for example, the standardization of machine parts) that were far in advance of their time. Although Leonardo's notebooks—unpublished until 1898—had little influence upon European science, they remain a symbol of the Renaissance imagination and a timeless source of inspiration: The comic book hero Batman, according to its twentieth-century creator Bob Kane, was born when Kane first viewed Leonardo's sketches of human flight.

Following Alberti, Leonardo maintained that proportional principles govern both nature and art. Indeed, Leonardo's belief in a universal order led him to seek a basic correspondence between human proportions and ideal geometric shapes, as Vitruvius and his followers had advised. Leonardo's so-called "Vitruvian Man" (Figure **17.26**), whose strict geometry haunts the compositions of High Renaissance painters and architects, is the metaphor for the Renaissance view of the microcosm as a mirror of the macrocosm. Yet, more than any other artist of his time, Leonardo exalted the importance of empirical experience for discovering the general rules of nature. Critical of abstract speculation bereft of sensory confirmation, he held that the human eye was the most dependable instrument for obtaining true knowledge of nature. When Leonardo wrote, "That painting is the most to be praised which agrees most exactly with the thing imitated," he was articulating the Renaissance view of art as the imitation of nature. Though Leonardo never established a strict methodology for the formulation of scientific laws, his insistence on direct experience and experimentation made him the harbinger of the Scientific Revolution that would sweep through Western Europe during the next two centuries. In the following excerpts from his notebooks,

Leonardo defends the superiority of sensory experience over "book learning" and argues that painting surpasses poetry as a form of human expression.

READING 3.12   From Leonardo da Vinci's *Notes* (ca. 1510)

I am fully aware that the fact of my not being a man of letters may cause certain arrogant persons to think that they may with reason censure me, alleging that I am a man ignorant of book-learning. Foolish folk! Do they not know that I might retort by saying, as did Marius to the Roman Patricians, "They who themselves go about adorned in the labor of others will not permit me my own." They will say that because of my lack of book-learning, I cannot properly express what I desire to treat of. Do they not know that my subjects require for their exposition experience rather than the words of others? And since experience has been the mistress of whoever has written well, I take her as my mistress, and to her in all points make my appeal.   1   10

I wish to work miracles. . . . And you who say that it is better to look at an anatomical demonstration than to see these drawings, you would be right, if it were possible to observe all the details shown in these drawings in a single figure, in which, with all your ability, you will not see nor acquire a knowledge of more than some few veins, while, in order to obtain an exact and complete knowledge of these, I have dissected more than ten human bodies, destroying all the various members, and removing even the very smallest particles of the flesh which surrounded these veins without causing any effusion of blood other than the imperceptible bleeding of the capillary veins. And, as one single body did not suffice for so long a time, it was necessary to proceed by stages with so many bodies as would render my knowledge complete; and this I   20

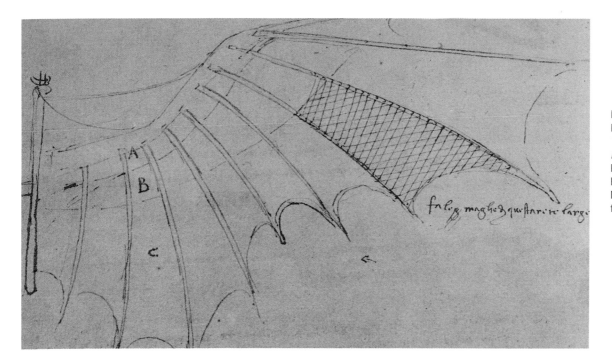

Figure 17.25
LEONARDO DA VINCI,
Wing Construction for a Flying Machine, ca. 1500. Pen and brown ink. Biblioteca Ambrosiana, Milan, Codex Atlanticus, f.309v–a.

Figure 17.43 TITIAN, *Venus of Urbino*, 1538–1539. Oil on canvas, 3 ft. 11 in. × 5 ft. 5 in. Uffizi Gallery, Florence. Scala, Florence.

a technique best described as "painterly." He preferred broken and subtle tones of color to the flat, bright hues favored by such artists as Raphael. Titian's painterly style became the definitive expression of the coloristic manner in High Renaissance painting and a model for such artists as Rubens in the seventeenth century and Delacroix in the nineteenth.

The Music of the Renaissance

Like Renaissance art, Renaissance music was increasingly secular in subject matter and function. However, the perception of the Renaissance as a time when secular music overtook ecclesiastical music may be due to the fact that after 1450 more secular music was committed to paper. The printing press, which was perfected in Germany in the mid-fifteenth century, encouraged the preservation and dissemination of all kinds of musical composition. With the establishment of printing presses in Venice in the late fifteenth century, printed books of lute music and part-books for individual instruments appeared in great numbers. (Most music was based on preexisting melodies, and manuscripts normally lacked tempo markings and other indications as to how a piece was to be performed.) Publishers also sold vernacular handbooks that offered instructions on how to play musical instruments. It is no surprise, then, that during the Renaissance, music was composed not only by professional musicians, but by amateurs as well. Indeed, Castiglione observed that making music was the function of all well-rounded individuals. Music was an essential ingredient at intimate gatherings, court celebrations, and public festivals (Figure **17.44**). And virtuosity in performance, a hallmark of Renaissance music, was common among both amateurs and professionals. Such Renaissance princes as Lorenzo de' Medici took pleasure in writing songs for the carnivals that traditionally preceded the Lenten season. On pageant wagons designed for holiday spectacles in Florence and other cities, masked singers, dancers, and mimes enacted mythological, religious, and contemporary tales in musical performance.

While the literary and visual evidence of classical antiquity was readily available to the humanists of the Renaissance, few musical examples had survived, and none could be accurately deciphered. For that reason, medieval tradition maintained a stronger influence in the development of music than it did in art and literature. (Not until the late sixteenth century did composers draw on Greek drama as the inspiration for a new genre: opera—discussed in chapter 20.) Moreover, perhaps because performing music was believed to be within everyone's reach, musicians were not held in such high esteem as painters, sculptors, or architects of the Renaissance. Most theorists, including Leonardo da Vinci (himself a

Figure 17.44 LORENZO COSTA, *The Concert*, ca. 1485–95, oil on poplar, 37½ × 29¾ in. National Gallery, London.

The snake, man's enemy, is not long-lived, yet the serpent that lives hidden will surely die old. Djata[4] was strong enough now to face his enemies. At the age of eighteen, he had the stateliness of the lion and the strength of the buffalo. His voice carried authority, his eyes were live coals, his arm was iron, he was the husband of power.

Moussa Tounkara, king of Mema, gave Sundiata half of his army. The most valiant came forward of their own free will to follow Sundiata in the great adventure. The cavalry of Mema, which he had fashioned himself, formed his iron squadron. Sundiata, dressed in the Muslim fashion of Mema, left the town at the head of his small but redoubtable army. The whole population sent their best wishes with him. He was surrounded by five messengers from Mali and Manding Bory rode proudly at the side of his brother. The horsemen of Mema formed behind Djata a bristling iron squadron. The troops took the direction of Wagadou, for Djata did not have enough troops to confront Soumaoro directly, and so the king of Mema advised him to go to Wagadou and take half of the men of the king, Soumaba Cissé. A swift messenger had been sent there and so the king of Wagadou came out in person to meet Sundiata and his troops. He gave Sundiata half of his cavalry and blessed the weapons. Then Manding Bory said to his brother, "Djata, do you think yourself able to face Soumaoro now?"

"No matter how small a forest may be, you can always find there sufficient fibers to tie up a man. Numbers mean nothing; it is worth that counts. With my cavalry I shall clear myself a path to Mali."

Djata gave out his orders. They would head south, skirting Soumaoro's kingdom. The first objective to be reached was Tabon, the iron-gated town in the midst of the mountains, for Sundiata had promised Fran Kamara that he would pass by Tabon before returning to Mali. He hoped to find that his childhood companion had become king. It was a forced march and during the halts the divines, Singbin Mara Cissé and Mandjan Bérété, related to Sundiata the history of Alexander the Great[5] and several other heroes, but of all of them Sundiata preferred Alexander, the king of gold and silver, who crossed the world from west to east. He wanted to outdo his prototype both in the extent of his territory and the wealth of his treasury. . . .

In the evening, after a long day's march, Sundiata arrived at the head of the great valley which led to Tabon. The valley was quite black with men, for Sosso Balla had deployed his men everywhere in the valley, and some were positioned on the heights which dominated the way through. When Djata saw the layout of Sosso Balla's men he turned to his generals laughing.

"Why are you laughing, brother, you can see that the road is blocked."

"Yes, but no mere infantrymen can halt my course towards Mali," replied Sundiata.

The troops stopped. All the war chiefs were of the opinion that they should wait until the next day to give battle because, they said, the men were tired.

"The battle will not last long," said Sundiata, "and the men will have time to rest. We must not allow Soumaoro the time to attack Tabon."

Sundiata was immovable, so the orders were given and the war drums began to beat. On his proud horse Sundiata turned to right and left in front of his troops. He entrusted the rearguard, composed of a part of the Wagadou cavalry, to his younger brother, Manding Bory. Having drawn his sword, Sundiata led the charge, shouting his war cry.

The Sossos were surprised by this sudden attack for they all thought that the battle would be joined the next day. The lightning that flashes across the sky is slower, the thunderbolts less frightening and floodwaters less surprising than Sundiata swooping down on Sosso Balla and his smiths.[6] In a trice, Sundiata was in the middle of the Sossos like a lion in the sheepfold. The Sossos, trampled under the hooves of his fiery charger, cried out. When he turned to the right the smiths of Soumaoro fell in their tens, and when he turned to the left his sword made heads fall as when someone shakes a tree of ripe fruit. The horsemen of Mema wrought a frightful slaughter and their long lances pierced flesh like a knife sunk into a paw-paw.[7] Charging ever forwards, Sundiata looked for Sosso Balla; he caught sight of him and like a lion bounded towards the son of Soumaoro, his sword held aloft. His arm came sweeping down but at that moment a Sosso warrior came between Djata and Sosso Balla and was sliced like a calabash.[8] Sosso Balla did not wait and disappeared from amidst his smiths. Seeing their chief in flight, the Sossos gave way and fell into a terrible rout. Before the sun disappeared behind the mountains there were only Djata and his men left in the valley.

The festival began. The musicians of all the countries were there. Each people in turn came forward to the dais under Sundiata's impassive gaze. Then the war dances began. The sofas[9] of all the countries had lined themselves up in six ranks amid a great clatter of bows and spears knocking together. The war chiefs were on horseback. The warriors faced the enormous dais and at a signal from Balla Fasséké, the musicians, massed on the right of the dais, struck up. The heavy war drums thundered, the bolons[10] gave off muted notes while the griot's voice gave the throng the pitch for the "Hymn to

---

[4]Sundiata.

[5]In Mali tradition, it is said that Alexander was the second great conqueror and Sundiata the seventh and last.

[6]Metalsmiths, within the clan, a powerful caste of men who were noted as makers of weapons and sorcerers or soothsayers.

[7]Papaya.

[8]The common bottle gourd.

[9]Sudanese infantrymen or soldiers.

[10]Large harps with three or four strings.

the Bow."[11] The spearmen, advancing like hyenas in the night held their spears above their heads; the archers of Wagadou and Tabon,[12] walking with a noiseless tread, seemed to be lying in ambush behind bushes. They rose suddenly to their feet and let fly their arrows at imaginary enemies. In front of the great dais the Kéké-Tigui, or war chiefs, made their horses perform dance steps under the eyes of the Mansa.[13] The horses whinnied and reared, then, overmastered by the spurs, **180** knelt, got up and cut little capers, or else scraped the ground with their hooves.

The rapturous people shouted the "Hymn to the Bow" and clapped their hands. The sweating bodies of the warriors glistened in the sun while the exhausting rhythm of the tam-tams[14] wrenched from them shrill cries. But presently they made way for the cavalry, beloved by Djata. The horsemen of Mema threw their swords in the air and caught them in flight, uttering mighty shouts. A smile of contentment took shape on Sundiata's lips, for he was **190** happy to see his cavalry manoeuvre with so much skill. . . .

. . . .

After a year Sundiata held a new assembly at Niani, but this one was the assembly of dignitaries and kings of the empire. The kings and notables of all the tribes came to Niani. The kings spoke of their administration and the dignitaries talked of their kings. Fakoli, the nephew of Soumaoro, having proved himself too independent, had to flee to evade the Mansa's anger. His lands were confiscated and the taxes of Sosso were paid directly into the granaries of Niani. In this way, every year, **200** Sundiata gathered about him all the kings and notables; so justice prevailed everywhere, for the kings were afraid of being denounced at Niani.

Djata's justice spared nobody. He followed the very word of God. He protected the weak against the strong and people would make journeys lasting several days to come and demand justice of him. Under his sun the upright man was rewarded and the wicked one punished.

In their new-found peace the villages knew prosperity again, for with Sundiata happiness had come into **210** everyone's home. Vast fields of millet, rice, cotton, indigo and fonio[15] surrounded the villages. Whoever worked always had something to live on. Each year long caravans carried the taxes in kind[16] to Niani. You could go from village to village without fearing brigands. A thief would have his right hand chopped off and if he stole again he would be put to the sword.

New villages and new towns sprang up in Mali and elsewhere. "Dyulas," or traders, became numerous and during the reign of Sundiata the world knew happiness. **220**

There are some kings who are powerful through their

military strength. Everybody trembles before them, but when they die nothing but ill is spoken of them. Others do neither good nor ill and when they die they are forgotten. Others are feared because they have power, but they know how to use it and they are loved because they love justice. Sundiata belonged to this group. He was feared, but loved as well. He was the father of Mali and gave the world peace. After him the world has not seen a greater conqueror, for he was the seventh and last **230** conqueror. He had made the capital of an empire out of his father's village, and Niani became the navel of the earth. In the most distant lands Niani was talked of and foreigners said, "Travellers from Mali can tell lies with impunity," for Mali was a remote country for many peoples.

The griots, fine talkers that they were, used to boast of Niani and Mali saying: "If you want salt, go to Niani, for Niani is the camping place of the Sahel[17] caravans. If you want gold, go to Niani, for Bouré, Bambougou and **240** Wagadou work for Niani. If you want fine cloth, go to Niani, for the Mecca road passes by Niani. If you want fish, go to Niani, for it is there that the fishermen of Maouti and Djenné come to sell their catches. If you want meat, go to Niani, the country of the great hunters, and the land of the ox and the sheep. If you want to see an army, go to Niani, for it is there that the united forces of Mali are to be found. If you want to see a great king, go to Niani, for it is there that the son of Sogolon lives, the man with two names." **250**

This is what the masters of the spoken word used to sing. . . .

How many piled-up ruins, how much buried splendour! But all the deeds I have spoken of took place long ago and they all had Mali as their background. Kings have succeeded kings, but Mali has always remained the same.

Mali keeps its secrets jealously. There are things which the uninitiated will never know, for the griots, their depositaries, will never betray them. Maghan Sundiata, **260** the last conqueror on earth, lies not far from Niani-Niani at Balandougou, the weir town.

After him many kings and many Mansas reigned over Mali and other towns sprang up and disappeared. Hajji Mansa Moussa, of illustrious memory, beloved of God, built houses at Mecca for pilgrims coming from Mali, but the towns which he founded have all disappeared, Karanina, Bouroun-Kouna—nothing more remains of these towns. Other kings carried Mali far beyond Djata's frontiers, for example Mansa Samanka and Fadima **270** Moussa, but none of them came near Djata.

Maghan Sundiata was unique. In his own time no one equalled him and after him no one had the ambition to surpass him. He left his mark on Mali for all time and his taboos still guide men in their conduct.

Mali is eternal. To convince yourself of what I have said go to Mali.

. . . .

---

[11]A traditional song among the people of Mali.
[12]Kingdoms near Mali.
[13]Emperor.
[14]Large, circular gongs.
[15]A crabgrass with seeds that are used as a cereal.
[16]In produce or goods instead of money.

---

[17]A region of the Sudan bordering on the Sahara.

The Arts of Native America

A holistic and animistic world view—one that perceives the world as infused with natural spirits—characterized early Native American culture. Indeed, the fact that there is no word for "art" in any Native American language reminds us that the aesthetically compelling objects of these (and many other) people were simply objects of daily use. Among Native Americans (as among Africans) ritual images took on special power and authority: they shared the magical powers of the fetish. The Hopi people of Arizona still produce small wooden *kachinas* ("spirit beings") for the purpose of channeling supernatural powers (Figure **18.14**). These "dolls" are also given to children in order to familiarize them with the tribal gods. Masks, bowls, rattles, and charms picture gods and mythological heroes whose powers are sought in healing ceremonies and other sacred rites. Weaving, beadwork, pottery, and jewelry-making remain among the most technical and highly prized of Native American crafts. The Haida folk of the Queen Charlotte Islands, located near British Columbia, have revived the ancient practice of raising wooden poles carved and painted with *totems*—that is, heraldic family symbols that served as powerful expressions of social status, spiritual authority, and ancestral pride. The Haida and Tlingit peoples of the Northwest

Coast make portrait masks of spirits and ancestors whose powers help their shamans to cure the sick and predict events (Figure **18.15**). Tlingit dance masks and clan helmets—which, like African masks, draw on the natural elements of wood, human hair and teeth, animal fur, seashell, and feathers—capture the metamorphic vitality of Northwest Coast creatures such as the raven (see Reading 3.19).

In various parts of the American Southwest, Native Americans raised communal villages, called "pueblos" by the Spanish. These communities consisted of flat-roofed structures built of stone or adobe arranged in terraces to accommodate a number of families. Among the most notable of the pueblo communities was that of the Anasazi (a Navajo word meaning "ancient ones"). Their settlements at Mesa Verde and Chaco Canyon in southwestern Colorado, which flourished between the eleventh and fourteenth centuries, consisted of elaborate multi-storied living spaces with numerous rooms, storage areas, and circular underground ceremonial centers, known as **kivas**. Large enough to hold all of the male members of the community (women were not generally invited to attend sacred ceremonies), *kivas* served as cosmic symbols of the underworld and as theaters for rites designed to maintain harmony with nature. The Cliff Palace at Mesa Verde, Colorado, positioned under an overhanging cliff canyon wall, whose horizontal configuration it echoes, is one of the largest cliff dwellings in America (Figure **18.16**). Its inhabitants—an estimated 250 people—engineered the tasks of quarrying sandstone, cutting logs (for beams and posts), and hauling water, sand, and clay (for the adobe core structure) entirely without the aid of wheeled vehicles, draft animals, or metal tools.

The pueblo tribes of the American Southwest, including the Anasazi and the Mimbres people who preceded them, produced some of the most elegant ceramic wares in the history of North American art. Lacking the potter's wheel, women handbuilt vessels for domestic and ceremonial uses. They embellished jars and bowls with designs that vary from a stark, geometric abstraction to stylized human, animal, and plant forms. One Mimbres bowl shows a rabbit-man carrying a basket on his back (Figure **18.17**): The shape of the creature, which subtly blends human and animal features, works harmoniously with the curves of the bowl and animates the negative space that surrounds the image. Mimbres pottery—usually pierced or ritually "killed" before being placed with its owner in the grave—testifies to the rich imagination and sophisticated artistry of pueblo culture.

Native American religious rituals, like those of all ancient societies, blended poetry, music, and dance. The sun dance was a principal part of the annual ceremony that celebrated seasonal renewal. In the Navajo tribal community of the American Southwest, the shaman still conducts the healing ceremony known as the Night Chant. ♪ Beginning at sunset and ending some nine

Figure 18.14 Butterfly maiden, Hopi Kachina. Carved wood, pigment and feathers. Courtesy Museum of Northern Arizona, photo archives.

♪ See Music Listening Selections at end of chapter.

Figure 18.15 Maskette representing a dying man, from a headdress worn in the healing ceremony, ca. 1850. Spruce, human hair, teeth of operculum, height approx. 6 in. American Museum of Natural History, New York. Photo: © McMichael Canadian Collection, Kleinburg, Ontario.

days later at sunrise, the Night Chant calls for a series of meticulously executed sand paintings and the recitation of song cycles designed to remove evil and restore good. Characterized by monophonic melody and hypnotic repetition, the Night Chant is performed to the accompaniment of whistles and percussive instruments such as gourd rattles, drums, and rasps. Its compelling rhythms are evident in both the Music Listening Selection and in the "Prayer of the Night Chant" reproduced below. Rituals like the Night Chant are not mere curiosities but, rather, living practices that remain sacred to the Navajo people.

READING 3.18   "A Prayer of the Night Chant" (Navajo)

Tségihi.   1
House made of dawn.
House made of evening light.
House made of the dark cloud.
House made of male rain.   5
House made of dark mist.
House made of female rain.

Figure 18.16 (opposite) Cliff Palace, Mesa Verde, Colorado, inhabited 1073–1272. Photo: Werner Forman Archive, London.

Figure 18.17 Classic Mimbres bowl showing rabbit-man with burden basket, from Cameron Creek village, New Mexico, 1000–1150. Black-on-white pottery, height 4⅜ in., diameter 10¾ in. Museum of Indian Arts and Culture/Laboratory of Anthropology, Santa Fe, New Mexico. Cat. 20420/11. Photo: Blair Clark.

House made of pollen.
House made of grasshoppers.
Dark cloud is at the door.   10
The trail out of it is dark cloud.
The zigzag lightning stands high upon it.
Male deity!
Your offering I make.
I have prepared a smoke for you.   15
Restore my feet for me.
Restore my legs for me.
Restore my body for me.
Restore my mind for me.
This very day take out your spell for me.   20
Your spell remove for me.
You have taken it away for me.
Far off it has gone.
Happily I recover.
Happily my interior becomes cool.   25
Happily I go forth.
My interior feeling cool, may I walk.
No longer sore, may I walk.
Impervious to pain, may I walk.
With lively feelings may I walk.   30
As it used to be long ago, may I walk.
Happily may I walk.
Happily, with abundant dark clouds, may I walk.
Happily, with abundant showers, may I walk.
Happily, with abundant plants, may I walk.   35
Happily, on a trail of pollen, may I walk.
Happily may I walk.
Being as it used to be long ago, may I walk.
May it be beautiful before me.
May it be beautiful behind me.   40

May it be beautiful below me.
May it be beautiful above me.
May it be beautiful all around me.
In beauty it is finished.

Myths and folktales, transmitted orally for generations (and only recorded since the seventeenth century), feature themes that call to mind those of Africa. Creation myths, myths of destruction (or death), and myths that describe the way things are served to provide explanations of the workings of nature. Usually told by men who passed them down to boys, myths and tales often traveled vast distances, and, thus, may appear in many variant versions. As with African folklore, Native American myths feature heroes or heroines who work to transform nature; the heroes/tricksters may themselves be humans who are transformed into ravens, spiders, coyotes, wolves, or rabbits (see Figure 18.17). As with the African trickster tale, which usually points to a moral, the Native American trickster story means to teach or explain; nonetheless, heroes whose strategies involve deceit and cunning are often held in high regard.

READING 3.19   Two Native American Tales

How the Sun Came

There was no light anywhere, and the animal people   1
stumbled around in the darkness. Whenever one bumped
into another, he would say, "What we need in the world
is light." And the other would reply, "Yes, indeed, light is
what we badly need."

At last, the animals called a meeting, and gathered
together as well as they could in the dark. The red-
headed woodpecker said, "I have heard that over on the
other side of the world there are people who have light."

"Good, good!" said everyone.   10

"Perhaps if we go over there, they will give us some
light," the woodpecker suggested.

"If they have all the light there is," the fox said, "they
must be greedy people, who would not want to give any
of it up. Maybe we should just go there and take the
light from them."

"Who shall go?" cried everyone, and the animals all
began talking at once, arguing about who was strongest
and ran fastest, who was best able to go and get the light.

Finally, the 'possum said, "I can try. I have a fine big   20
bushy tail, and I can hide the light inside my fur."

"Good! Good!" said all the others, and the 'possum set
out.

As he traveled eastward, the light began to grow and
grow, until it dazzled his eyes, and the 'possum screwed
his eyes up to keep out the bright light. Even today, if you
notice, you will see that the 'possum's eyes are almost
shut, and that he comes out of his house only at night.

All the same, the 'possum kept going, clear to the
other side of the world, and there he found the sun. He   30
snatched a little piece of it and hid it in the fur of his

fine, bushy tail, but the sun was so hot it burned off all the fur, and by the time the 'possum got home his tail was as bare as it is today.

"Oh, dear!" everyone said. "Our brother has lost his fine, bushy tail, and still we have no light."

"I'll go," said the buzzard. "I have better sense than to put the sun on my tail. I'll put it on my head."

So the buzzard traveled eastward till he came to the place where the sun was. And because the buzzard flies so high, the sun-keeping people did not see him, although now they were watching out for thieves. The buzzard dived straight down out of the sky, the way he does today, and caught a piece of the sun in his claws. He set the sun on his head and started for home, but the sun was so hot that it burned off all his head feathers, and that is why the buzzard's head is bald today.

Now the people were in despair. "What shall we do? What shall we do?" they cried. "Our brothers have tried hard; they have done their best, everything a man can do. What else shall we do so we can have light?"

"They have done the best a man can do," said a little voice from the grass, "but perhaps this is something a woman can do better than a man."

"Who are you?" everyone asked. "Who is that speaking in a tiny voice and hidden in the grass?"

"I am your Grandmother Spider," she replied. "Perhaps I was put in the world to bring you light. Who knows? At least I can try, and if I am burned up it will still not be as if you had lost one of your great warriors."

Then Grandmother Spider felt around her in the

40

50

60

darkness until she found some damp clay. She rolled it in her hands, and molded a little clay bowl. She started eastward, carrying her bowl, and spinning a thread behind her so she could find her way back.

When Grandmother Spider came to the place of the sun people, she was so little and so quiet no one noticed her. She reached out gently, gently, and took a tiny bit of the sun, and placed it in her clay bowl. Then she went back along the thread that she had spun, with the sun's light growing and spreading before her, as she moved from east to west. And if you will notice, even today a spider's web is shaped like the sun's disk and its rays, and the spider will always spin her web in the morning, very early, before the sun is fully up.

"Thank you, Grandmother," the people said when she returned. "We will always honor you and we will always remember you."

And from then on pottery making became woman's work, and all pottery must be dried slowly in the shade before it is put in the heat of the firing oven, just as Grandmother Spider's bowl dried in her hand, slowly, in the darkness, as she traveled toward the land of the sun.

(Cheyenne)

70

80

Raven and the Moon

One day Raven learnt that an old fisherman, living alone with his daughter on an island far to the north, had a box containing a bright light called the moon. He felt that he must get hold of this wonderful thing, so he changed

1

462

CHAPTER EIGHTEEN Africa, the Americas, and cross-cultural encounter

Figure 18.18 Reconstruction drawing of post-classic Maya fortress city of Chutixtiox, Quiche, Guatemala, ca. 1000, from Richard Adams, *Prehistoric Mesoamerica*. Boston: Little Brown, 1977.

with h
believ

Luther c
to reform
Church ab
instance, b
only two c
Church—E
the other
celibacy, ul
six childre
medieval o
the pope as
denied that
and claimec
human bei
Christians,
of believers
The ultima
doctrine, he
individual
Bible amon
New Testan
Luther's
defied both
Church of
excommuni
ly burned th
University c
moned to th
Diet—the C
heresy, Luth
tional temp
in this exce
call for relig
Worms and

READING

It has been de
monks are cal
artificers, and
an artful lie a
made afraid b
Christians are
difference am
says (1 Cor.: 1
member does
because we h
are all Christi
these alone m

*J. H. Robinson
Sources of Euro
Pennsylvania Pr

The Temper of Ref

The Impact of Technology

In the transition from medieva
technology played a crucial rol
cannon, and other military de
impersonal and ultimately more
Western advances in navigation
itime instrumentation brought
position in world exploration an
of the sixteenth century, Eur
change the map of the world.

Another kind of technology,
tionized the future of learning a
printing originated in China i
movable type in the eleventh,
not reach Western Europe unti
1450, in the city of Mainz, the G
Gutenberg (ca. 1400–ca. 1468)
press that made it possible to fa
ly, more rapidly, and in greater
(Figure 19.1). As information
mass production, vast areas c
the exclusive domain of the m
the university—became availab
ing press facilitated the rise c

1320	paper adopted for use in Eu been in use in China)
1450	the Dutch devise the first fi to be carried by a single per
1451	Nicolas of Cusa (German) u nearsightedness
1454	Johannes Gutenberg (Germ movable metal type

Figure 18.19
Castillo, with
Chacmool in the
foreground, Chichén
Itzá, Yucatán,
Mexico. Maya, ninth
to thirteenth
centuries. © Lee
Boltin Picture Library,
Crotin-on-Hudson,
New York.

himself into a leaf growing on a bush near to the old
fisherman's home. When the fisherman's daughter came
to pick berries from the wild fruit patch, she pulled at
the twig on which the leaf stood and it fell down and
entered into her body. In time a child was born, a dark-
complexioned boy with a long, hooked nose, almost like
a bird's bill. As soon as the child could crawl, he began   10
to cry for the moon. He would knock at the box and keep
calling, "Moon, moon, shining moon."

At first nobody paid any attention, but as the child
became more vocal and knocked harder at the box, the
old fisherman said to his daughter, "Well, perhaps we
should give the boy the ball of light to play with." The
girl opened the box and took out another box, and then
another, from inside that. All the boxes were beautifully
painted and carved, and inside the tenth there was a net   20
of nettle thread. She loosened this and opened the lid of
the innermost box. Suddenly light filled the lodge, and
they saw the moon inside the box; bright, round like a
ball, shining white. The mother threw it towards her baby
son and he caught and held it so firmly they thought he
was content. But after a few days he began to fuss and
cry again. His grandfather felt sorry for him and asked
the mother to explain what the child was trying to say. So
his mother listened very carefully and explained that he
wanted to look out at the sky and see the stars in the   30
dark sky, but that the roof board over the smoke hole
prevented him from doing so. So the old man said,
"Open the smoke hole." No sooner had she opened the
hole than the child changed himself back into the
Raven. With the moon in his bill he flew off. After a
moment he landed on a mountain top and then threw the
moon into the sky where it remains, still circling in the
heavens where Raven threw it.

(Northwest Coast)

Maya Civilization

The most inventive of the ancient Native American peoples were the Maya, whose civilization reached the classic

phase between 250 and 900 C.E. and survived with considerable political and economic vigor until roughly 1600. At
sites in Southern Mexico, Honduras, Guatemala, and the
Yucatán Peninsula, the Maya constructed fortified cities
consisting of elaborate palace complexes that are hauntingly reminiscent of those from ancient Mesopotamia
(Figure **18.18**; see chapter 2). Like the Mesopotamian
ziggurat (see chapter 2), the Maya temple was a terraced
pyramid with a staircase ascending to a platform capped by
a multiroomed superstructure (Figure **18.19**).

Figure 18.20 Facade of the late classic Maya temple called "the Nunnery,"
Uxmal, Yucatán, Mexico, 600–1000 C.E. Photo: Ancient Art and Architecture
Collection, Middlesex, U.K.

were infused with spiritual powe[r]
of the living was shared by the d
cyclical rather than as moving
goal. Essentially, they sought the
in nature and in the communi[c]
nature. Such attitudes, closer in
India and China than to those
would struggle to survive the
European expansion and the
Christian world.

SUGGESTIONS FOR REA[DING]

Bierhorst, John. *The Mythology of Me*
    New York: William Morrow, 1990.
Brody, J. J., et al. *Mimbres Pottery: A*
    Southwest. New York: Hudson Hills
Coquet. Michèle. *African Royal Court*
    Chicago: University of Chicago Pre
Feder, Norman. *American Indian Art*.
    1995.
Levathes, Louise. *When China Ruled*
    of the Dragon Throne, 1405–1433.
    Press, 1996.
Levenson, Jay A., ed. *Circa 1492: Art*
    New Haven: Yale University Press
Mbiti, John S. *African Religions and*
    Heinemann, 1992.
Moctezuma, Eduardo M. *The Aztecs*.
Penney, David, and George Longfish.
    York: Scribners, 1994.
Prussin, Labelle. *African Nomadic Ar*
    Gendcr. Washington, D.C.: Smiths

especially
betrayal o
religious r
ular senti[n]
son of a r
become a[n]
as a docto[r]
spoke out
and essays
misery and
    Luther
humankin[d]
medieval v
(see chapt
performan[ce]
intermedia
by the wo[r]
(Romans 1
gained onl
Human be
grace, argu
The purch
making pil

Figure 19.3 L
panel, 8 × 5¾

bestial and cankerous features of his forbidding escorts. Dürer's engraving is remarkable for its wealth of microscopic detail. In the tradition of Jan van Eyck, but with a precision facilitated by the medium of metal engraving, Dürer records with scientific precision every leaf and pebble, hair and wrinkle; and yet the final effect is not a mere piling up of minutiae but, like nature itself, an astonishing amalgam of organically related substances.

The Paintings of Grünewald, Bosch, and Brueghel

Whether Catholic or Protestant, sixteenth-century Northern artists brought to religious subject matter spiritual intensity and emotional subjectivity that were uncharacteristic of Italian art. With the exception of Dürer, whose monumental paintings betray his admiration for classically proportioned figures and the Italianate unity of design, Northern Renaissance artists shared few of the aesthetic ideals of the Italian Renaissance masters. In the paintings of the German artist Matthias Gothardt Neithardt, better known as "Grünewald" (1460–1528), naturalistic detail and brutal distortion produced a highly expressive style. Grünewald's *Crucifixion* (Figure **19.9**),

the central panel of the multipaneled Isenheim Altarpiece, emphasizes the physical suffering of Christ, a devotional subject that might have provided solace to the disease victims at the hospital for which this work was commissioned. In the manner of his anonymous fourteenth-century German predecessor (compare Figure 15.10), Grünewald rejects harmonious proportion and figural idealization in favor of exaggeration and painfully precise detail: The agonized body of Jesus is lengthened to emphasize its weight as it hangs from the bowed cross, the flesh putrefies with clotted blood and angry thorns, the fingers convulse and curl, while the feet—broken and bruised—contort in a spasm of pain. Grünewald reinforces the mood of lamentation by placing the scene in a darkened landscape. He exaggerates the gestures of the attending figures, including that of John the Baptist, whose oversized finger points to the prophetic Latin inscription that explains his mystical presence: "He must increase and I must decrease" (John 3:30). A comparison of this painting with, for instance, Masaccio's *Trinity* (see Figure 17.18) provides a study in contrasts between German and Italian sensibilities in the age of the Renaissance.

Figure 19.9 MATTHIAS GRÜNEWALD, *Crucifixion*, central panel of the Isenheim Altarpiece, ca. 1510–1515. Oil on panel, 8 ft. × 10 ft. 1 in. Museé d'Unterlinden, Colmar, France. Photo: O. Zimmerman.

More difficult to interpret are the works of the extraordinary Flemish artist Hieronymus Bosch (1460–1516). Like Grünewald, Bosch was preoccupied with matters of sin and salvation. Bosch's *Death and the Miser* (Figure **19.10**), for instance, belongs to the tradition of the *memento mori* (discussed in chapter 12), which works to warn the beholder of the inevitability of death. The painting also shows the influence of popular fifteenth-century handbooks on the art of dying (the *ars moriendi*), designed to remind Christians that they must choose between sinful pleasures and the way of Christ. As Death looms on his threshold, the miser, unable to resist worldly temptations even in his last minutes of life, reaches for the bag of gold offered to him by a demon. In the foreground, Bosch depicts the miser storing gold in his money chest while clutching his rosary. Symbols of worldly power—a helmet, sword, and shield—allude to earthly follies. The depiction of such still-life objects to symbolize earthly vanity, transience, or decay would become a genre in itself among seventeenth-century Flemish artists.

Bosch's most famous work, *The Garden of Earthly Delights*—executed around 1510, the very time that Raphael was painting *The School of Athens*—underscores the enormous contrast between Renaissance art in Italy and in Northern Europe. Whereas Raphael celebrates the nobility and dignity of the human being, Bosch contemplates the inconstancy and degeneracy of humankind. In Bosch's **triptych** (a three-paneled painting), the Creation of Adam and Eve (left) and the Tortures of Hell (right) flank a central panel whose iconographic meaning is obscure (Figure **19.11**). Here, in an imaginary landscape, youthful nude men and women cavort in erotic pastimes, dallying affectionately with each other or with oversized flora and fauna that teeter between the fantastic and the actual. The scene, a veritable "Garden of Delights," may be an exposition on the lustful behavior of the descendants of Adam and Eve. But in this central panel, as in the scenes of Creation and Hell, Bosch has turned his back on convention—a circumstance probably related to the fact that the triptych was commissioned not by the Church but by a private patron. His imagery, the subject of endless scholarly interpretation, derives from many sources, including astrology and alchemy, both pseudosciences of some repute in Bosch's time. Astrology, the study of the influence of heavenly bodies on human affairs, and alchemy, the art of distillation (employed by apothecaries as well as by quacks who sought to transmute base metals into gold), attracted new attention when Islamic writings on both were introduced into late medieval Europe. Both, moreover, became subjects of serious study during the sixteenth century. Symbolic of the Renaissance quest to understand the operations of the material world, astrology (the ancestor of astronomy) and alchemy (precursor to

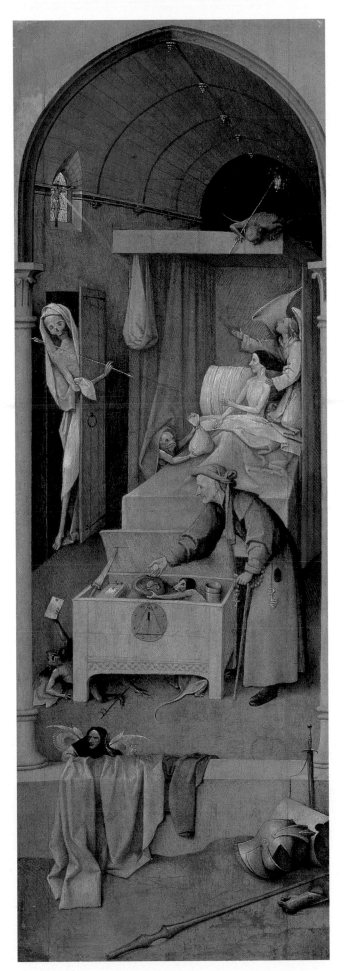

Figure 19.10 HIERONYMUS BOSCH, *Death and the Miser*, ca. 1485–1490. Oil on oak, 36⅝ × 12⅛ in. © 2000 Board of Trustees, National Gallery of Art, Washington, D.C. Samuel H. Kress Collection.

Figure 19.11 HIERONYMUS BOSCH, *The Creation of Eve: The Garden of Earthly Delights: Hell* (triptych), ca. 1510–1515. Oil on wood, 7 ft. 2⅝ in. × 6 ft. 4¾ in. (center panel), 7 ft. 2⅝ in. × 3 ft. 2¼ in. (each side panel). © Museo del Prado, Madrid.

[Handwritten annotations:]

flask
Conjunction, birds symbolize gloss → so in black, come out white

massage flask

Science of christianity

Conjunction stage
putting chemicals together

merging,
lots of sex
childs play stage

hermaphrodite
- everyone becoming one

the more i
more he w
pleases th
larger par
folly. If, th
both in hi
many, wh
discipline
cost him
make him
they will

In Engl
Thoma
Henry
Church
Christi
denou
religio
and Ch
tion as
king a

In
Europ
(the G
place'
ideal
accou

Figure
Oil on p
portrait
who di
convict

[handwritten annotations:]

looking
for fifth
element
(ice balls)

joining together of many
elements → all kinds
of people

pacification, Hell Stage

Hell you burn in science & you burn
in hell

Stingy
man
shutting
gold
coins

Flood Stage → empty land, starting over. white & grey, no color